INSIDE BARTLET'S WHITE HOUSE

An Unofficial and
Unauthorised Guide
to *The West Wing*

By the same author:

SLAYER: AN EXPANDED AND UPDATED
UNOFFICIAL AND UNAUTHORISED GUIDE TO
BUFFY THE VAMPIRE SLAYER

SLAYER – THE NEXT GENERATION: AN
UNOFFICIAL AND UNAUTHORISED GUIDE TO
SEASON SIX OF *BUFFY THE VAMPIRE SLAYER*

HOLLYWOOD VAMPIRE: AN EXPANDED AND
UPDATED UNOFFICIAL AND UNAUTHORISED
GUIDE TO *ANGEL*

HIGH TIMES: AN UNOFFICIAL AND
UNAUTHORISED GUIDE TO *ROSWELL*

By the same author with Paul Cornell and Martin Day:

THE NEW TREK PROGRAMME GUIDE

X-TREME POSSIBILITIES

THE AVENGERS DOSSIER

By the same author with Martin Day:

SHUT IT! A FAN'S GUIDE TO 70S COPS ON THE
BOX

INSIDE BARTLET'S WHITE HOUSE

An Unofficial and Unauthorised Guide to *The West Wing*
Revised and Updated

Keith Topping

This revised and updated edition first published in Great Britain in 2004 by
Virgin Books Ltd
Thames Wharf Studios
Rainville Road
London
W6 9HA

First published in 2002

A catalogue record for this book is available from the British Library.

ISBN 0 7535 0828 1

Typeset by TW Typesetting, Plymouth, Devon
Printed and bound in Great Britain by
Clays Ltd, St Ives PLC

Contents

Acknowledgements   vi

You Are Now Entering the Oval Office   1

Washington, Behind Closed Doors   5

All the President's Men (and Women)   8

Season One   14

Season Two   159

Season Three   260

Season Four   360

The West Wing and the Internet   401

Select Bibliography   403

Four More Years . . .?   417

Acknowledgements

The author wishes to thank Ian Abrahams, Michael Chlanda, Andy Cowper, Martin Day, Thomas Farley, Jeffrey Gainer, Dave G of Preston, Jeff Hart, Ian Rowbottom, Jim Sangster, Dan Smiczek, Patricia Smith, Graeme Topping, Michael Warren and Deborah Williams for their encouragement and support during the writing of this book. And a big shout-out to all of the contributors to the Ask Keith Topping forum on Outpost Gallifrey.

Thanks also to my outstanding editor, Kirstie Addis, who always had such faith in this project, and others, plus Suze Campagna, Diana Dougherty, Clay Eichelberger, Robert Franks, Tony and Jane Kenealy, Mike Lee, Ian Mond, Kathy Sullivan, Susannah Tiller and Jason Tucker for their outstanding research and contributions.

Inside Bartlet's White House was written, live, on location in Newcastle upon Tyne, Los Angeles, Madeira and Paris. And various airports and hotels in between.

This book is very definitely dedicated to Shaun Lyon.

You Are Now Entering the Oval Office

'Tonight, what began on the commons in Concord, Massachusetts, as an alliance of farmers and workers – of cobblers and tinsmiths, of statesmen and students, of mothers and wives, of men and boys – lives two centuries later as America. My name is Josiah Bartlet, and I accept your nomination for the presidency of the United States.'

– 'In the Shadow of Two Gunmen', Part 2

Political drama, whether straight or satirical, has always been a popular genre on TV, particularly if the subject is close to how we imagine our leaders behave, but *just* different enough to make us wish that real politicians were as decent and honest as those men and women depicted in fiction. That's one of the reasons why, for instance, the British comedy series *Yes, Minister* was so well loved around the world. Despite many flaws (and an abject lack of intelligence), a lot of people really wouldn't have minded living in a country run by someone like Jim Hacker.

So it is with *The West Wing*. I don't know about you, but a world in which the man with his finger on The Button is Josiah Bartlet seems immeasurably preferable to the one we've actually got.

The West Wing was created in 1999 by Aaron Sorkin, the author of *A Few Good Men*. It was the ailing NBC network's biggest hit drama in years and a winner of an unprecedented nine Emmy awards at the climax to its first season. Perhaps its greatest achievement, however, has been the praise that it has received from across the political spectrum. The series is proudly liberal, detailing the activities of a fictitious Democrat administration in an

America that is almost but not quite our own. It includes, among its consultants, Patrick Caddell, President Carter's policy and strategy adviser, Lawrence O'Donnell, a former adviser to senator Patrick Moynihan, and Dee Dee Myers, press secretary to the Clinton White House. However, the series' most vocal supporters have included many Republicans who seem to appreciate the balanced stance that *The West Wing* takes on many of today's important political issues. '*The West Wing* has no gratuitous violence or sex,' Sorkin told an online interview. 'It *has* featured the president of the United States kneeling on the floor of the Oval Office, praying. This, I think, would be exactly what conservative Republicans want to see on television.'[1]

The West Wing is a great series. Witty, inventive, experimental, influential. (Notice how many shows now use hand-held cameras and include scenes of multi-character dialogue? *Citizen Kane* was doing it fifty years ago, of course, but *The West Wing* is doing it now, and others are imitating it.) By its very nature the series focuses on the great issues of the day. Stuff that, however spasmodically, affects the lives of every person who watches TV no matter where in the world they are – racial awareness, drugs, gun control, homophobia, education, health, the economy, war. All within the context of a story about a group of extremely clever and idealistic people who work for a man who wants to make that world a better place. It's about the jaded politics of compromise versus the politics of idealism and how, even in an imperfect world, the latter isn't automatically squashed by the former.

I love this series. I think it's sexy and dangerous in an age when the only other shows to which such tags apply

---

[1] Some politicians consider it a greater victory to get an issue discussed on *The West Wing* than to appear on a talk show. The Californian Republican David Dreier notes that *The West Wing*'s audience is 'larger and clearly more diverse' than that to which politicians traditionally have access.

are teenage telefantasy series such as *Buffy*. They're strange bedfellows but aren't mutually exclusive. When *Buffy*'s creator Joss Whedon expresses a fan's admiration for Sorkin's brilliant use of dialogue and calls *The West Wing* 'the only programme I watch on TV', you know that you're dealing with something special.

Headings

A View from the Hill: A category that untangles the knotted web of political references that surround the president's relationship with Congress and the Senate.

American History X: Self-explanatory, but necessary for readers unfamiliar with some of the cultural allusions. Not to be confused with **References**, which highlight pop-culture and geographical terms.

Politics of Expediency/Compromise/Indulgence: Even men of integrity make occasional Faustian bargains. Scratch a liberal and you find a conservative. Scratch a conservative and you find a fascist. Scratch a fascist and you find yourself in hospital with a crowd round your bed.

The Encyclopedic Mind of Josiah Bartlet PhD: In addition to being the leader of the free world, Jed has a plethora of arcane, trainspotter-trivia in his brain, much to the annoyance of his staff. 'You're quite a nerd, Mr President,' notes Josh in **8**, 'Enemies'. He's being charitable.

Logic, Let Me Introduce You to This Window: The plot holes, continuity errors and bits of the episodes that simply don't work.

Quote/Unquote: Samples of the dialogue it's worth watching the video for.

Other categories regularly appear. Most should be self-explanatory. **Sex and Drugs and Rock'n'Roll**, for instance. **Oh, Donna!** deals with Josh's assistant and her unique outlook on life. **Critique** details what the press, viewers and real politicians made of it all. **Comments** from cast and crew have been added where appropriate. Each episode concludes with a review.

This second edition updates the first, published early in 2002, with details of the rest of Season Three and the early episodes of Season Four – up to and including Jed Bartlet's re-election for a second term in November 2002. Space restrictions, unfortunately, prohibit further episodes being covered in this edition. However, a volume is already planned to cover what happens next. See the final chapter, 'Four More Years . . . ?', for a small taste of what's in store.

   Many things have changed over the last year, both within *The West Wing* and in the real world, and not all of them for the better. But, at heart, Aaron Sorkin's creation – whilst having an element of wistful fantasy about it – remains a window into the complexities of politics. Ultimately, that's why people continue to watch it because, despite all the amputations, the world does not exist in black and white only but, rather, in vivid colour.

Keith Topping
Escaping By Canoe
Merrie Albion
September 2003

Washington, Behind Closed Doors

'This is a perfect metaphor. After you're gone and the poets write The Legend of Josiah Bartlet, *let them write you as a tragic figure. That he had the tools of greatness, but the voices of his better angels were shouted down by his obsessive need to win.'*

– 'The Crackpots and These Women'

'The show was originally based on the relationship between Sam and Josh,' notes the executive producer John Wells. 'But we kept finding other interesting characters. By the time the pilot was written, it was pretty much the way you see it.'[2]

The format: New England Democrat Josiah Bartlet is the US president. A liberal intellectual, he exudes a relaxed country-gentleman charisma that belies his brilliant mind and deep devotion to his responsibilities. Bartlet's closest friend and ally is his chief-of-staff, Leo McGarry, who possesses the backstreet savvy that enables him to stay in touch with the sentiments of the nation and (usually) one step ahead of his, and the president's, enemies. Leo's deputy, Josh Lyman, a wise-cracking Connecticut lawyer and gifted strategist, is far too opinionated for his, and the president's, good, but his sarcastic assistant, Donna Moss, is always there to bring him down to earth with a pithy comment. Adding to complexities, Josh's former girlfriend, Mandy Hampton, a forthright media expert, is also on the team.

---

[2] Rob Lowe and Bradley Whitford were originally cast as Josh and Sam respectively, but switched roles shortly before production began.

The press secretary CJ Cregg spends most of her time deftly deflecting awkward questions the administration doesn't want to answer, working alongside Toby Ziegler, the seen-it-all communications director, a career political animal whose dry, cynical humour masks a man of genuine integrity. In contrast to his boss, deputy director Sam Seaborn is less of a pragmatist and more an idealistic romantic, but his speechwriting skills are second to none. The president's plain-spoken yet astute personal aide, Charlie Young, is often the one person to inject a note of (sometimes unwelcome) reality into the theoretical flights of fancy of his colleagues.

The series' planned NBC debut in the autumn season of 1998 was scuppered, according to Wells, when the Monica Lewinsky scandal broke earlier that year while *The West Wing* was in development. 'There was justifiable concern over the political climate and whether it would pass "the snicker test",' Wells told the *Philadelphia Inquirer*. 'Would anyone be able to take a show about the president seriously given what was going on with the *actual* president?' NBC asked them to wait a year.[3]

'I wasn't going to [feature] the character of the president,' Sorkin told Scott Pierce. Sorkin saw the series as concerning the staff working in the president's shadow, and he would be seen only in glimpses. 'Then I felt that would become hokey,' he added. 'We'll constantly be just missing the president. As he walks around the corner, we'll see the back of his head. He'd be like the neighbor on *Home Improvement*.' So he created the character of Josiah Bartlet, an infrequent visitor to the show, and Martin Sheen was signed to appear in four episodes. 'We saw Mr Sheen's dailies,' John Wells noted. 'We said, "We had a great time. Did you?" ' Sheen agreed to join the regular cast. 'They realised that people might catch on that I'd be there only once a month, so they talked to me about a longer commitment.'

---

[3] Ironically, the Warner Bros-produced series was passed over by WB's boss Garth Ancier. 'It was a very expensive risk; it didn't feel like a WB show,' he noted.

Did You Know?: During an appearance on *Saturday Night Live* in the midst of the 2000 presidential elections, Charlie Sheen was asked, considering that his father is such a great president in *The West Wing*, whether he himself would fancy the job. 'I've used cocaine, I've been arrested, I'm not a very smart guy,' the actor replied. 'It's a big joke that people would want someone like me just because my dad was president.' Think about it!

All the President's Men (and Women)

'You want to see me orchestrate this right now? You want to see me mobilise these people . . . who would walk into fire if you told them to?'

– 'Let Bartlet Be Bartlet'

Martin Sheen: Despite his being one of the great actors of his generation, it wasn't a universally endorsed decision to cast Sheen as Jed Bartlet. John Wells was afraid the actor would try to inject some of his own well-documented radical agenda into the role and told Sorkin, who had lobbied hard for Sheen, 'This is a mistake.' Nevertheless, Wells is man enough to admit, 'Martin's really great. He tells us he's going to be arrested over the weekend but not to worry. He's arranged for someone to make bail and he'll be back on the set on Monday morning!'

Born, as Ramon Estevez, in 1940, Martin purposely flunked his entrance exam to the University of Dayton, Ohio, so he could pursue an acting career. His father wholeheartedly disapproved, remaining estranged from Sheen until he gained success some years later. He took his stage name from a bishop he admired. Early breaks came via TV, with appearances in the 1960s in *The Outer Limits*, *Ironside*, *Naked City*, *Mission: Impossible* and *Hawaii Five-O*. Hailed on Broadway for his performance as Timmy Cleary in *The Subject Was Roses*, Sheen recreated the role in the 1968 movie. Subsequently, he played Dobbs in *Catch-22*, Robby Navarro in *The Cassandra Crossing*, Frank Hallet in *The Little Girl Who Lives Down the Lane* and the psychotic Kit in *Badlands*. Other memorable appearances include the lead in *The Execution of Private*

Slovik, Bobby Kennedy in *The Missiles of October*, John Kennedy in *Kennedy*, the right-wing politician Greg Stillson in *The Dead Zone* (in which he was cast against type) and roles in *Wall Street*, *Firestarter*, *The Believers*, *Gandhi* and *Da*. To most readers, however, he will be familiar as Captain Willard in *Apocalypse Now*, the seemingly endless filming of which saw him suffer an almost fatal heart attack. He also directed 1991's *Cadence*. Sheen is a committed libertarian and an indefatigable activist for numerous social and environmental causes, activities that have seen him arrested on more than seventy occasions at marches and sit-ins. At the time of writing he is currently serving three years' probation for trespass at an Air Force base.[4] 'Part of the reason I'm playing this [role] is because of my involvement in social issues,' Sheen told *Radio Times*. 'I'm not a Democrat by accident. If a Republican had been president when we started filming, I don't think they would have offered me the job.' Sheen's four children, Charlie Sheen and Emilio, Renée and Ramon Estevez, have all followed their father into acting.

Did You Know?: Martin screen-tested for the role of Michael Corleone in *The Godfather*.

John Spencer: A native of New York, John Spencer was born, as John Speshock, in 1946. In his teens he played Henry in *The Patty Duke Show* and attended Fairleigh Dickenson University but dropped out to return to the profession he loved. A jobbing actor for many years, Spencer did not come to the attention of the wider public until the 1980s in movies such as *Sea of Love*, *Black Rain*, *Presumed Innocent* and *Green Card* (usually playing police or military officers). He was the director of the FBI in *The Rock* and Al Travis in *The Negotiator*, and is best known as Tommy Mullaney in *LA Law*. Like the character he plays, Spencer is an acknowledged recovering alcoholic.

Did You Know?: Spencer's other great love is gardening.

---

[4] Sheen is a strong advocate for closing the School of the Americas, which trains Latin American soldiers (allegedly in torture techniques).

Bradley Whitford: A native of Madison, Wisconsin, and a graduate of Wesleyan University, Middletown, Whitford was born in 1959 and always wanted to be an actor. His first big break was on stage appearing in *A Few Good Men*, and a friendship with the writer Aaron Sorkin led to his casting in *The West Wing*. On TV he was Norman Gardner in *NYPD Blue* and has appeared in *The X-Files*, *Tales from the Darkside*, *Ellen* and *ER*. Whitford also played Charles Palen in *Young Guns II: Blaze of Glory* and Jamey Collins in *Philadelphia*, and was in *Awakenings*, *Billy Madison*, *Scent of a Woman*, *Cobb* and *Bicentennial Man*. He is married to the actress Jane Kaczmarek (*Malcolm in the Middle*).

Did You Know?: During periods between acting work early in his career, Whitford waited tables at Panarellas restaurant in New York.

Richard Schiff: Like his alter ego, Schiff is from New York, though during his teens he lived a somewhat hippie lifestyle in Colorado. Returning, in 1975, to study theatre at CCNY, he initially disliked acting and trained to be a director, helming several off-Broadway plays, including *Antigone*, where he met his future wife Sheila Kelley. In the mid-1980s, Schiff conquered his fears and landed roles on TV series such as *LA Law* and *Murphy Brown*. Steven Spielberg saw him in *High Incident* and cast him in *Jurassic Park: The Lost World*. Other roles include Agent Stevens in *Roswell*, Mark Swarr in *Se7en* and Gene Reiss in *Doctor Dolittle* and appearances in *Deep Impact*, *Speed*, *The Hudsucker Proxy*, *The Bodyguard*, *Malcolm X*, *Murder One* and *Ally McBeal*.

Did You Know?: 'We don't ad-lib [much],' Schiff told an online interview. 'Aaron's words are like a musical composition and he wants it played a specific way. During the pilot, we got into arguments about being such a stickler for every syllable. Ad-libbing has been important to my work and most writers appreciate my input. But when I did *The Practice*, David Kelley was the same. Aaron's a playwright, he understands the importance of the script.'

Rob Lowe: Born in 1964 in Charlottesville, Virginia, Lowe grew up in Ohio and, in his teens, played Tony Flanagan in *A New Kind of Family*. A contemporary of Emilio Estevez and Charlie Sheen, Lowe was initially dismissed as an unctuous pretty boy, but a string of capable performances in movies such as *Class*, *The Outsiders*, *Oxford Blues*, *Hotel New Hampshire*, the Brat Pack ensemble-piece *St. Elmo's Fire*, *Masquerade* and *Youngblood* changed filmgoers' perceptions. Lowe was a sensation as a retarded youth in *Square Dance* (for which he was Golden Globe-nominated). He made headlines for all the wrong reasons in 1989, when explicit videotapes of him carousing with an underage girl while attending the Democratic Convention became public. He survived the notoriety, and twenty hours' community service, sought help for alcohol problems and has re-emerged in the 1990s as a sober husband and father. This also lent credibility to performances as slimy showbiz types in *The Dark Backward* and *Wayne's World* (Lowe credits his friend Mike Myers with helping save his career; he did a great job impersonating Robert Wagner as the young Number Two in *Austin Powers: The Spy Who Shagged Me*). On TV, he starred in *Suddenly, Last Summer* and *The Stand*, while recent films include *Mulholland Falls*, *Outrage* and *Proximity*. He directed 1997's *Desert's Edge*. Like many of the cast, Lowe is a committed Democrat who worked on the presidential campaign of Michael Dukakis. He boasts that he'd already read every book on the reading list suggested by Aaron Sorkin.

Did You Know?: Lowe is deaf in his right ear. He is brother-in-law of the Oscar winner Hilary Swank.

Allison Janney: Like Sheen and Lowe, Janney grew up in Dayton, Ohio. Her father is a jazz trumpeter and she has two brothers who are also musicians. As a child, she dreamed of becoming an ice skater before a freak accident with a glass door ended such hopes. Educated at Kenyon College and RADA in London, she won an Outer Critics' Circle award for her performance in *Present Laughter*

(1997). A role in the soap *Guiding Light* led to parts in *Ice Storm*, *Primary Colors*, *Six Days Seven Nights*, *10 Things I Hate About You*, *Drop Dead Gorgeous* and *Nurse Betty*.

Did You Know?: On her height, Janney notes: 'A casting agent told me that the only roles I could play were lesbians and aliens.'

Moira Kelly: Until she was eight, Kelly wanted to be a nun. She was born in Queens in 1968, and raised in Ronkonkoma. Her father was a concert violinist. She attended Connetquot High School and Marymount College and began acting in a school production of *Annie*. She was Cynthia in *Henry Hill*, Helen Keller in *Monday After the Miracle* and had the title role in *Entertaining Angels: The Dorothy Day Story*. She provided the voice of Nala in *The Lion King*. Her other movies include *Chaplin, Billy Bathgate* (as Rebecca) and *The Boy Who Cried Bitch*.

Did You Know?: When cast as Donna Hayward in *Twin Peaks: Fire Walk With Me*, Kelly sought the permission of her family priest to do her first sex scene.

Dulé Hill: A native of New Jersey and born in 1974, Hill is an excellent tap dancer and performed with Savion Glover at the 32nd NAACP Image Awards. His movies include *Men of Honor*, *She's All That* (as Preston), *The Ditchdigger's Daughters* and *Harlem*, in which he played the young Roemello Skuggs.

Did You Know?: Hill's first name is Karim but he goes by his unusual middle name, which was given to him by an aunt who had recently visited France.

Janel Moloney: Born in 1972, in Woodland Hills, California, Moloney is a niece of the actress Christine Ebersol. She played Pat White in *From the Earth to the Moon* and appeared in *Desperate Measures*, *Safe* and *Dream Lover*. 'Very early on, Aaron saw chemistry between Brad and me,' she notes. 'In the pilot, there's a scene Aaron wrote one morning and passed on to us to shoot the same day. I say, "Put this shirt on." He says, "No." I say, "All the girls think you look really hot in this shirt." He puts it on. I think that scene sparked something.'

Did You Know?: Moloney originally auditioned for the role of CJ.

The West Wing – Season One (1999–2000)

John Wells Television/Warner Bros Television
(a Time Warner Entertainment Company)
Created by Aaron Sorkin
Co-Producers: Michael Hissrich, Rick Cleveland (2–22)
Producers: Llewellyn Wells, Kristin Harms
Associate Producers: Robert W Glass III (2–8),
Julie Herlocker (6–22)
Consulting Producers: Jeff Reno (2–10), Ron Osborn (2–10)
Executive Producers: Aaron Sorkin, Thomas Schlamme, John Wells
Consultants: Patrick H Caddell (2–22),
Dee Dee Myers (2–22)
Executive Story Editors: Peter Parnell (2–22),
Lawrence O'Donnell Jr (9–22)
Story Editors: Paul Redford (2–22), Diana Son (21–22)
Theme and Music: WG Snuffy Walden

Regular Cast:
Martin Sheen (President Josiah Bartlet)
John Spencer (Leo McGarry)
Bradley Whitford (Joshua Lyman)
Richard Schiff (Toby Ziegler) Rob Lowe (Sam Seaborn)
Allison Janney (Claudia Jean Cregg)
Moira Kelly (Madelaine Hampton, 1–15, 18–22)
Janel Moloney (Donnatella Moss)
Kathryn Joosten (Delores Landingham, 1–13, 17, 19–20, 22)
Lisa Edelstein (Laurie Rollins, 1–2, 7, 10, 21)
Suzy Nakamura (Cathy, 1–3, 5–6, 13, 18, 20, 22)
NiCole Robinson (Margaret, 1–2, 4–5, 8–13, 15–16, 18–22)
Devika Parikh (Bonnie, 1, 3–4, 6, 8, 12, 14–15, 18, 20–22)
Allison Smith (Mallory O'Brien, 1, 6, 8, 12, 18)
Annie Corley (Mary Marsh, 1)
F William Parker (Reverend Al Caldwell, 1)
Melissa Fitzgerald (Carol[5], 1–2, 4–5, 7, 11–15, 17–22)
Peter James Smith (Ed[6], 1–2, 11, 16, 21)

---

[5] Credited as White House Staffer in **1**, 'The West Wing'.
[6] Credited as Congressional Liaison #1 in **1**, 'The West Wing'.

Bill Duffy (Larry[7], 1–2, 11, 16, 21)
Mindy Seeger (Chris[8], 1, 3, 7, 17, 20)
Jana Lee Hamblin (Bobbi[9], 1–3, 8, 10, 13)
Dafidd McCracken (Mike[10], 1, 11)
Molly Schaffer (Senior Staffer, 1)
Renee Estevez (Nancy, 2–3, 5–6, 8, 10, 13–14, 19, 21)
Tim Matheson (Vice President John Hoynes, 2, 4, 8, 16, 22)
Rose Rollins (Suzanne, 2–3)
Robyn Pedretti (Candy, 2, 8)
Bradley James (Donnie[11], 2, 4, 6, 10, 13)
Victor Love (Mike[12], 2–4, 15)
Steven M Gagnon (Officer #1, 2, 22)
Dulé Hill (Charlie Young, 3–22)
Timothy Busfield (Danny Concannon[13], 3, 7–10, 12–13, 15, 17–22)
John Amos (Admiral Percy Fitzwallace, 3, 11, 19, 22)
Kim Webster (Ginger[14], 3, 10, 13, 15, 17–22)
Marvin Krueger (Officer #1, 3, 12)
George McDaniel (Officer #2, 3, 22)
Ivan Allen (Roger Salier[15], 3–4, 12, 17)
Christopher Kriesa (Mitch[16], 3, 11–12)
Thom Barry (Mark Richardson, 4)
Penny Griego (DC Anchor[17], 4)
Mongo Brownlee (Secret Service Agent, 4)
Elisabeth Moss (Zoey Bartlet, 5–6, 11, 16–18, 22)

---

[7] Credited as Congressional Liaison #2 in **1**, 'The West Wing' and as Staffer in **2**, '"Post Hoc, Ergo Propter Hoc"'. The actor's name is given as William Duffy in **21**, 'Lies, Damn Lies and Statistics' and for all subsequent appearances.

[8] Credited as Reporter #3 in **1**, 'The West Wing' and as Reporter #2 in **17**, 'The White House Pro-Am'.

[9] Credited as Reporter #1 in **1**, 'The West Wing' and **13**, 'Take Out the Trash Day'.

[10] Credited as USS Officer (Mike) in **1**, 'The West Wing' and as Sec Officer in **11**, 'Lord John Marbury'.

[11] Credited as Secret Service Agent in **2**, '"Post Hoc, Ergo Propter Hoc"' and as Secret Service Agent #1 in **4**, 'Five Votes Down' and **6**, 'Mr Willis of Ohio'.

[12] Credited as Reporter (Mike) in **4**, 'Five Votes Down'.

[13] Uncredited in **3**, 'A Proportional Response'.

[14] Credited as Kim in **3**, 'A Proportional Response'.

[15] Credited as Newscaster in **3**, 'A Proportional Response', **12**, 'He Shall, from Time to Time . . .' and **17**, 'The White House Pro-Am', and as Newscaster #3 in **4**, 'Five Votes Down'. Character name given in a TV caption in one episode.

[16] Credited as Officer #3 in **3**, 'A Proportional Response'.

[17] Credited as Newscaster #1 in **4**, 'Five Votes Down'.

Michael O'Neill (Ron Butterfield[18], 6, 16, 18, 22)
Charley Lang (Matt Skinner, 6, 8)
Greg Wrangler (Secret Service Agent[19], 6)
Juan A Riojas (Secret Service Agent[20], 6, 14, 16)
Stockard Channing (Abigail Bartlet, 7, 12, 17)
Colin Gray (Bruce[21], 7–8, 11)
Jacqueline Torres (Sondra[22], 7, 13, 15)
JP Stevenson (Jonathan[23], 7, 15, 20)
DC Ford (Secret Service Agent[24], 7, 12)
Dennis Cockrum (Captain, 7)
Edward James Olmos (Roberto Mendoza, 9, 15)
Charles Noland (Steve[25], 9, 11, 13, 15, 17, 19–20, 22)
Diana Morgan (Jesse[26], 9, 15, 20)
Kris Narmont (Katie[27], 9, 15, 17, 19–22)
Roger Rees (Lord John Marbury, 11–12)
Ralph Meyering Jr (Tom, 11–12, 22)
Gary Cervantes (Bobby, 11) Tom Hall (Mike[28], 11)
Bill Stevenson (Jarworski, 11)
Marlee Matlin (Joey Lucas, 14, 16, 20–21)
Bill O'Brien (Kenny Thurman, 14, 16, 20–21)
Jorja Fox (Special Agent Gina Toscano, 16–18, 22)
John De Lancie (Al Kiefer, 16, 20)
Paul Provenza (Steve Onorato, 19–20)
Kathleen York (Andi Wyatt, 20)
Don Chastain (Reporter #2, 21)

---

[18] Uncredited in **18**, 'Six Meetings Before Lunch'.

[19] Credited as Secret Service Agent #2 in **6**, 'Mr Willis of Ohio'.

[20] Credited as Secret Service Agent #3 in **6**, 'Mr Willis of Ohio'.

[21] Credited as Tom in **7**, 'The State Dinner' and as Reporter in **8**, 'Enemies'.

[22] Credited as Reporter #2 in **13**, 'Take Out the Trash Day' and as Reporter #1 in **15**, 'Celestial Navigation'.

[23] Credited as Reporter in **7**, 'The State Dinner'.

[24] Uncredited in both **7**, 'The State Dinner' and **12**, 'He Shall, from Time to Time . . .'

[25] Credited as Reporter #2 in **9**, 'The Short List' and **15**, 'Celestial Navigation', as Reporter #1 in **11**, 'Lord John Marbury' and as Reporter #3 in **13**, 'Take Out the Trash Day'.

[26] Credited as Reporter #1 in **9**, 'The Short List' and as Reporter #3 in **15**, 'Celestial Navigation'.

[27] Credited as Reporter #3 in **9**, 'The Short List' and as Reporter #4 in **13**, 'Take Out the Trash Day'.

[28] Credited as Officer in **11**, 'Lord John Marbury'.

1
The West Wing
[a.k.a. Pilot]

US Transmission Date: 22 September 1999
UK Transmission Date: 10 January 2000 (Sky), 18 January 2001 (C4)

Writer: Aaron Sorkin
Director: Thomas Schlamme
Cast: Marc Grapey (Bill Kenworthy) David Sage (John Van Dyke)
Ossi Taylor (College Student #1) Tressa DiFiglia (College Student #2)
Wendell Wright (Economist #1)
Hamilton Mitchell (Economist #2)
Wendy Blair (Flight Attendant #2 and voice-over)
Elizabeth Greer (Flight Attendant #3) Marlene Warfield (Maid)
Dean Biasucci (Man) Diane Michelle (Woman's Voice-Over)
Marcus Boddie (DC Cop)

The White House sees frantic activity when President
Bartlet injures himself in a bike accident. Leo must cope
with a hostile reaction from right-wing Christians to
televised comments by Josh. Meanwhile, Sam, unwittingly,
spends the night with a prostitute.

A View from the Hill: Congress comprises the Senate and
House of Representatives. The Senate has 100 members,
two from each state[29], elected for six years with one-third
retiring biannually. The 435-member House is elected for
a two-year term from constituencies.[30] Executive federal
power is vested in the president, who serves a maximum of
two four-year terms. The president and vice president are
selected by an electoral college pledged to support individual candidates.

American History X: Sam tells a group of children that the
White House was built 'several years ago'. Mostly out of

---

[29] Each state, in turn, has a separate constitution and legislature.
Executive power is held by a directly elected governor.
[30] Additional nonvoting members are returned by the District of Columbia, Guam, Puerto Rico (see **31**, 'Galileo'), the US Virgin Islands and
American Samoa.

cement.[31] The room they occupy was 'named for our eighteenth president, Franklin Delano Roosevelt' and the chairs were 'fashioned from the lumber of a pirate ship captured during the Spanish-American war'. Unfortunately, he's mixed up Franklin Roosevelt (1882–1945), the 32nd president, with his distant cousin Teddy Roosevelt (1858–1919), the 26th. Ulysses Grant (1822–85) was the eighteenth. A portrait of George Washington (1732–99), the first president, hangs in the Oval Office.

Alger Hiss (1904–96) was a protégé of Felix Frankfurter and Wendell Holmes, an adviser at Yalta and a participant in the founding of the UN as temporary secretary general, subsequently convicted of perjury as part of the HUAC investigations in 1950 (see **38**, 'Somebody's Going to Emergency, Somebody's Going to Jail'). The 'secret pumpkin' refers to where evidence against him – a microfilm – was famously hidden (see **41**, 'Bad Moon Rising'). Toby mentions the Bill of Rights.[32]

Politics of Compromise: Leo tells Josh it's unwise to dump everyone on the Christian right in a pile labelled 'stupid', because 'we need these people'.

Approximately two thousand Cuban refugees embark from a village south of Havana heading for Miami. A discussion on the option to send them back has Sam noting that this will result in the administration getting 'whacked' in Florida's Dade County. 'With the clothes on their backs, they came through a storm,' Bartlet says of the 137 who finally reach America. 'And the ones that didn't die want a better life . . . Talk about impressive.'

---

[31] It was actually built between 1792 and 1800. The walls are sandstone.

[32] The name given to the first ten amendments to the Constitution, safeguarding individual rights against the federal government. Precedents came from three historic documents: Magna Carta (1215), the Petition of Right (1628) and the contemporaneous Declaration of the Rights of Man. Virginia (1776) and Massachusetts (1780) had already incorporated bills of rights into their constitutions and, along with New York and Pennsylvania, refused to ratify the Constitution unless it was amended.

A Little Learning is a Dangerous Thing: In relation to proposed gun control laws, Larry says each day seventeen thousand Americans defend themselves with a gun, including a 76-year-old grandmother in Chicago. She doesn't defend herself with a modified AK-47 assault rifle, Sam replies. Unless it's against Turkish rebels.

Office Gossip: Donna's heard that the president broke something in his fall. Leo confirms he suffered only a mild sprain.

Alternate Sexuality: Asked at a press conference about Josh's comments on learning that Mandy is dating her new client, Senator Lloyd Russell ('I always thought he was gay . . . He seemed effeminate to me'), Sorkin told reporters, 'I apologise if it came off as homophobic. My wife warned me it [might be perceived as such]. Every time I don't listen to her, I get in trouble for it.'

The Gospel According to Josh: On the TV show *Capital Beat*, Josh upsets right-winger Mary Marsh, saying, 'The God you pray to is too busy being indicted for tax fraud.'

Bartlet is a deeply religious man, says Leo. He's worked with the Southern Baptist Leadership Conference and Catholic Relief and spoke at Reverend Caldwell's church. He spent eight months travelling the country discouraging women from having abortions (presumably during the campaign). He doesn't, however, believe it's the government's place to legislate this issue (making him both pro-life and pro-choice, which isn't as contradictory as some readers may think). He's read his Bible from cover to cover (see **25**, 'The Midterms', **44**, 'Two Cathedrals').

References: Sorkin based his religious terrorists the Lambs of God on a real fundamentalist group, the Lambs of Christ, who, notes the writer, 'do violent things and harass people'. When a stewardess asks Toby to switch off his mobile, he says, 'We're flying in a Lockheed Eagle Series L10-11. Carries a Zim-5 transponder tracking system. You're telling me I can flummox [it] with something I bought at Radio Shack?' Leo says the only thing broken in the accident was 'a four-thousand-dollar Lynex Titanium touring bike I swore I'd never lend anyone'. Also, the *New York Times* crossword, State Farm insurance, the Red Cross, Centers for Disease Control, ABC's *Nightline*, the Cuban president Fidel Castro, the children's game Red Rover, the Dow Jones Index, the aircraft carrier the USS *Eisenhower*, the *Nina* and the *Pinta* (two of Columbus's three ships on his 1492 voyage) and the Immigration and Naturalization Service (see **30**, 'Shibboleth'). Bill tells Sam any information he gives will be 'strictly deep-cover', a possible reference to *All the President's Men*. The song heard when Mandy drives through a red light is 'Moment of Weakness' by Bif Naked. Mandy's car is a silver BMW (licence TDQ 019). Toby may have been named after Ron Ziegler, the press secretary to Richard Nixon.

'You May Remember Me From Such Films and TV Series As . . .': Suzy Nakamura was in *8mm*, *Daddio*, *Deep Impact* and *Strawberry Fields*. NiCole Robinson appeared in *Any Given Sunday* and *Friends*. Devika Parikh's movies include *Book of Love* and *Judgment Day*. Melissa Fitzgerald was in *Frequency*, *Love & Sex* and *Snitch*. Kathryn Joosten's CV includes *Code Blue*, *Phoenix*, *Murphy Brown* and *Buffy*. Lisa Edelstein was Bobbi in *Sports Night* and can be seen in *What Women Want*, *30 Days*, *The Doors* and *L.A. Without a Map*. Allison Smith played Sara Pratt in *Sweet Justice* and was in *Terror Tract*, *Jason Goes to Hell: The Final Friday* and *Switchback*. F William Parker appeared in *The Wedding Planner*, *He Said She Said*, *Jinxed!*, *Happy Days*, *Taxi*, *CHiPS* and *Starksy and Hutch*.

Annie Corley was in *The Cider House Rules*, *The Bridges of Madison County* and *Malcolm X*. Tressa DiFiglia appeared in *Pathos* and *Chance*. Jana Lee Hamblin was Janet in *Love is Strange*. Bill Duffy's movies include *Blast from the Past* and *The Two Jakes*. Marc Graphy was in *Big Girls Don't Cry . . . They Get Even*, *Pop Life* and *Chicago Hope*. Dave Sage was Senator Walter in *Dallas* and appeared in *Star Trek: The Next Generation* and *Babylon 5: The Gathering*. Hamilton Mitchell was in *Caddyshack*.

Diane Michelle provided the voice of Lashina in the animated *Superman*. Dafidd McCracken appeared in *Gang Related* and *Quantum Leap*. Molly Schaffer was in *Man on the Moon*. Mindy Seeger's CV includes *Fear*, *Father's Day* and *Baby Girl Scout*. Marlene Warfield was Victoria Butterfield in *Maude*, Laureen Hobbs in *Network* and appeared in *Hill Street Blues* and *Lou Grant*. Peter James Smith was in *Pearl Harbor*, *Dead Man on Campus*, *Silk Stalkings* and *Poker*. Wendell Wright played Lloyd Preston in *Days of Our Lives* and Sergeant Powell in *Highlander*. His movies include *The Onion Field*, *All the President's Men* and *The Howling*. A former place-kicker with the Indianapolis Colts and the St Louis Rams, Dean Biasucci was in *Jerry Maguire* and *Falcon Down*. Wendy Blair played Kelly in *Witchcraft XI: Sisters in Blood*.

Behind the Camera: Aaron Sorkin grew up in Scarsdale, New York. After graduating from Syracuse University he intended to pursue an acting career, but his talent lay in writing and he received the prestigious Outer Critics' Circle award for his third play, *A Few Good Men*, in 1989. The idea came from a conversation with his sister Deborah, a navy lawyer. Rob Reiner's movie adaptation appeared in 1993. Subsequently, Sorkin wrote *The American President*[33] and *Malice*, and did uncredited scriptwork on *Bulworth*, *Enemy of the State*, *The Rock* and *Schindler's List*. He also created *Sports Night*. In June 2001, he was sentenced to a drug-diversion programme after being arrested at Burbank airport for possession of marijuana, rock and hallucinogenic mushrooms.

John Wells was producer of *ER*, *China Beach* and *Third Watch*. In 1999 he became president of the Writers' Guild of America (West). Thomas Schlamme's acclaimed direction can be seen on series including *Ally McBeal*, *The Practice*, *Spin City*, *Friends*, *Mad About You*, *The Wonder Years* and *The Larry Sanders Show*.

---

[33] This 1995 movie, starring Michael Douglas and Annette Benning, represents a trial run for many of the ideas that Sorkin would explore in *The West Wing* (particularly in **4**, 'Five Votes Down').

Oh, Donna!: In the time Donna has worked for Josh she's never brought him a coffee. Until now (she does again when he's hung over in **14**, 'Take This Sabbath Day').

Sex and Drugs and Rock'n'Roll: Sam meets Laurie in a bar and they subsequently have sex, after which she smokes marijuana. All before the title sequence! 'It's not like I'm a drug person. I just love pot.' Laurie, it emerges, works for Cashmere Escort Service. 'Is it possible,' Sam asks when returning her pager, 'that in addition to being a law student and part-time bartender you are what I'm certain would have to be a very high-priced, call girl?'
    Toby quotes the Surgeon General (see **37**, 'Ellie') – that condoms reduce the risk of teen pregnancy and AIDS. So does abstinence, notes Mary Marsh, while Van Dyke adds, 'Show the average teenage male a condom and his mind will turn to thoughts of lust.' Toby is flabbergasted: 'Show the average teenage male a lug wrench and his mind'll turn . . .' The president considers five dollars too high a price to pay for pornography.

Cigarettes and Alcohol: In the bar a customer orders two Absolut Martinis and a Dewar's on the rocks. Laurie drinks white wine.

Logic, Let Me Introduce You to This Window: Toby says 'honour thy father' is the third commandment. It's the fifth in Judaism (though some Christian denominations regard it as the fourth). Leo claims the president might say 'economists were put on the earth to make astrologers look good' (a misquote of the economics guru Kenneth Galbraith) – seems a rather unlikely statement for an economist like Bartlet to make. There are actually several different spellings of Libyan dictator Moamar Gaddafi's surname (some with an 'h' and two 'd's, others without) depending where you are in the world.[34] The US military doesn't use

---

[34] *Guinness Book of Answers* (10th Edition, 1995) and *Chambers Biographical Dictionary* (1995 edition) both spell it Gaddafi – without an 'h'.

the Exocet, a French-built anti-ship missile whose uses against aeroplanes is limited, preferring sea-launched Tomahawk cruise missiles.

Quote/Unquote: Leo, on the president's accident: 'He was swerving to avoid a tree.' Donna: 'What happened?' Leo: 'He was unsuccessful.'

Leo, on the phone, concerning Gaddafi: 'You're spelling his name wrong. *My* name doesn't matter. I'm just an ordinary citizen who relies on the *Times* crossword for stimulation. I'm telling you that I've met the man twice and I've recommended a pre-emptive Exocet missile strike against his air force, so I think I know . . .'

Sam sums up the plot: 'Please believe me when I tell you that I'm a nice guy having a bad day. I just found out the *Times* is publishing a poll that says a considerable portion of Americans feel that the White House has lost energy and focus. A perception that's not likely to be altered by video footage of the president riding his bicycle into a tree . . . A good friend of mine's about to get fired for going on television and making sense. And, it turns out, I accidentally slept with a prostitute last night.' And, on discovering he's actually telling Leo's daughter all of this: 'Well, this is bad on so many levels.'

Notes: 'Seems to me we've all been taking a little break. Thinking about our personal lives or keeping our jobs.' Instant TV history. Minimalist introductions to the fore, as a pilot episode this is a work of genius. Highlights: CJ falling on the treadmill; Josh and Donna's brilliant badinage; Sam's bumbling performance with the kids and Mallory; Bartlet's first appearance.

The president was on vacation in Jackson Hole, Wyoming. The acronym POTUS (President of the United States) is used in beeper messages to staff. Location filming in Washington includes Leo and Caldwell walking along Pennsylvania Avenue and Mandy parking her car with the Capitol Building in the distance.

A New England: Bartlet, Leo and Josh all consider themselves New Englanders, a region of the northeastern

US comprising Maine, New Hampshire, Vermont, Rhode Island, Massachusetts and Connecticut.

Critique: ' "Nice morning, Mr McGarry," says the guard. "We'll take care of that," says Leo, as he passes through a corridor, an office, another office, a corridor, an office, five corridors, an office, a corridor, an office, a corridor, two offices, a corridor and two more offices, before settling behind his desk 3 minutes and 26 seconds later,' noted the *Philadelphia Inquirer*. 'He has 12 separate conversations, and 133 people pass in and out of the picture. That's more extras than populate some series in a whole season.'

'From the moment a disparate group of political high achievers receives the cryptic bleeper message "POTUS in a bicycle accident", the action never lets up,' added *Radio Times*. '*The West Wing* is a furious and frequently very funny ride through the corridors of power. It's a real "grown-up" drama with a script that crackles with wit and intelligence. The acting, by a cast of generally little-known actors, is as fine a piece of ensemble playing as we are likely to see this year. A real treat.'

Cast and Crew Comments: 'It wasn't my intention to paint the entire religious-right with one brush,' Sorkin told the *New York Post*. 'On the other hand, I admit that there are moments when I take a personal passion and let you all know about it.' On why he had Mandy use the term 'bitch-slapping', Sorkin informed the *St Petersburg Times*: 'I would never have a man saying it to a woman. But in that character, I find it endearing!'

Thomas Schlamme recalled haggling with Sorkin over the ending in *Entertainment Today*. The writer wanted to close the door on the Oval Office after the staff walked out; the director preferred to focus on the president alone with a shot that proclaimed, 'This is the arena we're going to be playing in from now on. My reason wasn't "Isn't that a cool shot?" It's that I think we can tell the story even better this way.'

Did You Know?: The inspiration for Sam's hopeless performance on White House history to the children may

have been Joe Lockhart, press secretary to President
Clinton, who told the *Chicago Tribune*: 'Having to [give
tours] on a regular basis, and frankly not knowing if that
room was named after Teddy Roosevelt or Franklin
Roosevelt, I'm pathetic. I haven't gotten caught yet, but
I've made up a few things.' Asked, subsequently, about the
series, Lockhart noted, 'In the premiere I saw a little bit of
myself in the absolute look of disdain on CJ's face when a
dumb question was asked. You can't learn that: you have
it naturally.'

The Left Wing?: 'You can look at the pilot and think this
is a left-leaning White House or a left-leaning writer who
took a roundhouse punch at the religious-right,' Sorkin
told the *Cleveland Plain Dealer*. 'But anybody who might
be upset, wait a week and you'll likely be cheering. I'm
looking forward to being unpredictable.'

New World Order: The Cabinet in the *West Wing* universe
includes Secretary of State Mickey Troop (**35**, 'Bartlet's
Third State of the Union'), Secretary of Defense Bill
Hutchinson (**3**, 'A Proportional Response', **24**, 'In the
Shadow of Two Gunmen' Part 2, **29**, 'The Portland
Trip'), Treasury Secretary Ken Kato (**21**, 'Lies, Damn
Lies and Statistics'), Attorney General Dan Larson (**21**,
'Lies, Damn Lies and Statistics', though see **3**, 'A Pro-
portional Response'), Secretary of Agriculture Roger
Tribby (**12**, 'He Shall, from Time to Time . . .', though
see **8**, 'Enemies'), Housing and Urban Development Sec-
retary Deborah O'Leary (**15**, 'Celestial Navigation'), Energy Secretary Ben Zaharian (**32**, 'Noël', his assistant,
Gerald Wegland is mentioned in **29**, 'The Portland Trip'.
In **39**, 'The Stackhouse Filibuster', the Secretary is Bill
Trotter) and National Security Advisor Nancy NcNally
(**23**, 'In the Shadow of Two Gunmen' Part 1). Other
high-ranking officials include: FBI Director Tom Connelly
(**3**, 'A Proportional Response'), CIA Director Rob Konrad
(**21**, 'Lies Damn Lies and Statistics', though a different
one, Rollie, is seen in **11**, 'Lord John Marbury' and
was presumably sacked after the agency's inability to

spot Indian troop movements), Chairman of the Federal
Reserve Ron Erhlich (**17**, 'The White House Pro-Am',
succeeding the late Bernard Dahl, who held the post from
1992 to 2000) and Chairman of the Joint Chiefs Admiral
Percy Fitzwallace (**3**, 'A Proportional Response'). There
have been four Republican presidents in the last thirty
years (**21**, 'Lies, Damn Lies and Statistics'), as in the real
world.

The Supreme Court has some differences (Crouch has
been on the bench for 38 years in **9**, 'The Short List')
though Judges Blackmun[35] (**14**, 'Take This Sabbath Day'),
Brennan[36] (**16**, '20 Hours in L.A.'), Black[37] (**7**, 'The State
Dinner') and Burger[38] (**9**, 'The Short List') are mentioned.
Similarly, Libya's Colonel Gaddafi exists in both worlds (**1**,
'The West Wing'), as does South Africa's President Mbeki
(**21**, 'Lies, Damn Lies and Statistics'), but Indonesia's
President Sugardo (**7**, 'The State Dinner'), the Indian
prime minster, Rikki Nohammid (**11**, 'Lord John
Marbury'), and the Bulgarian premier, Lucanov (**21**, 'Lies,
Damn Lies and Statistics'), are fictional. Bartlet names the
Israeli prime minister Benjamin in **6**, 'Mr. Willis of Ohio',
which could refer to Binyamin Netanyahu. Maybe here,
Ehud Barak didn't succeed him in 1999.

Bartlet's Background: From Manchester, New Hampshire
(**10**, 'In Excelsis Deo'), where his family has lived since at
least 1776 (Leo claims they 'founded the state' in **23**, 'In
the Shadow of Two Gunmen' Part 1). Jed is approximately
56 years old in **9**, 'The Short List' (Crouch took his seat on
the Supreme Court the year Bartlet began college –
probably 1962. Most college freshers are eighteen). Accep-

---

[35] Harry Blackmun (b. 1908). Appointed by President Nixon in 1970.
   Despite conservative credentials, was noted for his libertarianism,
   presiding over the landmark *Roe v Wade* case (see **9**, 'The Short List').
[36] William Brennan (b. 1906). Appointed by President Eisenhower in 1956.
[37] Hugo la Fayette Black (1886–1971). Associate Justice from 1937 (also
   mentioned in **9**, 'The Short List').
[38] Warren Burger (1907–95). Appointed by President Nixon in 1969 (also
   mentioned in **25**, 'The Midterms').

ted by Harvard, Yale and Williams, Bartlet chose Notre Dame because he was thinking of becoming a Catholic priest (confirmed in **29**, 'The Portland Trip', though he wears Notre Dame 'Fighting Irish' sweatshirts in **4**, 'Five Votes Down', and **5**, 'The Crackpots and These Women', and his Catholicism is central to **14**, 'Take This Sabbath Day'). Subsequently, he attended the London School of Economics (**9**, 'The Short List'. There, he wrote a controversial paper supporting the deregulation of Far East trade barriers). He is a PhD and a Nobel Laureate in Economics. He doesn't have a law degree (**41**, 'Bad Moon Rising') though he mentions his civil procedures professor (**22**, 'What Kind of Day Has it Been'). He's married to Abigail, a doctor (for 32 years when the series begins; they were dating while Abbey was in medical school, **12**, 'He Shall, from Time to Time . . .'). They have three daughters (alluded to in **16**, '20 Hours in L.A.', confirmed in **25**, 'The Midterms'), Elizabeth (**1**, 'The West Wing', who has a twelve-year-old daughter, Annie), Eleanor (**37**, 'Ellie') and Zoey (**5**, 'The Crackpots and These Women'). His mother seems to be alive (he speaks of her in the present tense in **4**, 'Five Votes Down'); his father, a school headmaster, wasn't Catholic and had a doctorate (**44**, 'Two Cathedrals'). He has a brother, Jonathan (**25**, 'The Midterms'), who once locked Jed in a steamer trunk. Jon now heads the Bartlet Presidential Library Commission (**38**, 'Somebody's Going to Emergency, Somebody's Going to Jail'). A brother-in-law is mentioned in **4**, 'Five Votes Down', but **44**, 'Two Cathedrals', confirms Jed doesn't have a sister, so this must be Abbey's brother. His grandmother was a teacher who began her career in a two-room schoolhouse and taught English to the children of Italian stonecutters (**29**, 'The Portland Trip'). Bartlet was a two-term governor (elected with a 69 per cent vote, **24**, 'In the Shadow of Two Gunmen' Part 2), a three-term Congressman (**2**, ' "Post Hoc, Ergo Propter Hoc" '; in his first Congressional race he beat Republican Elliot Roush, **25**, 'The Midterms') and a member of the New Hampshire State Legislature (**1**, 'The West Wing', where, 28 years ago, he came home from a

bad day at the State House and crashed his car). He may
have given up Congress to become governor. He didn't
lose his seat, since he has never lost an election (**20**,
'Mandatory Minimums'). He was elected president with 48
per cent of the vote (**19**, 'Let Bartlet Be Bartlet'). He has
'never spoken briefly in his life' (**15**, 'Celestial Navigation').
He is 'easy to like when you get to know him' (**24**, 'In the
Shadow of Two Gunmen' Part 2).

Bartlet has done no military service (**13**, 'Take Out the
Trash Day': at the height of Vietnam, he was safely in
London), though he *was* commander-in-chief of the New
Hampshire National Guard (**2**, ' "Post Hoc, Ergo Propter
Hoc" '). The president smokes occasionally ('two cigarettes
a day', **36**, 'The War at Home'), though he likes to pretend
he gave up years ago (**15**, 'Celestial Navigation'). He plays
basketball, tennis (**5**, 'The Crackpots and These Women')
and chess (**4**, 'Five Votes Down', **36**, 'The War at Home')
and was a trombonist in the school marching band (**31**,
'Galileo'). He doesn't play golf (**4**, 'Five Votes Down'),
even doubting its right to be called a sport (**34**, 'The Drop
In') and has probably never been trout fishing (**19**, 'Let
Bartlet Be Bartlet'). He enjoys watching sport on TV with
a beer (**22**, 'What Kind of Day Has it Been') and is a fan
of the Boston Celtics (**12**, 'He Shall, from Time to Time
. . .'; given the Celtics' rivalry with the LA Lakers, whom
Sam follows, that must make for interesting conversations). He is allergic to eggnog (**10**, 'In Excelsis Deo'). A
lover of classical music, he also admires Buddy Holly and
the Beatles (**31**, 'Galileo'). Around 1991 Bartlet began
feeling ill and had pains in his leg, which subsided after a
few months. The symptoms returned two years later and,
during an eye exam, a doctor detected abnormal pupil
response. Subsequent tests detected plaque on Bartlet's
brain and spine (**40**, '17 People') and he was diagnosed
with multiple sclerosis (**12**, 'He Shall, from Time to Time
. . .'). His life expectancy is normal and his course is
relapsing-remitting, meaning he should experience total
recovery after attacks (these have included one in Nan-
tucket and one at Abbey's parents' house). He once

accidentally ran over his former next-door neighbours, Herb and Marjorie Douglas, in his car (**17**, 'The White House Pro-Am'). Jed doesn't like vegetables (**19**, 'Let Bartlet Be Bartlet'), particularly green beans (**31**, 'Galileo'). He's given depositions in two lawsuits: when a meter-reader slipped in his drive and involving his great aunt's will. He has considerable personal wealth but no life or medical insurance (**41**, 'Bad Moon Rising'). When he was in tenth grade he and friends took his father's Ford Country Squire for a joyride to Vermont (**32**, 'Noël').

Capital Beat: The *West Wing* universe's current affairs TV show is probably based on CNN's *The Capital Gang*, a weekly political programme on Saturday afternoons.

2
"Post Hoc, Ergo Propter Hoc"

US Transmission Date: 29 September 1999
UK Transmission Date: 17 January 2000 (Sky), 25 January 2001 (C4)

Writer: Aaron Sorkin
Director: Thomas Schlamme
Cast: Ruben Santiago-Hudson (Morris Tolliver) Merrin Dungey (Daisy) Andy Umberger (Stevie) John Bedford Lloyd (Lloyd Russell) Gilles Savard (LaRouche) J August Richards (Bill) Mary Kay Wulf (Janet) Tammy Tavares (Woman) Chuti Tiu (Woman #2) Eric Fleeks (Officer #2) Chris Hendrie (Businessman) Paul Doherty (Aide #1) Neal Moran (Aide #2) Brad Van Grack (Pedestrian)

Despite warnings, Sam continues to pursue Laurie. CJ tries to defuse a public clash between the president and his vice president. Bartlet chooses a young naval officer as his personal physician.

A View from the Hill: One of Russell's staffers talks about keeping a bill in committee until after the midterms, allowing the president to veto it while no one is looking. Before bills are introduced to the House or Senate, they are argued in committee. Most of the legislative work is done here. However, the process also sees a lot of bureaucratic manoeuvring. Russell's price for this is to be offered a spot at the nominating convention, possibly a keynote speech.

American History X: The vice president mentions Article 2 of the Constitution concerning executive powers (in this case, whether the chief-of-staff can order him to do *anything*).

Politics of Compromise: The trade surplus causes Leo to note that the Japanese need to buy more American cars. '*Americans* need to buy more American cars,' notes the president.

A Little Learning is a Dangerous Thing: One of Russell's staff thinks Wagner was Italian.

The Encyclopedic Mind of Josiah Bartlet PhD: 'You have a once-in-a-generation mind,' says Tolliver. The episode title is a Latin phrase translated as 'After it, therefore because of it'. Which means, Bartlet tells his staff, that 'one thing follows the other, therefore it was caused by the other, but it's hardly ever true'.

Denial, Thy Name is Bartlet: The president believes he is an accomplished man who can sit comfortably with prime ministers and presidents, even the pope. 'Why is it every time I sit with the Joint Chiefs, I feel like I'm back at my father's dinner table?'

The Conspiracy Starts at Closing Time: An Air Force transport carrying Morris Tolliver and other doctors to a teaching hospital in Amman, Jordan, exploded 150 miles north of Tartus. What was first thought to be a mechanical failure was then claimed by a fundamentalist group after a keyhole satellite recorded a heat stream coming from a shoulder-mounted surface-to-air missile launcher. Hard intelligence suggests the order came from the Syrians.

References: 'Nessun Dorma' from *Turandot* by Giacomo Puccini (1858–1924), German composer Richard Wagner (1813–83), the Ryder Cup (a golf competition played biannually between the USA and Europe), the morning chat show *Live! With Regis and Kathie Lee* (Kathie Lee Gifford subsequently left; it's now called *Live! With Regis and Kelly*), the *Wall Street Journal* and *USA Today*, the superhero genre ('I didn't reveal my secret identity'), the breakfast cereal Cheerios, Central Indiana State, Nebraska, Purdue, Notre Dame and Yeshiva universities and Rocky Mountain College. Also, the Dallas Cowboys, Pasadena Rose Bowl, G-8 (formerly G-5, then G-7, an informal grouping of the leading Western economic powers, plus Italy and Russia) and Chris Matthews, host of NBC's *Hardball*. CJ makes a sarcastic reference to the Whiffenpoofs, the Yale Varsity singing quartet. A photograph of Senator Edward Kennedy can be seen on the wall directly opposite Toby's office.

'You May Remember Me From Such Films and TV Series As . . .': A child star as the voice of the Hanna-Barbara cartoon hero Jonny Quest, Tim Matheson grew up in San Fernando Valley. His TV debut was in *Window on Main Street* and was followed by roles on *The Twilight Zone*, *Leave it to Beaver* and *My Three Sons*. Soon after his first movie, *Divorce American Style*, he joined the Marine Corps reserves, pursued collegiate studies and appeared in many classic series, including *The Virginian*, *Bonanza* and *The Quest*. A small part in *Magnum Force* led to his best-known role as Otter, the oversexed frat brother, in *National Lampoon's Animal House*. He's now usually cast as smarmy but likable romantics, and his movies include *1941*, *Speed Zone!*, *Drop Dead Fred*, *A Very Brady Sequel*, *Catch Me If You Can* and *She's All That*. He produced the 1990 comedy *Blind Fury*, and briefly co-owned The *National Lampoon* magazine.

Merrin Dungey was Kitty Kenarban in *Malcolm in the Middle* and Joan in *Grosse Pointe*, and was in *The Sky is Falling*. Blink and you'll miss him in a two-word cameo, J August Richards is more famous as the teenage vampire hunter Charles Gunn in *Angel*. He also played Richard Street in *The Temptations*. Renee Estevez, aside from being

Martin's daughter, has a CV that includes *Heathers*, *A Murder of Crows*, *Addams Family Reunion*, *Good Girls Don't*, *Single White Female* and *MacGuyer*. Erik Fleeks's movies include *Campfire Tales*, *Deep Red* and *Virus*. Chris Hendrie was in *Fear and Loathing in Las Vegas*. Ruben Santiago-Hudson played Jimmy Groves in *Shaft* and Leamon Heath in *The Devil's Advocate*, and appeared in *Coming to America* and *Red Sneakers*. Gilles Savard was in *Pee-wee's Big Adventure* and *Scrooged*. Mary Kay Wulf was Aunt Rose in *Infinity*. Steven M Gagnon appeared in *The X-Files*, *Liar Liar* and *Escape from New York*. Tammy Tavares was Dr Bader in *Days of Our Lives*. Victor Love was in *Velocity Trap* and *Shadow of Doubt*. Bradley James's movies include *Cast a Deadly Spell*. Andy Umberger played D'Hoffryn in *Buffy the Vampire Slayer* and can be seen in *The X-Files* and *Tempting Fate*. John Bedford Lloyd was Louis in *Fair Game* and appeared in *Nixon*, *The Abyss* and *Spin City*.

Behind the Camera: The New York playwright Peter Parnell was Aaron Sorkin's writing teacher. His plays include *The Rise and Rise of Daniel Rocket*, *Hyde in Hollywood* and *Flaubert's Latest*. The producers Kristin Harms and Michael Hissrich both worked on *Third Watch* (Hissrich also produced *ER*). Llewellyn Wells was production manager on movies such as *Reform School Girl*, *That Night*, *Runaway Daughters*, *The Grifters*, *Confessions of a Sorority Girl* and *Girls in Prison*.

This is the first episode to feature WG Snuffy Walden's theme music. His scores can be heard on *Early Edition*, *My So-Called Life*, *thirtysomething*, *Roswell* and *Felicity*. He was also guitarist/musical director for acts as diverse as Chaka Khan, Laura Brannigan, Donna Summer and the former Animals' singer/songwriter Eric Burdon.

Oh, Donna!: Josh, gloating, asks Donna to bring him the finest muffins in all the land. 'It's gonna be an unbearable day,' she replies. Later, she walks in on Josh and Sam discussing the Laurie situation and, conspiratorially, asks them what they're talking about.

Sex and Drugs and Rock'n'Roll: Asked whether he's concerned about Sam's relationship with Laurie, Josh asks who among them hasn't known forbidden love. Sam says he's decided to become Laurie's friend. 'Am I supposed to strip down for you now?' she asks. Laurie says she wasn't abused as a child and likes what she does.

Cigarettes and Alcohol: Tolliver tells the president to cut down on Scotch. Daisy and Mandy contemplate a grim future drinking wine from paper cups. The bar where Sam met Laurie was the Four Seasons near Georgetown. This is the hotel where Sorkin lived for several months while writing *The American President* in 1995.

Logic, Let Me Introduce You to This Window: The vice president claims in **8**, 'Enemies', that he delivered the South in the election. But he's a Texan and this episode confirms that the Democrats got whomped in Texas. Perhaps their Republican opponent was also from Texas and, though they lost Hoynes's home state, they took the rest of the South because of his good-ol'-boy credentials. However, for the South as a whole to go Democrat is unheard of since the days of Roosevelt. Mandy says she worked with the Bartlet team for two and a half years. Given how long Donna has been Josh's assistant (**1**, 'The West Wing') and the timescale established in **24**, 'In the Shadow of Two Gunmen' Part 2, that isn't possible (see **19**, 'Let Bartlet Be Bartlet'). What are Toby, Sam and Josh doing in a meeting with military personnel before the president arrives? None of them usually have any involvement in foreign affairs. The euro is divisible by cents, not pennies.

Quote/Unquote: CJ, on the Ryder Cup team: 'In the world of sports, the White House just got dissed by twelve guys named Flippy.'

Mandy: 'I'm accomplished and brilliant. Yet, look how young and cute I am.'

Toby, to Sam: 'You accidentally slept with a prostitute? I don't understand. Did you trip over something?'

Leo: 'Can you think of a single reason not to use Mandy that isn't personal?' Josh: 'She used to be my girlfriend.'

Notes: 'Everybody's a critic today.' A furiously paced continuation of the themes of the pilot showing the labyrinthine levels of power within an administration (the vice president has his own agenda). Best bits: Leo distracting Margaret with a picture of Tolliver's baby; Josh's little victory dance at the beginning.

The president's doctor is Terry Wyatt, for whom Tolliver has been deputising. The White House chef is called Mario.

Cast and Crew Comments: 'My character is largely drawn from Bill Clinton,' Martin Sheen told *Radio Times*. 'He's bright, astute and filled with all the negative foibles that make him very human.'

'As a writer, I don't like to answer questions until I have to,' Aaron Sorkin notes. 'In the second episode, we find out our president was a three-term congressman, two-term governor and Nobel laureate. That's not something I jot down on a legal pad. It comes up naturally as you explore the episodes.'

Did You Know?: Owing to management nervousness about the leftish leanings of the pilot, Sorkin was stuck at NBC headquarters being grilled by petrified executives and missed much of the first day's filming of this episode. He was, however, there in spirit – in the form of a three-man mariachi band he hired to serenade the cast when they returned from lunch. 'Did Aaron do this?' asked Bradley Whitford grabbing Allison Janney for an impromptu dance.

Sam's Background: He's from Southern California (**2**, ' "Post Hoc, Ergo Propter Hoc" '), and his parents split in 2001 after his father's lengthy affair with a woman in Santa Monica was revealed (**38**, 'Somebody's Going to Emergency, Somebody's Going to Jail'). Sam's middle name is Norman (he's thinking of changing it to 'On Schedule', **18**, 'Six Meetings Before Lunch'). CJ doubts Sam was able to date girls in high school, though he claims this is untrue (**34**, 'The Drop In'). Toby's nickname for Sam is Princeton (**6**, 'Mr. Willis of Ohio'), the prestigious university that Sam attended. In his undergraduate thesis he argued for the alleged spy Daniel Gault's innocence (**38**, 'Somebody's Going to Emergency, Somebody's Going to Jail'). Princeton is also his Secret Service codename (**10**, 'In Excelsis Deo'). He was recording secretary of the Gilbert and Sullivan Society for two years (**27**, 'And it's Surely to Their Credit'). Sam attended Duke law school with Tom Jordan (**25**, 'The Midterms'), graduated eight years before **1**, 'The West Wing', and worked for Dewey-Ballantine. In four years of college and three years of law school, Sam spent $30 at Kinko's stationery store (**39**, 'The Stackhouse Filibuster'). He also worked as a congressional aide (**24**, 'In the Shadow of Two Gunmen' Part 2) but before joining the Bartlet team he was at Gage Whitney Page in New York protecting oil companies from litigation, was about to become a partner (**23**, 'In the Shadow of Two Gunmen' Part 1) and was making $400,000 a year. Sam brokered a deal for Kensington Oil to purchase the *Indio*, an aged tanker with faulty navigation systems. The *Indio* later ran aground off Delaware (**42**, 'The Fall's Gonna Kill You'). He was engaged to someone named Lisa in 1997 (**23**, 'In the Shadow of Two Gunmen' Part 1). They were due to marry in the September but something prevented this. Even at that stage, Josh and Sam were close friends, though it's yet to be revealed when they first met.

Sam describes himself as a counsellor to the president, mostly on domestic matters, generally not security-related. He, Toby and CJ work on 'crafting our message' (**1**, 'The West Wing'). During the campaign Sam wrote a significant portion of the president's speeches along with the Inaugural address and the State of the Union (**8**, 'Enemies'). He doesn't think he knows any state secrets. He's classified but doesn't have code-word clearance (**38**, 'Somebody's Going to Emergency, Somebody's Going to Jail'). He *can* recite the members of Congress in alphabetical order and knows a lot about capital gains tax (**2**, '"Post Hoc, Ergo Propter

Hoc"'). Leo's wife (see **4**, 'Five Votes Down') hates Sam
after he tried to chat her up at a fundraiser. He's something
of a klutz, stumbling over boxes in **9**, 'The Short List' while
references are made to his having once fallen overboard
('Hold on to a rope,' Leo suggests when Sam goes boating
in **14**, 'Take This Sabbath Day'). Congresswoman Reeseman meets Sam in the gym and says, 'I heard the clang and
the "ow". I figured it must be Sam Seaborn' (**17**, 'The
White House Pro-Am'). He dances like a white boy (**18**,
'Six Meetings Before Lunch'). When Laurie suggests she
makes more money than Sam, he replies, 'You and any kid
with a good paper route' (**2**, ' "Post Hoc, Ergo Propter
Hoc" ') though, in the private sector, he hires himself out
at $500 an hour (**7**, 'The State Dinner'). He is the lawyer
all the lawyers in the office turn to when they need legal
assistance (**11**, 'Lord John Marbury'). His favourite novelist is Charles Dickens (**39**, 'The Stackhouse Filibuster'). He
is 'nuts' about dental hygiene (**15**, 'Celestial Navigation').
He says he is less visually observant than others, but makes
up for it with cunning and guile (**41**, 'Bad Moon Rising').
CJ's occasional nickname for Sam is Spanky (**24**, 'In the
Shadow of Two Gunmen' Part 2). It's possible Sam once
played the clarinet (**38**, 'Somebody's Going to Emergency,
Somebody's Going to Jail').

3
A Proportional Response

US Transmission Date: 6 October 1999
UK Transmission Date: 24 January 2000 (Sky), 1 February 2001 (C4)

Writer: Aaron Sorkin
Director: Marc Buckland
Cast: Chad McKnight (Staffer #2) Jack Montoya (Floor Manager)
Andrew Shaifer (Reporter #4) Hunter von Leer (Officer #4)

Seeking vengeance for the downing of an American jet,
Bartlet overrules the Joint Chiefs' plan for a proportional
strike and demands a more severe response. CJ discovers

Sam's secret. Josh interviews Charlie Young as a potential aide to the president.

A View from the Hill: Among the questions Josh asks Charlie in his application is, 'Have you ever tried to overthrow the government?' Charlie says he hasn't. 'What the hell's been stopping you?' asks Sam.

American History X: 'We're behaving the way a super-power ought to,' Leo notes, but the president thinks such behaviour produces crappy results. He believes attacks on US personnel in Beirut, Somalia and Nairobi have been *caused* by inertia and the knowledge that they won't retaliate. 'Ratcheting up the body count's gonna act as a deterrent?' asks Leo incredulously. 'If you wanna start using American military strength as the arm of the Lord, you can do that, we're the only superpower left,' he adds. 'But you better be prepared to kill everyone and start with me.'

The Blue Room is a reception area, decorated with sapphire-blue fabric from which it acquires its name. It contains busts of Christopher Columbus (1451–1506) and Amerigo Vespucci (c.1451–1512) and a portrait of James Monroe (1758–1831), the fifth president.

Politics of Compromise: At dinner the previous evening the president snapped at the first lady (mentioned for the first time) while talking about blowing up half of North Africa. After the downing of the aircraft three days previously (see **2**, ' "Post Hoc, Ergo Propter Hoc" ') the Joint Chiefs prepare a scenario that meets the obligations of proportional response. The plan targets ammunition dumps, an abandoned railway bridge and the Syrian intelligence agency. The Syrians, however, know this and the areas have been abandoned. Asked what alternative to this plan there is, the president replies, 'The disproportional response. Let the word ring forth: you kill an American . . . we come back with total disaster.' Is he suggesting carpet-bombing Damascus? Bartlet orders that a plan be formulated that 'doesn't make me think we're just docking somebody's allowance'. Such a scenario is presented, involving attacking Hassan airport. The civilian causalities could be in the thousands. This would be seen abroad as a staggering overreaction, Fitzwallace says. 'You'll have doled out a five-thousand-dollar punishment for a fifty-buck crime.' Finally, the president opts for the proportional response.

A Little Learning is a Dangerous Thing: Josh calls CJ a 'paranoid Berkeley shiksta-feminista'. CJ retaliates, describing Josh as an 'élitist Harvard fascist missed-the-Dean's-list-two-semesters-in-a-row Yankee-jackass'.

The Encyclopedic Mind of Josiah Bartlet PhD: Two thousand years ago, the president notes, a Roman citizen could travel anywhere fearlessly, cloaked only in the words *Civis Romanis*. So great was the retribution should any harm befall one of its citizens. 'Where's the warning to the rest of the world that Americans shall walk this earth unharmed, lest the clenched fist of the most mighty military force in history comes crashing down on your house?' he asks. The president does not, in times of stress, suffer incompetence gladly (his phrase 'amateur hour' crops up again in **24**, 'In the Shadow of Two Gunmen' Part 2).

Office Gossip: After Josh assures Donna that she knows *everything* about what's going on in the White House, she says that CJ is looking for him: 'Best I can cobble together from the small shards of information I've been able to overhear in the restroom and the Danish cart. Is it possible there's a situation involving Sam, a woman and CJ being denied information?'

Denial, Thy Name is Mandy: Her present to Josh is a picture of them (taken the night they met). Someone has drawn over Josh's face with magic marker. 'That was me,' notes Mandy, 'during my period of hating you.' That could have been any time, Josh adds.

The Conspiracy Starts at Closing Time: Democrat Congressman Bertram Coles, appearing on the radio with officers from Cromwell Air Force Base, says the president is weak and suggests that if he visits the base he may not survive. Josh and Sam think it's a big joke. There ought to be a law against it, according to Leo. 'There is,' argues Toby. 'Threatening the life of the president. He was talking to other people. How about conspiracy? Those were military officers. How about treason?' Toby wants the Justice Department to press charges. 'What's the good of being in power if you're not gonna haul your enemies in for questioning?' asks Josh sarcastically. Toby gets his own way, however, telling reporters that the Secret Service investigates all threats made against the president.

References: The Pentagon, headquarters of the Department of Defense. Also, the American College Training Program, Pericles (490–429 BC: Athenian statesman responsible for the flowering of democracy and the construction of the Acropolis), Charlemagne (742–814, medieval King of the Franks) and the FBI (created in 1908 by Attorney General Charles Bonaparte). Josh enters his office to find CJ sitting with her feet on his desk, a visual reference to *The Graduate*. There's an allusion to *The Dating Game*.

'You May Remember Me From Such Films and TV Series As . . .': Instantly recognisable as Elliot in *thirtysomething*, Tim Busfield numbers among his other roles Woods in *First Kid*, Mark in *Field of Dreams*, Doug in *Family Ties* and JT in *Trapper John M.D.* He also appeared in *National Security* and *Quiz Show*. A TV legend as the adult Kunte Kinte in *Roots*, John Amos was Seth in *The Beastmaster*, Fred Wilkes in *The Fresh Prince of Bel Air* and the villainous Major Howard in *Die Hard II*. He played Gordon Howard in *The Mary Tyler Moore Show* and appeared in *Ricochet*, *The A-Team* and *Sanford and Son*. Kim Webster was Miss Drake in *The Glass House*. Ivan Allen appeared in *Melrose Place* and *Apollo 1*. Andrew Schaifer's movies include *Who's Your Daddy?*, *The Wedding Singer*, *The Cable Guy* and *Deuce Bigalow: Male Gigolo*. Chad McKnight played Wilson in *ER*. George McDaniel was Alan Caldwell in *Falcon Crest* and Niven in

General Hospital. He also appeared in *Cast the First Stone*, *This is Spinal Tap*, *Magnum P.I.* and *The Dukes of Hazzard*. Rose Rollins was in *13 Moons*. Marvin Krueger's movies include *Coyote Ugly* and *Problem Child 3*. Hunter von Leer was BD Calhoun in *Dallas* and appeared in *Charlie's Angels*, *Halloween II*, *High Anxiety* and *The Missouri Breaks*. Christopher Kriesa's CV includes *Blind Obsession*, *The Stepdaughter*, *Shocker*, *The Karate Kid* and *T.J. Hooker*.

Behind the Camera: Marc Buckland has directed episodes of *Popular*, *Felicity*, *Maximum Bob* and *Murder One* (which he also produced) and appeared in *Star Trek: The Next Generation*.

Oh, Donna!: Josh asks Donna why she can't tell him when there's someone in his office. Donna replies that the first time (CJ) she didn't know and the second time (Mandy) she didn't care.

Sex and Drugs and Rock'n'Roll: Josh argues that Sam didn't know Laurie was a call girl when he went home with her and didn't participate in anything illegal, immoral or unethical. 'None of that matters on hard copy,' replies CJ.

Cigarettes and Alcohol: The president smokes in the Situations Room.

Logic, Let Me Introduce You to This Window: Charlie isn't in college because he has to raise his sister. But his mother died when he was twenty, yet he doesn't seem to have been in college then. He should have been able to attend after his mother died without needing a part-time job to support it: because she was a police officer killed in the line of duty, her children should have access to death benefits and insurance. He would also have more time to raise his sister if he *was* in college than he does now with an up-to-twenty-hours-a-day, seven-days-a-week job.

Quote/Unquote: Leo: 'Do you have any problem with a young black man waiting on the president?' Fitzwallace: 'I'm an old black man and I wait on the president. You gonna pay him a decent wage? Treat him with respect in the workplace?' Leo: 'Yeah.' Fitzwallace: 'Then why the hell should I care?'

Toby: 'Ordinarily we get help from inside the Syrian intelligence.' Bartlet: 'So what's the problem?' Toby: 'We just blew up Syrian intelligence.' Bartlet: 'Somebody get on the phone to CNN and find out if we hit anything?'

Notes: 'The proportional response doesn't empty the options box for the future.' A first indication that Bartlet isn't quite the stereotypical soppy liberal that many viewers believed. A story about thirst for revenge and the responsibility of power, this is a cracking deconstruction of the last twenty years of American foreign policy (watching it in the aftermath of the events of 11 September 2001 is a chilling experience). John Amos is fabulous, and the persistent rain helps to maintain a miserable atmosphere throughout. Best bits: CJ and Sam's argument in which both make the mistake of saying three things that all mean the same; Leo and Fitzwallace talking the president down from an understandable desire for blood.

The tie the president wears was given to him by his granddaughter (see **1**, 'The West Wing'). Josh tells Charlie that being personal aide to the president is a very hard job. There will be times when he'll have to make himself invisible, as well as an undeniable force to those who want more of the president's time (including kings and prime ministers). Traditionally the role is filled by someone twenty to twenty-five who excels academically, has strong personal responsibility and discretion. The previous job holder was called Ted Miller. After the president shouts at Charlie, Josh says this has been a bad day. 'He's ordinarily an extremely kind man, placing a high premium on civility' (this *is* usually true, but see **24**, 'In the Shadow of Two Gunmen' Part 2). Danny has been a White House reporter for seven years. He knows that Sam's been seeing a $3,000-a-night call-girl.

Token?: Criticism from the National Association for the Advancement of Colored People caused the producers to re-evaluate their casting policy. 'We're looking awfully white,' noted Sorkin. 'We're in no way resentful of NAACP tapping us on the shoulder and pointing it out.' Hence the creation of Charlie. 'The show needs to look like America,' continues Sorkin.

Critique: 'Hardly anyone ever stands still to have a conversation in this fast-paced US drama,' noted *Radio Times*. 'Like some sort of speeded-up ballet, the characters whiz up and down corridors, constantly walking and talking . . . This series has hit the ground running, it may have taken viewers this long to get to grips with the characters and the dizzying speed of it all but it's addictive stuff. You can see why thirteen million Americans tune-in to every episode.'

Cast and Crew Comments: 'I believe in nonviolence as a way of life,' Martin Sheen told Bob Blakey. 'I'm playing the commander-in-chief of the most powerful military force in the world and this guy is anxious to use it.'

'Bartlet is often vengeful when it comes to the Arab world, which troubles me,' Sheen explained to *Irish American* magazine. 'I'm always fighting for diplomacy rather than military intervention. But we have to satisfy the other side sometimes.'

Did You Know?: The re-creation of the White House on soundstage 28 at Warner Bros' studios in Burbank is, according to observers, uncannily accurate. 'When I got to see the real Oval Office,' says Richard Schiff, 'I almost jumped on the couch and put my feet up because it's so similar to ours.' Highlight of the day for Schiff? 'I got to meet Bill Clinton's dog, Buddy. *That* was cool!'

Charlie's Background: Charlie is a native of DC. His father is long gone and his mother, a police officer, was killed on duty five months prior to **3**, 'A Proportional Response' (the incident is dated June 1999 in **25**, 'The Midterms'). His younger sister is called Deena. He has a driver's licence and owns a bike. Charlie's grandparents have a house on the Georgia coast (**7**, 'The State Dinner'). He hasn't read

Revelation (**11**, 'Lord John Marbury'). Josh notes that Charlie's grades are better than his (adding, 'Not really, but they're close' – **3**, 'A Proportional Response'). Nevertheless, Charlie seems insecure about not having gone to college (**6**, 'Mr. Willis of Ohio'). He caddied for two summers at Sandy Hooks golf course (**9**, 'The Short List') and was a waiter at the Gramercy, an all-white club (**21**, 'Lies, Damn Lies and Statistics'). His White House income is $600 a week (**19**, 'Let Bartlet Be Bartlet'). He plays basketball (**5**, 'The Crackpots and These Women'). His philosophy on self-defence involves 'running as fast as I can' (**41**, 'Bad Moon Rising'). The part of his job Charlie likes least is waking the president (**15**, 'Celestial Navigation', **33**, 'The Leadership Breakfast'). When the president asks if, when his mother's killer is found, Charlie wants to see them executed, Charlie replies he'd wish to do it himself (**14**, 'Take This Sabbath Day'). He blames himself for her murder: she wasn't supposed to be on that particular shift, but Charlie asked her to switch (**25**, 'The Midterms'). Charlie says he never gets a night off when Zoey asks him for a date. Charlie asks her father's permission and Bartlet is initially reluctant (not, he is quick to add, because Charlie is black but because he is *male*). He eventually gives his consent but tells Charlie to remember Zoey is nineteen, and that he has the 82nd Airborne working for him (**11**, 'Lord John Marbury').

4
Five Votes Down

US Transmission Date: 13 October 1999
UK Transmission Date: 31 January 2000 (Sky), 8 February 2001 (C4)

Teleplay: Aaron Sorkin
Story: Lawrence O'Donnell Jr, Patrick Caddell
Director: Michael Lehmann
Cast: Michael McGuire (Cal Tillinghouse) Jay Underwood (Chris Wick)
Mark Blum (Katzenmoyer) Sara Botsford (Jenny McGarry)
Jillian Armenante (Leela) Jackie Mari Roberts (Janeane)

Cynthia Abeln (Female Groupie #1)
Paige Taylor Adams (Female Groupie #2)
Hanna Cheek (Female Groupie #3) Sheila Frazier (Newscaster #2)
Mia Tate (Cocktail Waitress) Julia Pearlstein (Volunteer)

'Two things you never want to let people see how you
make 'em: laws and sausages.' Leo needs five more votes
to pass a bill restricting the sale of automatic firearms – but
the cost may be too high, especially if he requires the vice
president's help. The staff's financial disclosures prove
thorny for Toby. Leo's long hours cause an unforeseen
crisis at home and the president unintentionally mixes up
his medications.

A View from the Hill: Votes are expensive, Sam notes.
Congressman O'Bannon will want farm subsidies revisited
to secure his, while Katzenmoyer wants the federal-tax-
exempt metro link. Josh meets Katzenmoyer, who narrowly won his seat. 'From the moment I'm sworn in I need to
raise ten thousand dollars a week just to run a re-election
campaign . . . The NRA makes me a target in the next
election, I lose.' Josh tells the Congressman to vote yes, or
he will lose the primary, never mind the election. No
Democrat is running against him, argues Katzenmoyer.
There is, replies Josh. 'You won with fifty-two per cent, but
the president took your district with fifty-nine. I think it's
time we come back and say thanks. Do you have any idea
how much noise *Air Force One* makes when it lands in Eau
Claire, Wisconsin?' The President will, Josh says, drape his
arm around some assistant DA that the White House likes
and Katzenmoyer will be finished in politics. President
Bartlet is a good man, Josh continues. He doesn't hold a
grudge. 'That's what he pays *me* for.'
    Leo, meanwhile, has to deal with the more heartfelt
concerns of Mark Richardson, leader of the Congressional
black caucus, who is voting against the bill because it
doesn't go far enough. Guns are number one on his list of
priorities, Leo argues. On the contrary, keeping the White
House strong is, responds Richardson. Leo notes that the
bodies being wheeled into the emergency room are black.

'These guns aren't going to Scottsdale: they're going to Detroit [and] Philadelphia. An entire generation of African-American men are being eaten alive by drugs and poverty.' Richardson, sarcastically, says he's encouraged to hear the White House has discovered there's a drug problem. 'Your insight is matched only by the courage displayed in the authorship of this bill,' which is, Richardson says, a waste of the taxpayer's money.

In the event, the bill is passed by one vote and the restrictions, while not considered sweeping, do include several nasty weapons. But it's the vice president who receives most of the credit.

American History X: Josh says that Lyndon B Johnson (1908–73), the 36th president, 'never would've taken this kind of crap from Democrats. He'd have said, "You're voting my way, in exchange for which it's possible that I might remember your name." ' The Mural Room is more formally known as the Diplomatic Reception Room. The panoramic wallpaper, *Views of North America*, was printed in 1834 by Jean Zuber et Cie. The vice president has a portrait of Abraham Lincoln (1809–65), the 16th president, on his office wall.

Politics of Expediency: Josh helped his friend Chris Wick into Congress. Wick, however, is disappointed that he's had only one photo opportunity with the president since. A relationship with the White House is currency, he says. 'You're voting down a measure that would restrict the sale of deadly weapons because nobody invited you to the cool kid's table?' Josh asks angrily. They agree that Wick will join the president for a game of chess over brandy with the White House photographers.

Office Gossip: Josh gets congratulations from several staff because, as Donna tells him, he's won the award for best gift valued over $25 on the financial disclosure report with the $1,198 Viennatelli silk smoking jacket from Sarah Wissinger. He was also runner-up with a $345 antique scrimshaw cigarette holder, also from Ms Wissinger. We later discover he got these a week before he and Mandy broke up, much to Mandy's annoyance. Someone else has given Josh a year's supply of fruit.

Denial, Thy Name is Toby: Toby didn't own shares until the previous year, when he bought $5,000 stock in an Internet company. This is now worth $125,000; 71 per cent of the increase happened the day after professor Theodore McGregor testified to the Commerce Committee on the future of Internet stocks. Toby arranged for McGregor, who grew up on the same block, to testify. Sam suggests that, to avoid the appearance of impropriety, Toby agree to reduce his salary for one year to $1, and immediately cash in his stock issue, thereby relieving the taxpayer of the burden.

The Conspiracy Starts at Closing Time: CJ asks the press not to report that the president received an Armani cravat from his brother-in-law, as he gave it to the Salvation Army.

References: The music that accompanies Bartlet's leaving the stage is J Yellar and M Agar's 'Happy Days Are Here Again' (Sam says it's an odd juxtaposition with a speech about gun laws). Also, the exclusive jewellers Harry Winston, telegraph company Western Union, the Julliard (a New York school of music founded in 1905), the National Rifle Association, Italian fashion designer Giorgio Armani, the Holland Tunnel in New Jersey and the National Football League. CJ plays with a Magic Eight-Ball toy.

'You May Remember Me From Such Films and TV Series As . . .': Michael McGuire played Judah Zachery in *Dark Shadows* and appeared in *Bird*, *Shakedown on Sunset Strip*, *Cheers*, *M*A*S*H*, *Harry O* and *Kojak*. Thom Barry was in *Rules of Engagement*, *Space Jam*, *Independence Day* and *Apollo 13*. Jay Underwood played Bug in *Uncle Buck* and Ernest Hemingway in *The Young Indiana Jones Chronicles*, and appeared in *Millennium*, *The Girl's Room* and *Valerie*

Flake. Mark Blum was in *Emma and Elvis*, *Roseanne*, *Miami Rhapsody*, *The Sopranos*, *Crocodile Dundee* and *Desperately Seeking Susan*. Mongo Brownlee's movies include *Me, Myself & Irene* and *Bulworth*. Sara Botsford was in *Legal Eagles*, *Murder by Phone* and *Jumpin' Jack Flash*, and she directed *Dead Innocent*.

Jillian Armenante played Cynthia in *Girl Interrupted* and Donna Kozlowski-Pant in *Judging Amy*, and was also in *Delivered* and *Northern Exposure*. Paige Taylor Adams appeared in *Facade* and *Broken Reality*. Penny Griego was in *American Virgin* and *Enemy of the State*. Sheila Frazier played Georgia in *Superfly* and *Superfly T.N.T.* She was also in *The Hitter* and *California Suite*. Julia Pearlstein's movies include *The Net* and *Bean*. Mia Tate was in *O Brother, Where Art Thou?*

Behind the Camera: Michael Lehmann directed *My Giant*, *The Truth About Cats & Dogs*, *Airheads*, *Hudson Hawk* and *Meet the Applegates*, which he also wrote. He was producer of *Ed Wood*. Patrick Caddell was political consultant on *Air Force One* and appeared in *In the Line of Fire*.

Oh, Donna!: Donna tells Josh about several meetings he has, all of which he already knew. 'This entire conversation served only as a reminder,' she notes. 'Actually,' replies Josh, 'it only served as a colossal waste of time and energy.'

Sex and Drugs and Rock'n'Roll: Leaving the hotel via the kitchens, Bartlet sees a couple getting friendly: 'She deserves a nice room and some supper,' he notes.

The president takes the painkillers Vicadin or Percocet for a bad back.

Cigarettes and Alcohol: Leo's wife likes champagne, particularly Dom Perignon and Cristal. While having dinner, Sam and Josh drink beer.

Logic, Let Me Introduce You to This Window: Leo's home in **1**, 'The West Wing', had a lawn and appeared suburban.

Here, it's in a street and looks urban (Leo claims he can get to the vice president's office and back in 45 minutes, so it must be in the city). Toby claims to drive a 1993 Dodge Dart, but these were only produced from 1963 to 1976.

Cruelty To Animals: Katzenmoyer: 'You gotta understand the people in my district.' Josh: 'Your constituents go quail hunting with an Uzi?'

Quote/Unquote: CJ: 'Excuse me, Toby. I was heading out for lunch and I'm a little short. You wouldn't happen to have a hundred and twenty-five thousand dollars I could borrow?'

Toby: 'There's literally no one in the world that I don't hate right now.'

Notes: 'I'm so sick of Congress I could vomit.' PRACTICAL IDEALISM, the sign behind Bartlet at the rally, is the central theme. The pace slows, slightly, in this gripping story about the politics of compromise and the price of getting what you want. It's a fascinating example of the show, in that it hardly features the president at all. Best bits: the staff enjoying their Chinese meal; Josh's fury at Wick, plus the two sides of Hoynes, the sensitive, thoughtful guy who says all the right things to Leo after his break-up and then the calculating political animal who tells Tillinghouse that he should hand Hoynes a personal victory because 'I'm going to be president one day, and you're not'; a special mention for the camerawork, particularly the way it circles Josh and Wick during their confrontation.

The property value of the president's farm in Manchester has increased $750,000 owing to Secret Service improvements. It now includes a helipad and the ability to run a global war from the porch (see 46, 'Manchester' Part 1). Hoynes, like Leo, is a recovering alcoholic. He holds weekly Alcoholics Anonymous meetings with three senators, two cabinet secretaries, a federal judge and two agency directors.

Leo meets Congressman Richardson beside the Lincoln Memorial.[39] Josh and Katzenmoyer meet in front of the Capitol Building on the banks of the Potomac.

Critique: 'The scene where President Bartlet is "whacked out" on painkillers is an absolute delight,' noted *Radio Times'* Jane Rackman. 'As is one where Josh and Sam realise they've been so absorbed in their discussion that neither of them knows where they are going.'

Cast and Crew Comments: 'All the network asked us to do is present a balanced view of an issue,' John Wells noted to Bernard Weinrub. 'We only don't do that on gun control. Frankly, no one involved in the program feels there's a logical reason for streets to be flooded with automatic weapons.'

'If in the script there is an argument about gun control,' adds Lawrence O'Donnell to Faye Fiore, 'the most precious document you could produce at *The West Wing* that week is a passionate, intelligent case against gun control.'

Did You Know?: Could a White House staffer go to AA meetings as the chief-of-staff and vice president do? Yes, says John Podesta, chief-of-staff for President Clinton. 'If someone came to me and said, "I am an alcoholic and I am going to AA," I think that would be something I would accept. I don't think it would be a case for firing. It's about how much you're willing to take the initial attacks of your political opponents and the press. We know a lot about that.'

Leo's Background: 'You're Boston Irish Catholic,' Josh says in **9**, 'The Short List', though Leo himself claims to be

---

[39] Talk of a memorial began soon after Lincoln's death. The location finally chosen was in the newly created Potomac Park in DC. The last addition to Pierre L'Enfant's plan for the city, this served as the west end of the Mall midway between the Washington Monument and the Capitol. It was designed by the architect Henry Bacon with the sculptor Daniel Chester French creating the centrepiece statue, and construction began in 1914.

from Chicago (**41**, 'Bad Moon Rising'). His father, an alcoholic, committed suicide after an argument with Leo's mother when Leo was a child (**13**, 'Take Out the Trash Day'). He has two sisters, Elizabeth (**10**, 'In Excelsis Deo') and Josephine (**30**, 'Shibboleth'), a nephew who made him an ashtray at camp (**3**, 'A Proportional Response') and at least one other niece or nephew, as he refers to Josey's 'kids' (since she uses the surname McGarry, she may be divorced, widowed or a single mother). His wife, Jenny, asks for a divorce after decades of marriage (**4**, 'Five Votes Down') because, as Leo realises, he widowed her through his job (the papers arrive in **29**, 'The Portland Trip'). Their only daughter, Mallory O'Brien (there's no mention of her having been married or divorced, so it's unclear why she isn't called McGarry), is a fourth-grade teacher at Clearlake Elementary School (**1**, 'The West Wing'). Leo's known the president for forty years (probably an approximation. 'The president and I have a long history,' he says in **12**, 'He Shall, from Time to Time . . .' where he tells Bartlet, 'When I was lying on my face in the motel parking lot, *you* were the one I called.' It's a measure of the trust both Bartlet and Abbey have in Leo that, when Bartlet's sick, Abbey uses the fact that Leo is in the West Wing to calm him). **29**, 'The Portland Trip' suggests that Leo may have been educated at Michigan (the traditional rivals of Bartlet's beloved Notre Dame). He saw military service in Vietnam as a pilot (**3**, 'A Proportional Response', **9**, 'The Short List, **22**, 'What Kind of Day Has it Been', **34**, 'The Drop In').

Subsequently he entered politics and became a major player in the Democratic party. The vice president considers him a world class political operative (**2**, ' "Post Hoc, Ergo Propter Hoc" '). He was Secretary of Labor in 1993 (**9**, 'The Short List') and Josh addresses him as Mr Secretary in 1997 (**23**, 'In the Shadow of Two Gunmen' Part 1), suggesting that Leo had only recently left the Cabinet. 'You're bigger in the party than I am,' Bartlet tells him. Leo makes $40,000 a time on the lecture circuit (**4**, 'Five Votes Down'). He considers himself a wartime *consigliere* (**33**, 'The Leadership Breakfast'). He has been addicted to alcohol and valium (**9**, 'The Short List'). The latter isn't a recreational drug so it's possible he first used it to treat an injury or perhaps post-traumatic stress disorder (this may explain his willingness to help his protégé, Josh, with similar problems in **32**, 'Noël'). He was in treatment for substance abuse at Sierra Tucson for a month in June 1993 (**10**, 'In Excelsis Deo', **12**, 'He Shall, from Time to Time . . .'). After his separation, he lives in a hotel that charges $6.50 for a coffee (**8**, 'Enemies'). It could be the Watergate, which is within walking distance of the White House. Leo's wife said that *she* was staying there when she left in **4**, 'Five Votes Down', but he notes in **6**, 'Mr. Willis of Ohio', that he wanted Jenny to have the house. Leo doesn't think there should be instant-replay in football (**1**, 'The West Wing'). A waitress knows he likes tomato juice (**20**, 'Mandatory Minimums'). He tells Donna that if she goes to Phoebe's restaurant she should tell Dario that 'you work for me and you want the flash-seared escolar with foie gras butter' (**29**, 'The Portland Trip'). He was an old friend of Josh's father **23**, 'In the Shadow of Two Gunmen' Part 1. Both Sam and Josh consider that they owe Leo their total allegiance (**10**, 'In Excelsis Deo'). He frequently uses sporting metaphors including golf, football and baseball (**10**, 'In Excelsis Deo', **19**, 'Let Bartlet Be Bartlet', **20**, 'Mandatory Minimums'). He has golf clubs in his closet (**36**, 'The War at Home'). His suits are handmade (**31**, 'Galileo').

5
The Crackpots and These Women

US Transmission Date: 20 October 1999
UK Transmission Date: 7 February 2000 (Sky), 15 February 2001 (C4)

Writer: Aaron Sorkin
Director: Anthony Drazon
Cast: Guy Boyd (Dr Stanley) Sam Lloyd (Bob) Nick Offerman (Jerry)
Nicholas Cascone (Loomis) Rachel Singer (Marge)
David Fabrizio (Jonathan Lacey) Michele Marsh (Economist)
Juwan Howard (Mr Grant)

Josh receives a card informing him of where to go in the event of a nuclear attack – a privilege denied to most of his friends. Leo has the staff meet various special-interest groups. Toby is disturbed by a rumour that he wasn't the president's first choice for the job.

American History X: Andrew Jackson (1767–1845), the seventh president, had a large block of cheese in the foyer of his White House.[40] Jackson wanted the White House to belong to the people so, from time to time, opened its doors to those who wished an audience. Senator Joseph McCarthy (1909–57) was chairman of the Subcommittee on Investigations during the 1950s – a man described by Harry Truman as 'a pathological character assassin'. Nobody *looks* like McCarthy, Toby tells the president. That's how they get elected.

Politics of Indulgence: Leo's block-of-cheese day (also described as throw-open-our-doors-to-people-who-want-to-discuss-things-that-we-could-care-less-about day by Toby and total-crackpot day by Josh) is scheduled to be held on the first of each month. They've actually had two in a year.

A Little Learning is a Dangerous Thing:: A rise in the producers price index has sparked inflation concerns. Bartlet believes the economy remains strong, with declining unemployment. Mandy asks if he could avoid answering the question 'like an economics professor with a big old stick up his butt'. The president says, unfortunately, he *is* exactly that. Leo notes that, while he's the only person in the room who isn't an economist, the annual budget should be in balance, deficit or surplus. 'I don't know how I can sell Congress, to say nothing of people who

---

[40] A gift from the dairymen of Oswego County. Jackson announced in 1837 that he would hold a cheese tasting and invited the general public. Though the city marshal and his deputies tried to screen those entering, contemporary accounts describe 'rag-a-muffins of the city' infiltrating the gathering. The cheese was demolished in two hours. It's said the White House reeked of cheddar for months afterwards.

graduated eighth grade, on the idea there's anything in between.'

Watch the Skies!: Sam meets Bob from the United States Space Command, who would like the White House to pay more attention to UFOs. Sam wonders if they are paying *any* attention. He is told ATC in Honolulu picked up something unidentified crossing the Pacific towards California. Air Force and naval jets in the area were unable to establish visual contact. Doesn't the president need to know? There's an order to air defence command, Sam replies, and to jump from a radar officer to the commander-in-chief would skip several levels, such as the Pentagon and, perhaps, therapy. The president later reveals that it wasn't a spaceship but a long-abandoned Soviet satellite. 'A sad reminder of a time when two powerful nations challenged each other and then boldly raced into space.'

The Encyclopedic Mind of Josiah Bartlet PhD: Ten years previously, the federal budget had a deficit of $22 billion but the national debt rose from $5.2 trillion to $5.4 trillion in the same fiscal year, Bartlet notes. 'You knew those numbers in your head?' asks one of the economists. 'The president's startlingly freakish that way,' says Leo.

Office Gossip: According to Sam and Josh, the first lady has an interest in ouija boards.

In the Interests of National Security: When Aaron Sorkin met Clinton's policy adviser George Stephanopoulos while researching *The American President*, the aide showed him what looked like a bus pass. The card contained instructions of where he would be evacuated to in the event of war. During this episode Dee Dee Myers said, ' "You know, they don't have these cards," ' Sorkin told *Brill's Content*. 'Turns out *they* did, but *she* didn't!'

References: Richard Schiff wears a City College of New York sweatshirt, celebrating his old school. 'He came back as guest speaker at our honours convocation. We're terrifically proud of him,' noted CCNY's Charles DeCicco. 'We sent him the sweatshirt and he wore it in an episode.' The *New Yorker*, *Miami Herald* and *Chicago Sun-Times*; American Express; the New York fashion store Donna Karan. For some reason the Italian actor Roberto Benigni (*La Vita è Bella*) pushed CJ into a swimming pool during a fundraiser. Bartlet obliquely refers to John Gillespie Magee's poem 'High Flight'. Also, the Viennese composer Franz Schubert (1797–1828), game show *Hollywood Squares* and the Civil Liberties Union. Bartlet mentions the poet Lord George Byron (1788–1824). There's a first sighting of the silhouette gun target in Josh's office. Sam admires *The Godfather* (see **20**, 'Mandatory Minimums'), reads *USA Today* and has two posters concerning human rights on his wall. CJ says more people were killed last year getting change from vending machines than by wolves, a possible reference to the famous Internet 'Darwin Awards', honours given to people who do the gene pool the biggest favour by killing themselves – and thereby removing themselves from it – in spectacularly stupid ways (the 1995 winner was a man who died when a Coke machine he was attempting to shake a freebie from fell on him). A thinning gene pool, CJ notes, 'explains Buckingham Palace', referring to several centuries of inbreeding in the British royal family.

Cheat!: It isn't so much that Bartlet cheats, Toby notes, it's how brazenly bad he is at it. The president asks for examples. In Florida, says Toby, 'playing mixed doubles with me and CJ. You tried to tell us your partner worked at the American Consulate in Vienna.' Bartlet insists she did. 'You crazy lunatic,' shouts Toby, 'you think I'm not gonna recognise Steffi Graf when she's serving a tennis ball at me?' Bartlet then introduces Rodney Grant, the associate director of the President's Council on Physical Fitness, into the basketball game he's playing. The fact that, before this, Rodney played at Duke University is incidental.

'You May Remember Me From Such Films, TV Series and Basketball Play-Offs As . . .': Elisabeth Moss was a child star in *Bad Girls*, *Suburban Commando* and *The Last Supper*. She played Cynthia Parks in *Picket Fences* and Rachel in *Anywhere But Here*, and appeared in *Girl, Interrupted*. Guy Boyd was Dick Locher in *Knots Landing*, Matthew Barnes in *Jagged Edge* and Hackman in *Miami Vice*, and appeared in *The Dark Side of the Sun*, *Pacific Heights*, *Ghost Story* and *Body Double*. Sam Lloyd was in *My Generation*, *Rising Sun* and *Mad About You*. Nick Offerman's movies include *City of Angels* and *Groove*. Nicholas Cascone was in *Titanic*, *Moonlighting*, *Up Close & Personal* and *The Pornographer*. Rachel Singer played Chloe in *Fight Club* and was also in *What Lies Beneath*, *The Green Mile* and *Bull Durham*. David Fabrizio was in *Storm Catcher* and *Gods and Monsters*. Michele Marsh was Hodel in *Fiddler on the Roof* and appeared in *Mannix*, *Star Trek: The Next Generation*, *Quincy* and *Raven Hawk*. Juwan Howard is an NBA superstar with the Dallas Mavericks.

Behind the Camera: Anthony Drazon directed *Imaginary Crimes* and *Hurlyburly* (which he also wrote and produced).

Oh, Donna!: Josh comments on Donna's habit of telling him where he should be going when he's going there anyway. 'You don't find that adorable?' she asks. When she tells him that Donald hasn't called her, Josh replies, 'Can we clear up a few things about my level of interest in the revolving door of local gomers that you see, in the free time you create by not working very hard at your job?'

Sex and Drugs and Rock'n'Roll: The president is giving a speech to the entertainment industry on violence in film and TV the day before a fundraiser at the home of Larry Posner, a producer of notoriously violent movies. Toby sees this as hypocritical. It's not that Posner's movies have gratuitous sex and violence, the president notes. It's that they suck. But people go to see them *because* they have gratuitous sex and violence. 'If we could just get people to stop going to see crappy movies, Posner would stop making them.'

Cigarettes and Alcohol: Bartlet is looking forward to the arrival of Zoey so that he can have a beer-and-chilli party with the staff.

Logic, Let Me Introduce You to This Window: The staff discuss an upcoming fundraiser hosted by Larry Posner in LA. But, when they go to Hollywood (see **16**, '20 Hours in L.A.'), the event they attend is hosted by Ted Marcus. They could, of course, be talking about two different LA trips. It does, however, seem unlikely that the president would choose to attend a fundraiser held by a rival producer, considering Posner's ties to the administration. Josh's sister, Joanie, wanted to be a conductor and practised to 'Ave Maria', a slightly odd choice for a Jewish girl. Why is Josh getting his national security card now? They've been in government for almost a year.

Cruelty To Animals: CJ is told the story of Pluie the wolf, whom scientists have tracked for four years as she travelled from Banff National Park, Alberta, up and down the Rockies. In that time she made three round trips between Canada and Wyoming, covering 40,000 square miles. The wildlife protection group propose a wolves-only roadway covering 1,800 miles from Yellowstone to the Yukon. How are they going to teach wolves to follow road signs? CJ asks. Scientists are, apparently, working on a plan. An argument follows over whether ranchers are killers. CJ says they face falling stock prices, rising taxes, prolonged drought and a country that's eating less beef. Ranchers want to blame something, and, because they're ranchers, fight something. 'I'd rather it be a wolf than us, so unless Pluie registers to vote . . .' Unfortunately, Pluie can't, because she was shot by a rancher in British Columbia.

Quote/Unquote: Toby asks Leo, 'Wouldn't this time be better spent plotting a war against a country that can't possibly defend itself against us?'

Bartlet, to Toby: 'Ah, Mr Ziegler from the *Coney Island Killjoy*.' And: 'You are a wise and brilliant man.'

Josh returns his 'nuclear attack' card to the president: 'I want to be a comfort to my friends in tragedy. I want to be able to celebrate with them in triumph. And, for all the times in between, I just want to be able to look them in the eye.'

Bartlet: 'Did you mean what you said? My demons were shouting down the better angels in my brain? You think that's what's stopping me from greatness?' Toby: 'Yes ... Tell you what, though, sir. In a battle between a president's demons and his better angels, for the first time in a long while, I think we might have ourselves a fair fight.'

Notes: 'When smallpox was eradicated, it was considered the single greatest humanitarian achievement of this century. Surely, we can do it again. As we did in the time when our eyes looked toward the heavens, and with outstretched fingers, we touched the face of God.' One of the most beautiful pieces of TV ever made. A life-affirming story about friendship, trust and integrity. There is a real sense of magnificence about this. When Josh gives his security card back and Bartlet speaks about absent friends and 'these women' you want to kiss the screen. Other wonderful bits: the basketball game; CJ's discussion with the wildlife-protection people; Josh telling CJ about the horrors of smallpox ('That's how it's gonna be, a little test tube with a rubber cap that's deteriorating; a guy steps out of Times Square Station – *pshht!*'); the president and Toby's heart-to-heart; and dozens of others. The episode that will turn you from a casual viewer into a bona fide fan.

Josh asks if Sam considers himself close to Cathy. Sam confirms he hasn't seen her naked and says she's like a younger sister, only she gets paid. She frightens him, but he loves her, just like Josh and Donna. The first lady is in Pakistan. Mrs Landingham lost two sons in Vietnam (see **10**, 'In Excelsis Deo'). In fourteen years, she hasn't missed a day's work. Zoey is starting university in the spring, prior to medical school.

Critique: 'They say God is in the details,' noted *Newsweek*. 'At a conference table on the Warner Bros lot, director

Tony Drazan confers with Dee Dee Myers. "In the Roosevelt Room I want to have doughnuts, bagels and coffee, because it's a morning meeting," says the director. "It doesn't really happen." Drazan is amazed: "They don't provide food?" Sam's a stingy Uncle, Myers explains. "On Air Force One, you pay for your own lunch." '

Did You Know?: 'When we were kids, [Martin Sheen] whipped us on the basketball court every day,' Rob Lowe told *Smoke* magazine. 'He was proud of that. We have a court here on the lot, and we had a rematch for the first time in 12 years. It took me back to when I was 15. I won't say who won this time.'

Josh's Background: 'A smart guy,' notes the president (**10**, 'In Excelsis Deo'). Josh is the son of a Jewish Connecticut lawyer, Noah Lyman, a partner at the firm of Debevoise & Plimpton, who died from a blood clot on the night of the Illinois primary (**18**, 'Six Meetings Before Lunch', **24**, 'In the Shadow of Two Gunmen' Part 2). His mother is still alive (**39**, 'The Stackhouse Filibuster'). Josh had an older sister, Joanie, who was killed in a fire while babysitting Josh (**5**, 'The Crackpots and These Women'). It's clear that Josh still feels guilty that he survived by running out of the house. His grandfather, of whom Josh keeps a picture on his office wall, was in Birkenau during the Holocaust (**18**, 'Six Meetings Before Lunch'). Josh put on talent shows as a child (**2**, ' "Post Hoc, Ergo Propter Hoc" '). He scored 760 on his oral SAT (**21**, 'Lies, Damn Lies and Statistics'). He was a Fulbright scholar (an international exchange programme, which means he studied abroad and is clearly wicked-smart – **1**, 'The West Wing', **6**, 'Mr. Willis of Ohio') and a graduate of Harvard (**3**, 'A Proportional Response') and Yale (**15**, 'Celestial Navigation'). At one of these he and Chris Wick were in a fraternity (**4**, 'Five Votes Down'). He was floor manager for the House minority whip, chief-of-staff for Congressman Earl Brennan (**15**, 'Celestial Navigation'), held an important position on the presidential campaign of Senator Hoynes (**23**, 'In the Shadow of Two Gunmen' Part 1) and was senior political director for Bartlet's campaign. Sam doesn't consider him a 'real' lawyer (**11**, 'Lord John Marbury'). He is unmarried, though 'many have tried' (**21**, 'Lies, Damn Lies and Statistics'). According to Donna, Josh's romantic strategy consists of randomly tumbling into a girl and hoping she breaks up with him (**35**, 'Bartlet's Third State of the Union'). She thinks he has a crush on Joey Lucas and nags him about it (**16**, '20 Hours in L.A.'). He has problems holding his liquor and a very sensitive system (**14**, 'Take This Sabbath Day'). **1**, 'The West Wing', and **4**, 'Five Votes Down', suggest Josh has a fan club of college-age girl groupies who turn up at events to scream at him. Joey Lucas thinks he has 'the cutest butt in professional politics' (**35**, 'Bartlet's Third State of the Union'). He plays basketball and golf ('real golfers don't use carts' – **11**, 'Lord John Marbury') but he doesn't seem much of an outdoors type (having never climbed a tree – **8**, 'Enemies'). He likes his hamburgers well done (**13**, 'Take Out the Trash Day'). He claims to have spent half the nights of his life in hotels (**16**, '20 Hours in L.A.'). Josh has a psychologist, Stanley, whom he hasn't seen much since the election (**5**, 'The Crackpots and These Women'). He's never been on a movie set (**3**, 'A Proportional Response') and is a video club member (**5**, 'The Crackpots and These Women'). Josh has twice-weekly meetings with his deputies to delegate work (**39**, 'The Stackhouse Filibuster').

Josh was shot in the chest after a meeting in Rosslyn and suffered a collapsed lung and a ruptured pulmonary artery. His condition was critical but he survived after fourteen hours of surgery (**24**, 'In the Shadow of Two Gunmen' Part 2). He subsequently suffered post-traumatic stress disorder, diagnosed by Dr Stanley Keyworth, and was referred to a therapist (**32**, 'Noël'). His doctor advised him to stand with his back against a wall to relax (**34**, 'The Drop In'). He has his blood pressure checked twice weekly. The Surgeon General saw his scar when he was in the hospital and declared it beautiful. He has some back pain, but it's supposedly all in his head. Along with many other things (**37**, 'Ellie'). He claims never to get tired of the sound of his own voice (**40**, '17 People'). He takes sugar in his coffee (**41**, 'Bad Moon Rising'). Bartlet thinks of Josh like a son (**44**, 'Two Cathedrals').

6
Mr. Willis of Ohio

US Transmission Date: 3 November 1999
UK Transmission Date: 21 February 2000 (Sky), 22 February 2001 (C4)

Writer: Aaron Sorkin
Director: Christopher Misiano
Cast: Al Frann (Joe Willis) Kenneth Tigar (Gladman)
Blake Shields (Frat Boy #1) Justin Urich (Frat Boy #2)
Gathering Marbet (Waitress) Eric Balfour (Frat Boy[41])

Toby and Mandy try to persuade Congressmen to pass the Appropriations Bill without hindrance. CJ begs Sam for help to understand the census. Bartlet asks Josh to take Charlie out for the night, which almost ends in a brawl involving the president's daughter.

A View from the Hill: Some additions to the Appropriations Bill are $12,000,000 to establish an Appalachian transportation institute, $1,500,000 to study parking facilities at truck stops and $3,000,000 to produce a documentary on highway infrastructure. Mandy asks what's in this for the administration. Funding for 100,000 new public school teachers, notes Toby. The latest draft of the bill is 7,000 pages long. It includes $1,200,000 for a lettuce geneticist in Salinas, California, and $1,700,000 for manure handling in Mississippi. Eight states will divide $5,000,000 to research the uses of wood. After negotiations Congress agree to leave a census amendment in committee.

American History X: Article 1, Section 2, of the Constitution says, 'Representatives and direct taxes shall be apportioned among the several states which may be included

---

[41] Uncredited.

within this Union, according to their respective numbers, which shall be determined by adding to the whole number of free persons, including those bound to service for a term of years, and excluding Indians not taxed, three fifths of all other persons.' When Toby wants a copy of the constitution, Bonnie asks if it's still in print. Toby suggests she try Amazon.com. 'If they don't have it just bust into the glass display case at the National Archives.'

The Susan B Anthony House, the home of the social reformer and women's suffrage leader (1820–1906), is in Rochester.

Politics of Desperation: CJ doesn't understand the census, so Sam explains it in simple terms. The Constitution mandates that every ten years a count be held because representation at federal, state and municipal levels is based on population. The only way to find out how many Congressmen, for instance, California gets is to count the people there. The census has always been done by a door-to-door head count; 950,000 professionals are hired, the process costs $6,900,000,000 and is inaccurate. It is disadvantageous to inner-city populations and the homeless. There's also a large number of people who don't speak English, and others who simply don't want to answer personal questions. Sampling, statisticians believe, is a more effective way of getting a good census.

Politics of Integrity: After Joe Willis says he will delay the census amendment Toby asks what changed his mind. 'You did. I thought you made a very strong argument.' Toby says the merits of a particular argument generally take a back seat in politics. He admits that the process *is* partisan and that he isn't wild about the precedent. 'What's to stop us saying we don't need elections, we'll just use polling data? One thousand one hundred and fifty people will decide who runs the country.' This is OK by Willis as long as it's not the same people who decide what's on television.

The Encyclopedic Mind of Josiah Bartlet PhD: 'You should feel free to give us a quiz on inane trivia,' Josh tells the president during the cards game. So he does, asking which fruit has its seeds on the outside (the strawberry). Next, he asks for the fourteen punctuation marks in English grammar (the staff get them all, Toby impressively reeling off seven in a row) and the three words in the English language that begin with 'dw' ('dwindle, dwarf and dwell' is the answer given, though that's incorrect: 'dwale' is a fourth: it's another name for deadly nightshade). He knows lots about South American geography too but, thankfully, the Secret Service interrupt him.

In the Interests of National Security: Ron Butterfield, of the Secret Service, tells the president that, if anybody jumps the fence into the White House, they'll be going to jail. 'What they do once we get to them is what's gonna determine for how long.' The previous night's alarm was tripped by an armed and mentally unbalanced woman. Bartlet, however, wasn't her target; Zoey was.

References: Knute Rockne (1888–1931) was the Norwegian-born coach of Notre Dame's Fighting Irish football team in the 1920s. Thornton Wilder's play *Our Town* (Bartlet once played the stage manager in a production). The staff playing poker was a plot device used in *Star Trek: The Next Generation*. Toby mentions the game-show host and singer Wink Martindale. Also, *Saved By the Bell*, *Super Fly*, rappers LL Cool J, Ice T, Puff Daddy and Ice Cube. *Doctor Dolittle* and *Mary Poppins*. Among the magazines in a rack outside Toby's office are *Forbes* and the *New Yorker*. Sam has a US flag with DON'T TREAD ON ME written on it in his office.

'You May Remember Me From Such Films and TV Series As . . .': Al Frann was Felix in *Home Improvements*. His CV also includes *Stop! Or My Mom Will Shoot*, *The Fisher King*, *The French Connection*, *Turner & Hooch* and *The Incredible Hulk*. Charley Lang was Jarvis Powell in *Fire in the Sky*, Rob Stemkowski in *Days of Our Lives* and Dr Hilligan in *Dark Skies*. He's also been in *LA Law* and *The*

Flash. Michael O'Neill played Richard Walsh in *24* and was in *Traffic*, *The Mod Squad*, *The Legend of Bagger Vance*, *Sea of Love*, *Roswell* and *The X-Files*. Blake Shields appeared in *Boys and Girls*. Kenneth Tigar was in *Conspiracy Theory*, *Primal Fear*, *Rage*, *Lethal Weapon 2*, *Dynasty*, *Baywatch*, *Who's the Boss?* and *Wonder Woman*.

Greg Wrangler's movies include *Venus Rising*, *No Secrets* and *God, Sex & Apple Pie*. Justin Urich was in *Horror 101*, *Nutty Professor II: The Klumps* and *Scrapbook*. Eric Balfour was Jesse in *Buffy* and appeared in *Can't Hardly Wait and Shattered Image*. Juan A Riojas was in *The Rock*, *In the Line of Fire*, *Angel* and *Murder She Wrote*. Gathering Marbet appeared in *Claire of the Moon*.

Behind the Camera: Chris Misiano produced *ER* and directed *Nash Bridges* and *Law & Order*. He was a grip on *The Europeans*.

Oh, Donna!: In one of the series' best-running gags, Donna asks Josh about the budget surplus. Is it true that it's $32 billion for the first time in decades? Josh confirms this. Republicans want to use this money for tax relief, notes Donna. Essentially they're saying they want to give back the money. Why, therefore, don't the Democrats? She won't spend it right, replies Josh: suppose Donna's cut is $700, the government want to take her money, combine it with everyone else's and use it to endow social security. What does Donna want to do with it? 'Buy a DVD player,' she replies, arguing that her $700 would help to employ the people who manufacture and sell DVD players. However, the DVD player she buys might be made in Japan, Josh argues. 'I'll buy an American one,' pleads Donna. 'We don't trust you. We're Democrats. You shouldn't have voted for us!' Later Josh gives Donna $20 to buy some sandwiches. When he asks where his change is, Donna replies that, as it turns out, Josh gave her more money than she needed. However, knowing him as she does, she cannot trust that he will spend the change wisely. 'That was a little parable,' says Josh, as Donna leaves still demanding, 'I want my money back!'

Sex and Drugs and Rock'n'Roll: Mallory has told Zoey about Sam's friend. Sam asks, horrified, if either of their fathers knows. 'Not yet,' says Zoey, wickedly.

Cigarettes and Alcohol: During the card game, Sam drinks a bottle of lager, CJ, Mandy and Josh drink whisky and Toby smokes a cigar. The president asks Josh to take Charlie out and offers to give him some money before discovering he hasn't got any. At the bar, the Georgetowne Station, CJ orders a grasshopper (a crème-de-menthe-based cocktail) while Charlie, Sam and Josh drink beer and Mallory has a screwdriver.

Logic, Let Me Introduce You to This Window: In a Congressional roll call, the names are given in alphabetical order and those after Willis are mentioned, but Wyatt isn't one of them, even though Andi (see **20**, 'Mandatory Minimums') is a member of Congress. In reality, the House doesn't take voice roll calls any more, they vote electronically (the change happened in 1999). Joe Willis couldn't be appointed to the House of Representatives: Article 1, Section 2, of the Constitution notes that, when vacancies occur, an election is called. There's no such thing as a caretaker Congressman.

Quote/Unquote: Gladman: 'I thought we were here to talk about the census.' Josh: 'The White House just wanted to take this opportunity to point out that you're criminals and despots.'

Bartlet: 'Marriage needs attention, Leo. It can't run on autopilot. It's not your prom date we're talking about here.' Leo: 'Thank you for pointing that out. I tried to squeeze in as much time as I could between my wine-tasting club and running your White House.'

Notes: 'The president's daughter, chief-of-staff's daughter, a Georgetown bar and Sam. What could possibly go wrong?' Another cracker (it was probably around this stage, after – literally – six *great* episodes that most viewers started to realise this was something special). A story about conscience and not being afraid of what you don't know, it's a defining moment for Toby, as we see his shattered faith in decency and democracy restored. Love the bar sequences, as a quiet night threatens to descend into farce and then ends in a hugely satisfying way ('Now I'm enjoying myself,' says Charlie as the boneheads who racially taunted him are hauled off by the Secret Service). And Josh and Sam's bravado after the event (arguing about how many of the thugs they could each have taken). Other great bits: Donna and Josh bitching about the budget surplus and DVDs.

The president says his 'nightmare scenario' is Zoey being kidnapped (though he isn't crazy about the idea of getting shot himself, either).

Critique: According to *USA Today*, Cynthia Mostoller, National History Day teacher of the year in 1998, was enchanted with Joe Willis. 'I'm an eighth-grade social studies teacher from Ohio. The show was exactly on target with what we are teaching right now,' she noted. Scott Reid (communications director for Paul Martin, the Canadian Finance Minister) told the *National Post* that the discussion about tax cuts versus rebates punctuated by Donna repeatedly saying 'I want to buy a DVD' had impressed him. The line quickly became a favourite among staff in his office, who now use it whenever the subject comes up.

'A third of the episode involved a debate on census and statistical sampling,' Joe Lockhart told Terence Smith during *Online NewsHour with Jim Lehrer*. 'They did a better job of framing the issue, the politics and the passions on each side, than anybody in the broadcast world.'

Cast and Crew Comments: The census scenes work, Tom Schlamme told *Brill's Content*, because they're not about teaching. 'You're involved with the fact that Sam is the smarter one and CJ has to be the student,' he explained. 'From a directing point of view the essence is about how are these two people going to end up being closer by the end of this episode. If you start from that it's fascinating.'

'When we do the census, 13 or 14 million people watch,' Bradley Whitford told the *St Louis Post-Dispatch*. 'Somebody at the White House was saying, when they want to talk about something, if they get the news cycle, it's maybe a million people. And if they bring up the census, the channel changes.'

Did You Know?: In a revealing interview with Andrew Duncan, Martin Sheen declared himself a fan of President Kennedy: 'These stories of womanising that unravelled after his death made him more human to me. We idealise our leaders, raise them up so we have the power to knock them down. The American psyche is oddball – as soon as a man becomes president, suddenly there's no more original sin. There's a lot of hypocrisy and I'm proud of President Clinton for fighting it and not giving those bastards their day.' Of Clinton's successor, however, he was less charitable: 'George W Bush is like a bad comic working the crowd,' he notes. 'A moron, if you'll pardon the expression.'

Toby's Background: Toby is a New York Jew (**1**, 'The West Wing') from Brooklyn (**25**, 'The Midterms'), and his mother seems to be alive (**4**, 'Five Votes Down'). He has a brother named David, a payload specialist with NASA, who has postgraduate degrees in physiology and biology. There appears to be a schism between them (**22**, 'What Kind of Day Has it Been'). He has two older sisters (**38**, 'Somebody's Going to Emergency, Somebody's Going to Jail') who took him on protest marches in 1968. It implies that Toby had remarkable SAT scores (**31**, 'Galileo'). He proudly wears a CCNY sweatshirt (**5**, 'The Crackpots and These Women'), so probably spent part of his education there. He says he was raised on PBS (**13**, 'Take Out the Trash Day'). In fourth grade, Toby was beaten up because he sat out voluntary prayer (**30**, 'Shibboleth'). Congresswoman, Andrea Wyatt is his *ex*-wife, though he still wears a wedding ring (**20**, 'Mandatory Minimums'). Her nickname for him is Pokey. Toby says he and Andrea could 'talk about anything but why we couldn't live with each other' (**33**, 'The Leadership Breakfast'). Cynical about most things, he nevertheless regularly attends synagogue and is opposed to the death penalty (**14**, 'Take This Sabbath Day'). Though it is never specifically stated, there are suggestions he's been in the military (he correctly identifies a veteran's tattoo in **10**, 'In Excelsis Deo'), though he's far too young to have served in, for example, Vietnam. He's witnessed shooting before (**25**, 'The Midterms'). Toby claims to have been a professional political operative his whole life (apart from elementary school) but was never on a winning campaign until he worked for Bartlet (**23**, 'In the Shadow of Two Gunmen' Part 1). In addition to being communications director, Toby is a senior domestic policy adviser (**38**, 'Somebody's Going to Emergency, Somebody's Going to Jail'). After the election, Bartlet, despite pressure from Leo and Josh, wanted to drop Toby in favour of David Rosen, but the latter rejected the offer, to Bartlet's subsequent sincere relief (**5**, 'The Crackpots and These Women').

Toby and CJ were friends before working on the Bartlet campaign (**24**, 'In the Shadow of Two Gunmen' Part 2). 'I'm gonna be at the bar drinking a lot if anybody needs me,' he says in **16**, '20 Hours in L.A.' and both **7**, 'The State Dinner', and **23**, 'In the Shadow of Two Gunmen' Part 1, suggest he drinks in times of stress. He plays basketball and tennis (and probably anything else highly competitive – **5**, 'The Crackpots and These Women') and is a fanatical New York Yankees fan (**20**, 'Mandatory Minimums'). Toby proudly says he's cultivated a reputation for being a pain in the ass and that he likes winning (**17**, 'The White House Pro-Am'). He gets upset when the president deviates from the text Toby's written (**5**, 'The Crackpots and These Women') and is not fond of political expediency, and Bartlet sometimes disappoints him, but Josh notes that the president always listens to Toby (**9**, 'The Short List'). He has a stress ball, which he throws against his office wall, sometimes to attract Sam's attention (**37**, 'Ellie').

7
The State Dinner

US Transmission Date: 10 November 1999
UK Transmission Date: 28 February 2000 (Sky), 1 March 2001 (C4)

Writers: Aaron Sorkin, Paul Redford
Director: Thomas Schlamme
Cast: David Rasche (Carl Everett) John Kapelos (Seymour Little)
Peter Kors (Rahmadi Sumahidjo Bambang) Sal Landi (Chaffey)
William Lucking (Bobby Russo) Steve Rankin (FBI Agent #2)
Jeff Williams (Harold Lewis) Ariono Suriawinata (President of Indonesia)
Nelson Mashita (Minaldi) Tyler Bowe (Gomez)

A dinner honouring the Indonesian president looms but
Bartlet has other worries: an FBI hostage stand-off with
militant survivalists; a hurricane bearing down on a carrier
group; and an impending trucker's strike. Toby seeks a
favour from an Indonesian official and a surprised Sam
meets Laurie at the White House.

American History X: The Taft-Hartley Act was a 1947
amendment to the National Labor Relations Act (1935),
which gave employees the right *not* to belong to unions and
established certain presidential powers to be used in
emergency situations such as a strike that would threaten
national health. Bartlet refers to President Truman's
actions when, to avert a nationwide strike of steelworkers
in April 1952, which he believed would jeopardise national
defence, he issued an executive order, directing the Commerce Secretary, Charles Sawyer, to seize and operate steel
mills. In the event, the order was declared unconstitutional
by the Supreme Court.[42]

Gideon v. Wainwright was a landmark 1963 case in which
a Florida defendant, charged with a noncapital felony, was
without funds and asked the court to appoint his counsel.
He was denied, as state law permitted appointment of
counsel for indigent defendants in capital cases only,

---

[42] The Court noted that Truman could have used the Taft-Hartley Act to
delay the strike, but Truman disliked the law too much to employ it.

leaving the defendant to conduct his own defence. Subsequently, he applied to the Supreme Court for a writ of habeas corpus, on the ground that his conviction violated his rights under the Constitution. The appeal confirmed that the right of a defendant in a criminal trial to the assistance of counsel is essential and that a conviction without representation violates the fourteenth Amendment.

The Gold Room contains portraits of six first ladies along with the vermeil collection (bequeathed to the White House by Margaret Thompson Biddle), including the work of the silversmiths Paul Storr (1771 1844) and Jean-Baptiste-Claude Odiot (1763–1850). Many workers were blinded by mercury during the process, which is seen in some circles as a symbol of a government's tyrannical oppression of its people. The demonstration that Danny mentions turns out to be six people in Lafayette Park. 'I didn't say it was Selma, Alabama,' says Danny, referring to the civil-rights protests led by Martin Luther King in 1965.

A Siege is a Dangerous Thing: In McClane, Idaho, local law enforcement surrounded a farmhouse containing approximately forty survivalists (including children). Arguments have erupted among the Attorney General, the FBI and the Bureau of Alcohol, Firearms, and Tobacco about who's in charge (an almost certain reference to the real-life Waco siege[43]). The military (and Josh) argue that the FBI should storm the building; the president takes Mandy's advice and sends in a negotiator, who is shot.

The Encyclopedic Mind of Josiah Bartlet PhD: The first lady says that when she stays away too long Bartlet forgets that he doesn't have the power to fix everything. 'You have a big brain,' she tells her husband. 'A good heart. And an ego the size of Montana.'

---

[43] In 1993 a 51-day stand-off between law-enforcement officials and members of a religious group, the Branch Davidians, resulted in over 80 deaths.

Fashion Victims: The first lady will be wearing a Badgely Mischka silk Shantung gown with a beaded bodice and a Gabriel Sanchez pearl necklace with tourmaline beads, CJ tells the press. Her shoes will be black suede and velvet with Manolo Blahnik slides and a rhinestone and mother-of-pearl toe buckle and she will carry a Christina Bomba silk, pleated, burgundy drawstring bag. 'I love it when *In Style* issues press credentials,' she tells Josh. '*Mirabella* need to know what kind of wine is being served with the fish.'

Carol's Spelling: The first of many jokes about CJ's assistant Carol and her lack of spelling talent. It's a minor one: she checks with CJ that 'vermeil' ends 'e-i-l'.

References: The business parcel delivery services FedEx and UPS, the Federal Emergency Management Agency (a far less sinister organisation here than in *The X-Files*), fashion designer Carmen Marc Valvo, the Nuclear Test Ban Treaty, the Washington Redskins. The cellist Yo-Yo Ma (see **32**, 'Noël') is to play a Bach concerto at the reception. Also, the Norfolk naval shipyard in Portsmouth, the aircraft carrier USS *John F Kennedy* and the cruisers USS *Normandy* and USS *South Carolina*, the actor and dancer Fred Astaire (1899–1987), *Head* ('you're all crazy'), *Entrapment* and *Rambo*. Sam uses an Apple Mac laptop.

'You May Remember Me From Such Films and TV Series As . . .': A formidable actress, Stockard Channing gained notice via movies such as *The Fortune*, *The Big Bus*, *All-American Girl* and *The Fish That Saved Pittsburgh* and gave a memorable performance as Betty Rizzo in *Grease*. After starring in her own sitcom (*Stockard Channing in Just Friends*) she moved to Broadway and won a Tony award for *A Day in the Death of Joe Egg*. She spent the 1980s making appearances in movies such as *The Men's Club*, *Echoes in the Darkness*, *Perfect Witness* and *Without a Trace*. She was Oscar-nominated in 1993 for re-creating her Broadway role in *Six Degrees of Separation*, and her recent work includes *Smoke*, *Practical Magic* and *Where the Heart Is*.

Tyler Bowe was Slash in *Speak of the Devil*. Dennis Cockrum was in *Inherit the Wind*, *Life During Wartime*, *Uncle Buck*, *The Adventures of Brisco County Jr* and *Married ... With Children*. JP Stevenson appeared in *Spring*. John Kapelos played Don Schanke in *Forever Knight* and Carl in *The Breakfast Club*. His other movies include *L.A.X*, *Deep End of the Ocean*, *Johnny Skidmarks*, *The Craft*, *Sixteen Candles*, *Roxanne* and *Weird Science*. Sal Landi was in *The Alternative*, *Dark Breed*, *The X-Files* and *JAG*. He was associate producer on *Love & Sex etc*. Jacqueline Torres was Kira Sanchez in *F/X: The Series*. Jeff Williams appeared in *Golden Years* and *A Perfect Murder*. William Lucking's massive CV includes *Erin Brockovich*, *The Limey*, *10*, *The Magnificent Seven Ride!*, *Star Trek: Deep Space Nine*, *Tales of the Gold Monkey*, *The Waltons*, *Kung Fu*, *Bonanza* and *The High Chaparral*. He played Colonel Lynch in *The A-Team* and Roky Crikenson in *The X-Files*. Nelson Mashita was in *Independence Day*, *Eve of Destruction* and *Darkman*. David Rasche was Alan in *That Old Feeling* and Evan in *Suddenly Susan*, and appeared in *Off the Lip*, *Wicked Stepmother* and *Manhattan*. Steve Rankin was Tara's father in *Buffy* and has also been in *The Adventures of Rocky & Bullwinkle*, *Blue Streak*, *Mercury Rising*, *Men in Black* and *L.A. Confidential*. DC Ford, who appeared uncredited, was in *Rock Star*, *Blow* and *Gone in 60 Seconds*. Colin Gray was a driver in *Nuns on the Run* and a rigging gaffer on *Run*.

Behind the Camera: Paul Redford wrote *Partners* and *Ebbie*.

Oh, Donna!: Donna has been doing some reading. Josh wishes she wouldn't, because she tends to cull some bizarre fact from a less than reputable source and then blow it out of proportion. 'I do not,' argues Donna, before telling Josh that in certain parts of Indonesia people suspected of being sorcerers are summarily beheaded.

Sex and Drugs and Rock'n'Roll: Josh seems conversant with the contents of *Hustler*. Laurie is still working for the escort agency and turns up at the dinner with Carl Everett, who has raised a lot of money for the Democrats in the Midwest.

Logic, Let Me Introduce You to This Window: Indonesian *is* a language, despite what Minaldi says, albeit a synthetic one that uses Malay as a grammatical base. It's very unlikely that a State Department translator would be unable to communicate with a senior aide of the Indonesian president. Although the translator's language is Javanese while Bambang's is Batak (an ethnic group in Sumatra), they should *both* speak Indonesian, otherwise they would not occupy the positions they do. Bambang is not a Batak surname: rather it's Javanese. Bartlet says President Truman nationalised the coal mines in 1952; it was actually steel mills.

Quote/Unquote: Mandy: 'It really bugs you that the president listens to me.' Josh: 'You shouldn't take it personally. It bugs me when the president listens to anyone who isn't me.'

Sam: 'Do you think it a good idea to invite people to dinner and then tell them what they're doing wrong with their lives?' Toby: 'Absolutely, otherwise it's a waste of food.'

Toby, to the kitchen worker who speaks only Batak and Portuguese: 'You might want to take a crack at English, seeing as how you live here.'

Notes: 'I don't think we should remind people how friendly we were with dictators who oppressed their people while stealing their money.' One of the less successful episodes, which tries to do too much and sees potentially important aspects (such as the Toby plotline) pushed to one side. The FBI/siege situation is a fascinating one that probably deserved an episode on its own, but this, too, gets little attention and a rather undramatic ending. There are some great bits (Bambang's angry and justified rant about America attempting to lecture other countries on human rights after its disgraceful treatment of its own natives, for instance) but there's just too much going on. Good performances all round, though, particularly Stockard Channing, who brings the first lady to life in a delightful way. Best bits: Sam offering Laurie $10,000 not to go home with Everett; Josh and Sam congratulating each other on how cool they look in their tuxedos. Worst bit: the ending, the first time that *The West Wing* is mawkish and obvious.

A French friend of Toby is imprisoned for leading anti-government demonstrations in Indonesia. President Siguto was once almost assassinated by a CIA-trained operative.

Critique: Concerning Laurie's White House appearance: 'For a program that prides itself on political savvy, this was a surprising lapse: even invited guests at a White House dinner undergo background checks. No one, let alone a paid escort with a phoney name, gets inside 1600 Pennsylvania Avenue on a whim,' noted Matt Roush.

Did You Know?: Stockard Channing's appearance was originally a one-off, so she came in during a hiatus on a film shoot. After the episode aired, Aaron Sorkin took her to lunch. 'He said, "Everybody thought that was great. Also our ratings went up a lot when you were on," ' she told Brill Bundy on *zap2it.com*. 'Then, he said, "Do you want to be a doctor? I have this thing. [Bartlet] has a bad cold in the teaser and I'm thinking he might have MS." '

Mandy's Background: Mandy has a bachelor's degree in art history, a master's in communications and a PhD in political science (**2**, ' "Post Hoc, Ergo Propter Hoc" '). She was the media director on Bartlet's campaign (**19**, 'Let Bartlet Be Bartlet') but left to work for Lennox-Chase for $900,000 per year, and subsequently set up her own consultancy with Lloyd Russell as her client (**1**, 'The West Wing'). While working for Russell, Mandy wrote a memo outlining the weaknesses of the Bartlet administration. This was later leaked to the press (**19**, 'Let Bartlet Be Bartlet'). She was Josh's girlfriend during the election campaign (**1**, 'The West Wing'). They met at a seafood restaurant near the Democratic Leadership Conference (**3**, 'A Proportional Response') and broke up on 9 July (presumably 1999, which means they were still together after she left the administration – **4**, 'Five Votes Down'). Her White House salary is paid by the Democratic National Committee (**2**, ' "Post Hoc, Ergo Propter Hoc" '). Mandy wants to take on a new client, Mike Brace, a moderate Republican. She seems able to manipulate Sam easily, but is less successful with Josh and, especially, Toby (**11**, 'Lord John Marbury').

8
Enemies

US Transmission Date: 17 November 1999
UK Transmission Date: 6 March 2000 (Sky), 8 March 2001 (C4)

Teleplay: Ron Osborn, Jeff Reno
Story: Rick Cleveland, Lawrence O'Donnell Jr,
Patrick Caddell
Director: Alan Taylor
Cast: Shirley Y Scott (Court Stenographer) Seth Walker (Tony)

A banking bill is at risk when a rider to allow mining in Montana is attached. CJ tries to quash rumours that the president belittled the vice president during a cabinet meeting. Leo isn't keen on Mallory's dating Sam.

A View from the Hill: The bill will stop the banking lobby from getting whatever it wants, including deregulation. Josh agrees, but the rider to allow mining at Big Sky Federal Reserve outrages him. Not that he cares about Big Sky itself, but he *does* care about hanging a sign outside the White House saying, FEEL FREE TO SLAP US AROUND ANYTIME YOU WANT.

Leo's diary includes meeting the CIA director and receiving an intelligence briefing regarding plutonium stores in a country that, the president notes, 'is not on our Christmas card list'. He brokered a compromise among Democrats for army funding, then met with chief counsel to discuss whether the president has broken any federal laws. This was, apparently, a *very* light day.

American History X: Ulysses Grant (see **1**, 'The West Wing') is mentioned. The Antiquities Act of 1906 states, 'The President of the United States is hereby authorized, in his discretion, to declare by public proclamation historic landmarks, historic and prehistoric structures, and other objects of historic or scientific interest that are situated upon the lands owned or controlled by the Government of the United States to be national monuments.'

Politics of Compromise: Sam and Josh argue over what the president's position should be on the rider. Sam argues that he isn't abandoning the environmental lobby (probably true, given his position in **34**, 'The Drop In'). Josh suggests that, instead of accepting the rider, the president simply veto the bill.

The president's difficult relationship with his vice president is explored. Bartlet is bitter that Hoynes made him beg him to join the Bartlet ticket. 'You've just kicked my ass in a primary,' notes Hoynes, 'I'm fifteen years younger than you, I have my career to think of.' Nevertheless, says Bartlet, this weakened him (see **16**, '20 Hours in L.A.').

The Encyclopedic Mind of Josiah Bartlet PhD: The president is a national park buff, has visited all 54 of them and has the slides to prove it. He displays his expertise to Josh, CJ and Charlie and mentions Yellowstone (America's first national park, created in 1872), Everglades (which has extensive mangrove forests), Grand Canyon, Bryce Canyon, Badlands, Capitol Reef, Acadia (Bartlet considers it 'overlooked'), Dry Tortugas, Petrified Forest, North Cascades, Joshua Tree, Shenandoah, Yosemite and Glacier Park (grizzly bears inhabit this; hikers are told to sing along the trail to keep them at bay). Josh suggests the president make Big Sky a national park: 'I'm sure someone with your encyclopedic knowledge of the ridiculous and dorklike will be able to find a tree or a ferret the public has a right to visit.'

Office Gossip: Danny's heard that the president 'roughed up' Hoynes in the Cabinet meeting. Soon rumours are sweeping the White House. It appears that Mildred, the note taker, was the snitch.

References: The NASDAQ market, the Saturn V rocket (used by NASA on the Apollo missions), Ralph Kramden as played by Jackie Gleason in the 1950s sitcom *The Honeymooners*, *Monday Night Football* and Niccoló Machiavelli (1469–1527, Italian political and military theorist). Hoynes's comment that 'the Internet is not a fad' may be a reference to statements about the Net made by the former vice president Al Gore. Sam reads *The Washington Post*. Donna has a sticker on her filing cabinet that says, IF YOU THINK EDUCATION IS EXPENSIVE, TRY IGNORANCE. Sam owns a Newton's Cradle. Parts of the plot may be inspired by the *Simpsons* episode 'Bart's Comet', where a bill to provide emergency comet-relief funding for Springfield has a rider concerning obscene art attached.

'You May Remember Me From Such Films and TV Series As . . .': Shirley Y Scott was in *Bullet*. Seth Walker appeared in *Vegas Vacation*.

Behind the Camera: Jeff Reno and Ron Osborn were writer/producers on the 1980s series *Moonlighting* and wrote *Meet Joe Black*.

Oh, Donna!: Donna and Mandy appear at Josh's door while he's on the computer. Donna tells Josh that Mandy wants to see him. Without looking up, Josh asks, 'Can you tell her I'm not in?' No, replies Donna, 'I think the ship's pretty much sailed on that one.'

Sex and Chinese Opera: Mallory asks Sam to accompany her to the Beijing Opera, who are performing at the Kennedy Center. However, this is not a date. Sam asks in what way. There will be, under no circumstances, any sex, replies Mallory. Like most people, Sam says, he's an absolute nut for Chinese opera. And, what with Mallory's guarantee of no sex, he doesn't see how he can refuse. Her father has other ideas.

Logic, Let Me Introduce You to This Window: Hoynes says Mars is made of nitrogen. It isn't: it's made from the same basic elements as the Earth. It *is* true that nitrogen's in the thin Martian atmosphere, though there's more carbon dioxide. When Mallory is in Sam's office, directly behind his seat is a black baseball cap with the AFT logo (Bureau of Alcohol, Firearms and Tobacco). When she returns with Leo later, there's a different cap sporting a DEA logo (Drug Enforcement Administration).

Quote/Unquote: Bartlet: 'There are fifty-four national parks in the country.' Josh: 'Please tell me you haven't been to all of them.' And, Bartlet: 'We should organise a staff field trip to Shenandoah.' Josh: 'Good a place as any to dump your body.'

Toby: 'It's retaliatory.' Bartlet: 'For what?' Toby: 'The campaign.' Bartlet: 'What did I do to them during the campaign?' Toby: 'You won, sir.'

Notes: 'We talk about enemies more than we used to.' The only *West Wing* episode that doesn't feature Sorkin's name on the writing credits. Nevertheless, there's some good stuff – particularly Danny and CJ's flirting. The pre-titles, with Bartlet boring Josh, is a classic.

This is the third Cabinet meeting of the administration. Danny considers himself very good-looking. He likes seafood, is good at kayaking and is a lively conversationalist. He enjoys movies and music and, though not wild about ice-skating, he will do it. CJ says Mandy knows Danny well.

Did You Know?: The New York Republican Carolyn Maloney admitted to borrowing the *deus ex machina* from this episode when she asked President Clinton to use the Antiquities Act to preserve Governor's Island by declaring two of its ruins (Castle Williams and Fort Jay) national monuments.

CJ's Background: Since she calls Josh a Yankee (**3**, 'A Proportional Response') it's possible Claudia is from the South, although more likely she's Californian (her father lives in Napa, near San Francisco – **39**, 'The Stackhouse Filibuster' – and she doesn't think she sees enough of him). There's a picture on her desk of a young girl and two boys, possibly of CJ and her brothers (**14**, 'Take This Sabbath Day'). She went to school 'for twenty-two years' (**7**, 'The State Dinner'), including Berkeley (**3**, 'A Proportional Response'), where she was a merit scholar and achieved a master's degree (**30**, 'Shibboleth'). She had fine SAT scores (**31**, 'Galileo'). She is Catholic. Bartlet thinks of her as a daughter (**21**, 'Lies, Damn Lies and Statistics') and describes her as 'like a 50s movie star' (**5**, 'The Crackpots and These Women').

CJ is six feet tall (**5**, 'The Crackpots and These Women') and the president pointedly asks if she's getting taller (**19**, 'Let Bartlet Be Bartlet'). Between 5 and 6 a.m., CJ works out at the gym in the hope of meeting an interesting man (**1**, 'The West Wing'), though she bemoans that she can't remember the last time she got home before midnight (**13**, 'Take Out the Trash Day'). 'Do you think the joke reflex you use as a defence mechanism is why you have such trouble keeping a man?' Josh asks (**12**, 'He Shall, from Time to Time . . .') She once had a boyfriend who owned a Porsche. He dumped her after she drove it into a pond (**18**, 'Six Meetings Before Lunch'). She has an off/on/off-again 'girlish preoccupation' with Danny Concannon (their first date is arranged in **10**, 'In Excelsis Deo', they kiss in **12**, 'He Shall, from Time to Time . . .'; CJ appears jealous when Mandy flirts with Danny).

CJ has been an expert on polling trends since 1993 (**21**, 'Lies, Damn Lies and Statistics'). She worked for the Hollywood public relations firm Triton-Day (in TV and movies, which she hated) with an annual salary of $550,000, and was living in Beverly Hills before being recruited by Toby to work for Bartlet (**24**, 'In the Shadow of Two Gunmen' Part 2). She had run state campaigns before but never a national, though her work with Emily's List (a nationwide network of political donors helping to elect pro-choice Democrat women) impressed Leo. She wears glasses or contact lenses and has short sight without them. CJ plays tennis (**5**, 'The Crackpots and These Women'), loves Goldfish cheese crackers and drinks grass-hoppers (**6**, 'Mr. Willis of Ohio'). She has a pet fish named Gail, a gift from Danny, and a cat (**5**, 'The Crackpots and These Women'). She considers herself great in bed (**31**, 'Galileo'). Her party piece is lip-synching to 'The Jackal' (**18**, 'Six Meetings Before Lunch'). CJ chews gum (**8**, 'Enemies') and is afraid of dentists (**15**, 'Celestial Navigation'). Her Secret Service code name is Flamingo, much to her annoyance (**10**, 'In Excelsis Deo'). There is concern among some senior staff that CJ is too friendly with the press, specifically Danny (**11**, 'Lord John Marbury'). She believes her humour is very dry (**12**, 'He Shall, from Time to Time . . .'). She received the Matrix Award from Women in Communication (**34**, 'The Drop In').

9
The Short List

US Transmission Date: 24 November 1999
UK Transmission Date: 13 March 2000 (Sky), 15 March 2001 (C4)

Teleplay: Aaron Sorkin, Patrick Caddell
Story: Aaron Sorkin, Dee Dee Myers
Director: Bill D'Elia
Cast: Holmes Osborne (Peter Lillienfield) Mason Adams (Joseph Crouch)
Ken Howard (Peyton Cabot Harrison III)

The retirement of a Supreme justice hands the administration a public-relations triumph. But a study of their candidate's ideology reveals some frightening opinions. A headline-seeking Congressman accuses the White House staff of drug abuse – an uncomfortable issue for one member.

A View from the Hill: The Senate Committee on the Judiciary was created in 1816. The committee has the broadest jurisdiction in the Senate.

American History X: Harry Truman (1884–1972) was the 33rd US president, Dwight D Eisenhower (1890–1969), the

34th. Sam mentions that the third amendment says soldiers can't be quartered in private homes, the fourth provides protection against unreasonable searches and the fifth is against self-incrimination. The first amendment grants freedom of expression. In 1787, a sizable block of delegates was opposed to the Bill of Rights (see **1**, 'The West Wing'). One Georgia member noted, 'If we list the set of rights, some fools in the future are going to claim that people are entitled only to those rights.' Harrison asks if Sam is calling him a fool. 'I wasn't, sir,' replies Sam. 'The brand-new state of Georgia was.'

In the 1920s and 1930s the major underlying public concern was the role of government, Sam notes. In the 1950s and 1960s it was civil rights. The next two decades will, he believes, be about privacy over subjects such as the Internet, mobile phones, health records and who is gay and who isn't. 'In a country born on a will to be free, what could be more fundamental than this?'

Roe v. Wade (1973) concerned a pregnant woman who challenged Texas law, which prohibited abortion. The Supreme Court declared the statute infringed the plaintiffs' ninth- and fourteenth-amendment rights. *Amicus* briefs are aspects of legal cases where the court is advised by someone who is not a direct party to the case.

Among former White House staffers that Lillienfield mentions are Schlesinger[44], Sorenson[45] and Rumsfeld[46]. These 'best and brightest' have been replaced, he says, by Ivy League liberals and Hollywood darlings (the Ivy League is a name applied to eight universities – Brown, Columbia, Cornell, Dartmouth, Harvard, Pennsylvania, Princeton and Yale; Stanley Woodward, a *New York Herald Tribune* sports writer, coined the phrase).

Peyton Cabot Harrison III is said to have been educated at Walnut Park Country Day, Phillips Exeter Academy

---

[44] Arthur Schlesinger Jr, assistant to President Kennedy and author of *A Thousand Days*.

[45] Theodore Sorenson, consul to President Kennedy.

[46] Donald Rumsfeld, chief-of-staff to President Ford and Defense Secretary under President Bush Jr.

and Princeton, to have been a Rhodes scholar (which brings overseas students to Oxford), editor of *Harvard Law Review* and a clerk for Warren Burger. He was dean of Harvard Law School. His father was Attorney General to Eisenhower. He's a lifelong Democrat. Roberto Mendoza attended Public School 138 in Brooklyn and City University of New York. He was in the NYPD (1965–76) and was shot in the leg on duty. He took a desk job and went to law school at night. He was Assistant District Attorney, Brooklyn (1976–80), Assistant US Attorney, Eastern District, and is now a federal district judge.

Politics of Compromise: Crouch says that Bartlet ran a great campaign. Then he got elected and drove to the middle of the road. Crouch wanted to retire five years ago but he waited for a Democrat president. 'Instead, I got *you*.' He tells Bartlet that he will lose the next election. Voters like guts, he notes. Bartlet imagines that the view from Crouch's place in history must be different from his own – he reminds him that he has to negotiate an opposition Congress, special interests with power beyond belief and bitchy media.

A Little Learning is a Dangerous Thing: Where does Lillienfield get his information from? Donna asks. Josh notes he's involved in the Government Oversight Committee. This literally decides if the White House gets electricity, so it has access to background information.

Office Gossip: Mandy says Mendoza has ruled in favour of same-sex marriages. Josh corrects her – while not recommending it, he has ruled the state has no right to interfere.

The Conspiracy Starts at Closing Time: An unsigned note is a scholarly work that every member of Law Review must prepare. It's approximately forty pages, researched, footnoted and revised with faculty supervision, then published anonymously. Sam has spent three months reading everything Harrison has ever written and knows he is the author of the unsigned note, which he wrote 29 years ago when he was 26. A quote from the work says, 'While enjoying my privacy, I am compelled to admit that government has a right to invade it unless specifically prohibited by some specific Constitutional provision.' Judges are bound to interpret the Constitution within the parameters of the text, Harrison argues. That the framers enumerated specific protections (for instance, the third, fourth and fifth amendments) is reason to believe that they had no intention of making privacy a *de facto* right. They had just fought a revolution, they had no question about their freedoms, argues Sam. Harrison does not deny Toby's argument that there are natural laws. Only that judges are empowered to enforce them.

So as not to alert Mendoza that he's being considered for the bench, Mandy invites him to the White House for a place on the President's Commission for Hispanic Opportunity.

References: *Masterpiece Theatre* (a PBS television anthology, sponsored by ExxonMobile, which began in 1971 and, in its presentation of the cream of British drama, introduced American audiences to *The Forsyte Saga, Elizabeth R, Last of the Mohicans* and *I, Claudius,* among others). Random House publishing. Donna misquotes the aphorism 'There's many a slip twixt the tongue and the lip'. Josh says 'there for the grace of God', a misquote of a saying attributed to the penal reformer John Bradford (1510–55). Bartlet alludes to the book of Timothy ('let the good fight begin'). *USA Today* is on CJ's desk. Sam has a dartboard and an LA Lakers shirt on his office wall.

'You May Remember Me From Such Films and TV Series As …': Holmes Osborne played Mr Patterson in *That Thing You Do!* and was in *The Deep End, Bring it On* and *Nice Girls Don't Explode.* Mason Adams appeared in *Toy Soldiers, F/X – Murder By Illusion, Flamingo Road* and *The Happy Hooker.* Ken Howard was in *The Net, Strange Interlude, The Thorn Birds* and *Melrose Place.* Edward James Olmos's distinguished career includes roles in *Stand and Deliver, Blade Runner* (as Gaff), *Miami Vice, Hollywood Confidential, Evening in Byzantium, Starsky and*

Hutch and *Cannon*. He directed *American Me*. Diana Morgan was Mallory in *Murder One*. Charles Noland was in *ER*, *Wayne's World* and *Sunset*.

Behind the Camera: Bill D'Elia was director/producer on *Ally McBeal* and *Chicago Hope*. He also worked on *Picket Fences*, *Beverly Hills 90210* and *Doogie Howser M.D.*, and wrote episodes of *Judging Amy*.

Oh, Donna!: Donna tells Josh a maintenance crew's working upstairs. Josh doesn't seem interested until a chunk of masonry crashes down on his desk. Josh says that from now on he wants Donna to 'test' his office.

On the subject of drugs, Donna says Josh shouldn't feel uncomfortable interviewing her. Josh asks if she knows anybody who uses drugs. Donna says she does but won't say who. 'Good,' replies Josh, 'consider yourself interviewed.' He's seen her records and says she needs to learn what 'no parking' means.

Sex and Drugs and Rock'n'Roll: Peter Lillienfield alleges that one in three White House staffers uses drugs. Josh and Sam suggest a categorical denial. CJ says she can't, as more than 1,300 people work in the White House. If she denies that any of them use drugs it's perfectly possible that three guys in the photo lab blew a joint over the weekend or that the assistant to the deputy director of White House beverages is a closet junkie.

Mandy suggests mandatory drug tests for all staff to kill the story. Josh vehemently argues against this. Toby rejects the idea, but tells Josh to hold an internal investigation. An intern from Legislative Liaison tells Josh she made a bong out of an eggplant (aubergine). Josh admits he always used a potato.

Cigarettes and Alcohol: The president asks Charlie to find out what sort of cigars Harrison likes. Josh notes that the worst-kept secret in Washington is that Leo is a recovering alcoholic.

Logic, Let Me Introduce You to This Window: When Crouch says he wanted to retire five years ago but waited until a Democrat was elected, he's confirming something alluded to, if not stated, previously: the administration before Bartlet's was Republican and it served at least two terms. It, therefore, appears a contradiction that Leo was Secretary of Labor six years ago. It's unusual to have opposition members in the government, though not unique – for instance, the Secretary of Defense under Bill Clinton was a Republican. There are actually 3,300 full-time staff on the White House payroll, not 1,300 as CJ says. Why does Toby refer to Peyton Harrison as Ed? Toby notes that Harrison is 55 but says he wants to know about any girls whom the judge stood up for dinner in 1953. When he was eight?

Quote/Unquote: Josh: 'Five White House staffers in the room. I would like to say to the one point six of you who are stoned right now, it's time to share!'

Toby: 'We've been doing this for a year. All we've gotten is a year older. Our job approval's forty-eight per cent, I think that number's soft and I'm tired of being the field captain for the gang that couldn't shoot straight.'

Notes: 'You're Leo McGarry. You're not gonna be taken down by this small fraction of a man.' Fantastic stuff. An episode about how even when you're certain you've made the right decision something comes along to change your mind. Crouch's disillusionment in Bartlet is juxtaposed by Sam's (naïve but valid) belief that freedoms are fundamental. Best bits: everybody deciding 'who de man'; Sam grilling Harrison; Josh's description of Lillienfield as 'a hairdo'; Leo telling the president there'll be rough times ahead; and Bartlet's unstinting support. When Bartlet says, 'You've fought in a war, you got me elected, you run the country, I think we owe you one,' you'll have a lump in your throat.

Danny suggests watching a New York Knicks game with CJ in her office while he explains basketball in a patronising manner because he knows this is something women like. He can't spell 'subpoena' (he's probably lying) and has a good relationship with Josh (they occasionally feed each other information). Locations include outside the Supreme Court and Danny meeting Josh on the Mall. Episode **13**, 'Take Out the Trash Day', reveals that this one begins on 21 November 1999.

Critique: 'It's hard not to get caught up in the exuberance displayed by the staff,' noted *Radio Times*. 'Josh, in particular, is behaving like an American footballer scoring a touchdown, punching the air and shrieking, "I de man!" Keep a lookout for reporter Danny, who has his eye on CJ. The programme makers have said they intend to focus more on the characters' personal lives. As we don't count the daft relationship between Sam and a call-girl in episode one, could this be the series' first romance.'

Cast and Crew Comments: 'I wanted to start with "Everything's great, we got Mario Cuomo," '.[47] Sorkin told Matthew Miller. 'And to end with "It's a whole different guy." In other words, we're gonna have to discover a problem with our home-run candidate.' Sorkin didn't want this problem to be scandalous as with Clarence Thomas.[48] 'I didn't want this guy to have done anything wrong except that I was intrigued by [Robert] Bork[49] and those who agree the Constitution does not provide for a right of privacy.' Sorkin also wanted the action to take place over just a couple of days. 'The more you compress time, the more the heat goes up,' he explains. 'I was taught that you want to start your stories as close to the end as possible.' Lawrence O'Donnell supplied the résumé of the perfect candidate; Pat Caddell researched the privacy arguments.

---

[47] Mario Cuomo, governor of New York (1983–95).
[48] Clarence Thomas, nominated by President Bush in 1991. Thomas's nomination hearings were marred by accusations of sexual harassment against him by a former colleague, Anita Hill. His appointment was eventually confirmed by a Senate vote of 52 to 48, one of the closest margins in history.
[49] Robert Bork. Controversial right-wing judge, nominated by President Reagan in 1987. Senate rejected him following heated debates about his ideology. Author of *Slouching Towards Gomorrah: Modern Liberalism and American Decline* (1996).

Sorkin asked Dee Dee Myers what might undo the perfect candidate. She suggested an unsigned note he wrote as a young man that casts doubt on his commitment to privacy.

Did You Know?: *The West Wing* is miserly with guest stars, Edward James Olmos told Gail Shister. Olmos says he was asked to work for $4,500 per episode. '*West Wing* complained when they had to pay me,' Olmos added. 'They felt they had a top show, and wouldn't everybody do it for nothing? I said, "I don't do anything for commercial television for nothing. You don't need the help!" '

Did You Know?: The addiction storyline came from Aaron Sorkin's own, well-documented, problems with drugs. He's been in recovery since 1995, when he went to the Hazleden Institute, Minnesota, for a freebase cocaine habit. His sobriety since then has, he told *TV Guide*, been sporadic. He confesses to smoking marijuana to relax – usually after finishing a script. Sorkin, nevertheless, received an award from Phoenix House, a drug- and alcohol-abuse treatment organisation, for his personal commitment to the issue.

Donna's Background: Donnatella Moss describes herself as a farm girl (**29**, 'The Portland Trip') and spent two years at the University of Wisconsin in Madison, where she bonded with Stephanie Gault because of a shared loathing for the same ex-boyfriend (**38**, 'Somebody's Going to Emergency, Somebody's Going to Jail'). Her parents still live in Madison (**41**, 'Bad Moon Rising'). Donna dropped out to put her then boyfriend through medical school (**24**, 'In the Shadow of Two Gunmen' Part 2). She initially claimed to be a graduate, with a degree in political science and government, though later admits, 'When I said *graduated*, I may have been overstating.' She also majored in sociology, psychology and biology, with minors in French and drama. Josh hired her (**41**, 'Bad Moon Rising' dates this as February 1998) but she subsequently left to return to her boyfriend. Soon afterwards Donna was in a car accident and broke her ankle. Having ended her relationship for a second time, she returned to the team in April and has been Josh's assistant for a year and a half (**1**, 'The West Wing').

Her family are Protestant (**10**, 'In Excelsis Deo'), though Josh suggests she went to a catholic school (**40**, '17 People'). She dated Tod, an insurance lobbyist, but he was undeservingly full of himself. 'I have an excellent sense about these things,' she tells Josh concerning guys. 'You have *no* sense about these things,' Josh responds. 'You have terrible taste in men and your desire to be coupled up will forever drown out any small sense of self-worth you have' (**29**, 'The Portland Trip'). But he loves her really (see, especially, **32**, 'Noël', and **40**, '17 People'). Donna was a flautist in high school (**29**, 'The Portland Trip'). When things go wrong for Josh he usually ends up drunk in Donna's apartment yelling at her roommate's cats (**9**, 'The Short List'). Her handwriting is illegible but she never gets messages wrong (**18**, 'Six Meetings Before Lunch'). She's a huge fan of David Hasselhoff (**16**, '20 Hours in L.A.'). Her friend, Curtis, fixes chairs (**22**, 'What Kind of Day Has it Been').

10
In Excelsis Deo

US Transmission Date: 15 December 1999
UK Transmission Date: 20 March 2000 (Sky), 22 March 2001 (C4)

Writers: Aaron Sorkin, Rick Cleveland
Director: Alex Graves
Cast: Paul Austin (George Hufnagle) Tom Quinn (John Noonan)
Raynor Scheine (Homeless Man) Lance Reddick (DC Police Officer)
Christian Copelin (Jeffrey) Morina Pierce (Jessica) Becky Woodley (Aide)

As the president does some last-minute Christmas shopping, Toby learns that a Korean War hero died on the streets wearing a coat that Toby donated to charity. Sam and Josh ignore Leo's orders and ask Laurie about her clientele when a political rival hints at exposing Leo's former drug problems.

American History X: The US entered the Korean War as part of UN forces seeking to halt a North Korean invasion of the South in 1950. The War Memorial in Washington, dedicated in 1995 and seen in this episode, shows a group of servicemen of different ethnic groups. Toby says Hufnagle got better treatment at P'anmunjóm – where the truce was signed in 1953 – than in his own country.[50]

Arlington National Cemetery is on a hill overlooking Washington. It houses the Tomb of the Unknown Soldier and the grave of John Kennedy, as well as being the final resting place of honourably discharged members of the armed services.

Politics of Indulgence: Sam is going to Bermuda for Christmas. 'Just me, some sun-tan oil and six hundred and fifty-five pages of briefing memos.' Josh, meanwhile, is helping to prepare a strategy for the European economic summit in February, but the president tells him to blow it off and come shopping with him.

The Encyclopedic Mind of Josiah Bartlet PhD: Among the titles Bartlet claims for himself while talking to the children are: President of Bulgaria and of the great Kingdom of Luxembourg and His Royal Majesty the King of All England. He's in his element in the bookshop, gleefully telling Leo about *The Fables of Phaedrus*, a Thracian slave and the first translator of Aesop into Latin verse. Later granted his freedom by the Emperor Augustus, Phaedrus wrote animal fables in iambic verse. Bartlet also buys two volumes by the Greek philosopher Epicurus. With Zoey starting at Georgetown in two weeks (see **5**, 'The Crackpots and These Women'), Jed considers getting her a copy of *The Nature of Things: A Viviscalic Poem Translated from the Latin of Titus Lucrecius Carus*. Charlie notes, with

---

[50] Debate among fans concerned whether Toby says 'guy got better treatment at P'anmunjóm' or '*I* got' (it certainly sounds like the latter, though the former makes more sense). Sorkin cleared up the matter in February 2001, confirming that Toby was referring to Hufnagle being in Korea and not Toby himself.

no apparent sarcasm, that Zoey would much prefer this to a new stereo.

Office Gossip: Margaret tells Donna about Leo's predicament. Leo has heard rumours about Sam and Laurie.

The Conspiracy Starts at Closing Time: How does the president go shopping without a huge entourage? Simple: a couple of agents, an unmarked black Suburban. They tell the manager – in this case at a shop called Rare Books – who clears the store. He's in, he's out. Bartlet asks Josh if he knew that there's a secret underground tunnel out of the White House. Josh says he did. 'I haven't been able to find it,' notes the president. 'Even though I search almost every day.' Asked if he wants to come, Josh says, 'An hour with you in a rare bookstore? Couldn't you just drop me off the top of the Washington monument instead?' It's Christmas, the president notes – no reason they can't do both. Toby, meanwhile, uses the president's name to organise a guard of honour for the funeral of the homeless veteran. Bartlet doesn't mind but asks Toby to assure him that there isn't anything else he's arranged. 'We're still in NATO, right?'

Alternate Sexuality: Lowell Lydell, a gay high school senior from Minneapolis, was stripped naked, tied to a tree and had rocks thrown at his head by thirteen-year-old assailants. They made him say 'Hail Mary' as they beat him to death. 'This was a crime of entertainment,' says CJ. The debate on the subject of hate crime continues in **13**, 'Take Out the Trash Day'.

References: Namechecks for the NBC weatherman Al Roker, José Feliciano (best known for his cover of the Doors' 'Light My Fire'), the Chicago Cubs baseball star Sammy Sosa, the Spanish carol 'Feliz Navidad', which, Sam notes, outsold Bing Crosby's 'White Christmas', and Stephen Jay Gould (palaeontologist, science philosopher and author of numerous books on evolution). Josh would rather eat *The Adventures of James Capen Adams, Mountaineer and Grizzly Bear Hunter of California* than read it. He has a copy of *Fortune* magazine. Leo calls Sam's and

Josh's antics 'the Keystone Kops' after the characters created by Mack Sennett. An allusion to *Monty Python's Flying Circus* ('I'm arguing now, I'll call back'). The choir sing 'Little Drummer Boy'.

'You May Remember Me From Such Films and TV Series As . . .': Paul Austin was in *The Pope of Greenwich Village*, *Flirt*, *The Manhattan Project*, *Killer Image* and *Trading Places*. Christian Copelin appeared in *Delivering Milo*. Tom Quinn's movies include *To Die For* and *Monkey Shines*. Lance Reddick was in *The Fixer* and *Godzilla*. Raynor Scheine has been in *Book of Shadows: Blair Witch 2*, *Last Man Standing*, *My Cousin Vinny*, *The Handmaid's Tale*, *Insignificance*, *Return of Sabata* and *Matlock*.

Stun-Your-Friends Trivia!: One of the uncredited extras in the press conference is Rene Auberjonois (best known as Odo in *Star Trek: Deep Space Nine*).

Behind the Camera: Alex Graves directed episodes of *Ally McBeal* and the movies *The Crude Oasis* (which he also wrote and produced) and *Casualties*. Rick Cleveland was producer on *Jerry and Tom*. Since leaving *The West Wing*, he's worked on *Gideon's Crossing* and *Six Feet Under*.

Oh, Donna!: Josh hasn't bought Donna a Christmas gift yet. She believes this is because he's agonising over how best to express his affection. It's more, Josh notes, how he can find ten bucks. Donna has, helpfully, prepared a list of suggestions which includes ski pants, ski boots, ski hat, ski goggles, ski gloves and ski poles. 'I'm assuming you already have skis,' Josh says. 'Page two,' she replies. Ultimately, he buys her a book by Heimlich Beckengrüber called *The Art and Artistry of Alpine Skiing*. Donna is affected by what Josh writes in it. 'You spend most of our time being, you know, *you*,' she notes tearfully. 'Then you write something like this,' before adding, 'Skis would have *killed* you?'

Sex and Drugs and Rock'n'Roll: Josh and Sam ask Laurie for details of an influential Republican who likes kinky sex so they can scare Lillienfield into shutting up. She refuses.

Logic, Let Me Introduce You to This Window: Mrs Landingham mentions that her sons had low draft numbers in the lottery. They died in Vietnam on 24 December 1970. The first lottery was held on 1 December 1969 so even someone with quite a high number could easily have been in the field by December 1970. Laurie's apartment in **1**, 'The West Wing' (with a long hallway) is different from the one Sam and Josh visit here. Toby may be a pedant, but he *is* correct: the year 2000 is the *last* year of the millennium, not the first. What is Toby, a Jew, doing with a 'Merry Christmas' card on his office wall? Would the president really ring the parents of a murder victim – even one as horrific as this? If he did, it's a dangerous precedent to set. He'd never be off the phone, given the murder rate in the US. Sam tells CJ he's leaving for Bermuda tonight. The next morning he's still at the White House.

Cruelty To Animals: Josh asks Donna to stop looking at him 'like I just killed your hamster'.

Quote/Unquote: CJ: 'The president is scheduled to leave for New Hampshire tomorrow morning at precisely ten on the dot. Which means he ought to be leaving around noon.'

CJ, on Leo's Christmas plans: 'Want me to come cook you something?' Leo: 'What are you, my mother?'

Notes: 'You're the good guys. You should act like it.' An excellent story about honour and dignity. Best bits: Toby and Sam arguing over the millennium.

Mrs Landingham's twin sons (see **5**, 'The Crackpots and These Women'), Andrew and Simon, did everything together, including going to medical school. They finished their second year and were drafted to Vietnam. They could have got a deferment to finish school but they wanted to go where people needed doctors, despite their parents' objections. They joined up as medics and four months later they were killed by enemy fire in DaNang. Walter Hufnagle was a lance corporal in the Marines in Korea and was awarded the Purple Heart.

Controversy: In September 2000 this episode deservedly won an Emmy. At the ceremony, Sorkin made an acceptance speech while Rick Cleveland, who was with him on stage, said nothing. Cleveland had left the *West Wing* production team some months earlier.

Cleveland's father was a Korean veteran with an alcohol addiction who spent the last years of his life in flophouses. In an article in the Writers' Guild magazine in November 2000, Cleveland noted, 'When I finally had the courage to go through what few personal items he left, I found among his decorations were a Good Conduct Medal and a Purple Heart. I didn't know at the time but I could have had him buried at Arlington National Cemetery.'

Concerning the episode itself, Cleveland said that the earliest draft was entitled 'Bellwether', the name of the first lady's cat. This never made the final cut but his story about Toby's attempts to get a homeless Korean veteran buried in Arlington did. Rick was, he admitted, upset that Sorkin had not allowed him to speak during the ceremony. 'He has an actor's vanity about his work,' Cleveland wrote about his former employer.

In June 2001, an article by Bernard Weinraub in the *New York Times* alleged that Sorkin had stirred enmity among his writers, partly because he takes credit for every episode and partly for the incident with Cleveland. Days before the ceremony, wrote Weinraub, quoting 'people connected to the show', Cleveland had sent Sorkin an email saying that, if they won, he should be allowed to say a brief word in honour of his father because the episode was autobiographical. 'At the Awards, Sorkin conspicuously ignored him,' Weinraub alleged. Responding on *mightybigtv.com*, Sorkin noted that, on most TV series, plots are pitched and outlined by a group, assigned to staff writers, then polished by the show's creator. However, on *The West Wing*, Sorkin writes the scripts with the help of the staff, who provide research and kick ideas around with him. He explained that, by way of a gratuity, each is granted a 'Story by' credit on a rotating basis. Regarding 'In Excelsis Deo', Sorkin alleged, 'I gave Rick Cleveland an assignment. He

wrote a script called "A White House Christmas", wherein
the first lady's cat trips a Secret Service alarm. I can't
[remember] much else except mention was made of a
business card found in an old coat of Toby's. I threw out
Rick's script and wrote "In Excelsis Deo".' Because
Cleveland had worked for months on the episode, Sorkin
went on, he was given a 'Story by' credit for which he
subsequently received a Humanitas nomination, an Emmy
and a Writers' Guild award. Sorkin also said that each
Emmy nominee receives a letter from Don Mischer,
producer of the telecast, saying that only one person is
allowed to speak when accepting. 'All of this was explained
to Bernie Weinraub,' he added.

Two weeks later, Rick Cleveland responded, directing
interested parties to the three earlier drafts of his script –
available at the WGA archive. 'The "A" story is mine –
not just the idea – all the way down to the name of the
veteran,' he wrote. 'Other stuff is also mine – the new
millennium stuff in the teaser, as well as CJ's secret service
nickname – which was my wife's idea. Aaron's a great
writer, and did a great job rewriting the script – but he
didn't write it alone. And he didn't "give" me a written-by
credit. The script was arbitrated by the WGA – they
decided my work warranted a Co-Writer credit.'

Sorkin attempted to end the row by addressing Cleveland directly online, thanking him for his crucial contributions to the episode and saying that he was wrong to imply
otherwise. While he felt Cleveland's piece in the Writers'
Guide magazine had been unduly nasty, he was more
concerned about the way in which the story had been
presented in the *New York Times*. 'I reacted too quickly to
what I felt was an egregiously unfair characterization of
the way writers are treated on *The West Wing*. Further,
I'm remarkably and stupidly naive about the Internet, and
never imagined my response to a poster would be picked
up.' Cleveland, graciously, accepted Sorkin's apology.

'I was simply responding [on the Internet], not thinking
that there were more than a dozen people in the room,'
Sorkin told the *Washington Post*. 'I made a guy I like feel

bad,' he added in an interview with *TV Guide*. 'I'd gone below the belt in assassinating his work.'

Cast and Crew Comments: 'It was such a powerful and moving story,' Richard Schiff told Michele Sponagle. 'After every take, I cried.' In another interview, with the *Bergen Record*, Schiff noted, 'I don't watch the show very often, because I get too upset at the editing choices, but Aaron made me watch that one. It was too hard to be my favourite episode, but it was certainly the most challenging. I was moved by every aspect of it.'

The original ending of the script, according to Martin Sheen in *St Anthony Messenger*, was to feature the president attending the funeral. 'It was changed because it took away the power of Mrs Landingham and Ziegler, who were deeply affected by the incident: a woman who has lost two sons and a man who gave this guy clothes to keep warm. Had the president been there, it would have [reduced] the poignancy of the scene. That's why I like this show. We try to play honest moments with real characters.'

Did You Know?: 'The Pentagon has been phenomenally friendly to us and very supportive of this show and what it has to say,' John Wells told the *Globe and Mail*. 'They gave us the Arlington location and the Marines and set up the whole funeral for us because they read Aaron's script and felt touched by it.'

11
Lord John Marbury

US Transmission Date: 5 January 2000
UK Transmission Date: 27 March 2000 (Sky), 29 March 2001 (C4)

Teleplay: Aaron Sorkin, Patrick Caddell
Story: Patrick Caddell, Lawrence O'Donnell Jr.
Director: Kevin Rodney Sullivan
Cast: John Diehl (Claypool) James Hong (David)
Eric Avari (Pakistani Ambassador) David Doty (Military Officer)
Clyde Kusatsu (Joe) Iqbal Theba (Indian Ambassador)

Ryan Cutrona (CIA Director Rollie) Charles Hoyes (Thompson)
J David Krassner (Jack) Roger Ranney (Civilian)

An Indian invasion of Kashmir and the threat of nuclear confrontation with Pakistan pushes the president into calling on the help of Lord Marbury, an eccentric British diplomat. Josh is subpoenaed to testify on his investigation into substance abuse. The president is surprised when Charlie asks him if he can date Zoey.

A View from the Hill: Josh is asked to brief the Hill about the international situation.

American History X: The Freedom of Information Act was first passed in 1967.[51]
   Whenever the Indian Ambassador talks about colonial Western imperialism, Bartlet says he wants to remind him that the US is also a revolutionary country that threw off its colonial masters. So it's seemingly *all* Britain's fault. Sorry.

A Little Learning is a Dangerous Thing: Larry and Ed get most of their material on India and Pakistan from *Encyclopaedia Britannica*.

Carol's Spelling: She gets 'New Delhi' wrong, putting the 'h' in the wrong place.

Denial, Thy Name is America: Happily ensconced in the cocoon of their Cold War victory, Lord Marbury says, Americans are woefully ignorant of the powerful historical agents in Asia. The global triumph of the economic free market has created an assumption that the world is drawing together. Congress has been inept at halting the proliferation of nuclear weapons in this

---

[51] FOIA requires each government agency to publish descriptions of its operations that affect the public. Any person can obtain data from a government agency through a FOIA request. However, agencies may withhold nine categories of records, ranging from national defence information to medical files.

region and intelligence gathering is weak. It's about religion, Marbury concludes, and he assures the president that *they* do not share our fear of the bomb.

The Gospel According to Marbury: The president is unable to remember a specific quotation from the Book of Revelation. Lord Marbury supplies it: 'I looked, and I beheld a pale horse, and the name that sat on him was Death, and Hell followed with him.' (Revelation 6:8)

The Revolution Will Be Televised: Intense fighting occurs between Indian and Pakistani troops after the incursion (which may have been provoked by earlier Pakistani movement in the Neutral Zone), the ceasefire line being breached in two thrusts, north of Kargil and into Azhad. The CIA director says the nearest orbiting satellites have been diverted to the area. The KH-Super-Platform is going into stationary orbit over the subcontinent. The UN Security Council is in emergency session to try to effect a ceasefire. India has two intermediate-range ballistic missiles named Agni 1 and Agni 2 (*agni* means fire in Hindi), a 55-kiloton A-bomb (50 per cent more destructive than the Hiroshima bomb) and a thermonuclear device. Beijing instruct their ambassador to tell the president that China would like to see a peaceful solution but are prepared to use force if necessary. Despite some sabre-rattling by both sides when meeting the president, a two-week ceasefire resolution is brokered at the UN.

References: In reality Larry Klayman is leader of a litigious watchdog called Judicial Watch. In *The West Wing*, Harry Claypool is the head of a litigious watchdog called Freedom Watch. Stanley Kubrick's black comedy *Dr. Strangelove or: How I Learned to Stop Worrying and Love the Bomb*. Leo and Bartlet have a shared appreciation for Spencer Tracy (1900–67) and his performance in *Guess Who's Coming to Dinner*. Also, *Little Lord Fauntleroy* by Frances Hodgson Burnett (1849–1924), the doyen of English light opera William Schwenk Gilbert (1836–1911) and Arthur Sullivan (1842–1900) (see

27, 'And it's Surely to Their Credit'), allusions to *Scanners* ('without your head exploding') and Sherlock Holmes ('excellent deducing') and a misquote from R.E.M.'s 'Radio Song'. Josh is conversant with CB-speak ('that's a Big 10-4').

'You May Remember Me From Such Films and TV Series As . . .': Like a number of British actors of his generation, Roger Rees was originally trained in the visual arts. A member of the RSC, he won a Tony for *The Life and Adventures of Nicholas Nickleby*. A role in *A Bouquet of Barbed Wire* led to his movie debut in *Star 80*. Primarily a man of the theatre, a playwright and director, he's lived in the US since 1989 and appeared in *Jump*, *Suddenly Manhattan*, *Cheers*, *Robin Hood: Men in Tights* and *If Looks Could Kill*.

John Diehl was Cooper in *Jurassic Park III*, Joe DiMaggio in *The Rat Pack* and Gordon Liddy in *Nixon*, and appeared in *Anywhere But Here*, *A Time to Kill*, *Stargate* and *Whore*. David Doty can be seen in *Never Been Kissed*, *The Parent Trap* and *Star Trek: Voyager*. Gary Cervantes was in *Traffic*, *Scarface*, *The Wonder Years*, *Herman's Head* and *Chico and the Man*. Clyde Kusatsu was in *American Pie*, *Spy Hard*, *Jailbirds*, *Star Trek: The Next Generation*, *The Choirboys*, *Magnum P.I.*, *All in the Family* and *M*A*S*H*, and provided voices for *Batman Beyond*. Ryan Cutrona's movies include *Militia*, *Sliver* and *Kuffs*. Ralph Meyering was in *Born Bad* and *The American President*. Roger Ranney played Jimmy in *The Cape*. Bill Stevenson was Pete in *Suddenly Susan* and appeared in *The Last Seduction*, *The 'burbs*, *Outbreak* and *Parker Lewis Can't Lose*.

James Hong's career stretches back to the 1950s with appearances in *Epoch*, *Caged Fury*, *Go Tell the Spartans*, *Big Trouble in Little China*, *Blade Runner*, *Airplane!*, *Kung Fu*, *Chinatown*, *The Satan Bug*, *Colossus: The Forbin Project*, *The Streets of San Francisco*, *The Outer Limits* and *I Dream of Jeannie*. He did voice work on Disney's *Mulan* and produced and directed *Teen Lust*. Eric Avari was Tival in *Planet of the Apes*, Dr Bey in *The Mummy* and Kasuf in *Stargate* and *Stargate SG-1*, and also appeared in *Scam* and *3 Days of Rain*. Iqbal Theba played Iqbal in *Married ... With Children*, was Joey's doctor in *Friends* and appeared in *Driven* and *Indecent Proposal*. Charles Hoyes was in *M.A.N.T.I.S.*, *Field of Dreams*, *Molly* and *Twin Peaks*. David Krassner played Tiller in *Clean and Sober*. Tom Hall was in *Another Midnight Run*.

Behind the Camera: Kevin Rodney Sullivan directed *How Stella Got Her Groove Back* and *America's Dream*. As an actor, he played March in *Star Trek: Wrath of Khan* and Tommy in *Happy Days*.

Oh, Donna!: Josh tries to persuade Donna to be his caddie.

Sex and Drugs and Rock'n'Roll: Leo says that both his family and the president know about his drug problems.

Cigarettes and Alcohol: When the subject of Lord Marbury comes up, Leo asks if the president intends to let him loose where there's liquor and women. 'We can hide the women,' says Bartlet. 'But the man deserves a drink.' Upon arrival, Marbury says his flight was intoxicating. He smokes in the Oval Office.

Logic, Let Me Introduce You to This Window: Leo tells Marbury, 'We don't allow smoking in this part of the world.' But he *does* allow Toby to smoke cigars (see **6**, 'Mr. Willis of Ohio'). Of course, the fact that Leo doesn't like Marbury is purely coincidental. A common mistake, but a very surprising one for a deeply religious man like Bartlet, is to call the final book of the Bible Revelations instead of Revelation. When CJ enters the Oval Office to find the guys discussing Kashmir, Leo is the only one who speaks, so why is she subsequently so angry with Toby and why does Toby say that it was he who decided not to include her in the loop? Britain doesn't have ministers to India and Pakistan: it has ambassadors.

Uncanny!: 'Our India invaded Kashmir two weeks before the real one did,' Sorkin noted in the *New York Times*.[52]

Quote/Unquote: Bartlet: 'When you say "the Indian army", what are we talking about? Five guys in a Humvee?'

Leo: 'The people the president's talking about aren't defenceless, Mr Ambassador. They're carrying the M-16s *we* sold them.'

Sam, to Claypool: 'You're a cheap hack. If you come after Leo I'm gonna bust you like a piñata.'

Notes: 'You're all frightened. As well you should be. Not since the Protestant–Catholic wars in the sixteenth century has Western society known anything comparable to the subcontinent's religious malevolence.' Though it opens like an episode of *The X-Files*, 'Lord John Marbury' is a very down-to-earth story about what can happen when, in the words of Matt Johnson, 'all the planet's little wars start joining hands'. It's a fascinating take on the *West Wing* universe's opinion of America as the world's policeman (which is just as bewilderingly complex as our own). Also, we get a decent portrayal of a British character on US TV (not quite unique; *Buffy*'s managed a couple of half-decent attempts, but it's still pretty rare). In the hands of a lesser actor, Lord Marbury could have been a stereotypical upper-class twit, but Roger Rees manages to make him charming and raise him above caricature. Best bits: Josh and Sam at the hearing; the staff offering Leo their support; Leo and Marbury.

Bartlet was sworn in twelve months ago (January 1999). There is no current US Ambassador to Pakistan.

Critique: Madeleine Albright, former Secretary of State, said this was one of the best expositions on foreign policy she'd seen, Patrick Caddell told *Time* magazine. The magazine also noted that, while sitting in the Oval Office

---

[52] In reality, as Marbury notes, Pakistan and India have fought three wars since independence (1947–49, 1965, 1996) over Kashmir, with numerous intermittent skirmishes.

monitoring a briefing session with Clinton and his advisers, John Podesta jokingly slipped a note to Joe Lockhart saying, 'If this were *The West Wing*, CJ wouldn't be at this meeting.'

Did You Know?: Dee Dee Myers' involvement can prompt *The West Wing* to relive history. Her worst moment in the White House came after the assassination attempt on former President Bush in 1993. Myers told reporters one Friday that the FBI was still looking into whether Saddam Hussein was involved; President Clinton would decide on a course of action once he received the FBI's report. But Clinton already had the report and had decided to bomb Baghdad the next day. Myers came into work on Saturday and assured the press there would be no news. An hour later, with US missiles flying, she found herself paging reporters who were on their way to a Baltimore Orioles game, her credibility in tatters. 'I wanted to make CJ more angry,' Myers told Matthew Miller. 'To be some resolution, in order to preserve the strength of her character.' Instead, Leo brushes CJ off by saying, 'Just tell them you spoke without being informed.' 'I [told Aaron] this is like saying, "I'm an idiot; you can't trust me." '

Lord Marbury's Background: Lord Marbury, the hereditary Earl of Sherbourne, is the great-great-grandson of a former viceroy. For thirteen years he served as the Queen's 'minister' to either India or Pakistan and is an expert on the subcontinent. His mother was a descendant of the third of Queen Victoria's children and he mentions his royal heritage via Victoria's grandfather George III, the grandson of George I, the great-nephew of Charles I, the son of James I, to James's mother, Mary Queen of Scots.[53]

Leo considers Marbury a lunatic (as does Josh). The president thinks he's colourful. He has problems remem-

---

[53] Marbury could continue and claim a blood relationship, via Mary's great-grandfather, Henry VII, and *his* great-great-grandfather, John of Gaunt (the son of Edward III), to every English monarch as far back as William the Conqueror.

bering Leo's name (calling him Gerald in **34**, 'The Drop In'), and initially believes Leo is the butler, despite the pair having met on a dozen previous occasions. He was educated at Cambridge University and the Sorbonne (**12**, 'He Shall, from Time to Time . . .'). Although something of a ladies' man (both Donna and CJ are mesmerised by his charm) he and his assistant, Caprice, are definitely not an item (**34**, 'The Drop In').

12
He Shall, from Time to Time . . .

US Transmission Date: 12 January 2000
UK Transmission Date: 10 April 2000 (Sky), 5 April 2001 (C4)

Writer: Aaron Sorkin
Director: Arlene Sanford
Cast: Harry Groener (Roger Tribby) Madison Mason (Admiral Hacket)
David Spielberg (Congressman) Austin Tichenor (Raymond Burnsin)
Ronne Troup (Pratt) Roger Ontiveros (Officer #3)

Bartlet collapses as he prepares for the State of the Union address. While it is officially blamed on the flu, the first lady knows it's more serious. The disclosure of Leo's former substance abuse prompts a press conference.

A View from the Hill: The line of succession, in the event of the death of the president, comprises the vice president followed by the Speaker of the House, the president *pro tempore* of the Senate, the Secretaries of State, Treasury, Defense, the Attorney General, Secretaries of the Interior, Agriculture, Commerce, Labor, Health & Human Services, Housing & Urban Development, Transportation, Energy, Education and Veterans Affairs. An official can't become president unless he meets these Constitutional requirements. Someone from the line is required to be absent from the State of the Union address in case of terrorism. Bartlet tells Roger that, if anything should go wrong, the first priority is always national security.

Bartlet's second State of the Union address will include details of eighteen million new jobs, wages rising at twice the rate of inflation, the highest home ownership in history, the smallest welfare figures in thirty years and the lowest unemployment since 1957. America has created the longest peacetime economic expansion in its history. For the first time in three decades, the budget is balanced.

American History X: Knowing Bartlet's love of all things ancient, Roger brings him a translation of the Constitution into Latin and highlights the appropriate passage in Article 2, Section 3: 'He shall, from time to time, give to the Congress information on the state of the union and recommend to their consideration such measures as he shall judge necessary and expedient.'

Bethesda, in Maryland, is the home of the National Naval Medical Center.

The 49th Pursuit Group (Interceptor) was formed in 1940 and was among the first deployed in the Pacific Theatre during World War Two. Based, since 1968, at Holloman Air Force Base, the 49th is now home to the F-117 stealth fighters and has seen recent action in the Gulf and the Balkans.

Politics of Compromise: Toby meets three Democrat Congressmen about the State of the Union speech – specifically about federal funding for the arts. The arts budget for the US is equivalent to that of Sweden and amounts to less than 0.001 per cent of the total spent by federal government, Toby argues. It costs the taxpayer 39 cents a year.

Politics of Integrity: Toby wants to change the sentiments of a line Josh fought to get into the speech: 'the era of big government is over'. Toby knows they can score popularity points, admitting that he was the principal architect of the strategy. But they're in the White House now and they should be saying that government, disregarding past and future failures, can be a place where people come together and where no one gets left behind. Bartlet agrees, as does Josh, who says he never disagrees with Toby when he's right.

A Little Learning is a Dangerous Thing: One of the Congressmen doesn't know the difference between Hammerstein and Hart, or between Arthur Murray and Arthur Miller (see **References**).

The Revolution Will Be Televised: There have been steady but not egregious clashes in Kashmir. Four days of the ceasefire remain, placing these events ten days after **11**, 'Lord John Marbury'. Pakistan is concerned that, if the Indian offensive continues, it won't be able to defend its capital with conventional forces. Bazin (the Pakistani leader) has given control of some of his country's nuclear weapons to field commanders but, Fitzwallace believes, they're just trying to get America's attention. 'They got mine,' notes the president.

Lord Marbury looks to history to end the crisis. For centuries Britain ruled India with a stick and carrot. When they had a problem with someone, one solution was to make him a maharaja. In return, he would be loyal to the crown. Foreign aid, during the Cold War, was America financing dictators to be on their side, Marbury argues. They continue to pay Korea not to develop nuclear weapons. India wants a computer industry, Marbury notes. For that, they require an infrastructure. It's the price America must pay for the negligent behaviour of Congress in not checking the proliferation of nuclear devices.

References: The Ghost of Christmas Future from Dickens's *A Christmas Carol*. Steuben Glass (founded in 1903 by the English glassmaker Frederick Carder). CNN's *Crossfire* and *Larry King*. Also *Newsweek*, the movie comedians Bud Abbott and Lou Costello, Robert Mapplethorpe (1946–89), the New York photographer famous for his cover of Patti Smith's *Horses* and numerous homoerotic studies, *Oklahoma!* the musical by Richard Rodgers (1902–79) and Oscar Hammerstein II (1895–1960), Rodgers's previous musical collaborator, the lyricist Lorenz Hart, the ballroom-dance teacher Arthur Murray, the playwright Arthur Miller and his Pulitzer-prize-winning *Death of a Salesman*. In bed, the president watches a dreadful afternoon soap opera and picks holes in the plot ('don't any of these characters have *jobs*?').

'You May Remember Me From Such Films and TV Series As . . .': Three-times Tony nominated, German-born Harry Groener played Tam Elburn *Star Trek: The Next Generation*, Brockwell in *Mad About You* and Ralph Dang in the US version of *Dear John*, along with roles in *Amistad*, *Dance With Me* and *The Day the World Ended*. He'll be familiar to readers for his magnificent performance as Mayor Wilkins in *Buffy*. Austin Tichenor was Mark in *Y2K* and Samuel in *Felicity*, and appeared in *Roswell*. Madison Mason played Gene Brisco in *Days of Our Lives* and appeared in *Omen IV: The Awakening*, *The Day After*, *Malibu Shores* and *Knight Rider*. David Spielberg played Dr Bernstein in *ER*, and appeared in *Where Are My Children?*, *Christine*, *Mork & Mindy* and *Hart to Hart*. Ronne Troup was Barbara in *Knots Landing* and also featured in *Cannon*, *The Banana Splits Adventure Hour*, *The Partridge Family* and *Marcus Welby M.D.* Roger Ontiveros was in *Uniform Code* and *Almost Anything*.

Behind the Camera: Arlene Sanford directed episodes of *Friends*, *Caroline in the City*, *Go Fish* and *Gilmore Girls*.

Oh, Donna!: Donna and Josh discuss whom he'll pick from the line of succession. Donna thinks it should be her, believing she'd make a good president.

Sex and Drugs and Rock'n'Roll: Among numerous pills that Bartlet is taking (or at least carrying) are vitamin C, vitamin B and echinacea. He's given 100 mg of Flumadine for the flu symptoms. Betaseron is a drug for treating MS.

Abbey believes Mallory has 'an itch' for Sam, despite Mallory's denials. Don't go for the geniuses, Abbey tells her. They never want to sleep. Sam is confused by Mallory, and gets even more so when she kisses him for writing the speech in defence of her father.

Cigarettes and Alcohol: Lord Marbury flu remedies include liquorice root, bamboo sap and a strong shot of whisky, and ginger root, citrus peel and a strong shot of whisky. In fact, he continues, you can throw out the ginger root and citrus peel . . . He has whisky in his tea.

Logic, Let Me Introduce You to This Window: Bartlet's had regular medical check-ups (see **2**, ' "Post Hoc, Ergo Propter Hoc" ') and, as president, is expected to have a physical each year and make the results public. MS is, however, quite difficult to diagnose and, if he hid his symptoms, it's possible his doctors may never have looked for them. Roger Tribby is not the Secretary of Agriculture briefly seen in **8**, 'Enemies'. Leo refers to G-7, but the summit hasn't been called that since 1997, when the EU joined to make it G-8 (see **1**, 'The West Wing').

Cruelty To Animals: CJ is concerned when kissing Danny that they're careful not to knock over her fish bowl.

Quote/Unquote: Bartlet, quoting from his speech: 'We meant "stronger" here, right?' Sam: 'What's it say?' Bartlet: ' "I'm proud to report our country is *stranger* than it was a year ago?" Could go either way.'

The president's first encounter with Jerry Springer: 'I was watching a television programme with a sort-of roving moderator who spoke to a seated panel of young women who are having problems with their boyfriends. Apparently the boyfriends have all slept with the girlfriends' mothers. Then they brought all the boyfriends out and they fought right there on television. Toby, tell me, these people don't vote, do they?'

Bartlet's presidential advice to Tribby: 'You have a best friend? Is he smarter than you? Would you trust him with your life?' Tribby: 'Yes, sir.' Bartlet: 'That's your chief-of-staff.'

Notes: 'People have phenomenal capacity'. A quite wonderful episode. Touching, lyrical and brilliantly acted, this shatters the illusion of Jed and Leo as Olympian figures by making them utterly human through their frailties. Particularly, watch out for the charmingly scatty way CJ and Danny kiss, the fast-moving opening scenes and the wonderful coda of Bartlet and Roger in the Oval Office.

Mandy thinks Danny looked cute with the full beard. CJ doesn't (or, at least, feigns uninterest).

Critique: 'Wouldn't it be great if the President was *actually* Martin Sheen's Josiah Bartlet?' asked Frances Lass in *Radio Times*. 'His lack of cynicism, his obvious enchantment with his clever and immaculate wife and his ability to get the best out of his staff are qualities we would love and expect from the most powerful man on the planet. What a pity he's fiction.'

Mike McCurry, former press secretary for Clinton, considered the MS storyline 'a little far-fetched. Yet it does remind me of the excruciating experience I went through when the president had a ruptured knee tendon.'

Cast and Crew Comments: 'It wasn't there because I wanted to explore MS, or medicine,' Sorkin told Ellen Gray. 'Now it's part of the show's bible, and we'll live with it.' The plot started because Sorkin wanted the president to be in bed watching a soap opera, he told Tom Feran. 'I also wanted us to discover that the first lady is a doctor. Bartlet's particular course of MS is not severe. He can lead a normal life for the most part. When I wrote the pilot, I didn't have any idea what was going to happen in Episode 2, much less 12.' However, as Sorkin confirmed to *Rocky Mountain News*, 'I worried over the episode when Bartlet was diagnosed with MS. That wasn't a particularly strong show.'

'It rips on a lot of levels,' John Spencer added, particularly 'the disappointment and the hurt that my best friend didn't share something so great with me, and fear, because there's a duality now' – and a devotion and love for Bartlet and a desire to protect the presidency and the administration. 'With this particular disease, he could be in a wheelchair in four years,' noted Martin Sheen.

Did You Know?: 'We want to thank *The West Wing* for helping to enhance understanding about a disease that strikes someone every day,' said Mike Dugan, president of the National Multiple Sclerosis Society. 'This is a first on network television.' The group is especially pleased, Dugan noted, that the affected character is a world leader, that the show made clear MS is not fatal, and that Bartlet is taking advantage of medical breakthroughs to treat the more common and relatively mild form of the disease effectively. 'Since fiction often becomes more real to people than fact,' Dugan said, 'President Bartlet's life with MS has the potential for great good. If he does well, despite the challenges of the disease, the public will become more accepting of individuals with MS and individuals with MS will become more accepting of themselves and their abilities to lead fulfilling lives.'

13
Take Out the Trash Day

US Transmission Date: 26 January 2000
UK Transmission Date: 17 April 2000 (Sky), 12 April 2001 (C4)

Writer: Aaron Sorkin
Director: Thomas Schlamme
Cast: Dakin Matthews (Simon Blye) James Handy (Congressman Bruno)
Ray Baker (Jonathan Lydell) Liza Weil (Karen Larsen)
Linda Gehringer (Jennifer Lydell) Larry Sullivan Jr (Hamlin)
Sheryl Arenson (Lock) Kris Murphy (Reporter #4)

While the staff consider a sex-education study, there are fears that the father of a murdered gay teenager may not support a hate-crimes bill. Toby relishes a battle on Public Broadcasting. CJ is advised to release several embarrassing stories together to blunt their impact. The identity of the person who leaked Leo's addiction is revealed.

A View from the Hill: The term 'bully pulpit' stems from Theodore Roosevelt's reference to the White House as a platform to advocate an agenda persuasively.

Sam and Josh meet the Appropriations Subcommittee, who investigate whether Josh withheld information during his deposition to Freedom Watch. The president says he wants to pre-empt a hearing. He's confident that Josh and

Sam will be offered a deal. At the meeting Congressman Bruno says he too wants to avoid a hearing but that the price will be the delay of the sex-ed report until after the midterms. Bruno argues he's throwing them a rope, adding, 'This is what happens [when] you put teenagers in the White House.' He says they should have let the Counsel's Office investigate and that Josh came close to perjury.

Toby mentions that the Constitution specifically prohibits religious activity connected to government.

Politics of Desperation: Leo meets Simon Blye, who, he says, has been a good friend. The president warns that it isn't hard to like a guy when he's doing well, but that the measure of a man is how he behaves when things are otherwise. Blye advises Leo to resign. The president has a budget to pass, Mendoza has to be confirmed to the Supreme Court and, in nine months, a Democratic Congress has to be elected. Blye confesses that he has written an opinion piece in the *Washington Post* on the subject. Outraged, Leo says it probably won't get much attention and it will definitely not distract from the president's agenda.

A Little Learning is a Dangerous Thing: Zoey's sociology professor has been teaching, according to a student newspaper, borderline-racist ideology (examples quoted are too much funding for the Head Start education programme and for welfare mothers, which, while they're offensively right-wing, are hardly 'racist' *per se*). Toby subsequently reveals they are getting Zoey out of this class.

Office Gossip: Donna, Margaret, Carol, Cathy and Ginger gather round the photocopier, chatting conspiratorially. Mrs Landingham catches them and tells them they all work for very important people. Josh arrives and says, 'Here's a group of federal employees!' Donna asks if he and Sam know about an advance man for the vice president who took a navy helicopter to play golf (something that Danny had already told CJ the press was on to). Sam says his name is Chad Magrudian. He held the same position for the president but kept screwing up (spending half a day in Puerto Rico scuba diving, which wasn't on the president's itinerary, for instance) so was moved to Hoynes's staff. 'We know who leaked the story,' Donna tells them. The mole is Karen Larsen, who worked on the vice president's campaign. Aides thought she had a crush on Hoynes, so moved her to personnel. Sam thinks that her anger at the administration suggests a bigger target: it was she who gave Leo's personnel file to Claypool (a family friend). Sam takes delight in firing her. Leo subsequently gives her a second chance.

Carol's Spelling: She can't manage 'Senator'.

Bigotry, Thy Name is Leo: Concerning Lowell Lydell's father, Leo says he 'sells dental supplies in the Twin Cities. How enlightened do you think he's going to be?' Dental-supply retailers and Minnesotans are both famous for their homophobia?

Alternate Sexuality: Regarding 'the Matthew Shepard[54] story we did,' Sorkin told *The Advocate*, 'CJ assumes that the father is uncomfortable because he's embarrassed that his son was gay. In fact he's fumingly-pissed at the president's chickenshit attitude on gay rights [and] simply can't bring himself to be at this bill-signing.'

The Gospel According to Sam: Sam has discovered a town in Alabama that wants to abolish all laws except the Ten Commandments, some of which are going to be pretty hard to enforce – coveting thy neighbour's wife, for one. He tells Leo that, if he *were* arrested for this, he'd probably bear false witness. He later tells Cathy that if he doesn't honour his father, he goes to jail. Cathy asks how they'd know if Sam *wasn't*. 'I think they've overlooked that problem.'

---

[54] Matthew Shepard, a 21-year-old gay student, died in October 1998 after a brutal beating in Laramie, Wyoming. More than any other incident, Matthew's tragic death helped to focus attention on the subject of hate crimes.

References: Pebble Beach golf resort, the student newspaper the *Georgetown Hoya*, Public Service Broadcasting and some of its mainstays: *Sesame Street*, the cookery host Julia Child, Granada's 1982 adaptation of Evelyn Waugh's *Brideshead Revisited* (starring Jeremy Irons and Anthony Andrews), *Wall $treet Week*, introduced by Louis Rukeyser, and *Live from the Lincoln Center*. Also, the TV journalist Geraldo Rivera, CBS's *Face the Nation*, the banana suppliers Chiquita and Dole, the Nielsen's TV Rating index, Fozzie Bear, *The Muppet Show* and Inspector Javert from Victor Hugo's *Les Misérables*.

'You May Remember Me From Such Films and TV Series As . . .': Larry Sullivan Jr was in *Psycho Beach Party*, *Forbidden City* and *Defying Gravity*. Linda Gehringer played Vicki's mom in *American Pie* and Janet Reno in *Ally McBeal*, and was in *As Good As It Gets*. Dakin Matthews appeared in *Flubber*, *Revolver* and *The Fabulous Baker Boys*, and was the headmaster in *Gilmore Girls*. James Handy was in *Jumanji*, *Point of No Return* and *The Rocketeer*. Ray Baker's movies include *Girl, Interrupted*, *Anywhere But Here*, *Hard Rain*, *Hexed*, *Total Recall*, *Rain Man*, *Silkwood* and *Diamonds Are Forever*. Liza Weil played Paris Gellar in *Gilmore Girls* and appeared in *Stir of Echoes*. Kris Murphy was Sheryl in *Two Left Turns*.

Oh, Donna!: She asks what take-out-the-trash day is. Josh explains that any stories they have to give the press that they're not wild about are released, together, usually on a Friday. Donna asks why they don't spread out all the bad stories. Josh says that, if they're all released on the same day, coverage will be divided among them. And they do this on a Friday because no one reads the papers on Saturday.

Sex and Drugs and Rock'n'Roll: Congress are pressing for teaching abstinence in sex-education classes. Josh notes that a new report concludes that this doesn't work – teenagers are going to have sex whether they're cautioned against it or not. The report favours something called 'abstinence plus', which Sam has renamed 'everything but . . .' Josh adds that CJ must read 'pages twenty-seven to thirty-three – a couple of things every girl should know'.

Later, Mandy shares an uncomfortable meeting with the president reading the report, which says the majority of young people move from kissing to more intimate sexual behaviour, such as petting, during their teenage years. The president asks Mandy if that means what he thinks it means. Furthermore, he discovers that, by the age of fourteen, more than 25 per cent of boys have 'touched a girl's . . . I won't say that word'. Mrs Landingham tells a relieved Mandy that she's needed elsewhere. The secretary then asks Bartlet if he'd like to share what's in the report. 'With you?' he asks, horrified. 'No!' She asks why. 'Because I'd rather not be in therapy for the rest of my life.'

Cigarettes and Alcohol: Karen tells Leo that her father (like Leo, and his father) was an alcoholic.

Logic, Let Me Introduce You to This Window: Leo's 'where's your grave concern for country, party and president when you're out whoring for Atlantic Oil?' is clearly overdubbed. Was a real oil company name used but removed for legal reasons? Who was Danny's anonymous source? Karen, or somebody else in personnel?

Quote/Unquote: Bartlet: 'Unless a war breaks out, I'll be spending much of my day talking about bananas.'

Mr Lydell: 'I don't understand how this president, who I voted for, can take such a completely weak-ass position on gay rights. I want to know what quality necessary to being a parent the president feels my son lacked. I want to know, from this president, who has served not one day in uniform – I served two tours in Vietnam – I want to know what quality necessary to being a soldier this president feels my son lacked. Lady, I'm not embarrassed that my son was gay. My government is.'

Notes: 'The worst thing I'm empowered to do is fire you and I've already done that.' Dramatically not as certain as some of the previous episodes, this nevertheless builds to an excellent denouement as a bunch of well-executed plots merge. Best bits: Mr Lydell's articulate anti-homophobic outrage; Toby's committed defence of PBS; the president's horror at the content of the sex-ed report.

Josh uses a cricketing metaphor (maybe it's Marbury's influence), though, given the context of his conversation with CJ on sex-ed, 'sticky wicket' is, he notes, a regrettable pun. Toby says PBS is not television for rich people: one quarter of its audience is in households with incomes lower than $20,000 a year. Blacks comprise 11 per cent of both public and commercial TV audiences. Danny has worked with four previous press secretaries.

Cast and Crew Comments: 'I got three emails from the White House saying "That girl's ass stays fired!"' Sorkin told *Entertainment Weekly*. Emails from whom? 'Various staffers. I can't divulge their names.'

'This woman came up to me and said, "You must not hire that woman back. If she did this, she will be doing it again,"' John Spencer told the *Bergen Record*. 'I was so taken with this woman worrying about me. She thought I was being too optimistic about second chances. But Leo is a man who's been given a second chance himself.'

Did You Spot?: Martin Sheen's coffee cup is a white Think TV mug from Dayton's WPTD-TV (Channel 16). Martin was sent the cup by his brother John Estevez, Channel 16's corporate development manager.

14
Take This Sabbath Day

US Transmission Date: 9 February 2000
UK Transmission Date: 24 April 2000 (Sky), 19 April 2001 (C4)

Writer: Aaron Sorkin
Director: Thomas Schlamme
Cast: Noah Emmerich (Bobby Zane) David Proval (Rabbi Glassman)
Felton Perry (Jerry) Herb Mitchell (Public Defender)
Karl Malden (Father Tom Cavanaugh) Joe Cosgrove (Hayes)

Ellen Sugarman (Cantor) Richard Gross (Bailiff)
Carmela Rioseco (Sophia Cruz)

The Supreme Court refuses to stay the execution of a
federal prisoner and Bartlet must decide whether to
commute the sentence. Toby receives advice from his rabbi.
A campaign manager, Joey Lucas, demands an audience
with the president. It's left to Josh to deal with her.

American History X: The eighth amendment concerns
criminal trials: 'Excessive bail shall not be required, nor
excessive fines imposed, nor cruel or unusual punishments
inflicted.' Further to this, Article 2, Section 2, adds, '[the
president] shall have power to grant reprieves and pardons
for offences against the United States, except in cases of
impeachment'. A Writ of Certiorari is a decision by the
Supreme Court to hear an appeal from a lower court. The
Drug-Kingpin law allows for the execution of defendants
found guilty of offences 'referred to in section 408(c)(1) of
the Controlled Substances Act, committed as part of a
continuing criminal enterprise'. The last president to
commute a death sentence was Lincoln.

Politics of Murder: The US is one of only five countries
that execute people under the age of eighteen, Sam tells
Charlie. The other four are Nigeria, Pakistan, Saudi
Arabia and Iran. **52**, 'The Indians in the Lobby' suggests
that Somalia should also be on this list.

The Encyclopedic Mind of Josiah Bartlet PhD: Flying back
from Stockholm, CJ is seated next to the president and
subjected to a history of the fjords – followed by a *quiz* on
the fjords. She asks the president if he has any idea how
much she'd like to dress him in lederhosen and drop-kick
him into the fjords.

Carol's Spelling: She asks what sort of biographical
information CJ wants on Simon Cruz. 'How to spell his
name,' replies CJ.

The Gospel According to Bartlet: The president uses two
Old Testament verses normally referred to by those who

support capital punishment: 'Who sheddeth a man's blood by man shall his blood be shed' (Genesis 9) and 'Thou shalt not murder' (Exodus 20). They forget about 'Vengeance is mine sayeth the Lord' (Deuteronomy 32, Romans 12), notes Cavanaugh.

Toby hopes the president doesn't call the pope. This is because, Rabbi Glassman says, if he commutes the sentence after doing so, the worst fears of every non-Catholic who voted for him would be realised. Say what you want about the Catholic Church, Glassman continues, but their position on life is unimpeachable. No abortion, no death penalty. The Torah doesn't prohibit capital punishment, Toby argues. It says 'an eye for an eye' (Exodus 21). It also says a rebellious child can be brought to the city gates and stoned to death, adds Glassman. It says homosexuality is an abomination and punishable by death. It says men can be polygamous and slavery is acceptable. For all he knows, that reflected the best wisdom of its time, but it's wrong by any modern standard. Society has a right to protect itself, but it doesn't have a right to be vengeful (see **25**, 'The Midterms'). Even 2,000 years ago, the rabbis of the Talmud couldn't stomach it, Toby tells Bartlet. They came up with legal restrictions and made it impossible for the state to punish someone by killing them.

References: The aria Toby hears is called 'Hashkiveinu', arranged by Max Helfman. Also, the Gorton's fisherman logo, the pollsters Harris, Seder (the first two nights of the Jewish festival of the Passover), St Augustine of Hippo (354–430), Italian scholar and theologian St Thomas Aquinas (1225–74) and German philosopher and author of *Critique of Practical Reason* Immanuel Kant (1724–1804), all of whom supported capital punishment (those writings are from other centuries, argues Joey).

'You May Remember Me From Such Films and TV Series As . . .': Marlee Matlin became deaf after a childhood illness. 'I've always resisted putting limitations on myself, professionally and personally,' says Matlin, who played Sara, the isolated deaf girl, in a Chicago production of

Children of a Lesser God. Cast in the subsequent 1986 movie version, she won an Oscar. She was also nominated for an Emmy for her performance as Mayor Bey in *Picket Fences*. Her CV includes *Walker*, *The Player* and *Reasonable Doubt* and she was executive producer on *Where the Truth Lies*. In 1995, Matlin was heavily involved in the passing of a law that requires all US TV sets larger than thirteen inches to be manufactured with closed captioning devices. Noah Emmerich was Marlon in *The Truman Show*, and also appeared in *Blow*, *The Last Action Hero* and *Frequency*. Bill O'Brien was in *Vertical Flight*. Richard Gross was in *The Last Place on Earth* and *Baywatch*. Carmela Rioseco appeared in *Cold Heaven*. David Proval was Richie Aprile in *The Sopranos* and also featured in *Romeo is Bleeding*, *Zigs*, *The Hollywood Sign*, *The Shawshank Redemption*, *Mean Streets*, *Picket Fences* and *Fame*. Felton Perry was Johnson in *Robocop* and appeared in *Trouble Man*, *Hollywood Vampyr*, *Towering Inferno*, *McMillan and Wife* and *Magnum Force*. Herb Mitchell was in *Austin Powers: The Spy Who Shagged Me*, *Gettysburg*, *Innerspace*, *Big Man on Campus* and *Tuff Turf*.

The great Karl Malden's movie debut was in *They Knew What They Wanted* in 1940. He won an Oscar as Mitch in *A Streetcar Named Desire*, was Father Corrigan in *On the Waterfront*, Archie Lee in *Baby Doll* and Captain Wessels in *Cheyenne Autumn*, and appeared in *I Confess*, *One-Eyed Jacks*, *Birdman of Alcatraz*, *The Cincinnati Kid* and *Patton*. Also a TV legend, as Detective Mike Stone in *The Streets of San Francisco*, he won an Emmy for *Fatal Vision*. He was president of the Academy of Motion Picture Arts and Sciences from 1988 to 1993.

Joe Cosgrove was a teenager when he saw the 1974 TV movie *The Execution of Private Slovik*, about the only US soldier executed during World War Two. Martin Sheen played the title role. 'I was so moved by the injustice I decided to become a lawyer,' Cosgrove told Sharon Waxman. He spent his career defending people accused of capital crimes and, in doing so, became friends with Sheen, who invited Cosgrove to play what was basically himself, in this episode.

Cigarettes and Alcohol: Josh is going to a bachelor party, possibly with strippers. When Donna finds him in the office on Saturday morning he is hung over with a pair of red panties around his neck. Donna asks why he didn't go home after the party. Josh says he couldn't find his keys. Or remember where he lived. 'People were pouring champagne over each other,' he says. And wrestling in dirt? asks Donna. Josh can't remember, but it's certainly not out of the question.

Logic, Let Me Introduce You to This Window: The Supreme Court is sitting with all its members at 8 p.m. on Friday evening on a death row appeal. In reality, such a case would likely be handled by a single justice, and probably not at night. The rabbi of Toby's temple wears a yarmulke, though most of the men in the congregation, including Toby, don't. This is most unusual. Almost all Jewish denominations wear them as a matter of course. CJ threatens the president with physical violence. Even in jest, isn't that a sacking offence? Or treason, perhaps? See also Josh's threat to murder him in **8**, 'Enemies'. How does Cavanaugh know that Bartlet has received advice from a Quaker and (indirectly) a rabbi? He's only just arrived.

Quote/Unquote: Glassman: 'No matter how deep our desire to witness the sufferings of our enemies, we are commanded to relocate our humanity. Vengeance is not Jewish.'

Bartlet: 'We cannot execute some people and not execute others depending on the mood of the Oval Office. It's cruel and unusual.' Leo: 'If that's the only thing stopping you, I'll say this for the first time in your presidency. Let that be the next guy's problem.'

Sam: 'There are times when we are absolutely nowhere.'

Cavanaugh, on Bartlet's disappointment that his prayer for wisdom wasn't answered: 'He sent you a priest, a rabbi and a Quaker, Mr President. Not to mention his son, Jesus Christ. What do you want from Him?'

Notes: 'We don't execute people between sundown Friday and sundown Sunday.' How radical is *this*? Statistics suggest that 70 per cent of the audience watching this episode on its initial broadcast support the death penalty. If that's the case, and if just one of those people at the final credits had a few second thoughts about certainties and alternatives, then this remarkable piece of TV will have done its job. A multihanded look at the complexities of the issue with a number of religious and ethical viewpoints explored, this is a staggering work that is both balanced and, yet conversely, comes down strongly in favour of what turns out to be the losing side. Best bits: Toby and his rabbi (a wonderful performance by David Proval); Josh telling Joey that she has no chance of seeing the president just as he appears at Josh's door; and the extraordinary coda with Martin Sheen and Karl Malden – two of America's greatest living actors – intimately taking a story about faith to a new level.

The president's hometown priest is Thomas Cavanaugh of the Immaculate Heart of Mary Church in Hanover. He is surprised there isn't a red phone in the Oval Office any more. Bobby Zane went to high school with Sam and used to beat him up. After law school Bobby worked for Ross-Lipton (the implication is he wasn't a very good prosecutor) and has spent two years in the public defenders' office.

Simon Cruz was convicted of three murders by a Mexican court. During the penalty phase, the trial judge let the prosecutor introduce evidence of the Mexican convictions. His mother is called Sophia.

Behind the Scenes: Martin Sheen, John Spencer, Allison Janney and Dulé Hill were filmed on a tarmac at Dulles Airport. However, the plane they emerge from wasn't *Air Force One* but Virgin Atlantic complete with a painting on its side that was digitally removed in the editing room and replaced by a presidential seal. So, if they couldn't get *Air Force One*, why drag the cast from California to Washington? 'The actors' teeth wouldn't chatter as convincingly,'

Thomas Schlamme told *Entertainment Weekly*. 'We usually do get Air Force One, by the way.' The show films locations in DC about four times a year. In fact, *The West Wing* has inspired a mini-showbiz boom in the capital. One of the Virginia state troopers, part of the president's cavalcade, turned out to be a real trooper, Matt Hanley. 'I do this in my off duty,' he says. And when he's on duty? 'I escort President Clinton places.' On the other hand the guy in the black suit muttering into his lapel isn't a real secret service agent. He's an actor named Scott Goodhue. He and other Washington-based actors are hired by the day as extras. Goodhue is the agent who opens the limo door for Sheen and then slaps the roof of the car.

Cast and Crew Comments: 'I would disagree that this is a liberal show,' Sorkin told Ken Tucker. 'Bartlet is a Democrat, [but] we've seen him be very hawkish in response to a military attack and [he didn't] commute the sentence of the first federal prisoner executed since 1963.' This episode sparked heated debates on the set, especially between Sorkin, Schlamme and Sheen. The actor desperately wanted it to end with the president commuting the execution; Sorkin and Schlamme were adamant otherwise. They won; Joe Cosgrove told Sheen that the storyline was stronger that way. 'Maybe there's some kid in law school who'll watch it and learn the right message – they won't think they can rely on the president to save someone.' Sorkin's favourite moment from the season is the scene where Bartlet looks out of the window. 'Just for a moment, we see the guy who's about to be executed,' Sorkin recalled during a lunch with TV critics. 'His mother praying over the table he's being strapped to.' He credits Schlamme with creating the scene.

Sorkin consulted Rabbi Steven Leder at Los Angeles' Wilshire Boulevard Temple on aspects of the episode. In a sermon Leder had written, Sorkin found a phrase he liked: 'Vengeance is not Jewish.' He worked it into the episode and made sure Leder received a small fee and a special credit at the end of the show.

Did You Know?: The bible that Karl Malden carries was the actor's own, the same one he used 36 years earlier in *On the Waterfront*.

Although Bartlet decided not to commute the execution, shortly after this episode was broadcast President Clinton chose to postpone the execution of a federal prisoner, Juan Raul Garza, on whose case the episode was partly based.[55] Paul Redford provided a crucial part of the episode's plot when he casually asked Sorkin, 'Did you know we don't execute people on the Sabbath?'

Joey's Background: Josephine Lucas is campaign manager of the Californian Democrat Bill O'Dwyer. She's deaf. Her interpreter, Kenny Thurman, has worked with her for eleven years (**43**, '18th and Potomac'). From a Dutch Quaker family, she is against the death penalty. She was educated at UCLA and Stanford. She is running a campaign against a Republican who supports amending the Bill of Rights to prohibit flag burning. For the first time in three decades, they have a chance to beat him. That's why the DNC has cut her candidate's funding, Josh notes. His opponent is a preposterous figure and they want to keep him in Congress. Each time he speaks about 'brown people crossing the border', the DNC slaps it into a direct-mail campaign and he's good for $2 million. The president tells Joey that he feels her candidate is a schmuck who gives liberalism a bad name. Joey thinks so too, but she's a professional political operative and needs the work. She is having an affair with Al Kiefer in **16**, '20 Hours in L.A.', but this has ended by **20**, 'Mandatory Minimums'.

---

[55] Garza, a confessed drug-trafficker, was sentenced in 1993 for the murders of three rivals. Although given two stays by Clinton, Garza was eventually executed by lethal injection in June 2001 after pleas for clemency to Clinton's successor, George W Bush, failed. He became the second federal prisoner executed since 1963, his death coming eight days after that of the Oklahoma City bomber, Timothy McVeigh.

15
Celestial Navigation

US Transmission Date: 16 February 2000
UK Transmission Date: 1 May 2000 (Sky), 26 April 2001 (C4)

Teleplay: Aaron Sorkin
Story: Dee Dee Myers, Lawrence O'Donnell Jr
Director: Christopher Misiano
Cast: CCH Pounder (Debbie O'Leary)
Robert David Hall (David Nessler)
Vaughn Armstrong (Sgt MacNamara) Jason C Morgan (Peter)
Bob Thompson (Steward) Kelly Flaling (Pretty College Student)

Sam and Toby hurry to Connecticut to sort out a problem for Judge Mendoza, but get lost on the way. Meanwhile, Josh is a guest lecturer at a college class and talks about what a terrible week they've had.

American History X: Josh is taking part in the Marjorie Dupont lecture series.

Politics of Indulgence: Toby is in charge of the confirmation of Mendoza to the Supreme Court (see **9**, 'The Short List'). A failure is a body blow to a presidency. Nominees aren't supposed to speak publicly during their confirmation, something Toby's had trouble teaching Mendoza. In the eight weeks since the president named him, the judge has criticised the American Bar Association, the American Federation of Labor and Congress of Industrial Organization, and the New York state legislature, three organisations without which this president wouldn't have been elected. Mendoza is summoned to the White House from his vacation in Nova Scotia but decides to take three days as he's driving to DC, stopping in Connecticut to do some antiquing (when told he'll be here the day after tomorrow, the president asks whether he's coming from Neptune).

A Little Learning is a Dangerous Thing: Sam impresses the deputy at Wesley police station with the lie that he knows missile codes and stuff ('outstanding!').

Sam tells CJ that Mendoza has been arrested for drink driving but that the real reason is more likely to have been 'driving while being Hispanic'.

The Encyclopedic Mind of Sam Seaborn: Sam has a freakish ability with traffic directions. Except when it comes to something simple, such as finding a police station in Connecticut.

References: The cable TV company C-SPAN, Bullwinkle (Rocket J Squirrel's pal), Delta Airlines, LaGuardia airport in New Jersey, industrialist and philanthropist Dale Carnegie (1888–1955), *JFK* ('let justice be done'), *The Washington Post* and *Chicago Tribune*; Deputy Barney Fife, the character played by Don Knotts in *The Andy Griffiths Show*. Sam tries to use Polaris (the North Star) by which to navigate, causing Toby sarcastically to call him Galileo (see **31**, 'Galileo'). Josh mentions Socratic debate – relating to Socrates and the philosophical method of systematic doubt.

'You May Remember Me From Such Films and TV Series As . . .': CCH Pounder was Angela Hicks in *ER* and Cheryl Andrews in *Millennium* and appeared in *End of Days*, *Union City*, *Face/Off*, *Prizzi's Honor* and *Postcards from the Edge*. Bob Thompson appeared in *Storm*. Jason Morgan played Christian Holt in *UP, Michigan!*, which he also produced and wrote. Robert Hall was David Robbins in *CSI* and appeared in *Starship Troopers*. Vaughn Armstrong was in *The Theory of Everything*, *Family of Spies*, *Seinfeld* and *Saved By the Bell*. He holds the record for playing the most guest characters on the various *Star Trek* series.

Oh, Donna!: After Josh's terrible performance in the press briefing he emerges, shellshocked, to find Donna telling him that he has her full support. 'Tell me what you think I should do,' he says. 'Go into your office and come up with a secret plan to fight inflation,' she replies. Also, her translation of CJ's garbled rant to Josh.

Cigarettes and Alcohol: Mendoza has chronic persistent hepatitis, a nonprogressive liver inflammation. He doesn't drink, because alcohol would kill him.

Logic, Let Me Introduce You to This Window: How do the White House discover about Mendoza's arrest? Why send Sam and Toby all the way there? Why not simply ring the station (as the governor of Connecticut does anyway)? Surely some of the topics Josh discloses in his lecture aren't the kind of things that anyone in the administration would want to be public knowledge.

Quote/Unquote: Toby: 'So help me if you use the words "Pwesident" or "bwiefed" again . . .'

Charlie, to an almost comatose Bartlet: 'I need you to dig in. It wasn't a nightmare. You really are the president.'

Bartlet: 'You told the press I have a secret plan to fight inflation?' Josh: 'No, I did not . . . Except, yes, I did that. There was this idiotic round robin. It was sarcastic. There's no way they didn't know that. They were just mad at me for imposing discipline and calling them stupid.' And Josh: 'If anyone asks you, you quit smoking years ago and the cigarette you bummed on *Air Force One* was for a friend.' Bartlet: 'Get out.'

Notes: 'Depending on how you look at it, it started either with a Cabinet secretary losing her temper, a committee chairman baiting her during a hearing, the president answering a question he shouldn't have, a dentist appointment, or me being stupid.' Fine stuff, albeit with a rather odd nonlinear narrative structure. Best bits: Josh's merciless toying with poor CJ after her root-canal operation; Josh being systematically taken apart by Danny and the press corps; Charlie waking up the president.

The first lady is in Argentina. Mendoza's wife is called Laura. They have a nine-year-old son, Robbie. The headline in the *Hartford Chronicle* is PRESIDENT BARTLET DRAFTS LETTER TO SENATE LEADERS.

Critique: A future adviser to the show, Marlin Fitzwater, told Terence Smith on *Online News Hour*: 'I've only seen one that I thought was so far off the mark that it was really a mistake. That's when they had a Supreme Court nominee arrested for speeding and two members of the White House staff went and broke him out of jail. That's an impeachable offence.'

Cast and Crew Comments: Melissa Fitzgerald recalls the filming of the presidential photo opportunity. 'There were tons of extras.' Martin Sheen made a point of introducing himself to all of them. 'It was the most lovely thing. Everyone felt part of the scene. I thought, "He really looks like the president." '

Did You Know?: The plot of the HUD secretary accusing a Republican of being racist came out of a conversation between Sorkin and Dee Dee Myers which concluded with Myers, using the phrase 'If the shoe fits . . .' In the episode both Leo and Bartlet ask, if Debbie O'Leary was going to lose her cool, couldn't she have found some better insult than this? 'That kind of thing drives Dee Dee crazy because I spend the episode mocking her dialogue,' noted Sorkin.

16
20 Hours in L.A.

US Transmission Date: 23 February 2000
UK Transmission Date: 8 May 2000 (Sky), 3 May 2001 (C4)

Writer: Aaron Sorkin
Director: Alan Taylor
Cast: David Hasselhoff (Himself) Jay Leno (Himself)
Veronica Webb (Herself) Bob Balaban (Ted Marcus)
Chris Hogan (Mark Miller) Robert Pine (Greer)
Bart Braverman (Shapiro) Giovanni Sirchla (Carmine)
Bill Bolender (Man #1) Christopher Shea (Man #2)
Franklin Dennis Jones (Man #3) Mary Kathleen Gordon (Woman)

Bartlet heads to Los Angeles for a fundraiser hosted by the movie magnate Ted Marcus, who threatens to cancel unless the president announces his opposition to a bill banning gays in the military. In Washington, Leo tries to persuade the vice president to break a Senate tie. Josh learns that Joey Lucas is staying at his hotel.

A View from the Hill: Josh asks Marcus if he knows how many bills get introduced every day that are never voted upon. No one is going to pass a bill banning gays in the military, Josh argues. And, if the House and the Senate *did* pass such a bill, the president would never sign it. Marcus, nevertheless, is distressed by the president's silence and feels it's a betrayal of the gay community.

American History X: Reference is made to Justice Charles Black (1862–1948) who was appointed to the Supreme Court by President Taft in 1910. A Republican presidential candidate in 1916, he was narrowly defeated by Woodrow Wilson and returned to the bench.

Politics of Compromise: With a 50–50 tie in the Senate vote on an ethanol tax credit bill, the president needs the vice president to fulfil one of his constitutional responsibilities and break the tie. Ethanol accounts for twenty per cent of Iowa's corn crop, says Leo, though Larry adds that this doesn't mean a lot outside Iowa. The credit has created 16,000 new jobs and $4,000,000 has been invested in industrial plants and equipment because the credit made it economical. Hoynes, however, spent eight years in the Senate voting against this bill. It has accomplished none of its goals, he argues. Production will never be large enough to reduce America's dependence on foreign oil and it requires substantial energy to produce, which cancels out conservation effects. Also, the Republicans will use his voting in favour of this against him when he runs for president. Leo admits there's friction between Hoynes and the White House staff. Hoynes thinks that they don't respect him, but they do. They just don't *trust* him. And neither does the president. Ultimately, Leo and Sam broker a deal to let Hoynes off the hook by withdrawing their request that three Democrats vote in favour, deliberately losing the bill in the process. Leo reminds Bartlet it was he who persuaded the president to have Hoynes as a running mate.

Politics of Comedy: Jay Leno asks CJ if she could get the president to collide his bicycle with a tree again (see **1**, 'The West Wing') to provide him with more material.

A Little Learning is a Dangerous Thing: In conservative Orange County, the president meets civic leaders to discuss proposals to amend the Constitution to prohibit flag burning. Bartlet notes, after several speeches, that many people focus time and energy on this question and he's forced to ask if there's an epidemic of flag burning going on that he's not aware of.

The Encyclopedic Mind of Josiah Bartlet PhD: Amazingly, he mixes up the sports teams of the universities of West Virginia (the Mountaineers) and Virginia (the Cavaliers).

The Conspiracy Starts at Polling Time: The president could sew up re-election by backing a flag-burning amendment, the pollster Al Kiefer argues. Those who voted against him included white men, pool-and-patio types, who share an affinity with authority. They admire Bartlet's intellect and think he has vision but won't vote for him because they believe he's weak. Joey Lucas, however, thinks that Kiefer asked the wrong questions. His polls said that 80 per cent of people, when asked if they'd support such an amendment, said yes, which is roughly the same proportion of people who say they support sending litterbugs to prison. Kiefer never asked them how *much* they care. Fewer than half of those who said they'd favour the amendment rated the issue as important.

The Conspiracy Starts at Closing Time: The president meets Gina Toscano, Zoey's personal Secret Service agent. Gina was a second lieutenant with the military police, after gaining a degree in criminology. She is 27 and has trained for this assignment for eighteen months (she was the first agent to sign up for Zoey's protection team). Bartlet confirms Gina knows Zoey is dating Charlie and that there've been threatening letters. The president notes that Zoey wants to be a teenager. He doesn't blame her: he loved college. He wants Zoey to be comfortable with her protection. It isn't Gina's job to tell him if Zoey cut English lit, or that she's dyeing her hair blue, or going to a strip club. As Gina departs, Bartlet says, 'If she's cutting English lit, I want to know about it.' 'No deal, Mr President,' she replies.

References: Donna quotes from 'To the Virgins, to Make Much of Time' by the English poet Robert Herrick (1591–1674). Also, the cosmetic giants Clinique, Lancôme and Elizabeth Arden (both Donna and CJ have sensitive alabaster skin), the Southern Poverty Law Center, a nonprofit-making organisation that combats intolerance and discrimination, the African Methodist Episcopal Church in South Central LA (founded in 1902) and Matthew Perry (Chandler Bing in *Friends*). Donna mentions David Hasselhoff's career highlights, including *Baywatch*, *Knight Rider* and the less well-known *Nick Fury*, *Panic at Malibu Pier*, *The Cartier Affair* and *Pleasure Cove*. Joey quotes the Northumbrian scholar Alcuin (737–804): '*Vox populi, vox Dei*' ('The voice of the people is the voice of God').

'You May Remember Me From Such Films and TV Series As . . .': The 1980s TV icon David Hasselhoff was Michael Knight in *Knight Rider* and Mitch Buchannon in *Baywatch*. The ex-supermodel Veronica Webb has appeared in *Jungle Fever*, *Holy Man* and *Malcolm X*. Jay Leno became Johnny Carson's successor as host of *The Tonight Show* in 1992. Bob Balaban was Phoebe's father in *Friends*, and appeared in *Midnight Cowboy*, *Altered States*, *Bank Shot*, *2010*, *Close Encounters of the Third Kind*, *Bob Roberts*, *The Mexican*, *Clockwatchers* and *Jakob the Liar*. He also wrote, directed and produced *The Last Good Time*. Jorja Fox was Maggie Doyle in *ER* and Sara Sidle in *CSI*. She also appeared in *Happy Hell Night*. John de Lancie is best known as Q in the various *Star Trek* series, and as Colonel Simmons in *Stargate SG-1*. He was also in *The Hand That Rocks the Cradle*, *The Fisher King*, *The Bastard* and *The Six Million Dollar Man*. Chris Hogan was in *Monkeybone*, *Edtv*, *Hairshirt* and *That '70s Show*. Bill

Bolender was Skipper in *JAG* and appeared in *Dante's Peak*, *Suspect Device* and *JFK*. Christopher Shea was in *Star Trek: Deep Space Nine* and *Charmed*. Franklin Dennis Jones was Coach Brody in *Soccer Dog: The Movie*. Mary Kathleen Gordon was in *If I Die Before I Wake*. Robert Pine's CV includes *But I'm a Cheerleader*, *Independence Day*, *The Day of the Locust*, *The F.B.I.*, *Charlie's Angels*, *Munsters Go Home*, *Gunsmoke*, *Lost in Space* and *The Virginian*. He was also a director on *CHiPS*. Bart Braverman's debut was in 1955's *Cell 2455 Death Row*. He subsequently featured in *I Love Lucy*, *Have Gun, Will Travel*, *The Love Boat*, *Alligator* and *8 Heads in a Duffel Bag*.

Behind the Camera: Alan Taylor directed *Palookaville* and episodes of *The Sopranos*, *Sex and the City* and *Now and Again*.

Oh, Donna!: She terrifies David Hasselhoff.

Cigarettes and Alcohol: At the fundraiser Toby drinks whisky and CJ, Sam and Donna drink white wine.

Logic, Let Me Introduce You to This Window: Joey says she thinks the president should encourage people not to burn flags. Yet in **14**, 'Take This Sabbath Day', that was one of the issues supported by O'Dwyer's right-wing opponent that she used as an example of why the White House should be helping her candidate more. Does it really take *Air Force One* six hours to fly from DC to LA?

Quote/Unquote: Bartlet: 'All kinds of things in California. You've got your smog, your freeway shootings, brush fires, mudslides. Plus, apparently, there's a mad rash of flag-burning going on.'
   Toby: 'I just figured out who you were.' Kiefer: 'He's going to say Satan.' Toby: 'No. You're the guy that runs into the 7-Eleven to get Satan a pack of cigarettes.'
   Mark: 'CJ, I was wondering if my money buys me a few words alone with you.' Toby: 'Throw in a box of chocolates and a pair of nylons [and it'll] get you a lot more than that.'

Notes: 'If you don't mind my saying so, Mr President, you look more tired than you did a couple of months ago.' A story about the *real* Hollywood, with loads of movie-industry phoneys and the concept that money buys anything (including political influence). Best bit: David Hasselhoff's excellent debunking of his persona.

Los Angeles locations include the motorcade driving down Sepulveda Boulevard and the Sheraton near Universal Studio. The president has lunch at a restaurant in Santa Monica called the Playa Cantina.

Behind the Scenes: At the fundraiser, one of the secret service agents was played by Dan Smiczek, a regular background actor. Smiczek has a fascinating and humorous website, *The Adventures of Dan: Extra Extraordinaire*, at www.adventuresofdan.com, which details his experiences working on shows such as *Buffy*, *Angel*, *The X-Files* and *Roswell*. Smiczek notes that the exterior scenes were filmed at a house in Beverly Hills close to Hugh Hefner's mansion. Highlight of his time on the episode? Like Donna, 'I saw David Hasselhoff!'

Cast and Crew Comments: In retrospect, Sorkin was uncomfortable with the appearance of real-life celebrities. 'Where there is a Jay Leno, Bill Clinton is president, and we immediately know that,' he told Gail Shister. 'Moreover, for Leno to do a scene with CJ a week after Allison was on *Tonight* is strange . . . It started to feel like a *Larry Sanders Show*, trying to get mileage out of tossing around a contemporary name.'

Did You Know?: Martin Sheen agrees with the Democratic vice-presidential candidate Joseph Lieberman's criticisms of Hollywood. On a fund-raising trip for Democratic candidates, he said, 'He's one of the few politicians who's willing to stand up and say that. A lot of what we do has little to do with art. It has to do with sleaze and gratuitous sex and unnecessary violence.'

17
The White House Pro-Am

US Transmission Date: 22 March 2000
UK Transmission Date: 15 May 2000 (Sky), 10 May 2001 (C4)

Writers: Lawrence O'Donnell Jr, Paul Redford, Aaron Sorkin
Director: Ken Olin
Cast: Amy Aquino (Becky Reeseman) Nadia Dajani (Lilli Mays)
Rolanda Watts (Melissa) Richard Fancy (Congressman #1)
Kathleen Garrett (Congresswoman #2)
Brandon Hammond (Jeffrey Morgan) Joe O'Connor (Congressman #3)
Roger Eschbacher (Intelligence Officer #1)
David A Kimball (Intelligence Officer #2) Julie Pop (Aide)
Catherine Schreiber (Segment Producer) Laura Henry (Woman #1)
Valeri Ross (Woman #2)

The president's and first lady's staffs feud over rival agendas. The death of the Federal Reserve chairman is an added complication, as his obvious successor is Abbey's old boyfriend.

A View from the Hill: Abbey's press secretary, Lilli Mays, asks Sam if the president would cancel going to the Hill tomorrow. She explains that Abbey is scheduled to speak to the press and that her staff want the news cycle. One of the Congressmen Josh and Toby meet says, as they're Democrats, they don't like lowering taxes.

American History X: The statesman and presidential candidate Henry Clay (1777–1852) is mentioned.

Politics of Compromise: Abbey, no stranger to the fight for children's health around the world, reminds Congresswoman Reeseman that the president will support Reeseman if she runs for Senate, but that her child-labour amendment will kill the trade bill. Abbey explains that the vote will pass the House, but it will never pass the Senate.

A Little Learning is a Dangerous Thing: While Josh is on the phone, Donna starts pestering him about a book she's reading, *When My Grandmother Was a Child* by Leigh Rutledge. In those days the population of Las Vegas was

22. Donna explains that, even then, drive-by shootings were a problem in Denver and that popular girls' names included Florence and Bertha. Josh asks when Donna has time to read. She replies that it's important to make time for oneself. 'I notice you're able to do that here at the office,' adds Josh. Later, Donna reveals that medical authorities warned that seamstresses were apt to become sexually aroused by the rhythm of the foot pedal and recommended slipping bromide – thought to diminish sexual desire – into the drinking water. Josh asks why anyone would want to diminish that.

Fashion Victims: Charlie says he's picked up a powder-blue tuxedo with ruffles for his date with Zoey. If this *is* in jest, then it's pretty sick.

The Gospel According to Leo: He describes Bartlet's underhand manner of extracting information from Danny as 'Byzantine'.

References: The Rockefeller Center, an eleven-acre site in Manhattan named after the oil magnate and philanthropist John D Rockefeller (1839–1937), the Johns Hopkins medical school (see **37**, 'Ellie'), *Hawaii Five-O* and *Larry King* (see **12**, 'He Shall, from Time to Time . . .'). Also, the Japanese car manufacturer Toyota, the Range Rover, the Ford Explorer and the Hardy Boys (created by the publisher Edward Stratemeyer and a team of writers under the *nom de plume* Franklin Dixon). Charlie gives Zoey the book *Introduction to Advanced Trigonometry*.

'You May Remember Me From Such Films and TV Series As . . .': Julie Pop appeared in *Showgirls* and *Purgatory*. Laura Henry was in *Heavenly Bodies*. Roger Eschbacher featured in *Detention*, *Ellen*, *Nikki* and *Sabrina, the Teen-age Witch* and wrote episodes of *Star Trek: The Next Generation*. Catherine Schreiber was in *Volcano*. Valeri Ross's CV includes *Thirst* and *Joe's Rotten World*. David Kimball appeared in *The Firm* and *Sinatra*. Joe O'Connor played Marshall Darling in *Clarissa Explains it All*. Kathleen Garrett was in *Zen and the Art of Landscaping*.

Rolanda Watts began her career as an NBC news reporter in the 1980s. She fronted the chatshow *Rolanda* and appeared in *Sister Sister* and *7th Heaven*. Brandon Hammond played Anthony in *Dr Quinn, Medicine Woman*. He was also in *Mars Attacks!*, *The Fan* and *Menace II Society*. Richard Fancy appeared in *Nixon*, *Come On, Get Happy: The Partridge Family Story*, *Being John Malkovich* and *Tango & Cash*. Amy Aquino was in *ER*, *Moonstruck* and *Working Girl*. Nadia Dajani appeared in *Breathing Room*.

Behind the Camera: As an actor, Ken Olin played Abe Tingel in *The Advocate's Devil*, Cameron Quinn in *EZ Streets*, Father Christopher in *Falcon Crest* and Harry Garibaldi in *Hill Street Blues*, and appeared in *Y2K*. He has directed episodes of *Felicity* and *Freaks and Geeks*.

Sex and Drugs and Rock'n'Roll: 'I'm not willing to jump into bed with Ron Erhlich yet,' says Bartlet. 'Making me one of the few people in my family who can say that.'

Leo mentions that marijuana, morphine and heroin were available over the counter a hundred years ago and that one physician said heroin was a perfect guardian of health.

Logic, Let Me Introduce You to This Window: The president has been married for 32 years (see **4**, 'Five Votes Down'), but his wife had a boyfriend for nine months 30 years ago. It's unlikely that an extramarital lover would be called a 'boyfriend', so it's clear that Erhlich was someone Abbey dated before she married Jed. Bartlet says one of Abbey's friends thinks he's xenophobic because he doesn't like Mexican food. Yet in **16**, '20 Hours in L.A.', he ate in a Mexican restaurant. Maybe he likes guacamole but not other Mexican food. Congresswoman Reeseman is introducing a rider on an evening when the first lady remarks that Congress isn't in session. Zoey says Charlie left her sitting in the restaurant. He didn't: she was in the bathroom when he left. Gina has the same two posters on her dorm wall as Sam does on his office wall. Coincidence or budget cutbacks?

Quote/Unquote: Toby, after Josh suggests that they play good cop/bad cop: 'How about you be the good cop, I'll be the cop that doesn't go to the meeting?'

Gina: 'You're looking at the girl whose job it is to jump in front of the bullet. I like it when [Zoey] stays in her dorm and watches videos.'

Danny, to Mrs Landingham: 'You keep glancing over like you're afraid I'm going to steal something.'

Notes: 'I understand the *oeuvre*. I get the basic *mise en scène* of what you're saying.' One of the less successful episodes. The intermarital tension between Jed and Abbey that spills over into outright war between their staffs is amusing, but the plot is very slow-moving and the Josh-and-Toby subplot – the best bit of the episode – doesn't get nearly enough emphasis.

In her first semester at Georgetown, Zoey's taking introduction to cinema and nineteenth-century studies, but not maths (she may be studying French, too: see **18**, 'Six Meetings Before Lunch'). Her Secret Service nickname is 'Bookbag'. She used to attend school in overalls when she was five. She grudgingly agrees with Charlie's assessment that she is 'totally anal'. Abbey has a friend named Phyllis, who has never liked Jed; it is her friend Susan who Jed thinks is xenophobic. The president says he misses the late-night talks he had with Danny during the campaign. Danny also, literally, wrote the book on the first lady. He has a half-year salary invested in technology stocks.

Critique: 'If there's someone like those characters in Washington, I'd like to meet them,' Margaret Cone, a lobbyist for the Writers' Guild, told *St Paul Pioneer Press*. 'People in Washington are too stressed out to be witty.'

Cast and Crew Comments: 'There's a first-year enthusiasm on this show. The people here really care about it,' the director Ken Olin told Sharon Waxman.

'I go to lunch at the gym every day to keep my energy up,' Rob Lowe said in *Soap Opera Weekly*. 'Aaron [Sorkin] has always been fascinated. "You work so hard.

How can you go to the gym at lunch?" The next thing I know, I get an episode where Sam's at the gym!'

Did You Know?: Sorkin was embarrassed to find himself seated at the same table with the Federal Reserve Chairman Alan Greenspan at a White House dinner just weeks after Sorkin had given *his* Federal Reserve chief a heart attack. 'Alan was troubled because I killed the Fed chair and nobody on the show gave a damn that the guy was dead.'

18
Six Meetings Before Lunch

US Transmission Date: 5 April 2000
UK Transmission Date: 22 May 2000 (Sky), 17 May 2001 (C4)

Writer: Aaron Sorkin
Director: Clark Johnson
Cast: Carl Lumbly (Jeff Breckenridge) Lindsay Sloane (Stacy)
Christopher Wynne (Edgar Drumm)
Kenneth Choi (Secret Service Agent #1)
Todd Sandler (Secret Service Agent #2)
Kimiko Gelman (Secret Service Agent Kelly)
Heather Dawn (College Student #1)
Erin Leshawn Wiley (College Student #2),
Christopher Francis[56] (Student)

As Toby celebrates the confirmation of Mendoza, CJ struggles to keep an embarrassing story concerning Zoey from the press. Josh discusses slavery reparations with a civil-rights attorney. Sam and Mallory battle over school vouchers.

A View from the Hill: Sam's schedule includes a meeting on the Hill at noon, followed by meetings with the East Asia team, Medicare and the president.

Mallory argues that tax dollars should go to public schools, not aiding the shipment of students to private

---

[56] Uncredited.

schools, many being religious. She doesn't see how the administration can get around the separation of church and state. Sam argues that they have people on the payroll who are experts at obfuscating the Constitution.

Politics of Honesty: Jeff Breckenridge, the administration's nominee for Assistant Attorney General for Civil Rights, is a lawyer from Athens, Georgia. He worked at Debevoise and Plimpton with Josh's father. A soon-to-be-released book by Otis Hastings called *The Unpaid Debt* argues that African–Americans are owed monetary reparations for slavery. Breckenridge is quoted on the dust jacket. If asked, he says, he will tell his nomination committee that his ancestors were kidnapped outside a village called Wimbabwa, taken to New Guinea, sold to a slave trader from Boston and bought by a plantation owner in Wadsworth, South Carolina, where they worked for no wages. Josh asks if Jeff has a figure in mind. Harold Washington, the chief economist at the Manchester Institute, has calculated the number of slaves held and come up with a 'very conservative figure' of $1,700,000,000. This leads to a discussion on the Civil War in which Josh suggests 600,000 white men died over the issue of slavery. Jeff is dubious but Josh insists that many believed in the cause. Josh says that, to raise the kind of money suggested, the government would have to sell Texas and the navy. Jeff understands the predicament and notes he's willing to take his money in tax deductions and scholarship funds. How about in affirmative action, empowerment zones and civil-rights acts? Josh argues. Breckenridge asks Josh to look at a dollar bill. The pyramid is unfinished, he notes. With the eye of God looking over it and the words *Annuit Coeptis*, 'He favours our undertaking.' It is unfinished, because the country is meant to keep doing better.

American History X: Jeff says that slavery reparations aren't anything new. In January 1865, General William T Sherman (1820–91) issued Special Field Order 15, dividing up half a million acres from South Carolina to Florida into forty-acre plots, which were given to newly freed slaves. He also granted them the use of various decommissioned army supplies, including mules. The order was rescinded four years later by Andrew Johnson (1808–75, the seventeenth president). In the 1960s, during the Newark riots, black looters were heard shouting, 'That was my forty acres, I'll be back for the mule.' America also gave $1,200,000 to Japanese-Americans who were in internment camps during Word War Two.

The president reads *Rules of Civility and Decent Behavior in Company and Conversation* by George Washington, drawn from an English translation of a French book of maxims. Washington copied them down when he was fourteen. Having quoted a passage, Bartlet muses what a 'tight-assed little priss' the first president must've been. He asks Charlie if he thinks Bartlet could've 'taken' Washington in battle. Bartlet has the US Air Force under his command, Charlie notes, while Washington only had the Minutemen.

A Little Learning is a Dangerous Thing: Josh doesn't know the difference between a koala and a panda bear. Donna, he suggests, hasn't quite mastered the alphabet.

Zoey and her college friends are practising their French by conjugating the verbs *habiter* (to live) and *travailler* (to work).

Denial, Thy Name is Zoey: Having lied to Bartlet's nemesis Edgar Drumm, Zoey feels compelled to repeat the lie to CJ. Gina will not betray Zoey, however, telling CJ (as she told Bartlet in **16**, '20 Hours in L.A.') she is not permitted to discuss Zoey's behaviour. 'I can't protect her if she feels she has to do things behind my back.' However, she does give CJ a probable reason for the lie: Zoey thought she'd got her father into trouble.

White Power: Ron Butterfield tells his agents about Derrick Horgiboom, who threatened to blow up the Smithsonian unless Zoey agreed to meet him for a drink. He's now in custody. Butterfield says the Secret Service are adding the Aryan White Resistance, the Christian Defense League and the World Church of the Creator to their already extensive list of hate groups. Mike says that the Office of Protective Research has said that most recent letters have been signed with the slogan '14 words', which Gina explains means 'We must secure the existence of white people and the future for white children.' Two threats were received earlier in the week, made with letters cut from a magazine called *Resistance*, which recruits teenagers to far-right activity. They use the phrase, 'following the voice of blood', the title of a record by Graveland, a band popular among skinheads.

References: CJ lip-synchs to 'The Jackal' by Ronny Jordan. The title's an allusion to *Alice's Adventures in Wonderland*. Also, Leviticus 25 (Toby's 'day of jubilee'), the surrealist Salvador Dali (1904–89), *Happy Days* ('sit on it!'), Boston Latin, the oldest school in America, founded in 1635, Bronx Science high school and Birkenau extermination camp. Toby alludes to Carolyn Crawford's 'My Smile is Just a Frown Turned Upside Down' and sings 'Put on a Happy Face'. He seems to like Chinese food, referring to one of the pandas that Mandy is wittering on about as Dim Sum! (See **45**, 'Isaac and Ishmael'.)

'You May Remember Me From Such Films and TV Series As . . .': Carl Lumbly played the Martian Manhunter in *Justice League*, and was in *South Central*, *How Stella Got Her Groove Back*, *Cagney & Lacey* and *Taxi*. Lindsay Sloane was Valerie in *Sabrina, the Teenage Witch*, Marcy in *Grosse Pointe* and Big Red in *Bring it On*. Kenneth Choi was in *Deep Core*. Todd Sandler appeared in *Rainbow*. Christopher Wynne was in *Back to the Future Part III*, *1969* and *Speed 2: Cruise Control*. Kimiko Gelman played Trish in *The Bold and the Beautiful*. Erin Leshawn Wiley was Ilena in *Menace II Society* and Mona in *Reform School Girl*. Christopher Francis appeared in *Madison County* and *Little Nicky*.

Behind the Camera: Clark Johnson played Meldrick Lewis in *Homicide: Life on the Streets*, and acted in *Fear of Fiction*, *Rude*, *Skullduggery*, *Third Watch*, *Forever Knight* and *The Littlest Hobo*. He was a stunt man on *Night Stick*, provided special effects on *The Dead Zone* and directed *Boycott*.

Sex and Drugs and Rock'n'Roll: David Arbor, son of Bob Arbor, a major Democratic fundraiser, was arrested outside a frat party and is to be charged with felony possession and intent to distribute. He's a friend of Zoey, who insists he doesn't sell drugs, he just takes them.

Cigarettes and Alcohol: Ginger and Bonnie are opening the champagne, but Toby orders them to wait till all the votes are counted. Once Mendoza is confirmed, however, *everybody*'s drinking it. Toby smokes a cigar while CJ does 'The Jackal' (see **6**, 'Mr. Willis of Ohio').

Logic, Let Me Introduce You to This Window: David and Zoey were at a frat party at Georgetown and Mike mentions the girls of Kappa Kappa Gamma. That school, however, doesn't have any fraternities or sororities. CJ tells Bartlet that they, Charlie and Zoey are the only four people who know Zoey lied to the reporter. However, CJ also told Sam.

Cruelty To Animals: The panda Hsing-Hsing (1971–99) was a gift to Richard Nixon from the Chinese government in 1972. The Chinese also sent over a mate, Ling-Ling, who died in 1992. Mandy thinks, as a symbol of how serious America is about a relationship with China, they should ask for another two bears. Toby thinks it would be better if China stopped running over their citizens with tanks. When Mandy points out how rare pandas are Toby's solution is to get two regular bears and buckets of black and white paint. 'It's hard to believe the wildlife lobby was nervous about you,' says an exasperated Mandy (see **34**, 'The Drop In').

Quote/Unquote: Mandy: 'I think we should get a panda bear.' Josh: 'You say that now, but I'm the one who's going to end up feeding him.'
    Gina: 'I'm gonna look through an FBI photo album of teenage Nazis.' CJ: 'Why?' Gina: 'I'm on a break.'

Josh, on financial reparations: 'I'd love to give you the money, but I'm a little short of cash right now. Seems the SS officer forgot to give my grandfather his wallet back when he let him out of Birkenau.'

Notes: 'You can't kidnap a civilisation and sell them into slavery. No amount of money will make up for it.' An excellent multilayered story that mixes the serious (Josh and Jeff's debate on slavery) with the light-hearted (Mandy's pandas). Love the way Toby starts the episode singing, and two minutes with Mandy turns him back into a snarling beast.

The president's lunch with Mr Girardi has been postponed as the man has pneumonia. This is the first time anyone's cancelled on Bartlet since he took office. Toby doesn't usually say 'good morning' to colleagues, just growls something inaudible. Neither Bonnie nor Ginger has seen him sustain a good mood this long, while Margaret says he's scaring her. Danny has a police scanner, which he claims to listen to in the small hours. He was vice president of his school's audio-visual club (Bobby Pfeiffer was president). Edgar Drumm is a professional Bartlet-baiter with a fundraising newsletter for the radical right, the *Charlestown Citizen*. Mallory attended a private primary school, high school and college.

Cast and Crew Comments: Sorkin admitted to Eric Deggans that he was surprised by hate mail that came after Zoey and Charlie kissed. Developed on the fly to add 45 seconds to an episode, it provoked some ugly letters: 'Frankly, the most surprising thing is that these people were watching our show at all and not *WWF Smackdown*,' he said.

19
Let Bartlet Be Bartlet

US Transmission Date: 26 April 2000
UK Transmission Date: 29 May 2000 (Sky), 24 May 2001 (C4)

Teleplay: Aaron Sorkin
Story: Peter Parnell, Patrick Caddell
Director: Laura Innes
Cast: Richard Penn (Blakely) Aaron Lustig (Jerry Graham)
James DuMont (Major Thompson) Ted Marcoux (Major Tate)
David Brisbin (Ken) Andy Buckley (Mike Satchel)

Rumours of a memo that highlights the administration's weaknesses sweep the White House. CJ learns that its author was Mandy. Sam, Toby and Josh are involved in fruitless meetings on issues they know they cannot win. Leo confronts Bartlet and challenges him to be himself.

A View from the Hill: Two seats open up on the Federal Election Commission. Six commissioners are appointed and when a vacancy occurs, the party leadership on both sides always dictates the appointees. The president asks Josh to find him two candidates and Josh selects Democrat John Bacon and Republican Patty Calhoun (who worked in the White House under two former presidents and is director of the Roe Institute for Economic Policy Studies). Both favour aggressive campaign-finance overhaul. Soft money contributions render the 1974 Campaign Reform Act toothless, Josh tells the majority leadership aides. Such contributions, designed for party building, do nothing but eviscerate meaningful controls. America is, by definition, corrupt. This money comes from special interests whose interests aren't the same as those who don't have half a million bucks to spare. Josh is told it's called free speech, but he argues that it's really buying influence. Embarrass Congress like this, the aides threaten, and they'll give the same back to the president tenfold. Every piece of legislation the White House wants off the table will make a sudden appearance, including school prayer, Family Support Act, Entertainment Decency Act and English as the national language. Josh asks if, in addition to voting down their nominees, there will be a punishment beating for having nominated them in the first place. Steve Onorato rejects the suggestion that the best way to maintain free speech is by having government regulate it.

American History X: James Madison (1751–1836) was the fourth president. The tradition of the White House Easter Egg Roll seems to have begun during the administration of Andrew Johnson, when children of the president's family dyed eggs on Easter Sunday and held races on the White House lawn. Subsequent events moved to the Capitol but bad weather in 1876 took its toll on the grounds, a fact that didn't go unnoticed by Congress, which, mean-spiritedly, forbade its future use. On Easter Saturday 1878, president Rutherford Hayes was approached by some children who enquired about using the White House lawn to roll eggs. The president issued an order that should any child arrive with an egg, they be allowed to roll it. Successive presidents have continued the tradition.

Politics of Compromise: Mandy's memo argues that Leo drives the president to political safe ground. Leo argues the opposite is true. 'We're stuck in neutral because that's where you tell me to stay.' Too often the president's stance is to dangle his feet in the water, trying not to upset anyone. 'I'm the hall monitor,' argues Leo. 'It's my job to make sure nobody runs too fast.'

Office Technophobia: Margaret's friend Lynette, from the President's Council on Physical Fitness, sent an email about the calories in raisin muffins. Margaret forwarded the email to several hundred assistants and secretaries but Jolene Millman, from political liaison, hit 'reply', which clogged everyone's email box.

Alternate Sexuality: Sam and Toby conduct meetings with various staff from the Department of Defense, National Security Council and House and Senate Armed Services Committee. They feel hamstrung by the 'don't ask, don't tell' policy inherited from previous administrations regarding gays in the military. Major Tate says it takes an act of Congress to amend the uniform code and this still regards sodomy as a crime.

References: Baskin Robbins (the ice-cream manufacturers), the Boy Scouts, CNN and *USA Today*. Josh carries a copy of the book *A Necessary Evil: A History of American Distrust of Government* by Garry Wills. There's a reference to the Western genre ('keep the peace in Dodge'). A poster says WORKING WOMEN VOTE '96 in the bullpen near Josh's office.

'You May Remember Me From Such Films and TV Series As . . .': David Brisbin played Dr Babcock in *ER* and appeared in *Erin Brockovich*, *Life During Wartime*, *Leaving Las Vegas*, *Forrest Gump*, *Buffy* and *Five Corners*. Andrew Buckley was in *Body Waves* and *We Met on the Vineyard* (which he also wrote). Paul Provenza was Phil Capra in *Northern Exposure* and was also in *Nothing Sacred*. Richard Penn's movies include *Inspector Gadget*, *Volcano*, *Sleepwalkers* and *Lobster Men from Mars*. James DuMont was in *Primary Colors* and *Speed*. Aaron Lustig was in *Bedazzled*, *The Opposite Sex and How to Live with Them*, *L.A. Story*, *Edward Scissorhands* and *Ghostbusters II*. Ted Marcoux appeared in *Camp Stories* and *Ghost in the Machine*.

Behind the Camera: Laura Innes is best known as Kerry Weaver in *ER* and appeared in *Torch Song*, *Deep Impact* and *The Fury*. She wrote episodes of *Hey Dude* and began directing on *ER*.

Oh, Donna!: Another wonderful circular conversation. Josh returns to the White House to find Donna waiting in the lobby. Josh asks how she always knows when he's due back. Donna replies that she sees him from the window. But Donna doesn't have a window. '*You* have a window,' she says. What is she doing in his office when he isn't there? Josh asks. 'Looking for you at the window.'

Logic, Let Me Introduce You to This Window: Sam gets weather information from a First Lieutenant Emily Lowenbrau of the Coast Guard (see **41**, 'Bad Moon Rising'). There are no First Lieutenants in the Coast Guard – they use navy ranks. Also, the Coast Guard has no weather-forecasting responsibilities. Its forces rely on the National Weather Service, the same as everyone else. CJ says that Mandy 'worked for us for a year and a half', contradicting what Mandy said in **2**, ' "Post Hoc, Ergo Propter Hoc" '. Another timing issue: Josh says he's worked at the White House for fourteen months; since Bartlet was inaugurated in January 1999, it should be sixteen. Margaret says IT support has accused her of hacking. However, a hacker is someone who breaks into the computer systems of others rather than somebody who merely forwards junk mail – that's a spammer.

Quote/Unquote: Leo, to Margaret: 'I hung in there as long as I could, but you long since passed the point when I stopped caring.'

Fitzwallace: 'That's what they were saying to me fifty years ago. Blacks shouldn't serve with whites. It would disrupt the unit. You know what? It *did* disrupt the unit. The unit got over it.'

Danny: 'You guys are stuck in the mud. None of it's the fault of the press. I know you're frustrated but it ain't nothing compared to the frustration of people who voted for you.'

Leo's magnificent anger at Bartlet: 'If you ever told me to get aggressive about anything, I'd say I serve at the pleasure of the president. But we'll never know, sir, because I don't think you're ever gonna say it … [Charlie] gets death threats because he's black and he dates your daughter. He was warned: "Do not show up. Your life will be in danger." He said, "To hell with that, I'm going anyway." '

Notes: 'Why is everyone walking around like they know they already lost?' A wonderful look at disillusionment and the frustration of stalled idealism. Leo's attempts to raise the level of debate constantly suffocated by Bartlet's wish not to offend anyone. Best bits: Margaret's email problems; Leo and Jed's shouting match in the Oval Office.

The front page of the *Hartford Chronicle* from **15** 'Celestial Navigation' can be seen on the wall of Toby's office.

Cast and Crew Comments: Martin Sheen admits he had no idea who Laura Innes was during the first day of shooting. 'But my wife knew, and boy, did I get a beating for that,' he told *TV Guide Online*. 'She asked me who was directing,

and I said, "Some little girl. She looks about 14 years old," '
recalls Sheen. 'She looked at the call sheets and said, "She's
the best thing on *ER*. Behave yourself." ' He went on to
describe the scene in which he and John Spencer rather
overdid their verbal battle: 'She let it go for about six or eight
takes. And then she came in and began to take all the
decorations away and said, "Make it personal." The scene
got smaller and smaller and by the end of the evening we were
just looking at each other. It was phenomenal what she did.

'As president, just as in a marriage, you need one person
who tells you the truth,' says Sheen. 'That is the thing
between a president and a chief-of-staff.' In the hands of
Sheen and Spencer, friends off screen as well as on, the
relationship can be heartbreaking and heated as when Leo
accuses Bartlet of selling out the presidency for higher
approval ratings. John Podesta was asked by *TV Guide* if
he yells at the president. 'I could,' says Podesta mischiev-
ously. 'I'm tough with the president, but never condescending. But if he's wrong, I'll fight him. He's pretty good
about accepting that.'

Did You Know?: 'Martin's never made a comment about
my height,' Allison Janney told the *Atlanta Journal Constitution*. 'I can tell when men are threatened by [it], and they
don't act like Martin does.'

20
Mandatory Minimums

US Transmission Date: 3 May 2000
UK Transmission Date: 5 June 2000 (Sky), 24 May 2001 (C4)

Writer: Aaron Sorkin
Director: Robert Berlinger
Cast: Bruce Weitz (Senator) Chris Conner (Jack)
Michael Luckerman (Aide #1) Paul Emrmann (Aide #2)
Diane Nadeau (Aide) Karolyn Nishioka (Waitress)
Mark Weiler[57] (Onorato's Assistant)

---

[57] Uncredited.

Bartlet throws down the gauntlet and names the two campaign finance reformers to the FEC. He also proposes a controversial new drug policy. Joey Lucas arrives to help Josh form an argument against English as the national language. Toby seeks advice from his ex-wife.

Politics of Expediency: The president tells the Scholar Awards Dinner that he gets nervous around laws that assume Americans can't be trusted.

A Little Learning is a Dangerous Thing: Joey tells Josh, on the subject of English as a national language, that they have decent models in Marin County and the Bay Area. But San Jose is a mess and so are Orange County, Long Beach, Anaheim and San Diego.

Denial, Thy Name is Sam: Sam tells Toby and Josh that Steve Onorato came to see him and offered to 'warm things up for drugs' if they dropped FEC reform. Josh and Toby realise that Onorato knows about Laurie, and his people want to move Sam into the spotlight so that they can expose him.

References: Bartlet says his father was fond of the analogy of 'the Irish lads', whose journey was blocked by a wall. Throwing their caps over, they had no choice but to follow. This is a possible reference to a speech made in San Antonio by John Kennedy the day before he died, alluding to a story by the author Frank O'Connor. Sam mentioned *The Godfather* in **5**, 'The Crackpots and These Women'. Here, Josh sees parallels between Sam's wish for revenge on Onorato and the scene in the movie where Michael tells Sonny he intends to kill the cop who shot Don Vito. 'I'm James Caan,' says Josh (he *does* look a bit like him), Sam's Al Pacino and Toby is 'the guy who shows Pacino how to make tomato sauce' (Richard Castellano who played the Corleones' lieutenant Peter Clemenza). Also, Wheaties breakfast cereal, *Time*, *Newsweek*, the *Rambo* movies, *Taxi Driver* ('you talkin' to *me*?'), *The Terminator* ('I'll be back') and Girl Scout cookies. Andi has dated Victor Stipe, executive adviser for the Baltimore Orioles. Toby also mentions the Boston Red Socks.

**'You May Remember Me From Such Films and TV Series As
. . .':** Bruce Weitz played Mick Belker in *Hill Street Blues*,
and appeared in *Mach 2*, *Deep Impact*, *The Liars Club*, *The
X-Files* and *Happy Days*. Kathleen York was in *Dead Men
Can't Dance*, *I Love You to Death* and *Astronomy*. Chris
Conner appeared in *Teenage Tupelo*. Michael Luckerman
was Coyote in *Borders*. Diane Nadeau played Rebecca in
Voodoo. Mark Weiler was in *Pearl Harbor*.

Behind the Camera: Robert Berlinger's directorial work can
be seen on *Titus*, *Zoe Duncan Jack & Jane*, *Veronica's
Closet* and *3rd Rock from the Sun*.

Oh, Donna!: Donna embarrasses Josh over his 'Joey Lucas'
suit, forcing him to claim that he assigns his clothes to days
of the week. She likes waffles.

Sex and Drugs and Rock'n'Roll: Mandatory minimum
sentences are considerably higher for crack than for
powder cocaine. The majority of crack users are black,
while the majority of drug users are white. Mandatory
minimums could, therefore, be perceived as racist. Drug
control appropriations, $17,600,000, are divided into two-
thirds enforcement and one-third treatment. The administration wants to reverse that ratio. Al Kiefer argues it will
appear that they are soft on crime and don't care if kids
shoot up in the playground at recess. Leo gets together a
bunch of aides working for politicians who believe more
money should be spent on prisons. They all have guilty
secrets (a son arrested for carrying 25 grams of cocaine, a
daughter who was indicted by a jury in South Carolina for
conspiracy to distribute). The president wants a lively
debate, Leo tells them. He wants to hear opposition, but
he's not going to stomach hypocrisy.

Cigarettes and Alcohol: The majority leader says one of his
constituents can't tell the difference between cognac and
brandy.

Logic, Let Me Introduce You to This Window: Toby wears
a wedding ring but, when he meets with his ex-wife, there's

no mention of his having remarried. Fans have come up with several explanations for this discrepancy (he's gained weight and can't get the ring off; he still has feelings for Andi; he hates failure and divorce is a sign of this; his faith may regard divorce as untenable). Leo says Vicodin and Percocet are Schedule II drugs. Percocet is, but Vicodin is Schedule III.

Quote/Unquote: CJ, asked if the president has declared war on Congress: 'The president isn't empowered to declare war. I call it more of a police action.'

Sam: 'Is this what you meant when you said, "You're completely in charge of this"?' Toby: 'Yes, I meant you're in charge, in the sense that you're subordinate to me in every way.'

Bartlet, in bed, to his assembled staff: 'Let me tell you what I would like to have happen, right now.' Josh: 'Good evening, Mr President.' Bartlet, wearily: 'Josh walking in the door wasn't even close.'

Notes: 'Why don't you take your legislative agenda and shove it up your ass?' An episode short on drama but with some excellent comedy moments (Josh and Joey spend the episode bitching at each other; Josh's impotent anger and squirming embarrassment are a joy).

Bonnie is from Indiana; Ginger is from New Jersey. One of the seven people whom Leo threatens with exposure of drug-related family skeletons is Senator Stackhouse (see **39**, 'The Stackhouse Filibuster'). Sam's mother used the word 'hooleelya' a lot.

Andi Wyatt is a prominent House Democrat who has a voice on Campaign Finance Reform and is on the Ethics Committee. Locations include the Sheraton Center Hotel. Toby meets Andi on the banks of the Potomac opposite the Lincoln Memorial.

Critique: 'They wanted to know my opinion on who they ought to cast. They said it would be either Arnold Schwarzenegger or Woody Allen. Which do you think I picked?' The House Majority Whip Tom DeLay told a

National Press Club audience about this episode's DeLay-like character. One of the biggest endorsements for *The West Wing* as social comment comes from Robert Stutman, a former drug-enforcement agent who participated in a PBS *Frontline* special, 'Drug Wars'. 'The most intelligent discussion I've heard among politicians concerning the drug issue was on *The West Wing*,' Stutman volunteered.

Cast and Crew Comments: Richard Schiff created a back story for Toby by wearing his own wedding ring – something Sorkin and Schlamme failed to notice at first. 'They said, "Is Toby married?" I said, "No." They explained that they wanted to give Toby an ex-wife.' To Virginia Rohan Schiff said he believed Toby had more than one ex-wife. But concerning the ring: 'I had always imagined that his first wife had died, which accounts for his sadness, and why someone would devote himself to public service and be so singular about it. But Aaron and Tommy threw that out the window. I love that his personal life is not open to the public.'

Did You Know?: In real life Patricia Calhoun is the editor of Denver's *Westword*. Did *The West Wing* use the name deliberately? An NBC spokesman claimed it was 'a remarkable coincidence'. So, what would the real Calhoun do if she were appointed to the FEC? 'Condense the presidential campaign to about a day,' she told *Rocky Mountain News*.

21
Lies, Damn Lies and Statistics

US Transmission Date: 10 May 2000
UK Transmission Date: 3 July 2000 (Sky), 31 May 2001 (C4)

Writer: Aaron Sorkin
Director: Don Scardino
Cast: Thom Gossom Jr (Ted Mitchell) David Huddleston (Max Lobell)
Austin Pendleton (Barry Haskell)
Lawrence Pressman (Ken Cochran) Reiko Aylesworth (Janeane)

Justin Colvin (Rodney) Sherry Houston (Dan Larson)
Conrad Bachmann (Ken Kato) MG Mills (Rob Konrad)
Bruce Wright (Ross Kassenbach)

Bartlet begins a merry-go-round transfer of ambassadors and members of the Federal Election Commission designed to defuse an embarrassing incident overseas. Sam is photographed by a newspaper giving Laurie a gift.

A View from the Hill: In 1978 the FEC voted a regulatory rule that opened the door to soft money. The FEC can close it again with four of the six votes without the need to pass a law through Congress.

American History X: Theodore Roosevelt (see **1**, 'The West Wing') was a great exponent of a one-language nation: 'We have room for but one language here, and that is English. For we intend to see that the crucible turns our people out as Americans and not as dwellers in a polyglot boarding-house.'

Joey and Josh are working on a counterargument to the French historian and politician Alexis de Tocqueville (1805–59) in *L'Ancien Régime et la Révolution*. Josh asks what Joey says to the position that, with ethnic warfare spreading, particularly in Eastern Europe, it's only a matter of time before it reaches America, and making English the official language will safeguard against the destruction of national identity and help avoid ethnic strife. Joey blows a raspberry. This is what Josh has been dealing with all week, he tells the president. Joey says 72 per cent of Hispanics are strongly opposed to such a law. The Republicans will never push it because they'll risk losing the second largest ethnic block of voters in the country. But, if one needs a counterargument, then, aside from its being bigoted and unconstitutional, it's ludicrous to think that laws are needed to protect the language of Shakespeare.

A Little Learning is a Dangerous Thing: Josh thinks the term 'average people' is pejorative. CJ notes that 80 per cent of Americans would use the phrase to describe themselves. They don't find it deprecating. Indeed, being considered an average American is something they find positive.

The Encyclopedic Mind of Josiah Bartlet PhD: He knows that the Federated States of Micronesia consists of 607 islands and that, while the total land mass is only 270 square miles, it occupies more than a million square miles of the Pacific. The population is 127,000 and the US Embassy is located in the state of Pohnpei and not, as many people believe, on the island of Yap. Toby wonders why a person would have that information at their disposal. 'Parties,' suggests the president. He's also something of an expert on briefcases, mentioning Andare and Trieste of Milan.

The Conspiracy Starts at Closing Time: It takes CJ three hours to confirm that Sam was pictured with Laurie and another hour to find that the British *Mirror* newspaper paid Janeane, Laurie's waitress friend, $50,000 to set them up and confirm that she was a call girl.

References: *Funk and Wagnall*'s dictionary, the newspapers *Newark Star Ledger*, *Detroit Free Press*, *Washington Post* and *New York Times*, the magazines *Time*, *Newsweek* and *Popular Mechanics*; *Crossfire*, *Meet the Press*, *Charlie Rose*, *The Today Show* and *The Tonight Show*. Sam thinks that the Federated States of Micronesia is a country from a Marx Brothers movie.

'You May Remember Me From Such Films and TV Series As . . .': Reiko Aylesworth was in *Man on the Moon* and *You've Got Mail*. Thom Gossom appeared in *Senseless* and *Fight Club*. David Huddleston was the eponymous *Big Lebowski*, played Grampa Arnold in *The Wonder Years* and appeared in *Bewitched*, *Dirty Sally*, *When the Bough Breaks*, *Capricorn One*, *Rio Lobo*, *Petrocelli* and *Blazing Saddles*. Conrad Bachmann was Bing Crosby's stunt double in *Stagecoach*, and was also in *The Astronaut's Wife*, *Tremors*, *Tales of the Gold Monkey* and *Bedknobs and Broomsticks*. Don Chastain played Tom Baldwin in

General Hospital and appeared in *Hawaii Five-0* and *The Invaders*. MG Mills was in *Soldier*. Austin Pendleton's movies include *Catch-22*, *Clowns*, *Joe the King*, *2 Days in the Valley* and *Short Circuit*. Lawrence Pressman was Coach Marshall in *American Pie* and appeared in *Very Bad Things*, *The Hanoi Hilton*, *The Trial of Lee Harvey Oswald*, *The Man from Atlantis*, *Winter Kill*, *Shaft* and *Dark Angel*. Bruce Wright was in *Shogun Cop*, *Twister*, *Apollo 13*, *Speed*, *Battlestar Galactica* and *Buck Rogers in the 25th Century*.

Behind the Camera: Don Scardino directed episodes of *Cosby* and *Another World* (in which he played Chris Chapin). He also acted in *He Knows You're Alone* and *Squirm*.

Oh, Donna!: Donna knows the Federated States of Micronesia are located 2,500 miles southwest of Hawaii, where Josh has never taken her – it's something bosses do, she says. Micronesia has some of the best scuba-diving in the world and the mantas on the island of Yap are highly prized.

Sex and Drugs and Rock'n'Roll: The ambassador to Bulgaria, Ken Cochran, is having an affair with the daughter of the prime minister. Bartlet is a friend of Cochran's wife and doesn't want a scandal. Toby says they can create legitimate grounds for incompetence. 'There *are*,' notes the president. 'Come up with different ones.'

CJ asks Josh to stop distracting the female callers for the telephone poll. Josh asks them if he is, and they all say no. Josh seems a little upset.

CJ notes that the concept of mandatory minimums (**20**, 'Mandatory Minimums') requires a judge to sentence anyone convicted of possessing five grams of crack to at least five years in prison. It takes a hundred times as much powder cocaine and twenty times as much heroin to get that sentence. The White House is committed to reversing the devastating effects of drug abuse, believing the best way to treat addiction is as what the AMA has said it is, a medical problem.

Logic, Let Me Introduce You to This Window: The Attorney General was said to be black in **3**, 'A Proportional Response', but is white here. Once again, G-8 is referred to as G-7 (see **12**, 'He Shall, from Time to Time . . .'). The president tells Sam that Laurie probably has 'a cause of action' against the newspaper. For what exactly? All they did was photograph her (in the street, so there's no privacy issue at stake) and expose her as a prostitute (which she is). If she passes her exam, Bartlet goes on to say, the Attorney General will personally see to it that she's admitted to the Bar. Isn't that an illegal demonstration of grace and favour?

Margaret's Joke: 'You know why they only eat one egg for breakfast in France? 'Cos in France, one egg is an "oeuf".'

Quote/Unquote: Sam: 'You're not going to fire the ambassador. You're going to promote him.' Bartlet: 'To what?' Sam: 'Ambassador to Paraguay.' Bartlet: 'And what happens to the ambassador of Paraguay?' Sam: 'You make him ambassador to Bulgaria.' Bartlet: 'I like this. If everybody keeps moving up one, then I get to go home.'

Bartlet: 'We agree on nothing. Education, guns, drugs, school prayer, gays, defence spending, taxes. You name it, we disagree.' Lobell: 'You know why?' Bartlet: ' 'Cos I'm a lily-livered, bleeding-heart, liberal-egghead communist.' Lobell: 'Yes, sir. And I'm a gun-totin' redneck son-of-a-bitch!'

Cochran: 'I think it would be appropriate at this time to make a confession. I never voted for you.' Bartlet: 'Well, thanks for trying, but here I am anyway.'

Notes: 'It's nice when we can do something for prostitutes once in a while, isn't it?' A multitude of subplots that have brewed all season are resolved. A less than satisfying and unrealistic conclusion to the Sam/Laurie story is counter-balanced by some great moments (Leo manipulating Barry Haskell with the trappings of the White House, Bartlet shuttling from office to office hiring and firing).

Laurie has graduated from the George Washington law school. This episode takes place nine months after **1**, 'The West Wing'.

Critique: 'Where they fired an ambassador to make room for somebody else they wanted to move into that slot so they could hire somebody else in a third position. That happens often. I've been a part of those kinds of things myself, but the president never does the dirty work,' noted Marlin Fitzwater. 'He would make the decisions, but no one would ever see it. It's exactly how the White House works. For example, if a president of another country calls up our State Department and says, "I don't like your ambassador," they'll find a way to get rid of him, but he's not going to be fired. That guy will suddenly be given another post and we'll get a new ambassador. That happens quite a bit.'

Cast and Crew Comments: 'Sorry about the "Sing a song"/"Got it wrong"-joke,' Sorkin told fans on the Internet. 'I'm surprised Marlee didn't smack me as she usually does in those situations.'

22
What Kind of Day Has it Been

US Transmission Date: 17 May 2000
UK Transmission Date: 10 July 2000 (Sky), 7 June 2001 (C4)

Writer: Aaron Sorkin
Director: Thomas Schlamme
Cast: Linda Burden-Williams (Moderator) Emidio Antonio (Lou)
Christopher Dukes (Phil) Lisa Croisette (Patty) Larry Stahoviak (Steve)
Derek Triplett (Mikey)

The staff prepare for a speech by the president while the military race against time to find an American pilot stranded in the Iraqi desert. Meanwhile, Toby's brother is marooned on board a stricken orbiting shuttle. As the presidential entourage leave a town hall, shots are fired.

A View from the Hill: Josh uses a mixture of coercion and common sense to get Hoynes to support the president on finance reform (see **20**, 'Mandatory Minimums'). There are discussions on the fact that 40 million Americans (many of them children) don't have health insurance and on the administration's pursuit of constructive engagement with China even though it's a dictatorship that systematically suppresses dissent.

American History X: The president says he's been called a liberal, a populist and even a socialist but he's actually an economics professor. His ancestor, Josiah Bartlett, was the New Hampshire representative to the Second Continental Congress, which, in 1776, announced that they were no longer English subjects.[58] ' "We hold these truths to be self-evident," they said, "that all men are created equal." Strange as it may seem, that was the first time in history that anyone had ever bothered to write that down.' He reminds the audience that decisions are made by those who show up.

Politics of Expediency: Al-Jabar Air Base in Kuwait reports that an F117 Nighthawk didn't come back from a routine flight in the no-fly zone. The pilot, Scott Hotchkiss from Rhode Island, is stranded south of Basra, ten miles from the fourth corps of the Iraqi Republican Guard. If they get to him first, Leo tells Josh, and all he gives them is name, rank and serial number, they're going to beat and torture him. A daring rescue is undertaken by the 16th Special Ops unit using Saudi airspace.

A Little Learning is a Dangerous Thing: The current crop of 18–25-year-olds is *the* most politically apathetic generation in American history, says the president. In 1972, half that age group voted; in the last election, it was 32 per cent.

The Encyclopedic Mind of Josiah Bartlet PhD: He intends to watch a girls' softball game between Sacramento State and University of the Pacific on TV, as opposed to a game

---

[58] Josiah Bartlett (note the extra 't') was the first governor of New Hampshire (1790–94) and one of the signatories of the Declaration of Independence. It's not uncommon for family surnames to change spelling over several generations.

of cricket between Scotland and Bermuda. He's an educated man, the president tells Charlie, but, when someone tries to explain the rules of cricket to him, he wants to hit them on the head with a teapot.

Denial, Thy Name is Toby: Pride won't allow Toby to show his true feelings over his brother's predicament.

Brad Whitford, Comedy Genius: Best scene of the episode sees Zoey and Charlie using Josh's office for an argument. Josh walks in and says they can keep fighting, he just needs to find something. As Charlie says, 'I work in a building with the smartest people in the world,' Josh absent-mindedly sits down where his chair should be. Zoey and Charlie stop arguing as Josh yells, 'Donna!' from the floor behind his desk.

Carol's Spelling: Despite assuring CJ that her spelling is better than she's given credit for (and getting Saudi Arabia right), she spells Tel Aviv with two 'l's.

References: Filming location for the climax was outside the Newseum in Arlington. Also, NASA's space shuttles *Columbia* and *Atlantis* (see **31**, 'Galileo'), the soap opera *General Hospital*, *Clash of the Titans*, Shalamar's 'Take That to the Bank', MSNBC and CNN, King George III (1738–1820) and an allusion to Frank Sinatra ('with the mike, the stool and the jacket over my shoulder, I can do the meeting and then a couple of sets at the Copa'). Hoynes wears a United States Naval Academy T-shirt.

'You May Remember Me From Such Films and TV Series As . . .': Linda Burden-Williams was Mrs Feinberg in *Blast*. Emidio Antonio appeared in *The Deep End of the Ocean* and was a stuntman on *Jailbait*. Christopher Dukes was in *Diamondbacks*. Lisa Croisette appeared in *My Stepmother is an Alien*.

Logic, Let Me Introduce You to This Window: Despite what CJ subsequently remembers in **24**, 'In the Shadow of Two Gunmen' Part 2, someone other than Sam clearly pushes her to the ground (it looks like a Secret Service agent). Sam speaks with someone at NASA whom he identifies as the 'mission commander in Houston'. The mission commander is an astronaut in charge of the flight itself. Sam means the flight director. It isn't possible to launch a rescue shuttle in a couple of days, as Bartlet suggests. F117s are first-strike stealth bombers and are far too valuable for such mundane missions as this one was on. Fighters such as the F15 and F16 would have been more viable. The rescued pilot is said be on his way to Tel Aviv. In reality he would be taken to the nearest US Air Force base (America has no bases in Israel). Fitzwallace believes that the eagle on the presidential seal changes direction during wartime. However, a spokesman for the White House told *Entertainment Weekly* that President Truman instigated a policy in the 1940s that the eagle would always face the olive branch and never the arrows. At the window the shooters are backlit by a red exit sign (doesn't seem like the most inconspicuous place for an assassination attempt).

Cruelty To Actors: 'We were filming the assassination attempt scene and everyone had to duck and run,' Jorja Fox told *TV Guide*. 'I was lying on the ground waiting for the director to yell cut, when I felt something heavy on my leg. I turned as the wheel of the car was rolling over me.' Panic ensued and Fox was rushed to the nearest emergency room, where she was recognised for her former role on *ER*. 'Luckily, I wound up with just a few bruises.'

Cruelty To Astro-Newts: David Ziegler is accompanied on his space trip by four Japanese red-bellied newts. He wants to see how their inner ears, which are similar to those of humans, are influenced by the absence of gravity.

Quote/Unquote: Bartlet: 'If it ends up Fitzwallace has to call this kid's parents, I swear to God, I'm invading Baghdad.'

Hoynes: 'If I'd listened to you two years ago, would I be president now? You ever wonder that?' Josh: 'No, sir, I know it for sure.'

Mrs Landingham after Bartlet tells her that she's not going to spoil his fun: 'I think we both know from experience, that's not true.'

Notes: 'People down. Who's been hit?' A dramatic, heart-stopping end to a quite extraordinary year of TV. It was the only applicable climax with shades of Dealey Plaza and the Ambassador Hotel, and an all-too-horrible reminder that even in a supposedly civilised world in the twenty-first century, gun law is never more than a shot away. Best bits: Leo and Josh *not* hugging; Bartlet's extraordinary speech.

Sam was unaware that Toby had a brother. Danny has covered the White House for eight years with the *New York Times*, the *Washington Post*, *Time* magazine and the *Dallas Morning News*. There are continuity references to **3**, 'A Proportional Response' (Charlie telling Josh that Josh was right when he said the amazement that he's working for the president doesn't go away) and **11**, 'Lord John Marbury' (CJ and Leo's discussion about how she was kept out of the loop over Kashmir).

Cast and Crew Comments: According to Thomas Schlamme, who logged on to the Internet after the episode aired, 'people were studying the tape like it was the Zapruder film!'[59]

Sorkin, meanwhile, seemed to spend the summer talking about the climax. 'I promise you that moment happened for the same reason every moment on every show happens,' he told the *Calgary Sun*. 'I'd be fibbing if I told you we didn't get hammered by critics about the ending,' Sorkin added to *Rocky Mountain News*. 'Not many critics liked it. Was I hurt by bad reviews? A little bit. But this wasn't a spur-of-the moment decision. I actually planned this scenario last fall. It leads into a two-part season premiere, which provides a backstory about how Bartlet and his staff got together. Remember, in our story, Bartlet is at his midterm. From that perspective, the assassination attempt was important to show how he got to the White House.'

To the *Miami Herald*, he confessed, 'The first time I saw the final scene I said, "It doesn't look like our show." ' He

---

[59] The infamous 8 mm movie of John Kennedy's assassination taken by Abraham Zapruder.

told the *Toronto Star*, 'Those last two minutes kind of [confirmed] a lot of people's problem with TV. The cliché that there must be a cliffhanger.' But, by October, Sorkin was more positive. 'I read plenty of negative reaction but it's good that response wasn't universal,' he told William Larue. 'Lots of people [were] gripped by it and have spent all summer asking "Who got hit?" It, frankly, was as exciting a piece of film as I've ever been involved with.'

'There were complaints about the last scene,' Bradley Whitford told Mark Dawidziak. 'Interesting that people were upset about that, because assassination attempts are something that happened three times in my lifetime.'

Did You Know?: Sorkin told the *Globe and Mail* that the final moments were inspired by the legendary shoot-out in *Butch Cassidy and the Sundance Kid*.

Awards: Among the notable awards given to the first season were an almost unprecedented *nine* Emmys: Outstanding Drama Series; Outstanding Art Direction for Tony Fanning (art director), Jon Hutman (production designer) and Ellen Totleben (set decorator); Outstanding Casting for a Drama Series for John Levey, Barbara Miller and Kevin Scott; Outstanding Cinematography for Thomas Del Ruth; Outstanding Directing for a Drama Series for Thomas Schlamme; Outstanding Main Title Theme Music for Snuffy Walden; Outstanding Supporting Actor in a Drama Series for Richard Schiff; Outstanding Supporting Actress in a Drama Series for Allison Janney; and Outstanding Writing for a Drama Series for Rick Cleveland and Aaron Sorkin for **10**, 'In Excelsis Deo'. The series also picked up Golden Globes for Best TV Drama and Martin Sheen won the award for Best Performance by an Actor in a TV Series. Lawrence O'Donnell, Paul Redford and Aaron Sorkin won a Humanitas Prize for the script of **14**, 'Take This Sabbath Day'. The American Cinema Editors award for Best Edited One-Hour Series for Television went to Tina Hirsch for **22**, 'What Kind of Day Has it Been'. The 2000 Television Critics' Association Awards saw the series named Best Drama Program and

Best New Program, while the Viewers for Quality Television Awards named it Best Quality Drama Series, and gave awards to Martin Sheen (Best Actor in a Quality Drama Series) and John Spencer (Best Supporting Actor in a Quality Drama Series).

The West Wing – Season Two (2000–2001)

John Wells Television/Warner Bros Television
(A Time/Warner Entertainment Company)
Created by Aaron Sorkin
Co-Executive Producer: Kevin Falls
Producers: Llewellyn Wells, Kristin Harms,
Lawrence O'Donnell Jr (28–44), Michael Hissrich (29–44),
Neal Ahern Jr (35–36)
Co-Producers: Patrick H Caddell, Michael Hissrich (23–28),
Lawrence O'Donnell Jr (23–27), Peter Parnell, Paul Redford
Associated Producers: Julie Herlocker, Mindy Kanaskie
Executive Producers: Aaron Sorkin, Thomas Schlamme, John Wells
Advisers: Dee Dee Myers, Peggy Noonan, Marlin Fitzwater
Theme and Music: WG Snuffy Walden

Regular Cast:

Martin Sheen (President Josiah Bartlet) John Spencer (Leo McGarry)
Bradley Whitford (Josh Lyman) Richard Schiff (Toby Ziegler)
Rob Lowe (Sam Seaborn) Allison Janney (CJ Cregg, 23–39, 41–44)
Janel Moloney (Donna Moss)
Kathryn Joosten (Delores Landingham, 23, 27, 30–31, 34–37, 41, 43–44)
NiCole Robinson (Margaret, 23–31, 33–35, 37–38, 41–44)
Devika Parikh (Bonnie, 25, 28, 30, 34–36, 38, 41, 43-44)
Allison Smith (Mallory O'Brien, 31) Annie Corley (Mary Marsh, 30)
F William Parker (Reverend Al Caldwell, 30)
Melissa Fitzgerald (Carol, 23–37, 39, 41, 43–44)
Peter James Smith (Ed[60], 25, 33, 35, 37–42, 44)
William Duffy (Larry[61], 25, 33, 35, 37–42, 44)
Mindy Seeger (Chris, 23, 26, 35, 37, 39, 43)
Jana Lee Hamblin (Bobbi[62], 29, 32, 39)
Dafidd McCracken (Mike[63], 23)

---

[60] Credited as Staffer in **33**, 'The Leadership Breakfast', and as Staffer Ed in **35**, 'Bartlet's Third State of the Union'.

[61] Credited as Staffer in **33**, 'The Leadership Breakfast', and as Staffer Larry in **35**, 'Bartlet's Third State of the Union'.

[62] Credited as Reporter #1 in **29**, 'The Portland Trip', as Reporter in **32**, 'Noël', and as Reporter # 2 in **39**, 'The Stackhouse Filibuster'.

[63] Credited as Agent #1 in **23**, 'In the Shadow of Two Gunmen' Part 1.

Molly Schaffer[64] (Senior Staffer, 30–31, 35) Renee Estevez (Nancy, 34, 37)
Tim Matheson (Vice President John Hoynes, 23, 39)
Robyn Pedretti (Candy[65], 23, 39) Bradley James (Donnie[66], 23, 27, 35, 43)
Dulé Hill (Charlie Young)
Timothy Busfield (Danny Concannon, 23–24, 28–29)
Kim Webster (Ginger, 23, 25–27, 30, 33–38, 41, 44)
Marvin Krueger (Officer #1[67], 35–36)
Ivan Allen (Roger Salier[68], 23, 33, 44) Penny Griego (DC Anchor[69], 24)
Elisabeth Moss (Zoey Bartlet, 23–25)
Michael O'Neill (Ron Butterfield, 23–24)
Charley Lang (Matt Skinner, 29)
Greg Wrangler (Secret Service Agent, 32, 37)
Juan A Riojas (Secret Service Agent[70], 23)
Stockard Channing (Abigail Bartlet, 23–24, 27, 35–36, 42, 44)
JP Stevenson (Jonathan[71], 35)
Charles Noland (Steve[72], 24, 26, 28, 30, 33, 39, 41, 43–44)
Kris Narmont (Katie, 23–24, 26, 28, 32, 34, 37, 43)
Roger Rees (Lord John Marbury, 34) Ralph Meyering Jr (Tom, 35–36)
Gary Cervantes (Bobby[73], 23, 32, 43) Tom Hall (Mike[74], 26, 31, 34)
Bill Stevenson (Jarworski, 26) Marlee Matlin (Joey Lucas, 35–36, 42–43)
Bill O'Brien (Kenny Thurman, 35–36, 43)
Jorja Fox (Special Agent Gina Toscano, 23)
Kathleen York (Andi Wyatt, 37) Don Chastain (Reporter #2, 29)
Anna Deavere Smith (Nancy McNally, 23, 38, 43–44)

---

[64] Credited as Aide in **30**, 'Shibboleth', and as Staffer in **31**, 'Galileo', and **35**, 'Bartlet's Third State of the Union'.

[65] Credited as Senator's Aide in **23**, 'In the Shadow of Two Gunmen' Part 1, and as VP's Aide #1 in **39**, 'The Stackhouse Filibuster'.

[66] Credited as Agent #3 in **23**, 'In the Shadow of Two Gunmen' Part 1, and as Secret Service Agent in **35**, 'Bartlet's Third State of the Union', and **43**, '18th and Potomac'.

[67] Credited as Officer #2 in **35**, 'Bartlet's Third State of the Union', and **36**, 'The War at Home'.

[68] Credited as TV Anchor in **23**, 'In the Shadow of Two Gunmen' Part 1, and as Newscaster in **33**, 'The Leadership Breakfast', and **44**, 'Two Cathedrals'.

[69] Name given in an on-screen caption as Valerie Gordon.

[70] Credited as Agent #2 in **23**, 'In the Shadow of Two Gunmen' Part 1.

[71] Credited as Reporter #2 in **35**, 'Bartlet's Third State of the Union'.

[72] Credited as Reporter #1 in **30**, 'Shibboleth' and as Reporter in **44**, 'Two Cathedrals'.

[73] Credited as Civilian Adviser in **23**, 'In the Shadow of Two Gunmen' Part 1. Appears uncredited in **43**, '18th and Potomac'.

[74] Credited as Officer Mike in **26**, 'In This White House' and in **31**, 'Galileo'.

Daniel von Bargen (Ken[75], 23, 32) Andy Milder (Mark[76], 23, 39, 41, 43)
Peter White (Gage, 23–24) Ernie Lively (Loch, 23–24)
Jody Wood (Cameron, 23–24)
Randolph Brooks (Arthur Leeds[77], 23–24, 26, 29, 34, 39, 41)
Sean Moran (Dr Holbrook, 23–24) Jerry Sroka (Reporter, 23, 26)
Willie Gault (Agent Madsen, 23) Larry Carroll (TV Announcer[78], 24, 35)
Thomas Spencer (Military Aide[79], 23, 35–36, 43)
Victor McCay (Henry, 23, 43) Jane Lynch (Reporter[80], 23, 44)
Emily Procter (Ainsley Hayes, 26–29, 35–36, 40–41)
Ted McGinley (Mark Gottfried, 26, 35–36)
Sean Patrick Murphy (Floor Manager, 26, 35–36)
David Graf (Colonel Mark Chase, 29, 34)
Timothy Davis-Reed (Mark[81], 30, 32, 34, 37, 39)
Eric A Payne (Secret Service Agent[82], 32, 34, 43)
Gregalan Williams (Robbie Mosley, 32, 35–36, 43–44)
Corbin Bernsen (Henry Shallick, 33, 35) Patrick Falls (Billy[83], 33, 36)
Tony Plana (Mickey Troop, 35–36) Richard Riehle (Jack Sloane, 35–36)
Glenn Morshower (Mike Chysler, 35–36, 43)
Doris McMillon (Sandy[84], 35, 44) Emiko Parise (Carrie[85], 36, 42)
Shishir Kurup (Zach, 39, 41) Oliver Platt (Oliver Babish, 41–43)
Lewis Grenville (Reporter, 44)

---

[75] Assuming Daniel von Bargen plays the same character in his appearances – which seems likely – he undergoes a change of name between **23**, 'In the Shadow of Two Gunmen' Part 1, where he is credited as Jack, and **32**, 'Noël'. Perhaps it's something to do with national security.

[76] Credited as Senator's Aide in **23**, 'In the Shadow of Two Gunmen' Part 1, and as VP Assistant in **39**, 'The Stackhouse Filibuster'.

[77] Surname given in dialogue only.

[78] Credited as Newscaster #2 in **35**, 'Bartlet's Third State of the Union'.

[79] Credited as Aide #3 in **23**, 'In the Shadow of Two Gunmen' Part 1, and as Officer #1 in **43**, '18th and Potomac', an episode in which the character's name is given in dialogue as Jeff.

[80] Credited as Reporter in Briefing Room in **44**, 'Two Cathedrals'.

[81] Credited as Reporter #2 in **30**, 'Shibboleth', and as Reporter in **32**, 'Noël' and **34**, 'The Drop In'.

[82] Credited as Agent at Door in **43**, '18th and Potomac'.

[83] Credited as Steward in **33**, 'The Leadership Breakfast'.

[84] Credited as Newscaster in **35**, 'Bartlet's Third State of the Union'.

[85] Credited as Abbey's Aide #1 in **42**, 'The Fall's Gonna Kill You'.

23
In the Shadow of Two Gunmen
Part 1

US Transmission Date: 4 October 2000
UK Transmission Date: 12 June 2001 (E4)

Writer: Aaron Sorkin
Director: Thomas Schlamme
Cast: Michael Bryan French (Hospital Liaison)
Pamela Gordon (Woman in Hank's Tavern)
Andy Umberger (Cal Mathias) Jim Ortlieb (Dr Keller)
Elijah Marhar (Agent Dixon) Al Twanmo (Agent Cho) Ming Lo (Dr Lee)
Rhonda Stubbins White (Dr Whitaker) Carol Kiernan (Doctor)
Dan Gunther (Doctor #1) Maria McCann (Nurse)
Trisha Simmons (Nurse Debbie) Ted Garcia (TV Reporter)
David Ursin (Bartender) Matt Gotleib (Military Aide)
Kat Sawyer-Young (Sam's Secretary) V Kim Bush (Volleyball Player)
Scott Parrot (Paramedic #1) Sunita Koshy (Paramedic #2)
Shawn Woodyard (Paramedic #3) Chad Knight (Paramedic #4)
Tanya Linette Smith (Paramedic #5) Kivi Rogers (Paramedic #6)
Garrison Hershberger (Jerry) Peter Birkenhead (Steven)
Jenny Buchanan (Questioner #1) Harris Laskaway (Questioner #2)

In the assassination attempt's chaotic wake, Josh fights for his life and drifts in and out of consciousness, recalling how Bartlet's team came together during his campaign. Elsewhere, CJ is hounded by the media for news and a military crisis looms in Iraq.

A View from the Hill: Josh mentions that social security represents a quarter of the federal budget. Hoynes's staff were working on the ethanol tax-credit issue (see **16**, '20 Hours in L.A.') in 1997. Hoynes is voting in the annual resolution to ship nuclear waste to Nevada.

American History X: Danny asks CJ about the 25th amendment ('Presidential Vacancy, Disability, and Inability') and who was in charge while the president was under anaesthesia. In such circumstances, the president should sign a letter giving the vice president power (the Constitution doesn't grant it unless the president dies). It gets more complicated, continues Nancy McNally, the National Security Advisor. Section 202 of the National Securities Act (1947) says the Secretary of Defense will be the 'principal assistant' to the president on all matters relating to national security.

Politics of Prophecy and War: When the vice president and Leo discuss the assassination attempt, Nancy mentions that the whereabouts of various cell leaders, 'including bin Laden', is unknown. Few watching probably understood the reference to Osama bin Laden but, within a year, after the attack on the World Trade Center, everybody in the Western hemisphere knew all about the leader of Al-Qa'edah. She also notes a build-up of Iraqi forces along the Tigress and Euphrates. Thirteen hours ago they shot down an F117 and the rescue mission invaded their airspace (see **22**, 'What Kind of Day Has it Been'). Leo suggests (and the vice president orders) that a message be given to Iraq, via the King of Jordan: 'Don't mess with us tonight.'

Politics of Honesty: During the campaign Bartlet was asked why, when he was in Congress, he voted against the New England Dairy Farming Compact. He admits that it hurt lots of his constituents, but that one in five children in America lives in poverty. He voted against the bill because he didn't want it to be hard for people to buy milk. Josh, sitting in the audience, realises that he has found 'the real thing'.

The Conspiracy Starts at Closing Time: Abbey tells Dr Lee that he is the fifteenth person in the world who knows about her husband's MS. The others include Leo, Hoynes and Fitzwallace. 'When all this is over, tell the press, don't tell the press. It's entirely up to you' (see **35**, 'Bartlet's Third State of the Union', **40**, '17 People').

References: Los Del Rio's 'Macarena', the Walt Disney Corporation, Epcot theme park, Associated Press, Logan Airport in Boston and the Montreal Canadians ice hockey team.

'You May Remember Me From Such Films and TV Series As . . .': Randolph Brooks was in *Rocket's Red Glare* and *Reservoir Dogs*. Michael Bryan French appeared in *How to Get Laid at the End of the World*, *I Still Know What You Did Last Summer* and *The Drew Carey Show*. Ted Garcia was in *Ping!* The former Chicago Bears superstar Willie Gault has been in *Cottonmouth*, *In the Heat of the Night* and *Millennium Man*. Pamela Gordon was in *Frasier*, *My Favourite Martian*, *Weird Science* and *The Twilight Zone*. Matt Gotleib appeared in *Like Father, Like Santa*. Dan Gunther's movies include *Galaxy Quest* and *Slice & Dice*. Gary Hershberger was Snake Nelson in *Twin Peaks* and appeared in *Sneakers*. Carol Kiernan was in *Catfish in Black Bean Sauce* and *Grounded for Life*. Harris Laskaway appeared in *The Glimmer Man*. Trisha Simmons was Elaine in *Quick*. Sean Moran was one of the dancers in *Grease*. Robyn Pedretti appeared in *Border to Border*. Kat Sawyer-Young was in *Voyeur*. Jim Ortlieb played Nasedo in *Roswell* and also appeared in *Magnolia* and *Flatliners*. Ming Lo was in *Doctor Dolittle*. Andy Milder's movies include *Armageddon* and *Apollo 13*. Maria McCann was in *Zapped Again!* Ernie Lively appeared in *The Thirteenth Floor*, *Passenger 57* and *Scarecrow and Mrs King*. He also directed *Sandman*. Jane Lynch was in *What Planet Are You From?* and *The Fugitive*. David Ursin appeared in *Ready to Rumble* and *Die Hard*. Rhonda Stubbins White was in *Sunset Park*. Kivi Rogers's movies include *Romy and Michele's High School Reunion*.

Anna Deavere Smith was Robin McCall in *The American President* and appeared in *Philadelphia*. She's also a playwright, her work including *Twilight: Los Angeles*. Tanya Linette Smith was Lourdes in *Four Corners*. Jerry Sroka was in *Godspell* and *Nocturna*. Peter White's CV includes *Armageddon*, *Flubber*, *Dallas* and *The Colbys*. Jody Wood was in *Rules of Engagement*, *L.A. Confidential* and *The Rat Pack*. Shawn Woodyard appeared in *My Fellow Americans*. Daniel von Bargen's movies include *Silence of the Lambs*, *Crimson Tide*, *G.I. Jane* and *The Faculty*.

Behind the Camera: Two former White House staffers, Marlin Fitzwater and Peggy Noonan, joined the advisory team. Noonan was an assistant to President Reagan and chief speechwriter to (then Vice President) Bush, being behind his infamous 'read my lips' speech, before writing *What I Saw at the Revolution* and *The Case Against Hillary Clinton*. Fitzwater is the only press secretary appointed by two presidents. An accomplished lecturer and humorist, he provided political commentary during the 1996 election. His book *Call the Briefing!* is a memoire of his ten years in the White House.

Logic, Let Me Introduce You to This Window: The president's Secret Service code name was 'Eagle' in **2**, ' "Post Hoc, Ergo Propter Hoc" ', and 'Liberty' in **12**, 'He Shall, from Time to Time . . .' The service changes its codes periodically to prevent security breaches (mentioned, in connection with CJ's codename, in **10**, 'In Excelsis Deo'). But, in this episode, **32**, 'Noël', and **37**, 'Ellie', they're using 'Eagle' again. They would not revert to an old code name. Josh uses a Verizon payphone in NYC during a flashback set in 1997, before such phones existed. Outside Senator Hoynes's office there's a Tennessee flag, but he's from Texas (see **8**, 'Enemies'). Josh was by the iron railings (and seemingly facing away from the shooting), so how does he end up where he does, shot in the chest? Where's Mandy gone? She simply vanishes and is never mentioned again.

Cruelty To Animals: Josh's father used to shout at the squirrels because they ate seeds out of his bird feeder.

Quote/Unquote: Nurse: 'Do you have any medical conditions?' Bartlet: 'Well, I've been shot.'

Josh, on Hoynes's campaign: 'I don't know what we're for, I don't know what we're against. Except we seem to be for winning and against somebody else winning.'

Josh: 'Democrats aren't gonna nominate another liberal academic former governor from New England. We're not *that* dumb.' Leo: 'I think we're *exactly* that dumb!'

Leo, on why Jed must run: 'Because I'm tired of it year after year, having to choose between the lesser of "who cares"? Of trying to get myself excited about a candidate who can speak in complete sentences. They say a good man can't get elected president. I don't believe that.'

Notes: 'Somebody had to get them into that office. This was not a lonely guy who lived with his cats.' A fantastic reformatting, using multiple flashbacks to tell the administration's backstory. Best bits: Jed kissing Leo as he goes into surgery; Josh and Sam discussing 'the real thing'; Toby comforting Ginger.

The president's personal physician is Admiral Jarvis. His driver is named Coop. Someone called Shanahan was in the car with Leo (see **32**, 'Noël'). Vice President Hoynes attended the Southern Methodist University. One of his roommates was Drew Harper, a member of the 1972 Olympic volleyball team. Locations include the presidential motorcade speeding across the George Washington bridge. One of the stock shots of New York includes a brief glimpse of the World Trade Center towers.

Critique: 'This magnificent, literate drama pitches us straight into the chaotic aftermath of the assassination bid,' said *Radio Times*. 'The pace never flags and neither does the sharpness of the script nor the stunning direction as we are hurtled into the hunt for the would-be assassins. This is *brilliant* television – tense, involving and sometimes funny, even during the dark times. If there are occasional gung-ho moments, these are forgivable, mainly because the real magic of *The West Wing* is its ability to make even cynics care for the characters.'

Cast and Crew Comments: Sorkin told the *Toronto Star* that he'd watch the season premiere at home 'with everyone from the show, about 150 people. We're going to have huge flat-screen TVs in the backyard with hot-dogs and fried-chicken,' he said. 'You're going to know [who got shot] 90 seconds into the show. It'll be nice to actually get past that.'

Rob Lowe told the *Chicago Sun-Times* that the opener was 'very emotional. It's the best thing Aaron's ever written.'

The Real World: With the 2000 presidential election looming, Sorkin gave the *Toronto Star* his opinion of George W Bush: 'He's clearly not a very bright guy. I think the Republicans thought we weren't going to notice. If you run for president, at least you should be able to speak in complete sentences.'

Did You Know?: 'I was summoned to the office of Sandy Berger,' Sorkin told *Sky*, 'who chewed me out for not having a National Security Advisor. So I open next season with Anna Deavere Smith as National Security Advisor.'

24
In the Shadow of Two Gunmen
Part 2

US Transmission Date: 4 October 2000
UK Transmission Date: 19 June 2001 (E4)

Writer: Aaron Sorkin
Director: Thomas Schlamme
Cast: Grace Zabriskie (Isobel) Allen Garfield (Roger Becker)
Garret Wright (Skinhead) Richard Saxton (Boston Anchor)
Warner Saunders (Chicago Anchor) Laurie Hendler (Lawyer)
Harris Mann (Lawyer #2) Andy Brewster (Isobel's Assistant)
Chad McKnight[86] (Aide #5)

As the president recovers from his wounds, attention focuses on Josh's fight for life and the reasons behind the attack. CJ remembers who saved her life.

Politics of Integrity: Weeks after Bartlet was sworn in, Toby sent the Secret Service a memo saying the president wanted to enter and exit buildings in the open and that he wouldn't use a canopy. Toby doesn't want the service blamed for the shooting and wants to make this public. It

---

[86] The same actor appeared in **3**, 'A Proportional Response', as Staffer #2. It has not been possible to verify whether this is the character depicted here.

was an act of madmen, Ron Butterfield tells him. They got the president and Zoey in the car and at 150 yards, the shooters were down 9.2 seconds after the first shot. Ron says he won't let anyone not allow him to protect the president. 'You tell us you don't like something, we figure out something else. Anyway, the Secret Service doesn't comment on procedure.'

Gun Law: One of the shooters, a member of West Virginia White Pride, was using a 9mm Beretta, the other a 357 Desert Eagle. The Secret Service carry 357 Sig-Hauers. The agents on the roof used .726-calibre rifles referred to as JAR ('Just Another Rifle') made specifically for the service. There were 36 gun homicides last night, CJ tells the press corps. If anyone thinks those crimes could've been prevented if the victims themselves had been armed, she reminds them that the president was shot while surrounded by the best-trained armed guards in the world. The third victim (after the president and Josh) was Stephanie Abbott, a bystander who was shot in the thigh.

References: The oil company Chevron, *The Today Show*, the Golden Globes, *Premiere* magazine, New Coke, John Huston's *The Maltese Falcon*, *High Noon*, Emily's List. Sam doesn't want his heroic gesture to become like *I Dream of Jeannie* (with CJ following him 'with coconut oil and hot towels'). People drove past Exxon stations after the *Valdez* disaster, Sam notes, and also mentions other tanker disasters such as the *Amoco Cadiz* (which sank in the English Channel) and the *Braer* (a Liberian tanker that went down off the Shetland Islands). The Bartlet campaign HQ in Manchester contained Coke, Minute Maid and M&M machines. 'Happy Days Are Here Again' is played at the Bartlet victory rally (see **4**, 'Five Votes Down').

'You May Remember Me From Such Films and TV Series As . . .': Larry Carroll appeared in *Beverly Hills Cop II* and *Rocky*. Allen Garfield's movies include *The Ninth Gate*, *Bananas*, *The Candidate*, *Diabolique*, *Obsession* and *Dick Tracy*. Laurie Hendler was the eponymous *Little Lulu* and appeared in *High School USA*. Harris Mann was in *The Glass House*. Richard Saxton appeared in *Wag the Dog* and *Girls in Prison*. Grace Zabriskie played Sarah Palmer in *Twin Peaks*. She was also in *Gone in 60 Seconds*, *Even Cowgirls Get the Blues*, *Fried Green Tomatoes*, *My Own Private Idaho* and *The Executioner's Song*.

Sex and Drugs and MOR: When Bartlet wins the Illinois primary somebody puts on Kool and the Gang's 'Celebration'. Joss demands this be replaced by 'some Doobie Brothers'.

Cigarettes and Alcohol: The skinhead stubs out his cigarette in his fried egg.

Logic, Let Me Introduce You to This Window: In **16**, '20 Hours in L.A.', a producer tried to headhunt CJ to develop movies. She declared an ignorance of the industry, even saying she didn't know what a 'three-picture deal' is (it doesn't take much to work out). Yet prior to working on the Bartlet campaign, she was employed in movie public relations. She didn't enjoy it and asked to work on something else, but she still should've picked up a few terms. Josh and Sam persuade Bartlet to leave New Hampshire to campaign in South Carolina. Democrats usually go to Delaware next and there are several other primaries (including New York) before the Carolina caucuses. In one of the 1997 scenes, a June 2000 *Entertainment Weekly* (featuring Samuel L Jackson) can be seen. Why was Toby driving a car with a California licence when he visited CJ in 1997? Shouldn't it have been somewhere east coast? Leo was a good friend of Josh's father but he doesn't seem to be attending his funeral. To be fair he is trying to mastermind Bartlet's nomination in the forthcoming California primaries, so he probably has a justifiable excuse.

Cruelty To Animals: Somewhere in the middle of not a lot is the Dixie Pig Bar-B-Q diner.

Quote/Unquote: Becker: 'I dropped to ninth. Do you know how many people were ahead of me?' CJ: 'Eight?'

CJ, asked to join the campaign: 'How much does it pay?'
Toby: 'How much were you making before?' CJ: 'Five
hundred and fifty thousand dollars a year.' Toby: 'This
pays six hundred dollars a week.' CJ: 'So, this would be
less?'

Leo, when Margaret admits she can forge Bartlet's
signature: 'On a document removing him from power and
handing it to someone else?' Margaret: 'You think the
White House Counsel would say that was a bad idea?' Leo:
'I think the White House Counsel would say it was a *coup
d'état!*'

Josh: 'This is a campaign for the presidency. This can't be
a place where people come to find their confidence and start
over.' Donna: 'Why not? Why can't it be those things?'

Notes: 'Your husband's a real son-of-a-bitch, Mrs Bartlet.'
Even better than the previous episode, this effectively
completes our view of how all of the characters come
together. (Some of them, Donna for instance, arrive
exactly as expected. Others, such as Sam and CJ, have
more convoluted origins.) Best bits: CJ's sacking and
subsequent falling into the pool with Toby looking on
smirking; Bartlet's speech at the end – if you wouldn't vote
for him after that, you're a lost cause.

The third candidate for the Democrat nomination
besides Bartlet and Hoynes was Senator Wiley of Washington State. Locations: the sweeping shot of Los Angeles
includes most of the obvious landmarks (the Hollywood
Sign, Griffith Observatory etc.).

Cast and Crew Comments: *Daily Variety* reported during
the summer that this episode was scheduled to feature
scenes filmed at the Democratic National Congress in the
Staples Center. Unfortunately, according to Llewellyn
Wells, 'We weren't able to overcome logistical problems.'

Did You Know?: Delta Airlines generally doesn't approve
of product placement. This was an exception, allowing
producers to shoot in one of their terminals. 'It's a hit
show, obviously that helps,' said a spokesman.

25
The Midterms

US Transmission Date: 18 October 2000
UK Transmission Date: 26 June 2001 (E4)

Writer: Aaron Sorkin
Director: Alex Graves
Cast: Claire Yarlett (Jenna Jacobs) Rebecca Creskoff (Sarah Jordan)
Jamie Denton (Tom Jordan) Alfonso Freeman (Andrew Mackintosh)
Myles Killpatrick (Jeffery Mackintosh) Franc Ross (Sonny Saunders)
Jesse Corti (Dave Stewart) Alan McRae (Gary With A 'G')

As Josh recovers, the administration prepares for the
midterms. Toby wants to use the president's popularity for
a terrorism initiative. Bartlet seems obsessed with thwart-
ing an old political foe. Sam enlists a law-school classmate
to run for Congress.

Petty Politics: The president's former rival Elliot Roush is
seeking election to a board of education in the district in
Manchester where Bartlet's daughters attended school.
People like Roush aren't taken seriously because they don't
get anywhere nationally, Bartlet says, but they don't have
to. Bit by bit, they're elected to boards of education and
city councils where all the important governing happens.

American History X: The Pendleton Act (1883) prohibits
campaign donations being solicited on government property. Bartlet, therefore, makes campaign calls from the
residence. Zoey asks if this isn't also government property.
Leo confirms it is but Bartlet does so anyway because, as
Leo says, he's 'a demented man'.

The Encyclopedic Mind of Josiah Bartlet PhD: He asks if
his staff knows what 'acalculia' means. Sam replies it's the
inability to form arithmetic functions, then apologises,
realising Bartlet wanted to answer his own question.

Denial, Thy Name is Toby: He asks the president for
a leave-of-absence. Bartlet refuses. 'Why does it feel
like this? I've seen shootings before,' Toby asks. It

wasn't a shooting, Bartlet notes, it was a lynching. Bartlet has satellite photographs of the West Virginia White Pride HQ, a diner outside Blacksberg. Each night he picks up the phone prepared to order a raid. Then he hangs up because he knows it'll be better tomorrow.

The Conspiracy Starts at Closing Time: Toby wants to go after hate groups. His plan to avoid the appearance of randomly persecuting such groups in violation of civil liberties is that, because more than one person was involved, there was a conspiracy. This gives the FBI grounds to investigate the activities of all extremist organisations. This isn't an uncommon way to get around the Bill of Rights, Sam replies, and it's in blatant violation of their right to free association, he adds, noting that such laws were passed in the south during the Civil Rights movement to root out members of, for instance, the NAACP.

The Gospel According to Bartlet: The Bible says homosexuality is an abomination, Jenna Jacobs tells the president. Bartlet agrees (Leviticus 18). He then says he's interested in selling Zoey into slavery (Exodus 21). What would be a good price for her? Leo, he continues, works on the Sabbath (Exodus 35). Should he be put to death? Touching the skin of a dead pig makes one unclean (Leviticus 11). If they promise to wear gloves, can the Washington Redskins still play football? Does the whole town have to stone the president's brother for planting different crops side by side or burn his mother for wearing garments made from two different threads?

References: *Batman* ('Holy interruptus!'), CNN, *USA Today*, the Spanish Inquisition, the TV journalist Barbara Walters, the radio shock jock Howard Stern, 1970s rockers Fleetwood Mac, the MSNBC anchorman Don Imas, West Point military academy, Cleveland Cavaliers basketball team, Animal Crackers biscuits, the Consumer Price Index and the *New York Times*. Bartlet is watching rugby on TV.

You May Remember Me From Such Films and TV Series As . . .': Rebecca Creskoff was Gina in *Finding North*.

Claire Yarlett played Bliss Colby in *Dynasty*. Jamie Denton appeared in *Face/Off*, *That Old Feeling* and *The Pretender*. Alfonso Freeman was Morgan Freeman's assistant on *The Shawshank Redemption* and was in *Mad Song* and *Se7en*. Franc Ross was in *The 119*. Jess Corti's movies include *Last Mistake* and *High Stakes*. Alan McRae appeared in *3 Ninjas*, *Once Bitten* and *Shoot*.

Oh, Donna!: She thinks 'spatula' should be a Yiddish word.

Sex and Drugs and Rock'n'Roll: When Charlie tells Leo that he and Zoey are going out, Leo innocently asks if he's taking protection.

Chocolate and Alcohol: Bartlet discovers the wonders of egg cream (chocolate syrup, milk and seltzer). He appears to be drinking whisky when talking to CJ. She drinks red wine at the reception and also joins Toby, Donna, Sam and Josh in a beer at the end.

Logic, Let Me Introduce You to This Window: Tom Jordan is said to prefer all-white juries, using pre-emptive challenges to get them. These are actually called pre-emptory challenges and it would be virtually impossible for a prosecutor to use them consistently to remove jurors because of race (no judge would overlook such blatant racism). Tom attended Oberlin College and belonged to an all-white fraternity. Oberlin, however, has a ban on fraternities.

Josh claims that theoretical physicists at Caltech and Fermi National Accelerator Laboratory announced that string theory had produced a 'theory of everything'. Many physicists believe that superstring theory *has* succeeded in unifying all forces, including gravity (let's remember, however, that these are the same people who reckon the theory of relativity isn't consistent with quantum mechanics). There was nothing to suggest in **22**, 'What Kind of Day Has it Been', that those events didn't take place contemporaneously with the broadcast date (late May). However, this episode starts a week after the shooting, in August.

Quote/Unquote: Josh: 'It's called the theory of everything.'
CJ: 'Is it comprehensive?'

Sam, on the president's 81 per cent approval: 'When asked, "Whose approach on important national problems do you think is best, President Bartlet or the Republican leaders?" Bartlet gets sixty-one per cent.' Bartlet: 'Well, nineteen per cent of the country has clearly made up their minds about me; twenty per cent just feel sorry for me.'

Bartlet: 'While you may be mistaking this for your monthly meeting of the Ignorant Tightass Club, in this building, when the president stands, *nobody* sits.'

Andrew tells Charlie, 'If they're shooting at you, you're doing something right.'

Notes: 'Tell me democracy doesn't have a sense of humour. We sit here, we drink this beer on the stoop in violation of about forty-seven city ordinances. It's election night. What do you say about a government that goes out of its way to protect even citizens that try to destroy it? God bless America.' One of the best episodes, 'The Midterms' mixes political shenanigans but balances it with heartfelt concerns about freedom and democracy in an America that features people like those who tried to shoot Charlie, or who listen to (and agree with) bigots like Ms Jacobs. The ending, much misunderstood by overseas reviewers (see **Critique**), is beautiful. It might not be a perfect world, it says, but it's the one we've got. Best bits: Josh's frustration as CJ makes a mistake to the press; all of the politics-of-compromise stuff ('we can't afford all the things we want'); and CJ telling Bartlet that sometimes in a democracy the other guy wins.

Zoey speaks fluent Italian and always clears the table when it is her turn.

Critique: 'These people,' wrote David Binaculli of the *New York Daily News*, 'have developed language and imagery that can work in the post-Watergate, post-Monica era. They talk about politics in a sincere way.' Robert Thompson, director of the Center for the Study of Popular TV at Syracuse University, praised the episode, which ends with the staff saluting each other and the country. 'That was moving,' Thompson says. 'What they've captured is a language in which we can talk about our country, our nationhood, our responsibilities. We can, in fact, take it seriously again.' This comes in marked contrast to Jane Rackman in *Radio Times*, who found time to praise Bartlet's angry monologue to Dr Jacobs but criticise 'the overly-patriotic, slightly-nauseating ending'.

Cast and Crew Comments: 'You want to hear about lines being blurred?' Sorkin told *Zap2it.com*. 'Our office got a call from a woman wanting to know Josh Lyman's email to send him a get-well card. What's amazing is she had to call Warner Bros to get our number. So, there's obviously some acknowledgment that it's a TV show.'

Did You Know?: 'A friend forwarded me a copy of an anonymous Internet post in which the author sarcastically agrees with Dr Laura [Schlessinger, controversial talk-radio host] that homosexuality is an abomination,' Sorkin told Eric Mink. The author then pointed out several other Old Testament laws with extreme punishments. But Sorkin was unsure whether to use this material. 'If you're a writer the only thing worse than not getting credit for something you did is getting credit for something you didn't do. I wanted to make sure nobody thought I was trying to pull a fast one. Being called a plagiarist is like being called a sex offender. Even if it's not true, once the stench is out, it's not easy to get rid of.' Staff were assigned to identify the author. Efforts included infiltrating anti-Schlessinger chatrooms and contacting gay-oriented publications. 'We came up empty,' Sorkin notes, 'except that people said they'd seen several different versions of the same material.'

He has yet to hear from Schlessinger herself. 'I don't imagine I'll be getting a Christmas card from her,' he told *Entertainment Weekly*. 'To me, she is a staggeringly mean and ignorant person.'

26
In This White House

US Transmission Date: 25 October 2000
UK Transmission Date: 3 July 2001 (E4)

Teleplay: Aaron Sorkin
Story: Peter Parnell, Allison Abner
Director: Ken Olin
Cast: Zakes Mokae (President Nimbala)
Michael Chinyamurindi (President Nimbala's Interpreter)
Michael Cavanaugh (Pharmaceutical Company Executive)
Len Cariou (Alan Damson) Sam Jaeger (Bill Kelley)
Brigid Brannagh (Harriet) Tom Gallop (Bruce) Tracy McCubbin (Lily)
Lorenzo Callender (George)

A Republican lawyer, Ainsley Hayes, makes mincemeat of Sam during a TV debate. Bartlet gets Leo to offer her a job. The president of an AIDS-ravaged African country visits the White House for a confrontation with drug-company executives.

A View from the Hill: The House is voting on the president's education bill.

Politics of Compromise: Toby and Josh broker a deal for US drug companies to lower their prices but require President Nimbala to commit his military, customs and health ministry to stop the influx of black-market HIV drugs from Korea and Pakistan. Nimbala says 35 per cent of Kuhndu's adult population is infected. Josh explains that, if they don't honour patent regulations, Kuhndu may face trade sanctions. Toby notes that Congress could forgive the debt on loans to Kuhndu and the Import–Export Bank can offer a billion dollars to finance the purchase of American AIDS medication. Nimbala argues that it's a terrible thing to beg for your life.

A Little Learning is a Dangerous Thing: Sam says the town of Kirkwood is in Oregon. As Ainsley points out, it's actually in California. Later, he asks where the 1992 World Copyright Conference was held. Toby replies Geneva and

CJ adds, 'There's a bunch of women out there. Why don't you ask them whether [it's] in Switzerland or Oregon?'

The Encyclopedic Mind of Josiah Bartlet PhD: He tells Leo about dwarf wheat. 'Was it a hybrid?' Leo asks. 'What am I, Farmer Bob?' replies Bartlet.

Television, the Drug of the Nation: Mark tells Ainsley that Sam has been on *Capital Beat* several dozen times and usually wipes the floor with his opponent.

Denial, Thy Name is CJ: A cub reporter, Bill Kelley, asks CJ if she's heard about Bonamo Energy selling drilling equipment to Iraq, in violation of sanctions. CJ absent-mindedly replies that Grand Jury investigations are secret. Realising she's said too much, but unable to confide in anyone, CJ suffers insomnia. Ainsley discovers her secret and tells CJ that she could be prosecuted under Rule 6(e) of Federal Criminal Procedures and get eighteen months. Then says she's kidding: 'Attorneys and jurors are under a gag order. Witnesses are free to say whatever they want.'

References: The Nobel prize-winning author and agronomist Norman Borlang, Puccini (see **2**, ' "Post Hoc Ergo Propter Hoc" '), the *Cleveland Courier*, *Geraldo*, Paul Ehrlich, author of *The Population Bomb* (1968), the Gap, Lincoln High School in Dayton and Crenshaw High in South Central LA.

'You May Remember Me From Such Films and TV Series As . . .': Emily Procter played Tiffany Drawl in *Forever Fabulous* and appeared in *Kingdom Come* and *The Big Tease*. Brigid Brannagh was Claire in *Hyperion Bay* and Virginia in *Angel*. Sean Patrick Murphy appeared in *Jack Frost 2: Revenge of the Mutant Killer Snowman*. Tom Gallop played Frank in *Blossom* and Rob in *Will & Grace*. Lorenzo Callender was in *Planet of the Apes*. Ted McGinley was Roger Phillips in *Happy Days*, Jefferson in *Married . . . With Children* and Stan Cable in *Revenge of the Nerds* and appeared in *Cahoots*. Zakes Mokae was in *Waterworld*, *A Rage in Harlem* and *Cry Freedom*. Michael

Cavanaugh appeared in *When Billie Beat Bobby*, *The Enforcer* and *Five Fathom Full*. Michael Chinyamurindi played Claude in *Congo*. Len Cariou was Michael Hagarty in *Murder She Wrote*. His movies include *Executive Decision*.

Oh, Donna!: She and Josh discuss the average wage in Africa.

Sex and Drugs and Rock'n'Roll: Toby tells CJ that the same drug that costs $10 in Norway, where nobody needs it, costs $90 in Burundi, where everyone does. HIV drugs are a triple cocktail. Ten pills need to be taken every day at precise times: two protease inhibitors every eight hours, two combination RTI pills every twelve hours.

Logic, Let Me Introduce You to This Window: Ainsley knows a call is from the White House by the number 456-1414 appearing on caller ID. Though this *is* the real White House number, internal phones don't show up on caller ID. There isn't a Republic of Equatorial Kuhndu, nor a Sahelise Republic (the Sahel is a region of Western and Central Africa between the Sahara and the areas to the south). President Nimbala speaks Setswana, a language of South Africa and Botswana. When Nimbala says drug companies make billions selling Fluconazole, Toby adds, 'There's more money in giving a white guy an erection than curing a black guy of AIDS.' Fluconazole is a drug that treats fungal infections of the vagina. Bartlet has photos of Abbey and Zoey on his desk (previously unseen) but, seemingly, none of his other daughters.

Quote/Unquote: Josh rushing into Toby's office: 'Come quick: Sam's getting his ass kicked by a girl!' Toby: 'Ginger, get the popcorn . . .'

Charlie, when Bartlet asks if he should hire a Republican: 'Absolutely, Mr President. I'm told that theirs is the party of inclusion!'

Leo: 'You have an interesting conversational style.' Ainsley: 'It's a nervous condition.' Leo: 'I used to have a nervous condition.' Ainsley: 'How did yours manifest itself?' Leo: 'I drank Scotch.'

Notes: 'Say they like high taxes and spending your money. Say they want to take your guns and open your borders. But don't call them worthless. Their intent is good. They are righteous and they are patriots. And I'm their lawyer.' Another good episode, but, in its striving for political balance via the introduction of Ainsley (delightfully played with wide-eyed innocence by Emily Procter), some of the Democrat–Republican divisions are reduced in impact (for instance, Ainsley and Sam's argument over gun control descends into a childish shouting match). But the subplot about Nimbala (a dignified performance by Zakes Mokae) is the real meat. Best bit: Margaret eavesdropping on Leo's meeting with Ainsley.

Senator Stackhouse is mentioned again (see **20**, 'Mandatory Minimums', **39**, 'The Stackhouse Filibuster'). Toby considers Nimbala a great soldier: he has led his people for 28 years but is cursed by geography. 'If the ground won't grow anything, you don't have an economy.' Then there is a coup in his country. The AFRC takes the capital and, though the State Department will offer asylum, Nimbala says he must go home, and tells Bartlet he should trade Nimbala for the safe return of American Embassy staff. 'They'll shoot you the moment you step off the plane,' Bartlet argues, telling Nimbala that his brother and his two sons are already dead and his wife is being hidden in Kenya. Bartlet is right: Nimbala is executed at the airport. Admiral Fitzwallace and Nancy McNally are mentioned.

Critique: For South Africans concerned about international perceptions of their president and his views on AIDS, this episode was a humiliation. Bartlet says, 'You've got guys like Mbeki who say that AIDS isn't linked to HIV, it's linked to poverty.' It *is* linked to poverty, argues Leo, to which Bartlet replies, 'Would you like me to show you a list of dead millionaires?' 'It's an embarrassment,' said Mark Heywood, head of the AIDS Law Project in Johannesburg. 'This kind of thing can damage a country. It shows our president has become a subject of international ridicule.'

Cast and Crew Comments: 'It's a powerful episode,' Tom Schlamme told Terence Smith. 'It deals with the pharmaceutical companies, with AIDS as a form of genocide in Africa. The context is of the relationship between the president and a leader in an African nation. That's the drama that we're interested in.'

Did You Know?: 'I write a script about five weeks before it's on television,' Sorkin told Eric Deggans. 'Sometimes an event will happen almost exactly like what we did and it'll look like we stole it.' He cites both the India–Pakistan conflict, which broke days before **11**, 'Lord John Marbury', and this episode, which was repeated the day that the Congo's president was executed.

Ainsley's Background: A Republican political analyst, Ainsley is a lawyer who clerked for Supreme Justice Dreifort and became a media pundit by writing articles and, more recently, appearing on *Capital Beat*. Her grandfather was chairman of the North Carolina Republican Party. She doesn't have any pets. She's wanted to work in the White House since she was two (**26**, 'In This White House'). Ainsley attended Smith College (**40**, '17 People') and Harvard Law School (**28**, 'The Lame Duck Congress'). She played trombone in high school and likes to drink Fresca (**29**, 'The Portland Trip'), though alcohol makes her sick (**26**, 'In This White House') or a giggly party girl (**35**, 'Bartlet's Third State of the Union'). Her father is proud of her (**36**, 'The War at Home'). Her office in the White House is Room 442, the Steam Pipe Trunk Distribution Venue (**27**, 'And it's Surely to Their Credit'). She is an Episcopalian (**40**, '17 People'). She likes Chinese food (or, in fact, pretty much *any* food).

27
And it's Surely to Their Credit

US Transmission Date: 1 November 2000
UK Transmission Date: 10 July 2001 (E4)

Writer: Aaron Sorkin
Story: Kevin Falls, Laura Glasser
Director: Christopher Misiano
Cast: John Larroquette (Lionel Tribbey)
Daniel Roebuck (Lieutenant Buckley) Tom Bower (General Barrie)
Paul Perri (Steve Joyce) Steven Flynn (Mark Brookline)
Karen Lockhart (OEOB Staffer) Jack Shearer (Engineer)

Ainsley meets her new boss, Lionel Tribbey, and receives an assignment – sorting out the errors of two staffers who presented inaccurate testimony. Sam suggests Josh sue the hate group whose members shot him. CJ takes on a soon-to-be-retired general.

A View from the Hill: Steve Joyce and Mark Brookline, two arrogant staffers, testified to Governmental Affairs that the White House couldn't produce the Rockland memo. This isn't true and Congress could hold the White House in contempt. Ainsley sorts out the problems, but earns only spite from the pair. Sam is horrified and, with Tribbey's help, fires them.

American History X: General Barrie says he has ordered many men on assignment, to Hue City, Danang, Grenada, Haiti and Iraqi-occupied Kuwait. CJ responds that the Cold War ended ten years ago, and that America doesn't need to spend so much defending itself against a country that can't bake bread. Despite CJ's evidence that Barrie gained some of his decorations falsely, Bartlet tells her to allow him to air his grievances. He was the first in and the last out of a war Bartlet wanted no part of (Vietnam) and has earned his right to speak.

A Little Learning is a Dangerous Thing: The president once took eleven attempts to get his weekly radio address right (they're recorded on Friday for Sunday broadcast). Donna notes that he 'went on elocution safari during the word "protuberance".'

The Proceedings Start at Closing Time: The Southern Poverty Law Center wants Josh to sue the Knights of the Ku Klux Klan for $100 million. He could subpoena membership rolls, minutes of meetings, weapons inventory, computer downloads, depose everyone who's ever been to a meeting. Sam cites several cases in which hate groups were successfully sued. Josh declines, although he is keen to sue his medical insurance company.

References: The title alludes to 'He is an Englishman' from the opera *HMS Pinafore*. Other Gilbert and Sullivan works mentioned include *The Pirates of Penzance* and *Iolanthe* (see **11**, 'Lord John Marbury'). Also, the movie magnate Jack Warner (1892–1978), *Batman* ('the Bat Cave'), *Meet the Press*, ABC's *Sunday with Sam and Cokie* and *Late Edition*, Captain Queeg (as played by Humphrey Bogart in *The Caine Mutiny*), *This is Spinal Tap* (Tribbey's cricket-bat shenanigans), *Tonight* and its original host Johnny Carson, William Pierce, the extreme right-wing author of *Hunter*, MSNBC anchor Tim Russert and the singer Mel Tormé (1925–99). The pioneering journalist Nellie Bly (1865–1922), who, in 1890, circumnavigated the world in 72 days, besting, by more than one week, *Around the World in 80 Days* by Jules Verne (1828–1905). Verne's other great novel, *Twenty Thousand Leagues Under the Sea*, is mentioned. The first woman doctor, Elizabeth Blackwell (1821–1910); Belva Lockwood (1830–1917), the first woman to practise law; Ellen Swallow Richards (1842–1911), a pioneering chemist; and the American astronomer Maria Mitchell (1818–89). When Ainsley asks Tribbey for advice, he replies 'not speaking in iambic pentameter'.

'You May Remember Me From Such Films and TV Series As . . .': Steven Flynn was in *Scar City*. John Larroquette played Maltz in *Star Trek III: The Search for Spock* and appeared in *The 10th Kingdom*, *Night Court*, *Cat People* and *JFK*. Tom Bower was Everett Hubble in *Roswell* and Dr Willard in *The Waltons*. His movies include *Pollock*, *Nixon*, *Raising Cain* and *Die Hard 2*. Paul Perri was in *Live Nude Girls* and *Manhunter*. Daniel Roebuck was in *Final Destination*, *U.S. Marshals*, *The Fugitive* and *Matlock*. Jack Shearer appeared in *Star Trek: First Contact*, *The*

Negotiator and *The Usual Suspects*. Karen Lockhart was a stand-in on *Meet Joe Black*.

Behind the Camera: Kevin Falls wrote *Summer Catch* and *Scrubs*.

Oh, Donna!: She's looking after a group of visitors watching the president's radio broadcast. She tries a joke ('Form a horseshoe – not an *actual* horseshoe: that takes special training as a blacksmith') and is upset when it doesn't get a laugh, though the president is less surprised. It seems to be her birthday this Thursday, judging by a note on Josh's blackboard.

Sex and Drugs and Rock'n'Roll: Bartlet and Abbey frustratingly try to find time to have sex. It's been fourteen weeks and Jed is desperate. 'The writers said, "Here's an idea you're gonna hate. But sleep on it," ' says Sorkin. 'They were right.' So, did he think it wise to mix the presidency with sex, given previous real-life situations. 'I believe people will see Martin Sheen trying to have sex with Stockard Channing and not say, "Why doesn't he just grab an intern in the hallway?" '

Cigarettes and Alcohol: Jed prepares Scotch on the rocks for himself and Abbey.

Logic, Let Me Introduce You to This Window: The retiring army chief is a three-star general, whereas such a position is always held by a four-star general. His aide would not be a lieutenant (he should be a major at least). There's no Distinguished Combat Service Medal, which, anyway, Barrie is said to have won while on duty on the USS *Brooke*. What was a soldier doing in the navy? Why is Josh dealing with an insurance company? The first question on all US medical insurance forms asks if the injury was job related. If his injury wasn't job related, what is? Josh should be entitled to benefits under the Federal Employees Compensation Act. For the second episode running, a character suggests that a woman being ambitious is a bad thing, which seems somewhat sexist. Why would the Queen give Tribbey a cricket bat?

Quote/Unquote: Bartlet: 'Lionel Tribbey is a brilliant lawyer whom we cannot live without. Or there would be very little reason not to put him in prison.'

Abbey, on having sex: 'We'll find a free hour.' Bartlet: 'I don't think it's gonna take more than a couple of minutes, but I like your confidence.'

Leo: 'Sam Seaborn had this innocent relationship with a girl. Bam! Here comes the enemy. I'm a recovering alcoholic. Radio, TV, magazines, cameras in front of my house, people shouting at my daughter at the ballgame, editorials, op-eds.' Ainsley: 'I wrote one of those op-ed pieces.' Leo: 'I know.'

Notes: 'Tomorrow is Saturday. I'll be here. You can call me and be rude by phone or you can stop by and do it in person. 'Cos I think if I have to endure another disappointment today from this place that I have worshipped, I am gonna lose it.' The main theme of 'duty' and the Gilbert and Sullivan metaphors are nicely worked, while the episode also includes a tasty rad-fem agenda. Best bits: Bartlet's euphemism for sex to a group of schoolchildren ('a special meeting . . . of the government'); Donna's awful blacksmith joke.

Lionel Tribbey is the White House Counsel. A brilliant attorney with a reputation for what Leo describes as 'full-throated defence of the president' (or what Ainsley more accurately calls 'yelling and screaming on TV'). He owns a cricket bat, which was given to him by Her Royal Majesty Elizabeth Windsor. He was about to take a vacation somewhere warm, with a beach and people bringing him drinks with little umbrellas in them. He believes that Justice Dreifort is intolerant of gays, lesbians, blacks, unions, women, poor people, and the first, fourth, fifth and ninth amendments. The president is too moderate for Tribbey's taste, Ainsley notes, on affirmative action, capital gains, public schools and free trade. Yet he left a lucrative practice in Chicago and a seven-figure income out of a sense of duty.

Cast and Crew Comments: 'Allison Abner often has the unenviable task of calling the Pentagon for their input a week after CJ's dressed down the chief of staff. I've never seen her blink,' Sorkin told *mightybigtv.com*.

Did You Know?: Sorkin asked Dee Dee Myers for ideas on how the White House staff might torture a new recruit. Myers suggested they put her in a horrible office, citing the example of David Gergen, a Reagan and Nixon consultant who joined the Clinton staff, and was put in the old White House barbershop.

28
The Lame Duck Congress

US Transmission Date: 8 November 2000
UK Transmission Date: 17 July 2001 (E4)

Writer: Aaron Sorkin
Story: Lawrence O'Donnell Jr
Director: Jeremy Kagan
Cast: Eugene Lazarev (Vasily Konanov) Mike Starr (Tony Marino)
David Kaufman (Bob Fowler) Richard Tanner (Joe Fox)
Tegan West (Peter) Brian Stepanek (Senator's Aide #2)
Wayne Wilderson (Senator's Aide #3) Sima Kostov (Russian Woman)
Amy Turner (Waitress)

Josh, Toby and Sam want the president to consider calling a lame-duck session of Congress to pass a test-ban treaty, and CJ leaks the news to Danny. A Ukrainian politician arrives, drunk, to see the president.

A View from the Hill: Senator-elect Morgan Mitchell of Pennsylvania plans to seek a seat on the Foreign Relations Committee and, once there, will block a vote on the test-ban treaty, despite 82 per cent of the population being in favour of it. Danny asks whether the president has considered ordering a lame-duck session so the current Senate can ratify the treaty. Other countries are looking to the US to ratify first, Toby says, and, the longer they wait to do so, the closer they get to having unstable countries such as Pakistan develop a nuclear threat. The White House and Congress are exempt from the workplace laws they pass.

American History X: Article 2, Section 3, of the Constitution ('extraordinary circumstances clause') gives the president special powers. He tells Toby they sometimes forget, in all the talk about democracy, that they actually live in a republic. People don't make the decisions: they *choose* the people who make the decisions.

Politics of Integrity: Tony Marino, whom the president describes as a great public servant, lost his seat in the Midterms to Mitchell, having been a vocal advocate of the test-ban treaty. But he refuses to vote for it in a hypothetical lame-duck session. He'll do whatever the White House wants in terms of spadework, hoping that he can persuade colleagues to keep Mitchell off Foreign Relations. He believes that he was voted out largely because of his support of the treaty, and he chooses not to believe that his constituents were duped. Marino says he finds that more and more people expect less and less of each other, and he thinks that should change. He's going to respect the voters and what they want for the ten weeks he remains a senator.

Politics of Foreign Relations: The Ukrainian politician, Vasily Konanov, is not supposed to meet anyone of importance during his visit to the White House. Rather, he will be speaking with the president's advisers in the Balkans. However, when he arrives in the driveway, drunk, with a woman who Josh assumes is either a security attaché or a hooker, he refuses to leave until he sees the president. Leo arranges for him to meet the president accidentally.

Denial, Thy Name is Everyone: There's going to be an editorial in the *Post* tomorrow saying that the president's time isn't being used efficiently; schedules are abandoned before lunch; the West Wing resembles a high school; and Leo is compared to a substitute teacher.

References: *Hardball*, Barnum & Bailey's Circus, Boris Badenov and Natasha Fatale (the villains in *The Adventures of Rockie and Bullwinkle*), Santa Claus, Elvis Presley (1935–77, the Goddam King of Rock'n'Roll), the movies

The Man Who Came to Dinner (Bette Davis and Monty Woolley), *Norma Rae* (Sally Fields and Beau Bridges), David Lean's *Dr Zhivago* and *The Big Country*, the Dalai Lama and the former Indian prime minister Indira Nehru Gandhi (1917–84). Toby quotes Edmund Burke (1729–97): 'A representative owes not just his industry, but his judgment and betrays you if he sacrifices his judgment to yours.' Bartlet notes that he was voted out of office five years later by the people of Bristol. All the TV sets in the White House seem to be Samsung.

'You May Remember Me From Such Films and TV Series As . . .': David Kaufman played Dexter Douglas in *Freakzoid!* and provided Marty McFly's voice in the animated *Back to the Future* series. Eugene Lazarev is one of the foremost Russian stage-actors of his generation. He appeared in *The Saint*. Mike Starr was in *Summer of Sam*, *Hoodlum*, *James and the Giant Peach*, *Mad Dog and Glory*, *Radio Days* and *Ed Wood*. Brian Stepanek appeared in *Children of the Struggle*. Richard Tanner was in *Sexual Malice* and *Nails*. Amy Turner appeared in *I Hate You Now*. Tegan West's movies include *Bad Company* and *Hamburger Hill*. Wayne Wilderson was in *Independence Day*.

Oh, Donna!: Josh asks how Donna changes subjects so quickly. She replies, 'Because I'm me.' When Josh is less than interested in her rant about carpal tunnel syndrome she pinches his ear to demonstrate how painful it is. Josh notes that Republicans find the word 'ergonomic' silly. Donna replies that if they backed off from everything because of words the Republicans found silly, there would be a lot of pregnant teenagers and no healthcare.

Cigarettes and Alcohol: As Abbey is in New Hampshire, Jed invites Toby to share a cigar with him.

Logic, Let Me Introduce You to This Window: Sam has a 22-page position memo to summarise. Josh says he has staff for that and suggests getting Ainsley to do it. But Ainsley is not a member of Sam's staff. Sam asks her to write it because he has to attend a meeting on the Hill, a meeting that Ainsley accompanies him to, but, on their return, she has completed the memo. When did she have the time? Sam's office layout seems to have changed considerably since it was last seen (he's acquired a second window). Considering the way the last episode ended, Sam and Ainsley seem unusually bitchy towards each other. Donna reminds Josh that he's got an appointment at four o'clock. However, earlier scenes took place at 4.35. Sam and Ainsley get back to the White House around seven (at 8.25 she says they've been arguing for an hour and a half) but there's still bright sunlight outside. It should be dark by that time. The photo of Zoey on the president's desk is different from that seen in the previous episode. The next day's critical editorial in the *Washington Post* is the fourth such piece recently, yet, before the day is out, CJ mentions yesterday's editorial, last Thursday's and two others. That makes five. Josh slaps Donna's ass as he sends her into the meeting with Konanov (surely that's sexual harassment).

Cruelty To Animals: Leo says trying to get a hundred senators in a line is like trying to get cats to walk in a parade.

Quote/Unquote: Bartlet, to Charlie: 'Could I have a couple of aspirin, or a weapon of some kind to kill people with?'
    Josh on Donna's new-found interest in repetitive-strain injury: 'You're going to have to ask somebody else who, you know, *cares*.'
    Leo, after Donna organises a work-to-rule among the secretaries: 'Can you keep your people in line?' Josh: 'There's been no evidence of it so far.'

Notes: 'Oh, how I miss the Cold War.' This is one where the subplots are spread a bit too thinly to be really satisfying. Some fine sequences (Toby's rant about the test-ban treaty in front of a group of visitors, Josh trying hard to be nice to the drunken Ukrainian politician) are somewhat derailed by the slow-moving Sam-and-Ainsley scenes. Odd, downbeat ending, too. Best bit (by far): Leo's incandescent rage at Margaret's slow typing.

The presidential schedule includes a 7 a.m. jog. One of the Cabinet is named Schafer. Danny has been offered an editorship but turned it down, much to CJ's disappointment.

Cast and Crew Comments: 'One thing that I share with Ainsley is that I love to eat all the time,' says Emily Procter, who inherited her father's fast metabolism but also runs, bicycles, dances and weight-trains. 'It was in my second episode that [Ainsley] was eating everybody else's leftovers. I just sat there dumbfounded, thinking, "There's no way Aaron knows this about me."'

Did You Know?: Marlin Fitzwater provided an insider's version of Boris Yeltsin's first visit to the White House, on which the Konanov subplot is based. Yeltsin was in the Russian Parliament at the time, challenging Mikhail Gorbachev. He wanted to meet President Bush, but the president thought Gorbachev would take offence if he received Yeltsin in the Oval Office. 'Yeltsin refused to come in the building unless he could meet the president,' Fitzwater recalls. A compromise was struck and Yeltsin agreed to meet Bush in the national security adviser's office.

29
The Portland Trip

US Transmission Date: 15 November 2000
UK Transmission Date: 24 July 2001 (E4)

Writer: Aaron Sorkin
Story: Paul Redford
Director: Paris Barclay
Cast: Michael Tomlinson (Congressman) Gregg Daniel (Steve Adamley)
Richard Hoyt Miller (*Air Force One* Steward)
Timothy Dale Agee (*Air Force One* Steward)
Michael Cunio (Adamley's Aide)

The president is on *Air Force One* en route to Portland. Accompanying him are Sam, Toby and CJ, who is being punished for disparaging remarks about Bartlet's beloved Notre Dame. Josh spars with a gay Republican over a bill on homosexual marriage. Leo monitors a situation in the Gulf.

A View from the Hill: The Full Faith and Credit Clause obliges states to abide by the public acts and judicial proceedings of other states. So, Josh asks, how is the Marriage Recognition Act not unconstitutional? Ainsley says the clause also says Congress can proscribe the manner, which means they decide what being married means within the context of Article IV of the Constitution.

American History X: The founders based the country on Judaeo-Christian morality, says Matt. Josh talks about the separation of church and state. There's also a discussion of the fourteenth amendment ('Rights Guaranteed, Privileges and Immunities of Citizenship, Due Process and Equal Protection'). Josh says, 'A strict interpretation of the equal-protection clause would dictate that homophobia can't be made into a law.'

Politics of Bigotry: The Republican Majority Leader has compared homosexuality to kleptomania and sex addiction.

Politics of Integrity: Josh asks Matt how he can belong to a party that fundamentally disagrees with his sexuality. Matt replies that he agrees with 95 per cent of the Republican platform: individual rather than group rights, free markets and strong national defence.

Politics of Compromise: Knowing that the administration isn't going to win over the Marriage Recognition Act, Josh advises a reluctant Bartlet (who believes the act is legislative gay-bashing) to use his veto and delay its passage into law as a symbolic gesture to the gay community. Meanwhile, they can focus on the Employment Non-Discrimination Act, making gay spouses eligible for health and social-security benefits.

The Encyclopedic Mind of Josiah Bartlet PhD: The Tokyo Exchange has opened and Bartlet intends to gauge the impact on Pacific Rim banking reforms. A subject economics scholars could debate for years he will solve in twenty minutes, he boasts.

The Conspiracy Starts at High Tide: A Cypriot-registered tanker with a Sudanese captain was stopped leaving Qais (a notorious haven for Iraqi oil smugglers). When the US Navy attempted to land a helicopter they were fired on and, when the tanker was finally boarded, the crew threw the log and ship's manifest over the side.

References: A misquote from the Beatles' 'Help!' ('my life has changed in many ways') and an allusion to *Deputy Dawg*. Also, the fashion designer Max Mara, the Chinese dictator Mao Tse-Tung (1893–1976) and his red book, the French theologian and philosopher Pétrus de Alliaco (1350–1420), ex-president of Panama Ernesto Pérez Balladares, the St Louis baseball legend Joe Garagiola and Laurence Tribe (professor of constitutional law at Harvard). A presidential aide notes that, south of DC and west of Chicago, few places have subways and those that do (LA, Miami, San Francisco) have low usage. Ainsley's laptop is a Dell.

'You May Remember Me From Such Films and TV Series As . . .': The late David Graf was Tackleberry in the *Police Academy* movies. He also appeared in *Skeletons*, *Citizen Ruth* and *The Town Bully*. Michael Tomlinson was in *Atomic Train* and *Jacob's Ladder*. Gregg Daniel appeared in *Mars Attacks!* and *Pump Up the Volume*. Richard Hoyt Miller was in *Turbulence*. Timothy Dale Agee appeared in *Blue Streak*. Michael Cunio's movies include *Motorcrossed*.

Behind the Camera: The director Paris Barclay previously worked on *Sliders*, *ER* and *NYPD Blue*. As an actor, he appeared in *The Cherokee Kid*.

Oh, Donna!: She has a bizarre conversation with Josh about the difference between stealing and wearing a dress once and then returning it. And an even more weird chat with Ainsley about hair-dyeing (probable subtext: she thinks that they look alike and is worried Josh finds Ainsley attractive).

Sex and Drugs and Rock'n'Roll: Josh needs Donna back in an hour despite her plans with Tod. 'If you wanna have sex, you'd better do it during dinner,' he says.

Cigarettes and Alcohol: Toby asks the steward for a Jack Daniel's with his club sandwich. Josh shares a beer in the mess with Matt. At dinner, Donna had two whisky sours.

Logic, Let Me Introduce You to This Window: The CH-47 Seahawk sent to board the illegal oil tanker is an Army Chinook helicopter. The Seahawk H-60 is a Navy/Marine aircraft, more likely to be involved in such an operation.

Quote/Unquote: Sam: 'Oratory should blow the doors off the place. We should be talking about a permanent revolution.'

Charlie: 'If this was an idea, somebody would've had it already.' Bartlet: 'I find fault with that formula.'

Skinner: 'I never understand why you gun-control people don't all join the NRA. They've got two million members. You bring three million to the next meeting [and] call a vote.'

Notes: 'You know why late flights are good? Because we cease to be earthbound and burdened with practicality. Ask the impertinent question. Talk about the idea nobody has thought about yet.' A more linear story, which, in the beautifully played Josh–Matt scenes, includes some of series' finest work. Donna and Ainsley's odd double act is also worthy of attention.

The head of the White House Military Office (or WHAMO) is called Latham. Danny, like the president, went to Notre Dame.

Cast and Crew Comments: Some of the episode's ideas came from a conversation Charley Lang had with Sorkin. 'I was working on the *No on Knight* campaign,' Lang told

PlanetOut. The Knight Initiative, which became law in California in March 2001, prohibits same-sex marriages in the state. 'I called Aaron and said I wanted to talk about a topical idea for the show. He was already somewhat familiar with the issue. That evolved into the idea of gay Republicans. Both of us were curious about how they reconcile their orientation with their political values. I got a call this fall asking if I'd like to do another episode. When I got the script, it was all about what Aaron and I had discussed. In the course of the episode, my character comes out as gay.' So, why does Skinner, a gay man, support the Marriage Recognition Act? Lang was asked. 'Being gay myself and a Democrat, it was an interesting challenge to get inside the mind of a man who would support something like this. The beauty of Aaron's writing is that he doesn't write black-and-white characters. They're not good guys and bad guys. . . . He makes a case for Skinner, people ask him how he can be a member of a party that disagrees with who he is. The upshot is that he has a lot of other priorities; his life isn't all about being homosexual.'

30
Shibboleth

US Transmission Date: 22 November 2000
UK Transmission Date: 31 July 2001 (E4)

Writer: Aaron Sorkin
Story: Patrick H Caddell
Director: Laura Innes
Cast: Deborah Hedwall (Josephine McGarry)
Sam Anderson (John La Salle) Henry O (Jhin Wei)
John Prosky (Aide #4) John Mariano (Bertram) Sharon Omi (Gardener)
Jonah Rooney (Morton Horn) Joe D'Angerio (Russo)
Al Rodrigo (Commander Cale) Ivar Brogger (Aide #1)
Cameron Daddo (Aide #2) Rich Cooper (Aide #3)

Thanksgiving is coming and CJ has to choose a turkey for the president to pardon. A shipload of illegal immigrants from China land at San Diego and claim to be persecuted Christians.

A View from the Hill: Senate Republicans threaten to delay confirmation of other nominees over Josey, suggesting her nomination is an abuse of the recess appointment process. The Senate must confirm her, says Toby: she's too qualified. He says they can hold up the appointments all they want, and shut down the government because a teacher did as she was told. They'll have given the administration a second term as a consequence. 'Not because I'm right and you're wrong. Although I am and you are. But because I'm better at this than you.'

American History X: Article 2, Section 2, of the Constitution states, 'The president shall have the power to fill all vacancies that may happen during the recess of the Senate by granting commissions which shall expire at the end of their next session.'

Politics of Expediency: Expedited removal provisions are part of the Illegal Immigration Act (1996). Upon entry, the Immigration and Naturalisation Service (INS) conducts a 'credible-fear interview'. This is not a hearing on whether or not to grant asylum, just to determine if the detainee has reason to fear that they'll be harmed if returned to their country of origin. Bartlet says the US is trying to sell more 747s to China, while attempting to get them to crack down on violators of American copyrights and negotiate a settlement over Tibet, which makes the refugees issue problematic. A compromise is arranged whereby the 83 refugees, being held at an INS detention facility in Otay-Mesa, are allowed to stage a jailbreak.

A Little Learning is a Dangerous Thing: CJ's grasp of American history isn't as good as Toby's. She mixes up the dates of Jamestown, the *Mayflower* and the American Revolution.

The Encyclopedic Mind of Josiah Bartlet PhD: Leo is staying with the president for Thanksgiving. Josh, Toby and Sam are all eager to avoid an invitation, as they want to watch a football game. Something they'd sooner do, Josh says, than 'listen to a history of the yam in Latin' (the Latin word for yam is '*dioscorea*', Bartlet later tells him). The president takes carving knives very seriously, having Charlie shuttle backwards and forwards to the shop to get one he likes. At one time he wanted to be a chemistry professor but he never actually studied chemistry.

The Gospel According to Josey: The president wants a debate on the issue of school prayer. Toby decides to orchestrate this by appointing Josephine McGarry, Leo's sister, as Assistant Secretary for Primary and Secondary Education. She's a PhD from Cornell University, spent six years as a principal and four years as superintendent in Atlanta. She's on the board of visitors at her church and teaches Sunday mornings at the Immaculate Heart of Mary School. However, she is against organised prayer in public schools and, while superintendent, vigorously enforced the law that prohibits this (including an ugly incident at a high school football game).

The Gospel According to Sam: Mary Marsh says millions of Christians around the world won't stand by while religious freedom is threatened. Sam argues that a play called *Apostles*, in which Jesus is presented as gay, provoked threats to blow up the theatre. 'You're committed to religious freedom for all people unless you don't like what they have to say?'

The Gospel According to Bartlet: He quotes Judges 12: 'Then said they unto him, Say now "Shibboleth" and he said "Sibboleth" for he could not frame to pronounce it right.' This was a password the Israelites used to distinguish allies from impostors sent across the River Jordan. Jhin Wei names eleven of the twelve apostles (Peter, Andrew, John, Philip, Bartholomew, Thomas, Matthew, Thaddeus, Simon the Zealot, Judas Iscariot and James), which, the president remarks, is more than he'd be able to, and quotes from Paul in Romans 1:17 ('we hold that man is justified by faith alone').

The Conspiracy Starts at Closing Time: The INS agents suggest it's not uncommon for refugees to feign faith in order to claim religious persecution.

References: The Presidential Pardon of the Turkey (a Thanksgiving tradition dating back to Harry Truman), *All About Eve*, the Boys & Girls Clubs of America and the Big Brothers/Big Sisters of America, Amnesty International, the artist Norman Rockwell (1894–1978). CJ gets Donna to teach her the song 'We Gather Together' (arranged by Eduard Kremser, translated into English by Theodore Baker), Hershey's Milk Duds, the conductor Arturo Toscanini (1867–1957), the Waldorf Hotel, the Boston silversmith and patriot Paul Revere (1735–1818), *The Addams Family* ('show time!') and, obliquely, Tom Stoppard's *Rosencrantz and Guildenstern Are Dead* ('I was just flipping a nickel in my office: sixteen times in a row, it came out tails').

'You May Remember Me from Such Films and TV Series As . . .': Sam Anderson played Holland Manners in *Angel*, Kevin Davis in *The Cape* and Phoebe's Fonzie-loving gynaecologist in *Friends*. He was in *Forrest Gump*, *La Bamba* and *The X-Files*. Ivar Brogger was in *For Richer, For Poorer*. Rich Cooper appeared in *Home Invasion*. Henry O was in *Avatar* and *Shanghai Noon*. Joe D'Angerio's movies include *L.A. Johns*, *Naked Gun 33⅓: The Final Insult* and *True Romance*. Cameron Daddo appeared in *Anthrax* and *Models Inc*. Timothy Davis-Reed was Chris in *Sports Night*. Deborah Hedwall appeared in *Shadrach*. John Mariano played Johnny in *Caroline in the City* and was in *Cool Crime*. Sharon Omi appeared in *Terminal USA* and *Chicago Hope*. John Prosky was in *Bowfinger*, *Strip Mall* and *The Nutty Professor*. Jonah Rooney played Pinky Faraday in *Trevor*. Al Rodrigo was in *Brown's Requiem* and *Beverly Hills 90210*.

Oh, Donna!: She's involved in the conspiracy to put Eric and Troy, the turkeys, in CJ's office.

Logic, Let Me Introduce You to This Window: Toby says Jamestown (the first American colony) was established in the sixteenth century. It was founded in 1607, during the seventeenth. The president asks Jhin Wei to name the twelve apostles. He names eleven – there were actually two called James: one, the brother of John, the other the son of Alphæus (Matthew 10/Luke 6).

Cruelty To Turkeys: CJ: 'They sent me two turkeys. The most photo-friendly gets a presidential pardon and a full life at a children's zoo. The runner-up gets eaten.' Bartlet: 'If the Oscars were like that, I'd watch.'

Quote/Unquote: Donna, on how to lift a turkey: 'The guy said to support him under his hindquarters.' CJ: 'I don't know where his hindquarters are and I'm not gonna look that hard.'

Bartlet: 'Morton, I can't pardon a turkey. If you think I can, then you have got to go back to your school and insist that you be better prepared to go out in the world.' Donna: 'You can't pardon a turkey?'

Bartlet: 'You know what I get to do now? Proclaim a National Day of Thanksgiving. This is a *great* job.'

Notes: 'Christianity is not demonstrated through a recitation of facts ... Faith is the true shibboleth.' What a heart-warming episode. A pocket Frank Capra movie about doing the right thing even if it's not the *easy* thing. Bartlet compares the plight of the refugees to that of the pilgrims who founded the New World. The message here is that no one has to die in Bartlet's America, not even a Thanksgiving turkey. Best bits: Sam's crime series proposal, *Pilgrim Detectives*; CJ, Donna and the turkeys; the president giving Charlie his family knife.

CJ missed Thanksgiving last year, having a fever and flulike symptoms. She's turned down lots of Thanksgiving offers in the hope that Toby, Josh and Sam will invite her to watch football with them. Other recess appointments include James Alkins, Assistant Secretary of Transportation for Aviation, and Leslie Krier, Assistant Secretary of Commerce for Ecological Development. The president has known Josey for 25 years.

Critique: The *New York Times*' Laura Lippman wrote that *The West Wing* is 'wonderfully acted, well written and, contrary to what conservatives believe, more devastating to the Democrats than any right-wing conspiracy. It makes a counterproductive pact with its 20 million viewers: stay home, surrender to this fantasy of a Democratic president who never abandons his principles ... Sorkin has been praised for his uplifting world view. Yet what could be more cynical than spoon-feeding this Pollyanna presidency to disenfranchised liberals.'

Did You Know?: Peter Parnell suggested which questions Bartlet might ask a Chinese refugee to determine his Christianity.

31
Galileo

US Transmission Date: 29 November 2000
UK Transmission Date: 7 August 2001 (E4)

Writers: Kevin Falls, Aaron Sorkin
Director: Alex Graves
Cast: Troy Ruptash (Scott Tate) John Carroll Lynch (Jack Reese)
Charlotte Cornwell (Nadia Kozlowski) Colm Feore (Tad Whitney)
Duffy Epstein (Aide #1) Nigel Gibbs (Aide #2)
Nina Hodoruk (Military Aide) Ann Lim (Staff Aide) Steve Shin (Man #1)
John Leslie Wolfe (Man #2) Matthew Dickens (Man #3)

A Russian missile silo is ablaze but there's been a cover-up. It's reported that Bartlet doesn't like green beans. He is looking forward to a satellite link with children to watch NASA's latest Martian probe, but isn't eagerly anticipating a night at the symphonia.

American History X: The Citizen's Stamp Advisory Committee recommends that Marcus Aquino be put on a stamp. He's a Korean War hero (winning the Silver Star), but also a former Commissioner of Puerto Rico and a strong advocate of statehood for the island. To put his face on a stamp would be promoting that belief, Josh argues. Donna asks if anyone is worried that if the Puerto Ricans aren't given statehood, they'll want independence. Puerto Rico is dependent on US manufacturing, replies Josh. Donna says people won't suffer tyranny. Puerto Ricans have to register to be drafted to the armed forces, yet they're not allowed to vote and are expected to die for a commander-in-chief they had no voice in electing? 'We have colonised Puerto Rico and they will rise up against us,' she adds. 'I think we can take 'em,' says Josh confidently. The Jewish War Veterans lobbied to get a stamp, even though the criteria prohibit groups whose principal undertakings are religious; they were denied. The following groups *have* been issued stamps: Disabled Veterans of America, American Confederate Veterans, American Legion and its black soldiers who served as buffalo scouts.

Politics of Green Beans: Charlie's innocent answer to a question about the president's eating likes (steak, lobster, spaghetti, ice cream) and dislikes (green beans) is reported. It's a major story in Oregon, where green beans represent a significant percentage of state revenue. Bartlet won Oregon by 10,000 votes. Charlie thinks the whole thing is stupid – education, crime, jobs and national security are serious issues; green beans aren't.

A Little Learning is a Dangerous Thing: Toby knows that Mars rotates every 24 hours and 37 minutes. CJ calculates that, as a consequence, a Martian year is 687 days.

The Encyclopedic Mind of Josiah Bartlet PhD: For the telecast, CJ urges the president to act as moderator and pass the children's questions to the experts rather than answer them himself. After all, nobody likes a know-all. God forbid that, while talking to 60,000 students, the president should appear smart, replies Bartlet. He can't resist noting that Mars is 4.6 billion years old and the average temperature ranges from 15 degrees to minus 140. CJ believes he's wrong, but he adds that he converted it to

Celsius in his head. Mars, he notes, is colder and drier than
Earth, but has four seasons. Bartlet plans a quiet night in
with two books on Mars and one on Galileo.

BISHMILLAR!: The Italian astronomer and mathematician Galileo Galilei (1564–1642) sat in Pisa cathedral
watching a lamp suspended from the ceiling oscillate back
and forth. Using his pulse to keep time, he discovered the
period of oscillation was independent of the size of the arc.
Later he contradicted the theory that a heavier body falls
faster than a lighter one, which took some guts in 1609,
Bartlet remarks, considering the person he disproved was
Aristotle. Charlie adds that one example of Galileo's
extraordinary achievements is that he observed the rings
on Saturn. Others included the perfection of the refracting
telescope, which allowed him to discover, in 1610, four
moons of Jupiter (Ganymede, Callisto, Europa and Io)
and, by establishing that celestial objects orbit something
other than Earth, proved Copernicus's theory that the
Earth revolves around the sun. Arrested by the Inquisition
in 1632, and forced to recant his 'heresies', he lived his final
decade under house arrest.

Space Odyssey: NASA's great at naming things, the
president observes. He mentions Apollo (the moon
missions), Mercury (the first manned US space flights),
Atlantis (one of the space shuttles) and the Sea of
Tranquillity and the Ocean of Storms on the moon. Also
referenced: the Johnson Space Center and the Jet Propul-
sion Lab in California. The two moons of Mars, Phobos
and Deimos (discovered by Asaph Hall in 1877), were
named after the horses that pulled Mars's chariot.

Carol's Spelling: Amusingly, she has a copy of *Webster's
Dictionary* on her desk.

References: The *Milwaukee Journal*, the Beatles' 'Yellow
Submarine', Buddy Holly, the Greek philosopher Aristotle
(384–322 BC), Georgio Armani, the Algonquin Roundtable
(an informal gathering who met daily for lunch at the
Hotel Algonquin in New York during the 1920s, charac-

terised by its witty and urbane sophistication; members included Dorothy Parker, Alexander Woollcott, Robert Benchley, Harpo Marx, George S Kaufman and Russell Crouse), Wile E Coyote, Samuel Barber's Symphony No. 2, Stravinsky's *Variations on a Theme*, Schöenberg's *Enlightened Night for String Orchestra*, the singer Jackson Browne and the luna moth.

'You May Remember Me From Such Films and TV Series As . . .': Troy Ruptash was in *When It's Over*. John Carroll Lynch played Steve Carey in *The Drew Carey Show* and Norm in *Fargo*. The author John le Carré's sister, Charlotte Cornwell, appeared in many classic British TV series such as *Shoestring*, *Casualty* and *A Touch of Frost*. She was Anna in *Rock Follies* and Sally Porter in *Stardust*, and was also in *The Men's Room* and *The Krays*. Colm Feore played Rudolph Hess in *Nuremberg*, and was in *Pearl Harbor*, *La Femme Nikita*, *Titus* and *Due South*. Duffy Epstein can be seen in *Final Justice*. Nigel Gibbs was in *The Truth About Cats & Dogs*, *Pump Up the Volume*, *Quantum Leap* and *Roseanne*. Nina Hodoruk's movies include *The Lemon Sister*. Ann Lim was in *Fifty/Fifty*. John Leslie Wolfe appeared in *Black*.

Oh, Donna!: She argues with Josh about Puerto Rico. And lots of other (unrelated) things.

Sex and Drugs and Rock'n'Roll: CJ has hired a new deputy, Simon Glazer. Most of the others she interviewed were from the State Department. Tad Whitney (whom CJ dated for six weeks five years ago) suggests she overlooked him because he once dumped her.

After the picture of Sam and Laurie appeared in the press (see **21**, 'Lies, Damn Lies and Statistics') Sam didn't call Mallory. They haven't spoken since. Mallory's boyfriend is an injury-prone hockey player called Richard Andrewchuk ('We're having quite a lot of sex,' she says).

Cigarettes and Alcohol: Sam drinks white wine at the Kennedy Center.

Logic, Let Me Introduce You to This Window: There is no Reykjavik Symphony Orchestra – they're called the Icelandic Symphony Orchestra. Galileo was, indeed, the first astronomer to observe the rings of Saturn in 1610, though he'd no idea of their exact nature (his conclusion, that it was a 'triple planet', held until Christiaan Huygens confirmed they were rings in 1659).

Cruelty To Animals: Iceland is considering joining Norway and Japan in defying a ban on whale hunting imposed by the International Whaling Commission. There's a lucrative demand for Icelandic mink whale meat.

Quote/Unquote: Donna: 'About fifty thousand proposals a year are submitted to the Citizens' Stamp Advisory Committee, the acronym for which is . . .' Josh: 'Dork squad?'

Toby, after Sam has ranted about the problems of dating: 'That's twenty seconds of my life I'm never going to get back.'

Bartlet: 'Modern music sucks. Anything written after 1860 sucks.'

CJ, on the green-bean fiasco: 'He doesn't think they're bad for you and he doesn't think the people who make them are evil. They're simply not his cup of tea. Why do we think the adults of Oregon wouldn't be OK if we put it to them just that way? People stopped trusting the government during Vietnam, and it was because government stopped trusting them.'

Notes: 'We came out of the cave, looked over the hill and we saw fire. And we crossed the ocean, and we pioneered the West, and we took to the sky. The history of man is hung on the timeline of exploration.' A story about reaching for the stars (literally, as well as metaphorically), this is another brilliant episode. Best bits: Toby delegating; the president's Martian knowledge and his joyous review of the concert.

NASA's chief administrator Peter Jobson (see **22**, 'What Kind of Day Has it Been') is mentioned.

Critique: 'My sixteen-year-old daughter recently gave up *Dawson's Creek* for *The West Wing*,' wrote Michael Wolff in *New York Magazine*. The two aren't mutually exclusive, surely.

Did You Know?: President Clinton allowed the production use of the presidential box at the Kennedy Center.

32
Noël

US Transmission Date: 20 December 2000[87]
UK Transmission Date: 14 August 2001 (E4)

Writer: Aaron Sorkin
Story: Peter Parnell
Director: Thomas Schlamme
Cast: Adam Arkin (Dr Stanley Keyworth)
Paxton Whitehead (Bernard Thatch) Yo-Yo Ma (Himself)
Purva Bedi (Kaytha Trask) Robert Noble (Valet)
Deborah Snipes (Staffer) Michael Crider (David Housman)
Etyl Leder (Rebecca Housman)

Christmas is coming, but the holiday music Toby arranges irritates Josh. Things get worse as Josh investigates a suicidal pilot and raises his voice to the president. Leo orders therapy.

A View from the Hill: Asked about tapping into the Strategic Petroleum Reserve to help ease oil prices, the Energy Secretary responds that the idea had merit.

American History X: A portrait of Dolly Madison (wife of James Madison, see **19**, 'Let Bartlet Be Bartlet') hangs in the foyer. Woodrow Wilson, (1856–1924), the 28th president, is mentioned.

Politics of Excess: The president sends about 1,100,000 Christmas cards annually: 1,000 to the first family's list, 100,000 to campaign workers and contributors and almost 1,000,000 to everyone who writes to the White House (excluding those who make death threats).

---

[87] Originally scheduled for 13 December 2000, but pre-empted by the result of the 2000 presidential election.

Office Eccentrics: Bernard Thatch is an English member of the White House visitors' office. He's frequently unwell, doesn't like visitors touching things and would like his superiors to let him punish those who do. He calls CJ Claudia and sarcastically thinks her necklace is 'a monument to bourgeois taste'.

Denial, Thy Name is Josh: An F16 Falcon, armed with a 20mm Vulcan cannon and AIM sidewinder missiles, goes missing mid-flight. The pilot, Robert Cano, crashes the plane in Mexico. Cano was from Tallahassee, shared a birthday with Josh and was awarded a Purple Heart when his plane caught fire over Bosnia.

The Trauma Starts at Closing Time: The American Trauma Victims Association are called in to work with trauma victims. Examples of their work include the pipe bomb at Lancaster Middle School, Hurricane Beth, the Iowa tornadoes and the FBI raid in Rock Creek.

References: The cellists Pablo Casals (1876–1973) and Mstislav Rostropovich; Nellis, Edwards and Laughlin Air Force Bases; *The Cliffs at Etretat After a Storm* by Gustave Caillebotte, a less gifted contemporary of the French realist Gustave Courbet (1819–77); Johann Sebastian Bach (1685–1750); the carols 'Joy to the World', 'We Wish You a Merry Christmas', 'God Rest You Merry Gentlemen' and 'Carol of the Bells'. The bagpipes trio play 'Greensleeves'.

'You May Remember Me From Such Films and TV Series As . . .': Adam Arkin appeared in *Oceano*, *Dottie Gets Spanked*, *Full Moon High* and *All Together Now*. He was the director of *My Louisiana Sky*. Purva Bedi was in *American Desi*. Michael Crider appeared in *The Astronaut's Wife*. Robert Noble was in *Robin Hood: Men in Tights*, *Bill & Ted's Bogus Journey*, *Stir* and *Green Acres*. Paxton Whitehead played Hal Conway in *Mad About You*, and appeared in *Back to School* and *My Boyfriend's Back*. Gregalan Williams was in *Baywatch* and *Remember the Titans*. Eric Payne appeared in *Malcolm X*, *She's Got to*

Have It and *Gridlock'd*. Yo-Yo Ma provided the string arrangements for *Seven Years in Tibet*.

Oh, Donna!: Donna gives Josh the pilot's file before he asks for it. She claims to anticipate Josh's every need.

Sex and Drugs and Carols: For the last two Christmases Toby has been accused of not being in the proper spirit. This year he intends to fill the lobby with music, hiring a brass quintet, then the Capital Bluegrass Banjo Band and the Duncan McTavish Clarney Highland Bagpipe Regiment.

Cigarettes and Alcohol: Joss claims he cut his hand on a shattered whisky glass.

Logic, Let Me Introduce You to This Window: Josh says the White House has 1,100 employees (see **9**, 'The Short List'). What's Toby, a Jew, doing in charge of Christmas music in the White House (see **10**, 'In Excelsis Deo')? Where did CJ get the photo of Housman from? Donna claims she never asks Josh for any favours, which is patently untrue.

Cruelty: Augie Housman was a French Jew, a collector of minor impressionists including Caillebotte. Vichy Laws stripped him of his property. The painting was sold to a Swiss dealer and Housman died in Auschwitz. It made its way to the Musée d'Orsay, then the National Gallery, where the president spotted it. CJ and Bernard arrange for the painting to be returned to Housman's daughter, Rebecca.

Quote/Unquote: Bernard: 'The President, on a visit to the gallery, and possessing even less taste in fine art than you have in accessories, announced he liked the painting. The French government offered it as a gift to the White House. I suppose in retribution for EuroDisney. So here it hangs, like a gym sock on a shower rod.'
    Josh: 'There are only two things that ever stopped the government from doing anything. Money or politics.'
    Leo: 'This guy's walking down a street when he falls in a hole. The walls are so steep, he can't get out. A doctor

passes by, the guy shouts up, "Can you help me out?" The doctor writes him a prescription, throws it down the hole. Then a priest comes along and the guy shouts, "Father, I'm down in this hole, can you help me?" The priest writes out a prayer, throws it down in the hole. Then a friend walks by. "Hey Joe, it's me. Can you help me out?" The friend jumps in the hole. Our guy says, "Are you stupid? Now we're both down here." The friend says, "Yeah, but I've been down here before – I know the way out." '

Notes: 'I can hear the damn sirens all over the building.' An episode that's been coming for some time as Josh has to deal with the aftermath of the shooting just as his friends did in **25**, 'The Midterms'. This is glorious, juxtaposing the twisted emotions that lead Josh finally to acknowledge that he needs help with more trivial matters – such as the best bit of the episode, CJ's double act with Bernard.

Bob Shanahan, the staffer in the car with Leo in **23**, 'In the Shadow of Two Gunmen' Part 1, is mentioned.

Critique: 'I get into it with Aaron [Sorkin] when I think the aides are getting too cheeky,' Dee Dee Myers told *Newsday*. 'Even with Bill Clinton, who is fairly casual, there's still a line. You just don't make flip remarks.'

Cast and Crew Comments: 'When horrible things have happened in the White House, the tendency is for the staff to move beyond them quickly. I think that's especially true of Josh,' Bradley Whitford told Donna Petrozzello. 'Whatever emotional response he's feeling is less important to him than his job.'

Did You Know?: NBC's coverage of Al Gore conceding to George W Bush pre-empted this episode. Ironically, this was also the episode filmed on election day some weeks before. Bradley Whitford recalls cast and crew gravitating to TV sets after takes to watch. 'I'd worked hard on the campaign and was very anxious,' he said. 'Thank God it's an episode where I'm supposed to be emotionally discombobulated.'

33
The Leadership Breakfast

US Transmission Date: 10 January 2001
UK Transmission Date: 21 August 2001 (E4)

Writer: Aaron Sorkin
Story: Paul Redford
Director: Scott Winant
Cast: Felicity Huffman (Ann Stark) Bruce Winant (Henry Hanson)
Lesley D Van Arsdall (Reporter) Dude Walker (Simon)
Tom McCarthy (Senator Randall) Rhonda Overby (Reporter)
Tim Williams (Reporter) Marc Goldsmith (Staff Aide #1)
Kevin Fry (Staff Aide #2)

The White House plans a breakfast to encourage bipartisan cooperation. Toby meets Ann Stark, the Majority
Leader's chief-of-staff, to lay ground rules. Leo, Sam and
Donna all embarrass themselves with an influential columnist.

A View from the Hill: Things that *won't* be discussed at the
breakfast, much to Toby's disappointment, include the
patients' bill of rights and the minimum wage. Ann
complains that after breakfast the Majority Leader will
speak first and outside. CJ responds from a podium in
front of a big picture of the White House.

American History X: John Adams (1735–1826), the second
president, Andrew Johnson (1808–75), the seventeenth,
Benjamin Harrison (1833–1901), the twenty-third, and
Alexander Hamilton (1757-1804), Washington's aide-de-
camp and treasury secretary are mentioned. The Truman
Balcony was named after Harry Truman (see **9**, 'The Short
List'). The Monroe Doctrine (1823) was a rejection by
James Monroe (see **3**, 'A Proportional Response') of
threatened colonisation of the US by European powers.

Politics of Embarrassment: Karen Cahill is a *New York
Times* columnist whom Leo unintentionally insults. Josh
foists the task of apology on to Sam, who successfully
charms Cahill but mixes up Kyrgyzstan and Kazakhstan in

a discussion on nuclear weapons and Islamic extremism. He begs Donna to discover if Cahill noticed his slip. Donna fixes Sam's gaffe but suffers even worse embarrassment when her knickers end up in Cahill's possession.

A Little Learning is a Dangerous Thing: Sam displays expertise on different types of wood.

The Encyclopedic Mind of Josiah Bartlet PhD: He knows that the next person he's due to meet, Kim Woo, won a bronze medal for fencing, is a Buddhist and enjoys European history. He doesn't, however, know that Kim is a woman! He tells Charlie it's bad luck to toast with water, believing the superstition comes from Greek mythology.

Office Gossip: An efficiency expert suggests freeing up space by moving the Press Room. Sam argues such a move would be beneficial and has a question inserted into a telephone poll to see if the public would object. Unfortunately, by sheer bad luck, one of those spoken to is a reporter.

Denial, Thy Name is Toby: Ann Stark's had her current job for two weeks. Toby says, 'I know her a little.' The impression is that they've been involved in a previous relationship, possibly sexual. Ann accuses Toby of having lost his sense of humour.

The Conspiracy Starts at Closing Time: At the post-breakfast press conference the Majority Leader is missing, owing to a sore throat. CJ realises, too late, that Ann has manoeuvred the White House by quoting Toby as an unnamed source in a battle over the minimum wage, keeping Ann's boss out of the ensuing carnage and preparing him for a coming presidential campaign.

References: *The Godfather* ('a wartime *consigliere*'), *Ice Station Zebra*, Officer Krupke from *West Side Story*; *Washington Post* executive, Ben Bradlee, and his wife, the novelist Sally Quinn; the Rotary Club, the Washington Redskins, *Superman* ('my X-ray-vision is failing me'), Fred and Ethel Mertz (the Ricardos' neighbours in *I Love Lucy*, played by Bill Frawley and Vivian Vance); allusions to *Reach for the Sky*.

'You May Remember Me From Such Films and TV Series As . . .': The great Corbin Bernsen was Arnie Becker in *LA Law* and appeared in *Rubbernecking*, *The Cape*, *S.O.B.* and *Star Trek: The Next Generation*. Patrick Falls was in *There Are No Children Here*. Kevin Fry's movies include *Femme Fontaine: Killer Babe from the CIA*. Tom McCarthy was in *Beverly Hills Brats*, *Mannequin* and *Blow Out*. Rhonda Overby appeared in *Enemy of the State*. Felicity Huffman was Cynthia in *Magnolia* and Mimi in *Reversal of Fortune*. Tim Williams appeared in *The Mouse*. Bruce Winant played Bruce in *First Years* and was in *Mighty Aphrodite*.

Behind the Camera: Scott Winant worked on *Get Real*, *Earth 2* and *thirtysomething*.

Oh, Donna!: Donna considers that her conversation with Karen Cahill was pithy and erudite as Josh opens a package containing a pair of Donna's panties. 'I know it's your underwear,' Josh says: 'your name is sewn in the back, which obviously we'll talk about later.' A convoluted explanation follows on how she managed to drop these at the South Street Exhibit. Naturally, Cahill sent them back to Donna's boss with a note attached (well, you would, wouldn't you?).

Cigarettes and Alcohol: Ann mentions 'a spicy bouquet that suggests a fine Merlot'. Andrew Johnson's whisky drinking is quoted. Toby fondly remembers sharing bourbon with Ann.

Logic, Let Me Introduce You to This Window: It's half past midnight and there's no heat in the White House, so instead of letting maintenance handle it Sam and Josh build a fire? Yes, these boys *have* no life. The fireplace, with its flue welded shut a century ago, appears to be the one that had a fire burning in it in **18**, 'Six Meetings Before Lunch'.

Quote/Unquote: Charlie, with alarms sounding, to a bleary-eyed Bartlet: 'Remember how you told me not to wake you unless the building was on fire?'

Bartlet: 'Donna wants me to call Karen Cahill and make it clear she wasn't hitting on her when she gave her underwear.' Leo: 'That's 'cos I made fun of her shoes and then Sam said there were nuclear weapons in Kyrgyzstan and Donna went to clear up the mix-up and she accidentally left her underwear.'

Notes: 'Shake my hand. We just formed the committee to re-elect the president.' Leo advises Jed not to think too much about this story, which is good advice. This is a disappointing series of one-joke plots enlivened by odd moments of brilliance (Donna's knickers, chiefly, though Leo and Toby discussing political ideals is effective), but it's a very unsatisfying blend.

Leo says he intends to ask Josh regularly if he's all right (see **32**, 'Noël').

Critique: 'Applying Baryshnikov's precision to musical chairs was a political ballet we danced every day of the week,' noted the *Atlantic Monthly*'s Joshua King. 'President Clinton, like Bartlet, could not have cared less about such things. Put him in his seat, give him his talking points and let him go to work. Granite State-native Bartlet whines that Vermont maple syrup, rather than pancake topping from New Hampshire, has found its way onto the bill-of-fare. Forget the policy implications. Never mind the agenda. The president wants his favorite syrup served to his guests. In real-life, Clinton made sure that his hometown was on the map for more than just his birthplace.'

Cast and Crew Comments: 'You're going to see opposition and you're going to see them making strong, compelling arguments,' Sorkin told the *St Petersburg Times*. 'In our parallel universe, Bartlet's going to need to start running for re-election. And he's facing all kinds of opposition. Including [that] to his left.'

Did You Know?: Karen Cahill, the columnist everyone's trying to placate, may (according to the *Philadelphia Daily News*) be inspired by the *New York Times*' Maureen Dowd, of whom many politicians are, perhaps justifiably, terrified. In early drafts, Sorkin had actually referred to Dowd specifically, he admitted.

34
The Drop In

US Transmission Date: 24 January 2001
UK Transmission Date: 28 August 2001 (E4)

Writer: Aaron Sorkin
Story: Lawrence O'Donnell Jr
Director: Lou Antonio
Cast: Robert Clotworthy (Tom) Rocky Carroll (Corey Sykes)
Alberto Isaac (Tada Sumatra) Erik Holland (Peter Hans)
Jodie Hanson (Caprice) Elkin Antoniou (Bartender)
Eliott Goretsky (Staffer) Brian Watt (Staffer)

John Marbury is appointed Britain's ambassador to the US (to Leo's disgust). Toby and Sam wrangle over an environmental speech. CJ has to get a controversial comedian to decline an invitation to a presidential dinner.

A View from the Hill: Sam, Carl Towb and Jane Ziskin accept an invitation for the president to address the Global Defense Council (GDC), at which he will launch Clean Air Rehabilitation Effort. Toby is unhappy and believes a demonstration that the president isn't beholden to the environmental lobby would be advantageous ('We don't have to move to our right if there's an opportunity to spank the people to our left'). The GDC's failure to admonish acts of eco-terrorism is a suitable reason. Toby doesn't want this in the advance text and, to deal with Sam's objections, he suggests it should be 'a drop in'. Leo reminds Bartlet that he criticised Al Caldwell because the fundamentalists hadn't admonished extremists (see **1**, 'The West Wing'). Bartlet, reluctantly, says that it would be hypocrisy not to hold friends to the same standards. 'I'm not doing this for the politics,' he tells Toby. 'I'm doing it because it's the right thing to do.'

American History X: References to the frontiersman Daniel Boone (1735–1820) and the most decisive battle of the War of Independence, Yorktown (1781).

Swedish History X: Bartlet remarks that Swedes have lived in their country for 5,000 years longer than any other European people and that Swedish Gothic tribes played a role in the fall of the Roman Empire. Sweden has a 100 per cent literacy rate, though Leo suggests, 'Maybe they don't and they also can't count!'

Politics of Protocol: A reporter asks if there's a particular order in which ambassadors are received. CJ replies it's first-come-first-served. Recent arrivals include Peter Hans of Sweden, Renee Ernesto of Argentina, Noah Jola of Burkina Faso. A new British ambassador is also due, though Anthony Bratt had family obligations and Sir Christopher Nealing-Roach withdrew because of illness.

Politics of Compromise: The black comedian Cornelius Sykes has done much work for the Democrats, registering voters and making commercials. During the campaign at a fundraiser he told a joke about New York cops shooting black men, which caused a rumpus in the press. Bartlet's team still insist that Jed didn't laugh at the joke, but are worried that Sykes is due to host another presidential event and ask CJ to get him to withdraw. Sykes says he hoped that, when he was called 'Hollywood Sleaze' in the press, the president (for whom he voted) might have said something in his defence. For instance, that he is a world-class humorist and, though his material can be disconcerting to some, those who were making an issue of the joke were feigning concern to frighten white men. Bartlet *did* laugh at the joke, Corey concludes, but he graciously says he will decline the invitation.

A Little Learning is a Dangerous Thing: CJ has become an expert on ambassadors and the countries they're from, informing various people who couldn't care less that the longest-serving ambassador to the US is Prince Bandar-bin-Sultan of Saudi Arabia; that Burkina Faso has a population of 11,000,000; in even years, it hosts Africa's largest crafts market; and its chief crops are millet, sorghum, rice, peanuts and cotton. And that lumber, cocoa beans, aluminium and petroleum products are the major exports of Cameroon.

The Encyclopedic Mind of Josiah Bartlet PhD: Neither Leo nor Toby knows what a lynx is (Toby thinks it's a possum). Bartlet does.

The Pollution Starts at Closing Time: America is the world's biggest emitter of carbon dioxide. With 4 per cent of the population it's responsible for 25 per cent of greenhouse emissions.

References: The Oriental hotel in Bangkok, the *Centennial* author James Michener (1907–97), King Bhumibol Adulyadej of Thailand. There's a lengthy discussion on Leo's lack of familiarity with Charles Schulz's *Peanuts* (specifically Lucy's 'Football Gag' on Charlie Brown). Also, the Kwajalein Pacific Atoll, the Rat Pack comedian Joey Bishop, Davy Jones (*The Monkees* and *Coronation Street*), Sweden's King Carl Gustaf, Apollo 11 and its commander Neil Armstrong, 'God Save the Queen', *Catch a Rising Star*, the political commentator Cokie Roberts, ABC's *Good Morning America* anchorwoman Diane Sawyer, *60 Minutes*' editor Lesley Stahl and the environmental pressure group the Sierra Club. CJ quotes 'Theme from *New York, New York*'.

'You May Remember Me From Such Films and TV Series As . . .': Robert Clotworthy was in *Vampirella* and *V.I. Warshawski*. Rocky Carroll played Keith Wilkes in *Chicago Hope* and was in *Crimson Tide*. Erik Holland was Professor Langford in *Stargate* and appeared in *Torn Curtain*, *Ghostbusters II*, *The Outlaw Josey Wales*, *The Man from U.N.C.L.E.*, *The Invaders* and *Voyage to the Bottom of the Sea*. Jodie Hanson was Marianne Dwyer in

Brookside. Elkin Antoniou appeared in *CSI* and *Gypsy*. Eliott Goretsky was in *What Lies Beneath* and was casting assistant on *Shiloh*.

Behind the Camera: The director Lou Antonio has had a fascinating career working on *CSI*, *Dawson's Creek*, *American Gothic*, *Dark Skies*, *The Rockford Files*, *McCloud*, *The Flying Nun* and *The Partridge Family*. He also played Jack Ramsey in *Dog and Cat* and Koko in *Cool Hand Luke* and appeared in *Star Trek*, *Mission: Impossible*, *I Dream of Jeannie*, *The Monkees*, *The Fugitive*, *Route 66* and *Gunsmoke*.

Oh, Donna!: Donna grills Marbury about eligible royals. He cites Edward, Earl of Ulster. Does she date younger men, since he's five? Donna decides she may correspond with him, once he learns to read and write.

Sex and Drugs and Rock'n'Roll: Davy Jones once wrote CJ a letter. Marbury calls her 'Principessa'.

Cigarettes and Alcohol: Marbury says it's possible he was drunk when he agreed to become ambassador. He drinks champagne at the reception. Toby and an angry Sam share a beer.

Logic, Let Me Introduce You to This Window: Martin Sheen twice mispronounces 'plenipotentiary'. Richard, Duke of Gloucester, has three children (Alexander, Davina and Rose), but no Edward.

Quote/Unquote: Leo: 'We missed it by a hundred and thirty-seven miles?' Bartlet, sarcastically: 'When you consider the size of outer space, that's not so bad. By the way, the words you're looking for are, "Oh, good grief!"'

Bartlet, to Charlie: 'Two thousand environmentalists are gonna try to kill me tomorrow night. They're gonna come after me with vegan food and pitchforks. I'd like you to get between me and any boiled seaweed you see coming my way.'

CJ, after Toby has incredulously asked why she's getting an award: 'I discovered a *comet*!'

Notes: 'They say a statesman is a politician who's been dead for fifteen years.' Love Lord Marbury, he's so in your face (particularly, Leo's). A clever juggling of four interesting subplots. Best bit: Josh getting hit by the door he's 'relaxing' behind.

Marbury thinks Margaret is looking 'positively buxom' and tells Josh 'the prayers of millions were answered' (see **24**, 'In the Shadow of Two Gunmen' Part 2). He's said to be an expert in defence and notes that the NMD (a missile shield) is an absurdly wasteful military boondoggle that will *never* produce results. It violates the 1972 ABM Treaty, will compel China to strengthen their nuclear arsenal *and* it doesn't work. The environmental champion Seth Gillette is mentioned (see **36**, 'The War at Home'). There are continuity references to **33**, 'The Leadership Breakfast'.

Critique: CJ is to receive a Matrix Award, the New York Women in Communications' annual prize for 'women who change the world' in advertising, publishing and broadcasting. The NYWIC had no forewarning of the plug, but would gladly nominate CJ. 'She's smart, witty, sensitive, she shoots from the hip,' says Maurie Perl, the head of corporate communications at Condé Nast, who have sponsored the luncheon.

Did You Know?: Viewers may notice Bartlet is dealing with a group called the Global Defense Council, the same collective Sorkin used in his movie *The American President*.

35
Bartlet's Third State of the Union

US Transmission Date: 7 February 2001
UK Transmission Date: 4 September 2001 (E4)

Writer: Aaron Sorkin
Story: Allison Abner, Dee Dee Myers
Director: Christopher Misiano

Cast: Barbara Eve Harris (Gretchen Tyler) Kelly McNair (Pollster)
Jon Hershfield (Pollster #2) Keith Mills (Mr Finney)
Michael Francis Clarke (Congressman Satch)
Susan Krebs (Gail Schumer)

It's State of the Union and the White House hosts an
edition of *Capital Beat*. The first lady feels excluded from
her husband's intentions. Colombian guerrillas capture five
DEA agents. A policeman, cited for heroism, has a dark
secret. Josh can't get vital information from Joey.

A View from the Hill: In order for the president to address
Congress, he must first receive permission from the
Speaker. He announces a bipartisan Blue Ribbon Commis-
sion to study the future of entitlements programmes.

American History X: With the power out, Josh asks for 'a
lightning bolt, a key and a kite', a reference to electricity
experiments by Benjamin Franklin (1706–90).

Politics of a Liberal Democrat?: Bartlet challenges American schools to teach character, values and citizenship. If it
means children pay more attention to maths, English
literature, history, science and the arts than to designer
labels then students should be required to wear uniforms.

The Encyclopedic Mind of Josiah Bartlet PhD: While balancing
his chequebook, the president discovers an outstanding
cheque, written by the first lady, for $500 that was never
cashed. Charlie asks why the president does this balancing? To
relax, suggests Mrs Landingham. The cheque was sent to a
woman who was a victim of domestic violence and who
framed it. Charlie makes sure she gets the money in cash.

Denial, Thy Name is Abbey: Three years ago Abbey and
Jed made a deal that he would run for president for one
term. Abbey now realises that he's seeking re-election and
is angry at his change of heart.

The Conspiracy Starts at Closing Time: Jack Sloane, a
Detroit policeman, was invited to the State of the Union
after a recent heroic action at an elementary school.

Seventeen years ago, after he had pursued an armed robber called Walter Tapus, it was alleged that he broke the accused man's leg. Sloane denied this and both criminal and civil cases against him were dismissed. However, there was community pressure from black groups and Sloane received an official reprimand, which remains on file.

References: CNN's Bob Novak, C-SPAN, the English dramatist, composer and wit Noël Coward (1899–1973), Special Operations Command at Fort Bragg, the Lone Ranger's pal Tonto, Cassiopeia (the Greek goddess and mother of Andromeda) and the comedienne Gracie Allen. Joey obliquely refers to Sid and Marty Kofft's *Electra Woman and Dynagirl*. Josh reads *Vogue*.

You May Remember Me From Such Films and TV Series As . . .': Tony Plana played Bringuier in *JFK* and appeared in *Nixon*, *Three Amigos!* and *Valley Girl*. Richard Riehle's movies include *Fear and Loathing in Las Vegas*, *Casino*, *Fried Green Tomatoes*, *Office Space* and *Free Willy*. Glenn Morshower played Aaron Pierce in *24* and appeared in *Black Hawk Down*, *CSI*, *The Core*, *Godzilla*, *Air Force One*, *Buffy*, *Under Siege* and *JAG*. Barbara Eve Harris appeared in *Ignition* and *36 Hours to Die*. Kelly McNair played Caitlin in *Love Leprosy*. Keith Mills was Judge Green in *LA Law*. Michael Francis Clarke appeared in *The Rocketeer*. Doris McMillon's movies include *In the Line of Fire*. Susan Krebs was in *28 Days* and *Earth Girls are Easy*.

Oh, Donna!: She spends the episode trying to get Josh to ask Joey on a date (see **36**, 'The War at Home'). When the power fails, she expresses surprise at the lack of looting.

Sex and Drugs and Rock'n'Roll: After sitting on a freshly painted bench, Ainsley retires to her office, puts on a bathrobe, drinks a Pink Squirrel Suzy (a lethal cocktail) and dances to Annette Funicello's kitsch classic 'Blame it on the Bossa Nova'.

Colombian Marxist rebels abduct five US antidrug agents in Putumayo. The rebels are called The Frente ('the front') or the CRF.

Gun Law: Toby brilliantly argues down Shallick's anti-gun-control argument and the belief that the second amendment says federal government won't infringe the right to bear arms. Toby observes that it doesn't say that unless you take some words away. It *does* say: 'A well-regulated militia being necessary for the security of a free state, the government shall not infringe . . .' He doesn't think the framers were thinking of three guys in a Dodge Durango. He also notes that, if you combine the populations of Britain, France, Germany, Japan, Switzerland, Sweden, Denmark and Australia, you'll get a population roughly the size of the US, which had 32,000 gun deaths last year. All the others put together had 112. Does Shallick think it's because Americans are more homicidal by nature or because the other countries have gun controls?

Logic, Let Me Introduce You to This Window: The echo is missing from Bartlet's voice when he makes his speech, indicating that he was not in the Senate chamber, but a TV studio. Palm trees can be seen as the motorcade goes through the shot. When CJ is talking to Sam during a break in her TV slot, the floor manager is giving updates on the time before they're due to go back on air. The gap between ten seconds and five seconds is *very* long. Why does Charlie return to the White House before the end of the president's speech? One of the countries Toby mentions in connection with gun-control laws, Switzerland, actually has a very similar constitution to the US, all men of military age being trained by the government in the proficient use of privately held weapons.

Quote/Unquote: Joey: 'My plane had mechanical difficulties.' Josh: 'There was nothing you could do about it?' Joey: 'No. Because as a child I never paid attention during airplane mechanics class.'

CJ: 'You know why I'm not wearing pants?' Sam: 'I assumed it was the usual reason.'

Sam, to Ainsley: 'Remember, you're a blonde, Republican girl and nobody likes you!'

Toby: 'We gave Republicans plenty to be pissed about. The surplus, missile defence, capital gains. I was just on TV for the nine hundredth time and alienated gun owners, to say nothing of people who own Dodge Durangos.'

Notes: 'This was almost a good night.' Another terrific combination of big issues (education, drugs, foreign policy) and minor domestic trials. The Josh/Donna/Joey subplot is brilliantly played (and hysterically funny), while everyone gets plenty of lighter moments. Highlight: Bartlet meeting a drunk, dancing Ainsley.

During the address, the president was interrupted for applause 73 times.

Critique: 'To make this guy a practising Catholic who crosses himself before major events in his life creates a powerful sense of the earnest leader,' says Professor Robert Thompson. As Bartlet's character unfolds, Thompson notes, 'we get a sense that he really believes in God, that he's not using Him as a campaign consultant'. In a highly critical article, the *Seattle Post-Intelligencer*'s John Levesque wrote: 'Sorkin needs to know he's not doing women any favors, and that anyone who thinks his show is an intelligent alternative to the baseness of something like *Temptation Island* is likely to be disappointed.' He cited, as an example, CJ and Ainsley, 'placed in situations that made them look like victims of flighty femaleness after sitting in wet paint. More distressing: Sorkin's script belittled them in the presence of men who seemed to enjoy the women's discomfort like drunks at a bachelor party.'

Cast and Crew Comments: 'You're going to meet Ed Begley Jr., who [plays a character that] will remind you of Ralph Nader in that he's coming from the left,' Sorkin told Rob Owen. 'He's a junior senator from Dakota who is the darling of the environmental lobby and of liberal causes and is planning on causing trouble for Bartlet in terms of re-election.'

Did You Know?: Concerning the 'Bossa Nova' sequence, Emily Procter told an AOL chat: 'The scene was scripted but I, unfortunately, had to come up with the dancing. I spent many hours alone with myself in front of my mirror . . . I thought I had figured out a way to seem cool while I was doing it, but it just didn't happen.'

36
The War at Home

US Transmission Date: 14 February 2001
UK Transmission Date: 18 September 2001 (E4)[88]

Writer: Aaron Sorkin
Director: Christopher Misiano
Cast: Adam Alexi-Malle (Translator) Ed Begley Jr (Seth Gillette)
Lee Warren Jones (Aide) J Michael Flynn (Officer)

The Colombian crisis intensifies. A liberal Senator threatens to run as an independent against Bartlet and split the votes of the left. Joey's polling numbers are discouraging. Abbey feels betrayed by Jed.

A View from the Hill: Democrat Seth Gillette asks for White House support for his reform bill. Toby observes he got eighteen votes last year and points out that 'the president's not a member of your party. He's the *leader* of your party. If you think demonising people who are trying to govern responsibly is the way to protect our liberal base, then, speaking as a liberal, *go to bed.*' Gillette accuses Toby of 'running to the right' on the environment. Toby admits he admonished environmental terrorism (**34**, 'The Drop In'). It was a cheap shot, says Gillette and lost the president friends among seniors, environmentalists and African-Americans. Toby says Gillette has named three groups who will never desert the president.

Politics of Rhetoric: Five Congressional districts (Kentucky 3rd, Louisiana 4th, Missouri 6th and 9th and Ohio 12th)

---

[88] Originally scheduled for 11 September 2001 but postponed owing to the World Trade Center and Pentagon attacks earlier that day.

concern Josh. Bartlet is to introduce a crime bill that will require a five-day waiting period for gun purchase. The Congressmen for those districts are nervous and that's why he's anxious for polling figures. The issue polled well nationwide at 58 per cent. But in those districts it was much lower, to Josh's disappointment. Joey asks why, instead of softening the spin, they don't increase it. Josh refers to the numbers and what they indicate, but Joey responds that these are people who simply haven't been persuaded yet.

A Little Learning is a Dangerous Thing: The State of the Union address contained 8,747 words and was second only in length to Bartlet's inaugural address. It was 75 minutes longer than Washington's first address to Congress.

The Encyclopedic Mind of Josiah Bartlet PhD: Bartlet says that the US imprisons a higher percentage of citizens than Russia did under communism and South Africa under apartheid.

Denial, Thy Name is Donna: She continues her perverse mission to hook Josh up with Joey. She thinks they make a nice couple and, once married, would be Joshua and Josephine Lucas-Lyman and, thus, wouldn't need to get their towels re-monogrammed. In a revealing moment, Joey tells Josh that if he polled a hundred Donnas and asked them if they thought Josh and Joey should date, he'd get a high positive response. But it wouldn't tell him that it's because Donna likes him and knows it's beginning to show, so is covering herself with misdirection.

The Incursion Starts at Closing Time: A nineteen-man Special Forces unit is already on the ground in Tres Encinas. They head to Villacerreno, hike into the jungle and await sunset, when the hostages are to be moved. They are joined by further, helicopter-based, Delta commando units. However, radio communications were fake and one of the Blackhawks is shot down, killing nine men. For the kind of victory Americans are used to in war, Mickey tells the president, he will need a ten-to-one ratio, as in the

Gulf. The Frente has 20,000 well-armed soldiers, each with a financial stake in heroin and cocaine. The US would need to put 200,000 men into a jungle war and possibly lose as many as half.

References: The Irish playwright George Bernard Shaw (1856–1950), the *Washington Post* journalist and co-author of *All the President's Men* Bob Woodward, the CNN anchor Jeff Greenfield, the Hyatt hotel in Washington, *USA Today*, Gallup, elfin dancer Joey Heatherton, the Greek dramatist Euripides (*c.* 484–406 BC), the House of Atreus (the family tree of Zeus in Greek mythology), the 'Just Say No' campaign, novelist Truman Capote (1924–84). Toby makes an oblique reference to Elizabeth Barrett Browning's *Sonnets from the Portuguese*. Abbey misquotes *Hamlet* ('if wishing made it so').

'You May Remember Me From Such Films and TV Series As . . .': Adam Alexi-Malle was in *Bowfinger*. Ed Begley Jr appeared in *Get Over It*, *This is Spinal Tap*, *Streets of Fire*, *St Elsewhere*, *Ironside*, *Laverne and Shirley* and *Wonder Woman*.

Oh, Donna!: Josh has already sacked her twice tonight, but she says she's impervious to it.

Sex and Drugs and Rock'n'Roll: Josh tells Sam that when Donna has dates he isn't jealous, though he doesn't like it and usually does everything within his considerable capabilities to sabotage them.

Cigarettes and Alcohol: Toby smokes a cigar while drinking beer with Sam.

Logic, Let Me Introduce You to This Window: Why can Toby smoke inside the White House, but the president can't? Does the *New York Times* really use 'oftentimes' instead of 'often'? What's Sam doing in a foreign-policy meeting (see **1**, 'The West Wing')? Come to that, what are Donna, and several other rather low-level aides doing in such a meeting where military options are being discussed?

Quote/Unquote: Toby, on Gillette: 'He's a junior Senator from North Dakota, where nobody lives, 'cos it's too cold and they don't have a major sports franchise.'

Leo: 'How ya doing?' Ainsley: 'I'm concerned about peeing on your carpet.' Leo: 'OK. Now I am too.' When she emerges from a closet she thought was a bathroom, Bartlet says, 'They won't let me smoke inside, but you can pee in Leo's closet?'

Josh, on terrorist kidnapping: 'You don't think they're gonna kidnap another five people tomorrow and demand twelve months of free cable?' Donna: 'So you give them free cable.' Josh: 'How about the keys to the Situation Room?' Donna: 'You draw a line.' Josh: 'Where?'

Leo: 'If I could put myself anywhere in time it would be the Cabinet Room on August 4th 1964, when our ships were attacked by North Vietnam in the Tonkin Gulf. I'd say, "Mr President, don't do it. You're considering authorising a massive commitment of troops and throwing in our lot with torturers and panderers, leaders without principle and soldiers without conviction, with no clear mission and no end in sight."'

Notes: 'I inherited "War on Drugs" from a president who inherited it from a president who inherited it from a president before that. I'm not sure who we're fighting but I know we're not winning.' A remarkably mature look at the complexities of the political and military parts of foreign relations. Touching and effective scenes between Sheen and Channing, who credibly present a (loving) marital conflict very convincingly. The chess metaphor that Jed and Leo use is also a cunning touch. Listen to Bartlet's query about what's to stop him sending CIA black ops into Colombia to assassinate Aguilar and consider the events of autumn 2001, which were still months away when this episode was shown.

The *West Wing* universe's president of Colombia is Miguel Santos. Negotiations are through an intermediary called Nelson Güerra for the release of the imprisoned drug baron Juan Aguilar in exchange for the hostages (see

35, 'Bartlet's Third State of the Union'). Aguilar runs one of the largest drug cartels in the world, has produced fifteen billion dollars' worth of cocaine in two years and ordered the murder of eight Supreme Court justices, a pro-extradition prime minister and three federal police officers in Bogotá.

Cast and Crew Comments: For the scene of coffins returning, the idea was 'to barely show the image', said Thomas Schlamme. 'We don't want to be maudlin. There's a way to create that imagery and be powerful without going too far.'

Did You Know?: Each episode usually requires about a hundred hours of shooting for its 44 minutes of screen time.

37
Ellie

US Transmission Date: 21 February 2001
UK Transmission Date: 25 September 2001 (E4)

Writer: Aaron Sorkin
Story: Kevin Falls, Laura Glasser
Director: Michael Engler
Cast: Mary Kay Place (Surgeon General Millicent Griffith)
Nina Siezmaszko (Ellie Bartlet) Robert Knepper (Morgan Ross)
Paul Eiding (Labor Leader) John Capodice (Lenny)
Ned Schmidtke (Industry Leader #1) Greg Baker (Interviewer)
James Kiriyama-Lem (Industry Leader #2)

The Surgeon General controversially discusses marijuana and is supported by the president's daughter, Ellie. Charlie's choice of movie for the president proves controversial. Toby tries to enlist Andi to make peace with liberals over social security.

A View from the Hill: The American Association for Retired People (AARP) wants the president to put Seth Gillette (see **36**, 'The War at Home') on the Blue Ribbon

Commission. The White House would also like this since he can't attack it if he's on it. However, if they offer him the position and he turns it down it will be a massive slap in the face to the administration.

Politics of Sneakiness: Toby discovered that he is on the benefit committee for the Child Leukemia Foundation by reading about it in the paper (Andi put him on without asking him first). This gives Toby an idea how to get around the problem that Gillette might turn down the offer by announcing that he's *accepted* it. He tells CJ to inform the press that Gillette put the party above personal differences, that he's a patriot, and, when asked to serve, he answered the call.

A Little Learning is a Dangerous Thing: Margaret notes that red meat, maraschino cherries and mobile phones have all been found to cause cancer in white rats. Has anyone examined the possibility, she wonders, that cancer might just be *hereditary* in rats?

The Encyclopedic Mind of Josiah Bartlet PhD: He has the kind of knowledge of different areas of medicine that you'd expect from the husband of a doctor.

Denial, Thy Names are Jed and Ellie: The father–daughter relationship is complicated. Millie suggests that Ellie has always been frightened of Bartlet, that she quickly decided she wasn't his favourite and that she is uncomfortable around him.

The Conspiracy Starts at Closing Time: A newspaper advert by the Family Values Leadership Council congratulates prominent people, including the president, for denouncing a controversial movie, *Prince of New York*. Its producer, Morgan Ross, spoke to Charlie about screening it at the White House. Charlie didn't think the movie, a version of Dostoyevsky's *The Idiot*, about a Christlike epileptic who embodies goodness, but encounters sex, crime and family dysfunction, would be the president's thing, and chose *Dial M for Murder* instead (as Ross points out, Hitchcock used plenty of sex and violence in *his* movies). Ross, subsequently suggested Bartlet was cowardly for siding with puritanical censors.

References: The Allman Brothers, *The Today Show*, Tim Russert (see **27**, 'And it's Surely to Their Credit'), the International Date Line and Greenwich Mean Time, Alfred Hitchcock's *Dial M for Murder* and its stars Ray Milland, Grace Kelly, Robert Cummings and John Williams; also Don Imus (see **25**, 'The Midterms'), the 1930 Hawley-Smoot Tariff Act, the Great Depression, Pringles, Twinkies, the 1970s comedians Cheech and Chong, San Francisco's Golden Gate Bridge, NFL, National Hockey League, the V-Chip and *King Lear*.

You May Remember Me From Such Films and TV Series As . . .': Mary Kay Place appeared in *Junk, Girl, Interrupted, Being John Malkovich, Teresa's Tattoo* and *The Big Chill*. She co-wrote several episodes of *M*A*S*H* and has directed *Friends*. Nina Siemaszko was Beth Wade in *The American President* and Suzzi in *Airheads* and appeared in *Jakob the Liar*. Robert Knepper was in *Jaded* and *Phantoms*. Paul Eiding was a voice artist on *The Iron Giant, A Bug's Life* and *Transformers*. John Capodice appeared in *Enemy of the State, Jacob's Ladder, Angel, Speed* and *The Doors*. Ned Schmidtke was in *Mercury Rising* and *Roswell*. Greg Baker played Elliot in *Sports Night*. James Kiriyama-Lem was in *Magnolia, Space: Above & Beyond* and *Babylon 5*.

Behind the Camera: Michael Engler directed episodes of *Once and Again, Party of Five, My So-Called Life* and *Dream On*.

Sex and Drugs and Rock'n'Roll: During an online chat, the Surgeon General suggests that she favours the decriminalisation of marijuana, saying it poses no greater public health risk than nicotine or alcohol and doesn't share the same addictive properties of heroin and LSD.

Logic, Let Me Introduce You to This Window: LSD isn't physically addictive (although a psychological dependency is likely).

Quote/Unquote: Josh: 'Did you know sixty-nine per cent of Americans oppose legalisation? Only twenty-three per cent support it.' Millie: 'The number gets a lot higher than that if you ask people under thirty.' Josh: 'That's a shock. Did you know that the number gets even higher than that if you limit the polling sample to Bob Marley and the Wailers?'

CJ: 'I'm the enforcer. I'm gonna crush him, make him cry, and then tell his momma about it.'

Donna: 'In a free society. You don't need a reason to make something legal: you need a reason to make something illegal.'

Bartlet: 'Who's coming to her defence?' Josh: 'The Cannabis Society, the Cannabis Coalition, E-Cannabis-Unum, the American Hemp League and Friends of Mary Jane!'

Notes: 'I've got to hand it to you guys: you've pulled off a political first. You've managed to win me the support of the Christian Right and the Cheech and Chong Fan Club in the same day.' A much more serious episode than normal, about the difficulties some parents have with their children. That Bartlet, a loving and gentle man whom his other daughters seem to adore, has such a strained relationship with Ellie is interesting.

Eleanor is 24 and a medical student at Johns Hopkins in Baltimore, considering specialising in oncology or neurology. She likes her professors, especially her pathophysiology teacher. She clashed with her father over public statements she made in support of the Surgeon General, Millicent Griffith, her godmother. She wasn't around much during Bartlet's presidential campaign. Danny is mentioned (it was he whom Ellie called to make her show of support). One of the White House clocks is always set to the time wherever the president is.

Critique: 'It was a realistic portrayal,' says John Rother, AARP's Director of Legislation and Policy, about the subplot concerning a commission on social security. It reminded Rother of many White House negotiations he's taken part in. The only difference: 'Meetings usually take place in small offices with only a few people, not in the Roosevelt Room,' said Rother. 'And I have a beard and the actor who played me didn't.'

38
Somebody's Going to Emergency, Somebody's Going to Jail

US Transmission Date: 28 February 2001
UK Transmission Date: 2 October 2001 (E4)

Writers: Paul Redford, Aaron Sorkin
Director: Jessica Yu
Cast: Roma Maffia (Rhonda Sachs) Jolie Jenkins (Stephanie Gault)
Clark Gregg (Mike Casper) John Billingsley (John Fallow)
Jordan Baker (Cynthia Sayles) Brent Hinkley (Donald Huke)
Christopher Neiman (OMB Staffer) Richard Stay (Terry Webber)
Shana O'Neil (Protester #1) Free Brooks (Protester #2)
Michael Charles Vaccaro (Protester #3)
Shirley Jordan (FBI Receptionist) John Strand (Cop)

Toby meets anticapitalist demonstrators. CJ encounters Cartographers for Social Equality. A friend of Donna's asks Sam to pursue a pardon for her grandfather.

American History X: More McCarthy/HUAC horrors (see **1**, 'The West Wing'). The FBI rounded up some pretty dangerous TV comedy writers, Sam tells Josh's friend Mike Casper of the FBI. The Bureau have had moments in their past they're not proud of, Mike concedes. But their failures are public and their successes private: 'When we learned it wasn't the Secret Service who ordered the canopy down at Rosslyn, we kept it to ourselves' (see **24**, 'In the Shadow of Two Gunmen' Part 2). General George Marshall (1880–1959), Eisenhower's mentor, created the

Marshall plan for postwar reconstruction in Europe. Falsely accused victims of HUAC include the sinologist Owen Lattimore (1900–89), journalist IF Stone (1907–89) and blacklisted Oscar-winning screenwriter Ring Lardner. Abraham Lincoln signed an executive pardon on the day he was assassinated (14 April 1865) for a Union deserter named Patrick Murphy.

Politics of Compromise: It's Big-Block-of-Cheese day again (see **5**, 'The Crackpots and These Women').

Everything You Know is Wrong: CJ objects to her assignment, meeting Cartographers for Social Equality, since she can't see what map makers find socially unequal. Their presentation astonishes her. The 1569 map, drawn by the Flemish cartographer Gerardus Mercator (1512–94), remains the standard world map despite being inaccurate in terms of relative size between continents. It has helped to foster European imperialist attitudes and created an ethnic bias against the Third World. An alternative, developed by the German historian Arno Peters, was introduced in Europe in 1973.

The Encyclopedic Mind of Josiah Bartlet PhD: Charlie explains that the proposed site for the Bartlet Presidential Library violates the Historic Barn and Bridges Preservation Act, which requires that farm and ranch structures built prior to 1900 be preserved unless destroyed by an act of God. Bartlet asks, 'What plaid-flannel-wearing, cheese-eating yahoo of a milkman-governor signed that idiot bill into law?' Then concludes, 'It was me, wasn't it?'

In the Interests of National Security: Daniel Gault, Stephanie's grandfather, was a special economic assistant to Roosevelt in the 1940s. He was jailed for perjury under HUAC and died in prison six months later. There was only one witness against him: Earl Lydecker, a low-level State Department staffer, who confessed to FBI counterintelligence that he and Gault conspired to send economic analysis documents to Soviet agents. According to a retired KGB colonel, Oleg Prosorov, a search of the files in

Lubyanka revealed one reference to Gault. That he was approached in 1943 and labelled highly uncooperative and a poor prospect for recruitment. Stephanie's father requested Gault's FBI file in the 1970s under the Freedom of Information Act. The judge ruled the file couldn't be completely disclosed, since it breached three of the nine exemptions allowed: National Defense and Foreign Relations Information, Internal Agency Rules and Practices and Personal Privacy.

Nancy McNally, however, confirms to Sam that Gault was indeed a spy, an agent called Blackwater. He was a delegate at Yalta and returned to the US by way of Rostov, where he was given the Order of Lenin. He was responsible for, among other things, the death in 1952 of a translator in the Hungarian trade mission named Shaba Demsky, who was murdered as she was about to reveal Blackwater's identity.

The Conspiracy Starts at Closing Time: The World Trade Organisation is a group of 140 countries who agree to specific trade policies. Toby tells Rhonda that the benefits of this include cheaper food, clothes, cars and phone services. It lowers prices, it raises income. And, best of all, free trade stops wars.

References: The title is from the lyric of 'New York Minute' by Don Henley. Also, the World Bank, the National Geographic Society, dissident Russian author Aleksandr Solzhenitsyn, *Brigadoon*, *The Adventures of Robin Hood* ('merrie men') and *Sam and Cokie*. Sam alludes to *Santa Claus is Coming to Town*. Leo boasts he's fired people before breakfast, a reference to *Alice in Wonderland*.

'You May Remember Me From Such Films and TV Series As . . .': Roma Maffia was in *Double Jeopardy*, *Kiss the Girls*, *Profiler* and *Smithereens*. Jolie Jenkins appeared in *Psycho Beach Party* and *Shasta McNasty*. Shirley Jordan was in *General Hospital*. Clark Gregg's movies include *The Usual Suspects* and *Magnolia* and he wrote the screenplay for *What Lies Beneath*. John Billingsley plays Dr Phlox in *Star Trek: Enterprise*. Shana O'Neil appeared in *Not My Kid*. Jordan Baker played Willow's mom in *Buffy* and appeared in *Escape from L.A.* Brent Hinkley was in *The Silence of the Lambs*, *Bob Roberts*, *Carnival of Souls* and *Ed Wood*. Christopher Neiman appeared in *The X-Files*. Richard Stay was in *Teenage Bonnie and Klepto Clyde*.

Behind the Camera: A member of the 1986 USA fencing team, Jessica Yu stumbled into film production when looking for a job that had flexible hours to allow her to continue her sporting career. She directed *Better Late* and *Sour Death Balls*.

Sex and *Double Entendre* and Rock'n'Roll: Professor Huke quotes Salvatore Natoli of the National Council for Social Studies: 'In our society we unconsciously equate size with importance, and even power.' Josh looks at CJ for confirmation and she nods that this is true.

Cigarettes and Alcohol: Josh, Toby and Donna intend to take Sam out and get him drunk.

Logic, Let Me Introduce You to This Window: White House sugar packets don't have labels or manufacturers' names on them, only a presidential seal. Stephanie is a professor of international relations at the Maxwell School and is consulting on macroeconomic policy for a trade forum. It's unlikely that an IR professor would consult on macroeconomic policy.

Cruelty To Animals: Ed offers to trade his meeting with NIH (National Institutes of Health) representatives seeking funding for research on cancer treatment involving shark cartilage. Larry says he'll swap for 'Citizens for DC Statehood'. Ed isn't keen. Donna mentions she's meeting the Kemps-Ridley Sea Turtle Society, but she's keeping it.

Quote/Unquote: Toby, on the deficiencies of modern-day protesters: 'Cops know exactly where they're gonna be and what's gonna happen by logging on their website. We had the underground, we had rapid response.' CJ: 'And, by

God, you were home by supper on a school night.' Toby: 'These people are amateurs. What's my assignment?' Leo: 'Meeting with the amateurs!'

Toby, to Rhonda: 'How many different ways do you know to kill a man?'

Toby: 'They claim to speak for the underprivileged, but here in the blackest city in America, I'm looking at a room with no black faces, no Asians, no Hispanics. Where the hell's the Third World they claim to represent?' Rhonda: 'Lot of Third-Worlders in the Cabinet Room today, were there?'

Sam, on Gault and betrayal generally: 'It was high treason . . . This country is an idea, and one that's lit the world for two centuries. Treason against that idea is not just a crime against the living. This ground holds the graves of people who died for it.'

Notes: 'I don't know if this is the best time to tell you, but, according to CJ, I wouldn't be so sure about longitude and latitude.' Utterly magnificent, an indirect sequel to **5**, 'The Crackpot and These Women', and, in its own way, every bit as good. A story about dealing with betrayal and the sins of the father and discovering that what you've always believed is a lie. Multilayered, hugely amusing in Toby and CJ's subplots, but a descent into hell for Sam. This is *The West Wing* at its very best.

Lionel Tribbey is mentioned (see **27**, 'And it's Surely to Their Credit'). Staff aren't allowed to give tours until after 10 p.m., once the president is out of the West Wing.

Critique: Rich Mills, spokesman for the US Trade Representative Robert Zoellick, rejoiced when Toby gave the antitrade protesters an earful. 'I was pumped,' Mills told Faye Fiore.

Cast and Crew Comments: 'Paul Redford said: "Why don't we do a story about a pardon?" ' Sorkin told the *New York Times*, 'But there's controversy surrounding the pardon, and it doesn't have anything to do with influence peddling.'

'New facts are particularly devastating for those who say Richard Nixon made his name as a Commie-basher and tore down Alger Hiss for his own good,' Rob Lowe told Phil Rosenthal. 'Nixon was right about Hiss and people don't realize that. I'm no fan of Nixon, but it turns out that he was right. Julius and Ethel Rosenberg, too. They were both *cause célèbres*, for Democrats.' In another interview, with Scott Pierce, Lowe added, 'Sam often gets righteously indignant and he's almost always right. One of the things I loved about this episode was that he gets the carpet yanked from underneath him. I was swept away with the character's disillusionment and betrayal.' The episode also gave Lowe and Janel Moloney, who aren't often in scenes together, an opportunity to interact. 'I loved that Donna was the one to comfort Sam. There was something unexpected and it feels right,' Lowe said. 'Aaron knows his stuff. I thought maybe he would've put me with Allison Janney. He chose Donna, and I think it worked really well. She's a wonderful actress.' And he told *TV Guide*: 'I've always been unabashedly romantic and patriotic about this system, even when it was uncool to be. When Sam gives a speech to Donna about why treason is so terrible, that sort of gives voice to that part of myself.'

Did You Know?: As a direct consequence of this episode, sales for Peters projection maps rocketed in the US.

39
The Stackhouse Filibuster

US Transmission Date: 14 March 2001
UK Transmission Date: 9 October 2001 (E4)

Writer: Aaron Sorkin
Story: Pete McCabe
Director: Bryan Gordon
Cast: George Coe (Senator Howard Stackhouse)
Cara DeLizia (Winifred Hooper) Pete Leal (Stewart)
Darren Foreman (VP's Aide #2) Larry Stahoviak[89] (Staffer #1)

---

[89] Actor appeared as Steve in **22**, 'What Kind of Day Has it Been' – this may be a different character.

Lisa Croisette[90] (Staffer #2) Jessica Pennington (Sally)
Harrison Young (Senator Grissom) Dilva Henry (News Anchor)
Ron Harper (Chairman)

Weekend plans are interrupted by a Friday-night filibuster on a children's health bill. Toby is surprised when Hoynes offers to attack oil companies. CJ fears she's the victim of a curse.

Politics of Integrity and Stubbornness: The $6 billion Family Wellness Act is an omnibus health bill aimed at diseases that disproportionately affect children. After much bargaining *everybody*'s happy with it. Except the 78-year-old Minnesota Senator Howard Stackhouse, who uses a filibuster, reading from a cookbook (the recipe for deep-fried fantail shrimp sounds terrific), the rules of cards and *David Copperfield*. The filibuster's been a part of parliamentary strategy for centuries and the rules are simple: you have the floor as long as you don't stop talking, don't eat, don't drink, don't visit the bathroom, don't sit down and don't lean on anything. Stackhouse wanted to add an amendment allocating money for autism care, research and a programme to educate doctors to reduce misdiagnoses, but was refused, for the best of motives, by Josh. Stackhouse argues that during negotiations money was allocated for Alzheimer's, glaucoma and erectile dysfunction. Leo believes Stackhouse is a decent, honourable man though Bartlet isn't a fan ('he's a curmudgeon, a grouchy old crank'), probably because Stackhouse calls him 'Bartlet the Inert'. Donna learns that one of Stackhouse's seven grandchildren has autism. She also comes up with a solution: the Senator is allowed to take a question without yielding the floor. Answering a plea from the White House, Senator Tom Grissom of Washington State raises a point of order and Stackhouse is given a rest and the opportunity to answer questions about autism. Thus, the bill runs out of time, and Josh can return to the conference chairman and reopen it to include the amendment next week.

---

[90] Actor appeared as Patty in **22**, 'What Kind of Day Has it Been' – this may be a different character.

A Little Learning is a Dangerous Thing: A sassy intern, Winifred Hooper, seems to be an expert on everything, particularly municipal solid waste and the pay rates for garbagemen.

The Conspiracy Starts at Closing Time: Philip Sluman, chairman of the Petroleum Producers, says the administration's relentless pursuit of stricter emission standards is the cause of higher oil prices. Leo suggests that Bill Trotter, the Energy Secretary, respond. Toby would like to mention that to the vice president, who is a friend of the oil companies. Hoynes, surprisingly, is warm to the idea and says it shouldn't be Trotter because his rants against corporations are familiar, and he volunteers for the job himself. He's holding a press conference and is sure he'll be asked about Sluman. Subsequently he makes a strong statement in support of government policy, which has resulted in the cleanest air in California in fifty years. Hoynes readily admits that some of those CEOs are old friends, but adds that they know how to turn a profit. Josh is reminded of how close Hoynes came to being elected president. Toby is also impressed, but very suspicious of Hoynes's motives. He knows about private polling that shows a significant number of voters to be concerned about Hoynes's ties. He asks Hoynes what he knows that Toby doesn't. 'The total tonnage of what I know that you don't could stun a team of oxen in its tracks,' replies the vice president (see **40**, '17 People'). Bartlet, meanwhile, suggests to Leo that Hoynes knows about the president's illness and believes Bartlet may not seek re-election.

References: The architect Frank Lloyd Wright (1867–1959), fashion designer Tommy Hilfiger, the New York sport teams the Mets, the Jets and the Knicks, *Gilligan's Island*, the California Aqueduct, the US railway Amtrak, the stationery retailer Kinko's, Route 66 (the highway from Chicago to LA) and the song '(Get Your Kicks On) Route 66' by Bobby Troup (famous versions include those by Nat King Cole, Chuck Berry and the Rolling Stones), Provençal cuisine (cassoulet, duck with green olives, saffron chicken and *tomate du saltambique*), the former vice president Hubert Humphrey (1911–78). Sam plays computer solitaire. There's a Norwegian flag in Stackhouse's office.

'You May Remember Me From Such Films and TV Series As . . .': George Coe appeared in *Big Eden*, *Cousins*, *Max Headroom*, *The Entity*, *The Stepford Wives*, *Hill Street Blues* and *Star Trek: The Next Generation*. Cara DeLizia was in *So Weird*. Darren Foreman appeared in *Digital Man*. Shishir Kurup worked on *Anywhere But Here*. Jessica Pennington's movies include *Ed*. Harrison Young played Old Ryan in *Saving Private Ryan*. Ron Harper was Alan Virdon in *Planet of the Apes*. Pete Leal appeared in *Hotel Oasis*.

Behind the Camera: Bryan Gordon was a director on *Boston Public*, *Freaks and Geeks* and *The Wonder Years*. He wrote *Pie in the Sky* and has acted in *Corrina Corrina* and *Panic in Echo Park*. Pete McCabe wrote *If Looks Could Kill*.

Pussy Galore: CJ explains to Donna the history of cat worship in ancient Egypt, particularly during the 22nd Dynasty (*c.* 900 BC). Unfortunately, CJ accidentally breaks a priceless statue of Bast, the Egyptian cat-goddess of the Dead.

Oh, Donna!: CJ describes Donna as 'someone whose criminal mind is equal to my own' as Donna helps her fix the statue with Krazy-Glue.

Watch Donna's reaction to the revelation that Josh's mother bought him some shoes.

Sex and *Double Entendre* and Rock'n'Roll: CJ tells Sam, 'I hear you got spanked by some fourteen-year-old intern.' The president's euphemism for his illness is 'my thing'.

Weekend Plans: Sam is staying in Sag Harbor in the Hamptons with friends; Josh is going to Port Saint Lucie to watch the New York Mets spring training (is that *sad* or what?); Toby has something to do in Telluride; and CJ is going to her father's seventieth-birthday party in Napa.

Pizza and Alcohol: CJ tells Carol they're going to need a whole load of pizza for the press corps and some Cuervo 1800 for CJ. Bartlet has a brandy after dinner. Josh and Donna share a bottle of beer in the office.

Logic, Let Me Introduce You to This Window: Winifred says she's read all the reports the White House receives from Congress. *All* 3,000 of them? There are not enough hours in the day for that, even if they *do* let her come in early and stay late. CJ's fishbowl appears to be empty. Has Gail escaped? Why does someone off screen have Josh's wallet?

Quote/Unquote: Sam wonders how many recipes there can be. CJ: 'Altogether? I can't cook, but I think there are probably, like, twenty or thirty.'

Josh: 'Mike Piazza's gonna be standing in the batting cage. He's gonna turn, see me and say, *"Dude!"*' CJ: 'I wouldn't want you to miss a legitimate dude sighting.'

Sam, on a report on Route 66: 'Anything in there I don't get from the song?'

Bartlet tells Leo that he'd expected to have dinner with Abbey: 'We'll just pretend there's no candlelight.' Leo: 'Or, that we're not paranoid homophobes.'

CJ: 'Tonight I've seen a man with no legs stay standing. And a guy with no voice keep shouting. And, if politics brings out the worst in people, maybe people bring out the best.'

Notes: 'Don't *ever* underestimate the will of a grandfather. We're madmen. We'll make enemies, we'll break laws, we'll break bones. But you will not mess with the grandchildren.' This is gorgeous, with a nonlinear plot and an interesting narrative style (CJ, Sam and Josh writing emails to their parents). Some great comedy nuggets (CJ's panic over the broken statue in her possession, Bradley Whitford's physical comedy as Josh does a pratfall, Sam being told by a cheeky intern that he should come to her for a job when she graduates). And a heart-warming variant on *Mr Smith Goes to Washington* for the main story.

The Egyptian head of state is called Hassan Ali, and he has 38 wives. The relationship between Sam and his father has improved since the last episode. CJ refers to Sam and Josh as 'my spin boys'.

Did You Know?: Bradley Whitford pestered Sorkin into including autism in this episode. As a member of Cure Autism Now, the actor had lobbied in Washington for the Children's Health Act. 'Autism is underdiagnosed and exploding,' Whitford explains. 'No celebrities have it, so it's not a disease that gets attention and research is underfunded.' A novice to the political process but fascinated with how a bill becomes law, Whitford told John Morgan that the biggest hurdle was preventing the bill from becoming 'a Christmas tree. Everyone wants to hang an ornament on it in the form of riders. People were trying to attach tobacco and abortion legislation.' Through skilful lobbying, the bill passed unanimously and was signed into law. Sorkin was already working on a show about a filibuster, felt the autism issue would play perfectly and incorporated it. 'It's not precisely what I pitched,' says Whitford. 'But who's going to argue with the best writer in Hollywood?'

40
17 People

US Transmission Date: 4 April 2001
UK Transmission Date: 16 October 2001 (E4)

Writer: Aaron Sorkin
Director: Alex Graves

Toby's suspicions are confirmed when the president tells him about his MS. A terrorist threat tightens airport security. Sam and Ainsley squabble over the Equal Rights Amendment. Josh discovers a secret about Donna.

A View from the Hill: Articles of Impeachment have been issued only against Andrew Johnson (1867) and Bill

Clinton (1999), though there were numerous calls for Richard Nixon's impeachment over Watergate. The Freedom of Information Act is mentioned (see **11**, 'Lord John Marbury'), as is the 1964 Pay Equity Act.

American History X: Toby asks if Hoynes is to be dropped as vice president, describing such moves as an 'Eisenhower/ Nixon thing'. This refers to Eisenhower's often uneasy relationship with his vice president and the 'Dump Nixon' discussions in Republican circles prior to the 1956 election.

A Little Learning is a Dangerous Thing: MS, notes Bartlet, is a chronic disease of the central nervous system. Symptoms can be as mild as numbness or as severe as paralysis and loss of vision and of cognitive function. Sam believes self-deprecation is the appetiser of charm.

Office Gossip: The vice president is giving a speech at a semiconductor plant in Nashua on 'Clean Air Industry in the High-Tech Corridor of the Industrial Northeast'. It's clear to Toby that Hoynes has started an unannounced campaign for the presidency.

In The Interests of National Security: An Algerian-born terrorist, Reden Hassam, is arrested at the Canadian border carrying nitroglycerine. On advice from State and Intelligence departments, Bartlet closes US embassies in Tanzania and Brussels. The Federal Aviation Administration want the president to heighten airport security, but it's a holiday weekend and he's reluctant, as this will mean hand-searching luggage (and causing delays) and discontinuing kerbside check-ins.

The Conspiracy Starts at Closing Time: When told that one of those who know of the president's illness is Dr Lee (see **23**, 'In the Shadow of Two Gunmen' Part 1), Toby asks if the doctor is currently under surveillance.

References: Ado Annie from *Oklahoma* (see **12**, 'He Shall, from Time to Time . . .'), the feminist writers Rebecca Walker, Gloria Steinem, Phyllis Schlafly and Naomi Wolf, right-wing analyst Ann Coulter, Bill Maher

host of *Politically Incorrect*. Charlie reads a book by
Cornel West. Also Bloomberg, an allusion to Joshua 6
('the walls came tumbling down'), John Wayne (1907–79)
and Fortune 500 (America's largest-corporations list).
Ainsley wears an FBI sweatshirt. Josh uses Joey's *Friends*
catchphrase: 'How *you* doin'?' Jay Leno is on TV (see **16**,
'20 Hours in L.A.'). Yosemite National Park is mentioned
(see **8**, 'Enemies').

Oh, Donna!: Josh sends Donna flowers to celebrate the
anniversary of her starting work for him. He considers her
'hysterically funny'.

Sex and Drugs and Rock'n'Roll: Donna: 'I'm gonna give
you a little gift.' Josh: 'If you've got your old Catholic-
school uniform on under there . . .'
   Sam seems about to aim a swipe at Ainsley's butt as she
passes him.

Cigarettes and Alcohol: Bartlet and Toby drink bourbon,
no ice, in the Oval Office. Donna considers her dry wit to
be like a fine martini.

Logic, Let Me Introduce You to This Window: Why close,
specifically, embassies in Tanzania and Brussels? It's an
odd combination.

Quote/Unquote: Donna, to Josh: 'You're the kind of guy
who sends a woman flowers to be mean. You're the only
person I've met who can do that.'
   Toby, on who was in charge after the president's
shooting: 'I wasn't in the Situation Room that night but
I'll bet all the money in my pockets . . . that it was Leo.
Who no one elected. For ninety minutes that night there
was a *coup d'état* in this country.'
   Ainsley: 'If men were biologically responsible for procre-
ation, they'd fall down and die at the first sonogram.'

Notes: 'Are you pissed because there were fifteen people
who knew before you did? I feel fine, by the way. Thanks
for asking.' A dramatic Toby-centric episode with a highly
claustrophobic atmosphere.

Continuity references to: **12**, 'He Shall, from Time to Time . . .', **31**, 'Galileo', **23**, 'In the Shadow of Two Gunmen' Part 1, **21**, 'Lies, Damn Lies and Statistics' ('Knock-knock.' 'Who's there?' 'Sam and his prostitute friend!') and **33**, 'The Leadership Breakfast'.

Cast and Crew Comments: 'Toby's on a mission,' Richard Schiff told Mike McDaniel. 'He confronts the president. The result will change the nature of this White House for ever. His reaction is volatile and personal. George Stephanopoulos was at the read-through that day. He said, "We've never dealt with anything like this." He was very helpful to me in realising the gravity and the potential disastrousness of this situation.'

Did You Know?: The jury in the trial of Ahmed Ressam, a suspected Islamic terrorist who allegedly intended to blow up LA airport, were instructed not to watch this episode. Judge John Coughenhour told them, 'It has subject matter that touches a little too close to this case.'

41
Bad Moon Rising

US Transmission Date: 25 April 2001
UK Transmission Date: 23 October 2001 (E4)

Writer: Aaron Sorkin
Story: Fellicia Willson
Director: Bill Johnson
Cast: Jacqueline Kim (Emily Lowenbrau)
Robert Curtis Brown (Congressional Staffer)
Scott Lawrence (Congressional Staffer)
Michael Mantell (Jamie Hotchkiss) Eric Stonestreet (Staffer #1)
Scott Atkinson (Staffer #2) Jossie Harris Thacker (Staffer #3)
David Ackert (Babish Staffer) Tracy Beaulieu (Cal)

Bartlet confers with his counsel, Oliver Babish, on whether his MS cover-up is a conspiracy. An oil spill has special significance for Sam. Josh deals with a Mexican economic crisis. Toby asks CJ to find an unnamed source.

American History X: References to the third, fourth, seventh and eleventh amendments (quartering soldiers, search and seizure, civil trials and suits against states, respectively). Oliver refers to *amicus* briefs on sovereign immunity (see **9**, 'The Short List').

Politics of Honesty: The president is told he doesn't enjoy attorney–client privilege with Oliver, who advises him to go public and then have the Attorney General appoint a Special Prosecutor – ideally, a Bartlet-hating Republican. If the president invokes executive privilege, Oliver will resign.

A Little Learning is a Dangerous Thing: Josh gives Donna a social studies lesson on Europe in 1939. Apparently they're at war, but America has taken an isolationist stand and refuses to get involved. France, Austria and England are getting pounded by the Germans but Josh thinks they're being hysterical. 'This son of a customs agent with the Charlie Chaplin moustache ain't going anywhere.' Franklin Roosevelt, however, devised the Lend-Lease Act famously remarking, 'If your neighbour's house is on fire, you don't haggle over the price of your garden hose.'

The Conspiracy Starts at Closing Time: An anonymous White House quote on school vouchers puts Toby in a vile mood. He gives CJ the impossible job of finding the source. Leaks happen, she tells Toby, there's no malicious intent. Junior staffers try to impress reporters by showing they're in the know. There's no group of people in the world that large that can keep a secret. CJ finds it comforting.

References: The title is a song by Creedence Clearwater Revival. Josh sings 'The Wells Fargo Wagon' from *The Music Man*. The *Baltimore Sun*, Bach's 'Air on a G String', the Lindbergh baby, the Teamsters leader Jimmy Hoffa (1913–75), *Who Framed Roger Rabbit?*, Whittaker Chambers and the secret pumpkin (see **1**, 'The West Wing'), Dairy Queen, *Spartacus*, *Roswell* ('it's how I know for sure the government isn't covering up aliens in New Mexico'). Bartlet calls Abbey Lady Macbeth. Also *Bring It On*, allusions to Arthur Miller's *The Crucible* ('I saw Lizzie Proctor speakin' with the devil!') and *Monty Python and the Holy Grail* ('If you dunk the suspect in a deep well, and they drown, it means they're not a witch').

You May Remember Me From Such Films and TV Series As . . .': Oliver Platt's movies include *Bulworth*, *A Time to Kill* and *Flatliners*. Jacqueline Kim appeared in *Brokedown Palace*, *Star Trek: Generations* and *Xena; Warrior Princess*. Robert Curtis Brown was in *Trading Places* and *Legal Eagles*. Scott Lawrence worked on *Brimstone*. Michael Mantell appears in *The Velocity of Gary*, *Quiz Show*, *Passion Fish*, *The Brother from Another Planet*, *Charmed*, *Party of Five*, *When Billie Beat Bobby*, *Angel* and *Matlock*. He was Howard Sewell in *Space: Above and Beyond*. Eric Stonestreet was in *Almost Famous*. Scott Atkinson appeared in *Alien Hunter*. Jossie Harris Thacker was in *The Players Club*. David Ackert's movies include *Sucker*. Tracy Beaulieu was Clayton Forrester in *Mystery Science Theater 3000*.

Behind the Camera: Bill Johnson directed *Infinity*, *The Counterfeit Contessa* and *The Tower*.

Oh, Donna!: She pesters Josh about the Mexican bail-out until he tells her to close the door. With her on the other side of it.

Sex and Drugs and Rock'n'Roll: Josh and Donna are at it again. 'I'm not cheap, nor am I xenophobic. I just think it's time for some *tough love*,' she tells him, concerning Mexico. 'Not here in front of everybody, but if you want to run home and get your equipment . . .' quips Josh.

Logic, Let Me Introduce You to This Window: Sam asks Charlie how many AP (Advanced Placement) credits he has. Charlie replies English, maths and calculus, European history and French, which would give him approximately twenty. Most degrees require around 124. To be a junior (as Sam suggests) Charlie would need sixty at least. This episode seems to take place about a month after **38**, 'Somebody's Going to Emergency, Somebody's Going to

Jail', in which Tribbey was still White House Counsel. Yet Oliver has been in the job for three months. Josh's history is flawed: by 1939 Austria had already been occupied by the Nazis in the bloodless *Anschluss*. The president has told his wife, brother and children about his illness but not, seemingly, his mother, if she's still alive (see **4**, 'Five Votes Down'), or Elizabeth's husband (assuming she's not a single mother, see **1**, 'The West Wing'). Why did Zoey fill out her college entrance forms when she was seventeen, but not start at Georgetown until she was nineteen?

Quote/Unquote: Oliver, on his malfunctioning Dictaphone: 'It won't stop recording things. It's just what you want lying around the White House Counsel's Office.'

Oliver: 'I have more questions. Is there time now?' Bartlet: 'The Mexican economy crashed, an oil tanker busted up about a hundred and twenty miles from here and thirteen per cent of Americans are living in poverty. So, yeah, I can hang out with you and answer insulting questions for a while.'

Josh: 'The number of people whose permission I need before I can do whatever the hell I want . . . Let me tell you something: there's a lot to be said for fascism.'

Notes: 'There's a bad moon rising, Oliver. We both know it. They're gonna take me out for a walk.' A fabulous introduction for Babish. Some of the subplots are slightly inconsequential, but CJ's brilliantly incompetent investigation and Josh and Donna's running battle make up for it. Best bits: Bartlet telling Oliver he needs advice on whether he engaged sixteen people in a criminal conspiracy; Oliver looks at his malfunctioning Dictaphone, picks up his gavel and smashes it, as Leo and Bartlet look startled; Donna and Zack's 'confessions'.

Oliver Babish is the White House Counsel, the fifth in two years (his predecessors were Cochran, Gates, Solomon and Lionel Tribbey – see **27**, 'And it's Surely to Their Credit'). He's a friend of the Bartlets (though **42**, 'The Fall's Gonna Kill You', suggests his relationship with Abbey is less than friendly and Jed admits to being 'scared' by him). He 'built hospitals' with the president and was Midwest finance chairman on the campaign. He is from Chicago. He owns a gavel given to his grandfather by Justice Louis Brandeis (1856–1941). Henry Shallick, Ann Stark and Seth Gillette are name-checked (see **33**, 'The Leadership Breakfast'). Emily Lowenbrau was previously mentioned in **19**, 'Let Bartlet Be Bartlet'. Margaret may have practised fencing. The Bartlet family lawyer is called Pat Carr (also mentioned in **43**, '18th and Potomac'). CJ alludes to past PR disasters such as Leo's alcoholism (**9**, 'The Short List'), Sam and Laurie (**21**, 'Lies, Damn Lies and Statistics'), India and Pakistan (**11**, 'Lord John Marbury') and Colombia and a failed rescue mission (**36**, 'The War at Home'). Charlie uses Leo's emergency phrase 'an old friend from home' (previously heard in **35**, 'Bartlet's Third State of the Union').

Did You Know?: Rehoboth Beach officials happily cooperated with production staff and provided information and items native to the town. Michael Long, *The West Wing*'s costume supervisor, said he could have recreated the resort without speaking to anyone but enjoyed the research. 'Their web site is most impressive,' he noted.

42
The Fall's Gonna Kill You

US Transmission Date: 2 May 2001
UK Transmission Date: 30 October 2001 (E4)

Writer: Aaron Sorkin
Story: Patrick H Caddell
Director: Christopher Misiano
Cast: Lee Wilkof (Martin Connelly) Rosalind Chao (Jane Gentry)
Spencer Garrett (Richard Will) Douglas Roberts (Congressional Aide #1)
Lucia Vincent (Congressional Aide #3) Lenore Foster (Staffer)
Debbie Ann Thomas (Speechwriter) Barry Livingston (Speechwriter #2)
Julie A Koehnen (Abbey's Aide #2) Ariel Felix (Bobby)
Shannon Nelson (Staffer #2) Jon Wolfe Nelson (Dale Bracket)
Katie Rimmer (Waitress)

Oliver interrogates CJ and Abbey about what they withheld. Josh enlists Joey to devise a telephone poll. A Chinese satellite falls from orbit. No one but Donna seems concerned.

A View from the Hill: The law allows the Justice Department's civil division to transfer funds from the budgets of Commerce, Health and Human Services, and Veterans' Affairs to finance their suit against big tobacco firms. However, it requires such transfers be approved by various House committees, each of which has a chairman elected with the help of tobacco companies.

American History X: James Polk (1795–1849), the eleventh president, and Daniel Webster (1782–1852), Benjamin Harrison's Secretary of State, are mentioned.

Politics of Integrity: The Progressive Caucus want Sam to add a line to a finance speech concerning tax cuts for working families to pay for higher education while their opponents want 'to help the rich pay for bigger swimming pools and faster private jets'. Sam refuses, mainly because it's bad (it 'sounds like it was written by a high school girl'), but also because he doesn't agree with the sentiment. He's in favour of such tax cuts but dislikes rhetoric. When he left Gage-Whitney (see **23**, 'In the Shadow of Two Gunmen' Part 1) he was paying 27 times the national average in income tax. He paid his fair share and the fair share of 26 other people, and was perfectly happy to. But, he says, it didn't mean he got 27 votes on election day or that the fire department comes to his house 27 times faster.

A Little Learning is a Dangerous Thing: Learning that a satellite called Zodiac is crashing to Earth, Donna thinks it's an emergency. Josh doesn't tell her otherwise so that he can get a day's entertainment without leaving the office. Things fall out of the sky all the time, he remarks.

Office Gossip: Josh was told about the president's MS two days after **41**, 'Bad Moon Rising', CJ four days after that, which was the evening before this episode begins.

Denial, Thy Name is Abbey: Oliver believes Abbey has no idea how bad things are going to get for the president. The look on her face suggests he's right.

The Conspiracy Starts at Closing Time: Josh asks Joey to create a poll quickly and collate the results herself. Not even the callers should understand the question they're asking. Joey devises a question concerning a hypothetical degenerative disease given to the governor of an industrial state, perhaps Michigan.

References: NASA's Office of Space Flight, Steuben Glass (see **12**, 'He Shall, from Time to Time . . .'). Toby compares Sam and himself to Batman and Robin or, more accurately, to Bruce Wayne and Dick 'Something' (Grayson). Also referenced are the Dallas Cowboys, *Arsenic and Old Lace*, *Austin Powers* ('how was your day?'), the British parliamentarian Benjamin Disraeli (1804–81), PBS journalist Jim Lehrer, Tim Russert (see **27**, 'And it's Surely to Their Credit'), Barbara Walters (see **25**, 'The Midterms'). The title alludes to *Butch Cassidy and the Sundance Kid*.

'You May Remember Me From Such Films and TV Series As . . .': Lee Wilkof was in *Ally McBeal* and *Private Parts*. Rosalind Chao played Keiko in *Star Trek: The Next Generation* and *Deep Space Nine* and appeared in *Kojak*, *Diff'rent Strokes* and *Denial*. Spencer Garrett was Stark in *The Invisible Man*. Douglas Roberts appeared in *Postcards from the Edge* and *Blind Justice*. Lucia Vincent was in *Sweet Jane*. Debbie Ann Thomas appeared in *First Watch*. Julie Koehnen was in *Losing Grace*. Shannon Nelson's movies include *Drop Dead Gorgeous*. Kate Rimmer was Tiffany in *Girl Interrupted* and appeared in *Jesus' Son*.

Sex and Drugs and Rock'n'Roll: During the election in Manhattan, Kansas, CJ came to the president's suite to tell Abbey they had an interview with *Nightline*. 'I was almost sure I saw you giving the president an injection,' she says. Abbey admits it was Betaseron, to reduce the frequency of the attacks.

Cigarettes and Alcohol: Abbey's had a medEvac helicopter named after her – An AS335F1 Twinstar, which she got to break a bottle of cider over.

Logic, Let Me Introduce You to This Window: Why did Leo alone tell CJ about the MS, when the president himself told Toby, Josh and Sam? Abbey has been practising medicine for 26 years, which means (from other dating information) that she didn't begin until several years after she graduated. Leo and Bartlet have both met Joey Lucas on several occasions (notably **21**, 'Lies, Damn Lies and Statistics') and appear to be on first-name terms with her, yet in this episode both speak as if she were someone they barely know.

Quote/Unquote: CJ, when Oliver asks about the president collapsing and what she believed had happened: 'At first glance, I thought he might have a virus contracted from a rare African tsetse fly. I'm not an expert, but I did meet a man once in India. It could be anything with these presidents. James Polk had diverticulitis, couldn't digest nuts. I'll tell you what else, one in forty American men wear women's clothing and we've had well over forty presidents.'

Donna: 'A thing the size of a garbage truck is gonna be in a two-thousand-mile-an-hour free fall and no one knows where it's gonna hit.' Charlie: 'I'm rooting for Zurich. I've had it up to here with the Swiss!'

Donna, to Abbey: 'There's a giant object hurtling its way toward us at devastating velocity.' Abbey: 'Tell me about it.'

Notes: 'The sky is falling.' A tough nut to crack: an unremittingly downbeat and sombre episode, enlivened by some first-class Donna shenanigans and more good work on CJ.

Continuity references to previous occasions when CJ's given public reports on the president's health (**1**, 'The West Wing', and **23**, 'In the Shadow of Two Gunmen' Part 1).

Oliver has been divorced four times. The president's current physician is Admiral Leonard Morrow. Bartlet tells Abbey that Zoey will 'ace' her exams and that he hates Ellie's boyfriend. Kenny is on vacation, and Joey's replacement interpreter is Dale Bracket (Josh thinks he sounds like a TV detective). Abbey studied at Harvard. She is board-certified in internal medicine and thoracic surgery and is on the staff of Boston Mercy Hospital and Columbia Presbyterian.

Did You Know?: 'Laura Glasser said to me "Man-made objects fall out of the sky at a rate of one-per-week, think there's anything you can do with that?' Sorkin told *mightybigtv.com*.

43
18th and Potomac

US Transmission Date: 9 May 2001
UK Transmission Date: 6 November 2001 (E4)

Writer: Aaron Sorkin
Story: Lawrence O'Donnell Jr
Director: Robert Berlinger
Cast: John Rubinstein (Andy Ritter) Peter Michael Goetz (Paul Hacket)
Richard McGonagle (Warren) Robert Walden (Rossiter)
Ana Mercedes (Sally) Roger Ontiveros[91] (Sidney)
Wendy Haines (Abbey's Agent)

With disastrous polling figures from Joey, the president prepares to announce his MS. Sam readies Abbey for the broadcast. A crisis erupts in Haiti. Josh deals with Senators opposed to the tobacco-industry lawsuit. Charlie gives Mrs Landingham car advice.

A View from the Hill: Section 2,635 of the Standards of Ethical Conduct for Employees of the Executive Branch concerns gifts that can be accepted by government employees.

---

[91] The same actor appeared in **12**, 'He Shall, from Time to Time . . .' Officer #3. It's proved impossible to verify whether this is the same character.

Politics of Compromise: The Justice Department case against tobacco companies continues to exercise Josh's diplomacy (see **42**, 'The Fall's Gonna Kill You'). Two Democrat members of the Appropriations Subcommittee, Warren and Rossiter, have ideological problems with the case, believing that even though tobacco companies knew of the addictive properties of nicotine, so did smokers themselves. Josh suggests the American people deserve their day in court and the administration shouldn't let members of Appropriations choke funding for a lawsuit aimed at the perpetrators of hundreds of thousands of negligent homicides. Leo agrees, telling Josh, 'Stick some dynamite up Warren and Rossiter's ass.'

A Little Learning is a Dangerous Thing: Every Surgeon General since 1964 has warned the public of the dangers of smoking and cigarette packets have carried warning labels since 1966. Sam, after talking to Abbey, knows that fluid accumulating in the semicircular canals of the vestibulo cochlear nerve is usually what accounts for dizziness.

'On the Brink . . .': A military crisis erupts in Haiti after recent elections. Colonel Bazan's forces surround Carrefour Liberté, citing improper permits for a victory rally by supporters of President Dessaline. Some of the crowd refuse to disperse and two are killed. The new Justice Minister, René Ducasse, is arrested and the home of the Chief Justice is besieged by soldiers claiming they're protecting him from death threats. Intelligence suggests he's actually under house arrest. Haitian troops also occupy police stations in Port-au-Prince, indicating a full army coup. Leo suggests evacuating the embassy of nonessential personnel. Such a move will signal that the US has no confidence in Dessaline's government but, as the president notes, 'there is *no* Dessaline government'. The president orders that Dessaline be given asylum and he's smuggled inside the embassy in a car as some staff are evacuated. Haitian soldiers attempt to board the plane but are shot by Marines and it takes off. The embassy is then surrounded by the military, who demand Dessaline be handed over (see **44**, 'Two Cathedrals').

The Conspiracy Starts at Closing Time: The password 'Sagittarius' is used by senior staff when discussing the president's MS.

References: The doyen of political commentators Walter Cronkite; *Dateline* and its host, Stone Phillips; Ted Baxter, the egotistical anchorman played by Ted Knight on *The Mary Tyler Moore Show*; the Baltimore Orioles; *Petticoat Junction*; Marine boot camp at Parris Island; the USS Enterprise. Also Bob Cratchit from Dickens's 'A Christmas Carol' and Mammy Yokum from the *Lil Abner* comics. An oblique reference to evidence given by seven CEOs from tobacco companies in 1994 that nicotine is not addictive. Mrs Landingham quotes a line usually attributed to Julius Caesar (102–44 BC): 'Caesar's wife must be above reproach'.

'You May Remember Me From Such Films and TV Series As . . .': John Rubinstein played Harrison Fox Jr in *Crazy Like a Fox* and appeared in *The Boys from Brazil* and *The Car*. The son of the piano virtuoso Artur, John Rubinstein is a composer on series such as *China Beach* and *Harry O*. Peter Michael Goetz was in *Father of the Bride*, *Glory* and *Twin Peaks*. Richard McGonagle appeared in *Mighty Joe Young* and *Innerspace*. Robert Walden played Donald Segretti in *All the President's Men* and appeared in *Kiss of a Stranger*, *Capricorn One* and *Lou Grant*. Ana Mercedes was in *Rikki the Pig*.

Oh, Donna!: She's the first person at assistant level to be told about the president's MS (by Toby).

Sex and Drugs and Rock'n'Roll: Herman Vikram was the original specialist treating the president. He prescribed prednisone. Four years later, Abbey changed this to Betaseron. Oliver notes that Abbey violated the medical ethics rules of three state boards, didn't keep proper medical records and shouldn't, in any case, be treating a member of her family.

Logic, Let Me Introduce You to This Window: Leo invokes '1070 OAS' – the Organization of American States doesn't usually refer to resolutions by number, though there is a resolution 1080, which requires the convening of the Permanent Council within ten days of a coup or other interruption of a democratically elected government. This has been used four times: Haiti (1991), Peru (1992), Guatemala (1993) and Paraguay (1996). Why would Mrs Landingham be at 18th and Potomac? It's in South Washington, a significant distance from the White House. The president says there will be seven people at the basement meeting, but there are actually eight (including himself). There's no *Dateline* on a Wednesday. Sam says Hoynes 'signed off on the president's health and joined the ticket'. However, it's never been confirmed that Hoynes knew about Bartlet's health *prior* to the election. The fact that Leo didn't even know until **12**, 'He Shall, from Time to Time . . .', suggests otherwise.

Quote/Unquote: Leo: 'We're not going to soften, detour, postpone, circumvent, obfuscate or trade a single one of our goals to allow for whatever extracurricular nonsense is coming our way in the next days, weeks and months.' Toby: 'When did we decide this?' Leo: 'Just now.'

Nancy: 'You guys need some adult supervision? Leo: 'No, we need the cavalry.'

Notes: 'There was an accident at 18th and Potomac. Mrs Landingham was driving her car.' A clever and well-structured episode right up to the final, shocking moments when the series pulls the carpet from under viewers' feet by killing a popular character.

Admiral Fitzwallace is mentioned. Continuity references to 'Pulling nine bodies out of Colombia' and the Blue Ribbon Commission (see **35** 'Bartlet's Third State of the Union'). Leo calls the Secretary of State Scott on the phone, indicating Mickey Troop has vacated the job since **36**, 'The War at Home'. The president calls Mrs Landingham Delores for the first time in the series. Her late husband was called Henry.

Critique: The San Francisco Democrat Kevin Shelley adjourned the California Assembly session after this episode in memory of Mrs Landingham. Shelley called her a 'great American' whose 'contributions to the nation were numerous'. The announcement caught many legislators by surprise. 'Nobody knew if she really died or fake-died,' said a Shelley aide, Terri Carbaugh. Hearing about the statehouse eulogy, Thomas Schlamme commented, 'This power problem in California will never be solved by this group of people!'

Cast and Crew Comments: Kathryn Joosten was told her character's death was a creative decision by Sorkin and Schlamme. 'There's only one reason you get called into the producer's office,' she told David Bauder. Sworn to secrecy, Joosten went on vacation before the broadcast. She returned to find fifteen phone messages and eighty emails. 'Even the fellow who sold me a car two years ago called,' she said. He enquired about Joosten's health and whether she was interested in a trade-in. 'It's been tremendous for me. Being on *West Wing* has been a delight on every level.'

'People hated me for a while,' Sorkin told Mike Hughes. 'My dentist – who is not someone I want to be mad – was very upset.' But the worst part of the plot device, he confided to Walt Belcher, was 'losing Kathryn from our cast'. He recalled that the idea to kill the character occurred when the cast attended a charity banquet and he and Joosten went outside for a cigarette. 'I kept thinking about it and saw Mrs Landingham's death as a way to take the president to the edge. Now the joke on set is, "Don't take a smoke break with Aaron".'

Did You Know?: 'There were many times in the past two seasons when they'd call me and alert me that I'd be in the next episode, only to be re-called and hear "Aaron changed his mind," ' Tim Matheson told *Entertainment Weekly*. But *the actor* takes it in his stride. 'I'm ready to serve my country and my president!'

44
Two Cathedrals

US Transmission Date: 16 May 2001
UK Transmission Date: 13 November 2001 (E4)

Writer: Aaron Sorkin
Director: Thomas Schlamme
Cast: Kirsten Nelson (Young Delores) Jason Widener (Young Jed)
Don McManus (Greg Summerhays) Lawrence O'Donnell (Dr Bartlet)
John Bennett Perry (Bill) Fred Ornstein (Congressman Wade)
Bill Gratton (Adviser #1) Patrick Thomas O'Brien (Hanson)
Christopher Murray (Tony Phillips) Shelley Malil (Renfro)
Angelo Tiffe (Greenway) EE Bell (Adviser #2)
Robert A Becker (Monohan) Trevor Eddy (Young Bartlet's Friend)
Wendy Poole (Staffer)

A tropical storm bears down on Washington on the day
Bartlet will publicly disclose his MS – also the day of Mrs
Landingham's funeral. The staff prepare two responses to
the question 'Will the president seek re-election?'

A View from the Hill: Two Democratic Party representatives who've learned about Bartlet's MS tell Leo it's not
just about the president getting re-elected, but that Democrats are going to 'take it in the throat'. They're also
concerned the campaign will be about Bartlet's illness and
the cover-up and that their numerous valid issues against
Republicans (tax cuts, education, environment) will be
shunted aside.

American History X: A list of prosecutors is, according to
CJ, given to a three-judge panel. The prosecutors, as well
as the panel, were all appointed by Republican presidents.

Politics of What's the Point?: The female driver who
crashed into Mrs Landingham's car fractured her wrist.
Two passengers suffered only scratches and bruises. Abbey
says the driver will be charged with vehicular manslaughter.

A Little Learning is a Dangerous Thing: Delores feels that
Bartlet's father never got over the fact he wasn't as smart
as his brothers.

The Encyclopedic Mind of Josiah Bartlet PhD: He knows there's a season for tropical storms and that this isn't it. Donna confirms there hasn't been a storm like this in May for at least a hundred years.

'On the Brink . . .': Leo asks what conditions are like inside the Haitian Embassy. Nancy notes they still have water, but the power's been cut. There haven't been injuries, but the deputy chief is diabetic and running out of insulin. Outside are 1,200 troops and four Howitzers. Nancy suggests sending Fitzwallace to meet a Haitian general, Frances St Jacques, and, hopefully, to exploit a schism in the military.

Denial, Thy Name is Bartlet: Calling God a feckless thug, Bartlet lists his achievements as president: 3,800,000 jobs created, bailing out Mexico, increasing foreign trade, 30 million new acres of land for conservation, putting Mendoza on the bench, *not* fighting a war, and raising three children. 'That's not enough to buy me out of the doghouse?' Crushing his cigarette on the floor of the church he tells God, 'You get Hoynes.'

True Faith: 'There was nothing Standards and Practices found objectionable in the Latin,' Sorkin told *mightybigtv.com.* 'As for the clergy, many were on set. I was introduced to a minister and said, "You know he's about to renounce God, right?" The minister said, "I saw rehearsal, it's gonna be great." I said, "But am I going straight to hell?" He said, "Maybe for other stuff, but not for this." Then he gave me a good talking-to about how people of faith are supposed to question God. How those who don't are usually the ones who send their money to guys with cable TV shows.' Sorkin believes there's plenty of evidence that Bartlet's faith is important to him – the meeting with Cavanaugh (**14**, 'Take This Sabbath Day'), dressing down Jenna Jacobs (**25**, 'The Midterms'), meeting the Chinese refugee (**30**, 'Shibboleth') and his friendship with Al Caldwell (**1**, 'The West Wing') – but nowhere does he believe it was more strongly expressed than here.

Bartlet, notes Sorkin, is 'the son of a man who, we learn, is an intellectual Fredo. The father, obviously convinced he married some Catholic whore, treats his son terribly for a number of reasons, not the least of which is that he adopted his mother's religion.' The speech in the cathedral, therefore, was directed as much to his father as it was to God. But Bartlet is ultimately reconciled with God. Mrs Landingham's appearance in the penultimate scene isn't as a ghost: rather Bartlet is using memories of her to coax himself to make the right decision. 'When the scene was done,' noted Sorkin, 'he looked out at the storm that he was sure God had sent to mess with him, and realised it was God sending him strength. He baptised himself in it. And as he passed the church in the motorcade, a custodian picked the cigarette butt off the ground, and we cut back to Bartlet, who senses something move inside of him. I meant the episode as a tribute to faith.'

The Conspiracy Starts at Closing Time: CJ tells the press that she imagines subpoenas will be issued to most senior White House staff, including herself.

References: The Lord's Prayer, Mozart's *Requiem*; the guitar music is from 'Brothers in Arms' by Dire Straits; Ed Wood (1925–78), director of gloriously bad movies such as *Plan 9 from Outer Space*; Associated Press, Reuters and Agence France; the naval academy at Annapolis. Also a quote from Graham Greene (1904–91) author of *The Third Man*: 'you can't conceive, nor can I, the appalling strangeness of the mercy of God'. Josh suggests the president would sooner have his family 'dance the tarantella on the Truman Balcony' than seek re-election (see **33**, 'The Leadership Breakfast'). Also referenced are Lawrence Altman, the *New York Times*' chief medical correspondent; bohemian writer Henry Miller (1891–1980); the novelist DH Lawrence (1885–1930), best known for *Lady Chatterley's Lover*; James Baldwin's *Giovanni's Room*; science fiction author Ray Bradbury and his masterpiece *Fahrenheit 451*.

'You May Remember Me From Such Films and TV Series As . . .': Don McManus was in *Hannibal*, *Magnolia* and *The Shawshank Redemption*. Kirsten Nelson was in *The Fugitive*. Jason Widener's movies include *Out of the Black*. John Bennett Perry was in *Circles* and is probably best known for a series of adverts for Old Spice. Fred Ornstein was in *Gang Related*. Bill Gratton appeared in *The Green Mile* and *Jagged Edge*. Patrick O'Brien was in *Dead Man on Campus* and *Pleasantville*. Christopher Murray appeared in *Dante's Peak*. Shelley Malil's movies include *Just Can't Get Enough*. Angelo Tiffe appeared in *3 Ninjas Kick Back* and *Almost Pregnant*. EE Bell appeared in *Storm*. Lewis Grenville worked on *Murder at 1600*.

Cigarettes and Alcohol: Bartlet's smoking is central to the episode.

Logic, Let Me Introduce You to This Window: The motorcade passes the National Cathedral carrying the president from the White House to the State Department. However, State is just a few blocks from the White House, while the church is several miles away. Charlie reads from the Book of Wisdom, part of the Apocrypha (books of the Bible used only in certain versions and read almost exclusively by Catholics), at Mrs Landingham's memorial service. Why? It's established Mrs Landingham wasn't Catholic and there's no indication that Charlie is, either.

Quote/Unquote: Young Jed: 'In my family, we don't talk about money.' Young Delores: 'That's because you *have* money.'

Young Delores: 'You're a Boy King. You're a foot smarter than the smartest kids in the class. You're blessed with inspiration.'

A translation of Bartlet's Latin rant: 'Am I to believe these are the acts of a loving God? A just God? I was your servant on Earth. I spread your word and did your work. To hell with your punishments. To hell with you.'

Notes: 'God doesn't make cars crash and you know it. Stop using me as an excuse.' A quite remarkable, grim, apocalyptic, demanding hour of television. Bartlet is, like Job, tested to the limits of his faith and then, in the waters of a tropical storm, rebaptised.

The scenes of Young Jed and Young Delores take place in 1960, judging from a car number plate, which would make Young Jed approximately sixteen. There's a reference to the climax of *7*, 'The State Dinner' and a confirmation that the tender ship sank with 68 lives lost.

Critique: 'If Bartlet doesn't run, it's the wrong message,' says Eileen Curras of West Kendall, who has been diagnosed with MS. Curras saw her life mirrored in the way the president's staff treated him in the moments before the press conference. 'That was realistic, like he was no longer in control.'

'Rather than dropping a religious character in where it seems out of place, this guy is really dealing with cosmic questions of faith,' Quentin Schultze, communication professor at Calvin College, noted. 'It came out of that struggle and seemed a totally natural fit.'

Cast and Crew Comments: On the actress who uncannily replicated the young Landingham in the flashbacks, Kathryn Joosten said, 'She's a friend. I recorded all of her lines so that she could hear the cadence. She was very good. My children were sitting there going "Whoa! Has she got you pegged!"' Bartlet's father was played by the producer Lawrence O'Donnell. One of the mourners in the funeral scene, Andrea Sachs, wrote a piece about her experiences for the *Washington Post*. 'I watched it with much anticipation. The film crew shaved 15 hours off the funeral scene – reducing it to 15 minutes, with two commercial breaks. Yet, with my nose pressed to the screen, I could have sworn that the shadowy figure in the background was I. If only the president had moved a little to the left, you would have seen me, too.'

Did You Know?: NBC has been the most public of the networks in discussing the realistic language conundrum facing the industry. NBC's solution has been greater leniency. 'What's happening is a transformation to normalization,' notes professor Robert Thompson. 'It's commonplace to hear erection jokes on *Friends*.' An NBC executive, Alan Wurtzel, initially refused to let Sorkin have Mrs Landingham describe Bartlet's father as 'a prick'. Just days before the episode was to be broadcast, however, Wurtzel relented. 'I know this character,' he observed. 'The very fact that you would never think she'd say that is significant. There's a resonance to that dialogue.'

Awards: The West Wing won seven Emmys for Season Two including a best supporting actor for Bradley Whitford and a second successive award for Allison Janney.

The West Wing – Season Three (2001–2002)

John Wells Television/Warner Bros. Television
(A Time/Warner Entertainment Company)
Created by Aaron Sorkin
Producers: Michael Hissrich, Llewellyn Wells, Kristin Harms, Alex Graves
Co-Executive Producer: Kevin Wells
Supervising Producer: Christopher Misiano
Co-Producers: Paul Redford, Neal Ahern Jr
Associated Producers: Mindy Kanaskie, Patrick Ward
Executive Producers: Aaron Sorkin, Thomas Schlamme, John Wells
Advisers: Dee Dee Myers, Patrick H Caddell, Marlin Fitzwater,
Peggy Noonan, Frank Luntz, Gene Sperling
Executive Story Editor: Julia Dahl
Theme and Music: WG Snuffy Walden

Regular Cast:

Martin Sheen (President Josiah Bartlet) John Spencer (Leo McGarry)
Bradley Whitford (Josh Lyman) Richard Schiff (Toby Ziegler)
Rob Lowe (Sam Seaborn) Allison Janney (CJ Cregg)
Janel Moloney (Donna Moss)
Kathryn Joosten (Delores Landingham, 54)
NiCole Robinson (Margaret, 46–49, 52, 54–55, 57, 59–62, 64, 66)
Devika Parikh (Bonnie, 48–49, 51, 58, 61, 64)
Melissa Fitzgerald (Carol, 48–53, 55–56, 59, 61, 63–64, 66)
Peter James Smith (Ed, 46–47, 49, 53, 55–56, 59, 62, 65)
William Duffy (Larry, 46–47, 49, 53, 55–56, 59, 62, 65)
Mindy Seeger (Chris, 46, 50, 59, 61, 63, 66) Jana Lee Hamblin (Bobbi, 48)
Reneé Estevez (Nancy, 46, 50, 52, 57, 61, 63, 66)
Tim Matheson (John Hoynes, 50, 54, 62) Dulé Hill (Charlie Young)
John Amos (Admiral Percy Fitzwallace, 63–66)
Kim Webster (Ginger, 46, 48, 50–53, 55–58, 61–65)
Ivan Allen (Roger Salier,[92] 46) Penny Griego (DC Anchor,[93] 64)
Thom Barry (Mark Richardson, 48)
Mongo Brownlee (Secret Service Agent, 45)
Michael O'Neill (Ron Butterfield, 45, 63, 66)
Stockard Channing (Abigail Bartlet, 45–47, 50–54, 60)
Jacqueline Torres (Sondra,[94] 46)

---

[92] Credited as Reporter in **46**, 'Manchester' Part 1.
[93] Credited as TV Reporter in **64**, 'The Black Vera Wang'.
[94] Credited as A.F.1 Reporter # 3 in **46**, 'Manchester' Part 1.

JP Stevenson (Jonathan,[95] 46)
Dennis Cockrum (Captain,[96] 46, 51, 59)
Charles Noland (Steve,[97] 46, 48–50, 59, 63, 66) Diana Morgan (Jesse,[98] 61)
Kris Narmont (Katie Witt,[99] 46, 49, 53, 58–59, 61, 63, 66)
Roger Rees (Lord John Marbury, 60) Ralph Meyering Jr (Tom, 64)
Marlee Matlin (Joey Lucas, 46–47, 56)
Bill O'Brien (Kenny Thurman, 46–47, 56)
Kathleen York (Andi Wyatt, 58)
Anna Deavere Smith (Nancy McNally, 46–47, 49, 51, 53, 59)
Randolph Brooks (Arthur Leeds,[100] 45, 49–50, 53, 61, 66)
Willie Gault (Agent Madison,[101] 45)
Emily Procter (Ainsley Hayes, 48, 58, 61)
Timothy Davis-Reed (Mark, 48–49, 52–53, 58–59, 61, 63, 66)
Gregalan Williams (Robbie Mosley, 46, 51, 59)
Glenn Morshower (Mike Chysler, 46–47, 65–66)
Doris McMillon (Sandy,[102] 46) Oliver Platt (Oliver Babish, 46, 48, 51)
Lewis Grenville (Reporter, 48)
Ron Silver (Bruno Gianelli, 46–48, 51–52, 64)
Evan Handler (Doug Wegland, 46–48)
Connie Britton (Connie Tate, 46–48, 51) Victor McCay (Henry, 46–47)
Aaron Michael Lacey[103] (Officer Baron, 46–47, 53)
John Emmanuel (Agent, 46–47)
Mark Feuerstein (Cliff Calley, 48, 50, 54–55)
Richard Saxton (Boston Anchor,[104] 49, 64)
Rick Cramer (Officer, 49, 51, 59)
Jeff Mooring (Phil,[105] 49, 59, 61, 63)
Thomas Kopache (National Security Adviser, 49, 59, 64–66)
Hal Holbrook (Albie Duncan, 51)
Mary-Louise Parker (Amy Gardner, 53, 55–57, 60, 65–66)
Elizabeth Liang (Staffer, 53, 57, 63)
Joanna Gleason (Jordan Kendall, 54–55) Clark Gregg (Mike Casper, 54)
James Handy (Congressman Bruno, 54) Sam Lloyd (Bob Engler, 57)

---

[95] Credited as A.F.1 Reporter # 2 in **46**, 'Manchester' Part 1.
[96] Credited as Officer in **51**, 'Gone Quiet'.
[97] Credited as Reporter in **46**, 'Manchester' Part 1.
[98] Credited as Reporter # 2 in **61**, 'The U.S. Poet Laureate'.
[99] Credited as Reporter in **46**, 'Manchester' Part 1 and **61**, 'The U.S. Poet Laureate'. Surname given in dialogue.
[100] Credited as Reporter in **46**, 'Manchester' Part 1 and **61**, 'The U.S. Poet Laureate'.
[101] Credited as Agent #2 in **45**, 'Isaac and Ishmael'.
[102] Credited as Reporter in **46**, 'Manchester' Part 1.
[103] Uncredited.
[104] Credited as Alan in **49**, 'On The Day Before' and as TV Reporter in **64**, 'The Black Vera Wang'.
[105] Credited as Reporter in **61**, 'The U.S. Poet Laureate'.

Ted Garcia (Newscaster, 57) Adam Arkin (Dr Stanley Keyworth, 58, 66)
James Hong (David, 59) Tim Van Pelt (Harry, 62)
Mark Harmon (Simon Donovan, 63–66) Kurt Fuller (Adviser, 65–66)
William Thomas Jr (David, 65–66) SE Perry (Marine Officer, 65–66)
Lily Tomlin (Debbie Fiderer, 66) James Brolin (Robert Ritchie, 66)
David Huddleston (Max Lobell, 66)
Andrew McFarlane (Anthony Marcus, 66)

45
Isaac and Ishmael

US Transmission Date: 3 October 2001
UK Transmission Date: 20 November 2001 (E4)

Writer: Aaron Sorkin
Director: Thomas Schlamme
Cast: Ajay Naidu (Raqim Ali) Jonathan Nichols (Agent Cleary)
Jeanette Brox (Student) Cyd Strittmatter (Joan)
Frantz Turner (Agent Greg) Susie Geiser (Marjorie Mann)
Josh Zuckerman (Boy #1) Ben Donovan (Boy #2) Marcus Toji (Boy #3)
Arjay Smith (Boy #4) Kristine Woo (Girl #1) Chastity Dotson (Girl #2)
Dan Horton (Agent #1) William J Jones (FBI Agent)
Mark Oxman (Benji)[106]

During a security alert Josh talks to high school students
and, with the help of his friends, delivers an impromptu
lesson on the modern world.

A View from the Bunker: Billy Fernandez says the Constitution makes the Executive the weakest of the three
branches of government. Josh replies 'technically, *constitu-
tionally*, the Legislative Branch is the most powerful, but
we get a motorcade.'

American History X: The Boston Tea Party (1773) and the
Cuban Missile Crisis (1962) are mentioned. Also, Benjamin
Franklin (see **35**, 'Bartlet's Third State of the Union') and
the Blacklist (see **38**, 'Somebody's Going to Emergency,
Somebody's Going to Jail').

---

[106] Uncredited.

Politics of Fear: Recently arrested terrorist, Khuram Sharif, names a co-conspirator, Yaarun Nabi, who operates under various aliases, including Raqim Ali. A man with this name works in the White House so Leo interviews him. Raqim was arrested at a rally two years previously. When asked what he was protesting against, Raqim says the presence of US troops in Saudi Arabia which, he adds, houses two of Islam's holiest mosques (the Ka'aba in Makkah and the Prophet's Mosque in Madinah): 'How'd you like it if I camped in front of the Vatican with a stockpile of M-16s?' Leo claims the troops were there to make sure Iraq didn't seize Saudi territory. Raqim believes he actually means Saudi *oil*.

A Little Learning is a Dangerous Thing: Josh and his college roommates got a fish registered for eighteen credits. It made the Dean's List.

A Little Religious Difference is a Very Dangerous Thing: Jews (and Christians) and Muslims have separate accounts of the story of Abraham and his sons via The Old Testament and the Koran – the main difference is which son was to be sacrificed.

God Said to Abraham, 'Kill Me a Son': The Jewish and Christian versions agree that Abraham was told by God that he would father many nations. His wife Sarah, knowing she was past childbearing age, allowed Abraham to father a son (Ishmael) by her handmaid, Hagar. God then told Sarah and Abraham that they would have a son (Isaac) together. After Isaac was weaned, Ishmael and his mother were sent away. God then ordered Abraham to sacrifice Isaac as a test of his faith but then stopped him before he could.

The Koran says that, before *Ishmael* was weaned, Abraham took the child and his mother to Mecca assuming Allah would care for them. Abraham had a dream that told him to sacrifice Ishmael but God prevented him. Traditionally, Isaac's descendants became the Jews and Ishmael's the Arabs.

Office Gossip: One Secret Service agent's primary function is to get in the way of any bullet headed for the president.

Denial, Thy Name is Leo: Raqim notes: 'It's not uncommon for Arab–Americans to be the first suspected when [a bomb threat] happens.' Leo replies: 'I'm trying to figure out why anytime there's terrorist activity, people always assume it's *Arabs*.' Raqim says: 'I don't know the answer to that, but I can tell you it's horrible.' 'That's the price you pay,' Leo continues. He later apologises for his insensitivity.

The Gospel According to Josh: Josh equates Islamic fundamentalism with the Ku Klux Klan 'gone medieval and global'. On why such people target America, Josh says, right or wrong (and he believes they're wrong) one has to acknowledge they have specific complaints. 'The people we support [Israel], the troops in Saudi Arabia, sanctions against Iraq.' Islamic extremism, he continues, is strict adherence to an interpretation of seventh-century Islamic law as practised by Mohammed. For instance, men are forced to pray, grow their beards a certain length and there's only one acceptable cheer at a soccer match: '*Allah-u-akbar*: God is great.' 'Things are less comic for women, who aren't allowed to attend school or have jobs, and get publicly stoned for crimes like not wearing a veil.' So, on the other hand, what bothers them about America? Josh suggests it's religious and press freedom and women being able to do anything they want, including taking a rocket ship to outer space, vote and *play* soccer.

The Conspiracy Starts at Closing Time: Terrorist organisations mentioned include the Taliban, the IRA, Spain's Basque separatists, Italy's Red Brigade, Germany's Baader-Meinhof Gang and the anti-capitalist Weathermen in the US.

References: Buffalo Springfield's hippie anthem 'For What it's Worth' plays over the credits. The National Crime Information Center, Presidential Classroom, Wile E Coyote, composer Irving Berlin (1888–1989), LaGuardia airport, Massachusetts Institute of Technology, the Yankees (**20**, 'Mandatory Minimums') and the Knicks (**39**, 'The Stackhouse Filibuster'), the Boston Red Sox, LA Lakers and their cheerleaders, the Laker Girls and steak and seafood restaurant the Palm. Also Indian spiritual and political leader Mahatma Gandhi (1869–1948), Soviet Premier Nikita Khrushchev (1894–1971) and John Wayne (see **40**, '17 people'). There's a misquote from *Bill & Ted's Excellent Adventure* ('Be good to each other').

'You May Remember Me From Such Films and TV Series As . . .': Ajay Naidu appeared in *Hannibal, Office Space* and *Pi*. Jonathan Nichols was in *Pay it Forward*. Jeanette Brox's movies include *Teacher's Pet*. Cyd Strittmatter was in *Lost Souls*. Frantz Turner appeared in *Wait Till Your Mother Gets Home!* and *Elephant Parts*. Josh Zuckerman's films include *I Was a Teenage Faust*. Marcus Toji was in *Jingle all the Way*. Arjay Smith appeared in *Malcolm in the Middle*. Chastity Dotson was in *Kingston High*.

Oh, Donna!: She calls Josh ridiculous twice in a sentence, though she notes this is hardly a record.

Sex and Drugs and Rock'n'Roll: Charlie lives in Southeast DC, which he compares to Compton, South Central LA, Detroit and the South Bronx – containing, as it does, 'dilapidated schools, drugs, guns and gangs'.

Logic, Let Me Introduce You to This Window: You can't enter Vermont from Ontario, only from Quebec. Sam is a 'knowledgeable terrorism expert'. If so, then one has to fear for the administration's foreign policy. He says terrorism has a one hundred per cent failure rate. That depends on how one defines the term. For instance, in World War Two the Nazi's regarded the French Résistance as terrorists; ditto the British with the Minutemen (as Sam reluctantly acknowledges); the rest of the world, for decades, regarded Soviet Bolsheviks as terrorists. The history of post-war colonial Africa and Indochina is full of states winning independence from Britain, France and Belgium, often including what amounted to terrorist campaigns. If the ANC in South Africa isn't an example of an organisation succeeding in their aims through border-line terrorism then what is?

Josh writes, 'Islamic extremist is to Islamic as _____ is to Christianity'. It should be 'to Islam'. A suggestion for the missing term is Jehovah's Witnesses. To equate this apolitical church with the Christian Right (as Josh subsequently does) is off target. The Witnesses won't even vote in elections. The placement of them in such a context becomes more offensive when Toby compares the people of Afghanistan to 'Jews in concentration camps' – thousands of Jehovah's Witnesses also found themselves in Belsen and Dachau. Josh says, 'The Christian Right may not be your cup of tea but they're not blowing stuff up.' Apart, that is, from the ones who bomb abortion clinics.

In striving for balance it was inevitable that someone would be required to put the case for intelligence gathering, but CJ's 'the CIA, our maligned little brother' speech is hopelessly off target. For most of the last thirty years the CIA's interest in foreign affairs hasn't been the Middle and Far East as she suggests, but in propping up a collection of dodgy right-wing dictatorships in Central and South America – some democratically elected (though one can question the legality of many such elections), others placed in power via coups with active CIA aid. Let's consider Pinochet's Chile, Fujimori's Peru, over 10,000 *desaparecidos* in a succession of Argentinian regimes, the Contras in Nicaragua and the death squads in El Salvador. CJ says, with regard to international relations: 'We're gonna have to partner with some people who are the lesser of evils.' Contrast this with her attitude to just such a strange bedfellow in **53**, 'The Women of Qumar'.

At the FBI office it's suggested that Nabi has four aliases. Ron Butterfield later tells Leo he has five. A student asks what was the first act of terrorism. Toby gives an essay on the eleventh century Shi'ite cult of *al-Hasan ibn al-Sabah*, who allegedly murdered fellow Muslims while under the influence of hashish (this may be the etymology of the word 'assassins'). This was about a thousand years *after* elements of the notorious Jewish religious sect, the Zealots, were murdering Romans and anybody who collaborated with them. As has been noted, one man's terrorist is another man's freedom fighter. There are, seemingly, only three Raqim Ali's in the whole of the US.

Quote/Unquote: Toby: 'There's nothing wrong with a religion whose laws say a man's got to wear a beard or cover his head. It's when violation of these laws become a crime against the state and not your parents that we're talking about lack of choice.'

Toby, concerning a family friend who'd been in a concentration camp: 'He once saw a guy kneeling and praying. He said "What are you doing?" The guy said he was thanking God. "What could you possibly be thanking God for?" "For not making me like *them*."'

Student: 'What do you call a society that has to live every day with the idea that the pizza place you are eating in could blow up without any warning?' Sam: 'Israel.'

Notes: 'The variety of cheers coming from the cheap seats in Giants' Stadium is enough for a *jihad*.' Written, made and broadcast within a fortnight of the attacks on the World Trade Center and the Pentagon on 11 September, 'Isaac and Ishmael' forgoes *The West Wing*'s usually incisive critique to deliver a tidal wave of soapboxy rhetoric. It kind-of works, too, as a vast statement-of-accord. It was probably important that someone in America at this particular moment said many of the things that this episode does about what a big and dangerous world we live in. Sadly, in striving for some balance when (for once) a hint of myopia may have been a more human response, the episode in places falls between two stools. Nevertheless, it's a concerned piece with a quite literal bleeding heart, and a brave and thoughtful attempt at taking a step back and commenting on hugely complex issues. Despite several faults, and CJ being horribly out-of-character, 'Isaac and Ishmael' challenges us to keep asking the difficult questions. Eleven out of ten for trying.

Josh's mother (see **39**, 'The Stackhouse Filibuster') wants him to quit politics as family members have a habit of dying before their time (see **24**, 'In the Shadow of Two Gunmen' Part 2). She makes him keep a box of various supplies in the trunk of his car. He doesn't favour the death penalty (see **14**, 'Take This Sabbath Day'). He once owned a cap signed by Yankees baseball legend, Joe Pepitone. Abbey had her first child, Elizabeth, when she was 'very young' (see **1**, 'The West Wing'). Toby likes Italian and Chinese food as well as the Palm's steaks. Raqim is from Patterson, New Jersey. Other men with the same name live in Spokane and Los Angeles. He was at the shooting in Rosslyn (see **22**, 'What Kind of Day has it Been'). This was the first episode broadcast in widescreen. The title sequence is replaced by addresses for the Twin Towers Fund and the American Red Cross.

Critique: Predictably, this episode drew much press comment. *New York Post*'s headline was '*West Wing* wimps out on terror,' with Adam Buckman saying: 'The liberal Democrats took on terrorism last night and did little but make pompous speeches. Sorkin made sure that most of the bases were covered, but barely mentioned the military.' A positive view came from the *Toronto Star*: ' "Isaac & Ishmael" contained more insight into "America's New War" than the windstorm of opinion since the catastrophe.' *Orlando Sentinel*'s Hal Boedeker described the episode as 'more pedantic than dramatic' and, though Sorkin's attempt was bold, 'the results were like a high-falutin after-school special.' The *New York Daily News* liked it: 'Sorkin and his team, on an astonishingly tight schedule, provided a service similar to the one David Letterman did for fellow comics: that it's possible to deal with terrorism in fictional drama, to do so in a sensitive, sensible and intelligent way and to do it *now*.' However, *USA Today*'s Robert Bianco found the episode 'a crashing and often condescending bore. You could be forgiven if you feared a quiz would be given at the end.'

'Earnest in tone, admirable in its charitable intent and God-awful in its condescending pedantry,' noted James

Poniewozik in *Time*. 'For better or worse, *The West Wing* has always been a didactic series, but it took the urgency of recent news events for Sorkin to write an episode that was literally didactic by setting it in what was, for all intents and purposes, a classroom.' The *Columbus Dispatch* felt the episode motives were good, 'but Sorkin's slender premise didn't seem strong enough to bear the weight of what turned out to be a pedantic script. Too pat and perhaps too confident that it would offer the nation comfort and insight, this fiction couldn't support the weight of real events. Perhaps *The West Wing* would serve viewers better by returning to what it does normally: providing entertainment.'

Cast and Crew Comment: NBC Entertainment president Jeff Zucker believes Sorkin 'is a brilliant writer who has something to say. We have great faith in his abilities to interpret [the events of 11 September] in a manner that make this an important hour of television.' Given the series' setting, 'I don't think it was possible for us to proceed without pausing to acknowledge what happened,' John Wells told the *Sydney Morning Herald*.

'In the actual Oval Office are several red phones that say "Crash" on the handle,' set decorator Ellen Totleben told *Entertainment Weekly*. 'We asked the Secret Service what that meant. They said, "We can't tell you."' Bradley Whitford claims: 'It's for when there's a major problem at the gate.' 'There are large contemporary things that you can't reference because you blow the illusion,' Sorkin told the Writers' Guild of America. 'Eisenhower is the most recent president I'll mention. But when September 11 happened, it was an event too large to ignore. Either you were living in this world or you were in a comic book. That needed to be contended with.'

Did You Know?: An astonishing 24.5 million Americans watched this episode. The original broadcast was prefaced by the cast addressing the audience, explaining that 'Isaac and Ishmael' takes place outside the series time line and giving some hints on plots to come in Season Three. This is missing from overseas prints.

46
Manchester
Part 1[107]

US Transmission Date: 10 October 2001
UK Transmission Date: 22 August 2002 (E4)

Writer: Aaron Sorkin
Director: Thomas Schlamme
Cast: Jim Beaver (Carl) Earl Boen (Paulson)
Dayna Devon (AF1 Reporter) Lois Foraker (Bartender)
Jill Remez (Reporter #4) Kirk Kinder (One Star General)
Mark Henderson (Driver)

Bartlet announces he's running for re-election. CJ makes a gaffe to the press. The president has problems with Abbey who is still upset that she was not consulted about his decision.

American History X: References to the French and Indian War (1755–60).

Politics of Desperation: Two weeks after the announcement, with no sign that Bartlet's figures are significantly improving, Leo hires spin guru Bruno Gianelli, together with assistants Doug and Connie to work with Toby, Sam and CJ on the re-election.

A Little Learning is a Dangerous Thing: In the four weeks since Bartlet made his health disclosure he has, according to Leo and Bruno, educated the public about MS, saved Haiti for democracy, funded the Justice Department's tobacco lawsuit and watched the market rebound. Everything, in fact, but apologise for lying to the American public.

Office Gossip: Leo: 'We don't need to be marriage counsellors.' Toby: 'We should, cos you and I would be really good at it.'

---

[107] Originally scheduled for 19 September 2001.

Denial, Thy Names Are Josh and CJ: CJ tells the press that the president is relieved to be focusing on something important like a potential war with Haiti. Josh, meanwhile, prepares to leak his statement against big tobacco firms (see **42**, 'The Fall's Gonna Kill You') despite warnings from Joey, Leo and Sam.

The Conspiracy Starts at Closing Time: The Haiti rescue operation (see **44**, 'Two Cathedrals') is known as 'Swift Fury', deploying a Landingship Helicopter Assault to evacuate American personnel and President Dessaline from the Embassy to the USS *Enterprise*. It's successful, despite shots being fired by Haitian troops. A message is relayed to General Bazan, via the Canadian Prime Minister, that the US intend to restore Dessaline and that, if he doesn't step down, they will take military action.

References: 'Instead' by Abandon Jalopy, 'Evolution Revolution Love' by Tricky and 'Rock the Boat' by The Hues Corporation are heard during the bar scenes. Also M&Ms, *Oprah*, singer Andy Williams, the historic John Goffe's Mill built in 1744, Guantanamo Bay and Up With People. Sam alludes to *Bill & Ted's Bogus Journey* and Donna to Handel's *Messiah*. Doug wears a Ralph Lauren shirt. When Charlie and Toby are playing pool, on the TV behind Toby is a football match involving England.

'You May Remember Me From Such Films and TV Series As . . .': Ron Silver's CV includes *Kissinger and Nixon*, *Blue Steel*, *Love is Strange* and *Veronica's Closet*. Evan Handler was Miles Roberts in *Ransom* and David in *Natural Born Killers*. Connie Britton played Nikki in *Spin City*. Jim Beaver appeared in *Magnolia* and *Silkwood*. Earl Boen was in *Alien Nation*, *The Terminator* and *The Man With Two Brains*. Lois Foraker appeared in *M*A*S*H*, *The Exorcist II* and *The Candidate*. Jill Remez was in *Slappy and the Stinkers*. Kirk Kinder's movies include *Boyz N the Hood*. Aaron Lacey was Martin Sheen's stand-in in *Shadow Conspiracy*.

Oh, Donna!: Josh complains that Donna always says she doesn't want any food then picks at his. Donna notes: 'You'd think you'd have learned that by now.'

Sex and Drugs and Rock'n'Roll: CJ is told that the Federal Drug Agency is ready to announce its support for Mifepristone (RU-486) an abortifacient drug which can be used as 'morning after' contraception. Josh says Donna seems to think this would mean more sex for her. She replies that *less* sex would be impossible.

Cigarettes and Alcohol: In the bar, Doug has an Absolut martini, Toby drinks Jack Daniel's, Sam and Charlie have beers and CJ drinks what looks like a white wine.

Logic, Let Me Introduce You to This Window: What's a 12 ball doing on a pool table during a 9-Ball game? Pease Air Force Base closed in 1991. Victor McCay's character is referred to in dialogue as Peter when, in previous appearances (**23**, 'In the Shadow of Two Gunmen' Part 1 and **43**, '18th and Potomac'), he'd been Henry.

Quote/Unquote: Abbey: 'It's all over the news. This crazy man got up in front of millions of people and totally screwed his wife.'
    Toby: 'Thank you all for coming round to the self-evident point I made five minutes ago.'
    Bartlet: 'You think it's a sign of strength to invade Haiti? *Missouri* could invade Haiti.'

Notes: 'What if he has to *invade*? It's gonna look like he ordered a military operation to cover up.' Serving a similar purpose to last season's shot-'em-up opening, 'Manchester' is a slow, often ordinary reacquaintance with the characters. Best bits: Sam's girly strop on Air Force One. CJ and Toby playing pool. Leo and Jed on the farm.
    Bartlet's farm is called *Awasiwi Odanack* – an Abenaki term meaning 'beyond the village'. Toby's a good pool player but Charlie is a hustler. The outdoor scenes were shot in Middleburg, Virginia. The hotel that Josh and

Donna park near and where Leo and CJ are seen, in **47**, 'Manchester' Part 1, is called the Red Fox Inn.

Cast and Crew Comments: 'They've got to convince the public that MS isn't fatal, and that the president isn't going to have an attack in the situation room and bomb Heidelberg during Oktoberfest,' Sorkin told Ed Bark. 'They're all still shell-shocked. The president whom they loved and trusted so much has surprised them.' To David Zurawik, he quoted Orson Welles on jealousy being like seasickness, ' "For the person it's happening to, they want to kill themselves. For everybody else, it's hysterical." ' Everyone, including the press, feels a sense of betrayal and is reacting. The press in Bartlet's world – which by and large has been very supportive and sympathetic because he's their kind of guy – have come down on him like a brick bank.'

Did You Know?: After a couple of anxious days with filming delayed due to a set boycott, the press-dubbed '*West Wing* Four' settled their salary differences and returned to work. Janney, Schiff, Whitford and Spencer each received a healthy pay rise, from $30,000 to more than $70,000 per episode, *Variety* reported. After the third season they will also be entitled to five per cent incremental rises. The deal meant that the four committed themselves to stay with the show through to *West Wing*'s seventh season, in 2005–6. 'It's a good deal for them and a fair deal for Warner Bros,' a source close to the negotiations said.

47
Manchester
Part 2

US Transmission Date: 17 October 2001
UK Transmission Date: 22 August 2002 (E4)

Writer: Aaron Sorkin
Director: Thomas Schlamme
Cast: Kris Arnold (Staffer)

Staffers continue to clash with Bruno and his aides. Josh is upset because Leo won't let him postpone an FDA announcement. The press senses there may be a problem with the Bartlets' marriage.

American History X: Roosevelt and Churchill were, according to Bartlet, men who used big words for a big purpose. 'Manifest destiny' was a phrase used by US politicians in the 1840s to explain continental expansion.

A Little Learning is a Dangerous Thing: Jed thinks he could have been a great astronaut. Abbey notes he is afraid of heights, speed, fire and small places, so he probably couldn't.

Foreign Policy: In Haiti, Bazan's demands for allowing democracy to be restored include a private plane, a guarantee he won't be prosecuted and asylum for himself and sixty family members. A compromise is brokered via Canada: Bazan is to go to Venezuela, though he doesn't get the private plane ('if he's very good we won't shoot him in the head'). France help diplomatically during the crisis. Meanwhile, a trade deal is struck with Argentina.

References: Dr Jack Kevorkian – the advocate of doctor-assisted suicide, the International Court of Justice in the Hague, Sears Tower in Chicago, Stratocaster guitars (famous players include Jimi Hendrix, Hank Marvin, Eric Clapton, George Harrison and Kurt Cobain), the Hay-Adams hotel, 'Columbia Gem of the Ocean' by David T Shaw, *shivah* the seven-day Jewish period of mourning, the Rotarians, Starbucks coffee house and the *Boston Globe*. 'New Hampshire; live free or cheap' is a pun on the state's motto 'Live free or die'. Bartlet alludes to Fatboy Slim's 'Right Here, Right Now'. He is reading *American Animal Factories*.

'You May Remember Me From Such Films As . . .': Kris Arnold was in *Eat Me!* and *Buttcrack*.

Oh, Donna!: She helps a troubled Josh get changed.

Sex and Drugs and Rock'n'Roll: 'I never drank the Kool-Aid' refers to the Jonestown mass suicide (November 1978).

Cigarettes and Alcohol: Abbey decides not to give CJ home-made cider. Josh leaks his statement on tobacco to the press and the administration is given the money it wants to continue its lawsuit. But, as Bruno points out, the timing is dreadful. Had Josh waited, he would have got not only the money, but some political capital too.

Logic, Let Me Introduce You to This Window: Leo tells Bruno that Joey Lucas has been polling every day for two months. However, four weeks from the MS announcement brings us to the Manchester scenes in the previous episode and, prior to that, Joey only had 96 hours to do her fake polling (see **43**, '18th and Potomac').

Cruelty To Animals: When Bartlet is rehearsing his speech in the barn, CJ spots a snake. Sam asks what kind it is. 'I don't know and I don't want to ask him,' replies CJ. 'Can somebody shoot it, please?' Josh, too, seems to be afraid – what a girl.

Quote/Unquote: Bruno: 'We will work hard and we will work *together* or, so help me mother-of-God, I will stick a pitchfork so far up your asses you will, quite simply, be dead.'

Doug: 'It's a simple equation: Bartlet rules America. America rocks, therefore Bartlet rocks.' Toby: 'Bartlet *rocks*?' Josh: 'He really *doesn't*, that much.'

Abbey: 'Just one time . . . instead of "according to unnamed sources", I'd like to see, "according to tweaky little ill-informed chicken-ass wannabe . . ." '

Notes: 'Republicans talk about how arrogant you guys are. I always thought it was the natural reaction that comes from not getting the girl.' Better, as the pace picks up and we get an idea of where the story's going. Best bits: Doug giving Toby some harsh truths. Toby disgustedly changing a sign from BARTLET FOR PRESIDENT to BARTLET *IS THE* PRESIDENT. Jed telling CJ he needs her.

Josh worked for two years as Legislative Director in the House and two years as Floor Director in the Senate. Bruno's helped five senators, three governors and a Prime Minister of Israel get elected, though it's possible he himself has never voted. He's worked with Joey Lucas before and rates her highly. He knew Mrs Landingham. Doug is from Oregon.

Did You Know?: The Loudoun town of Bluemont is the location used for Manchester.

48
Ways and Means

US Transmission Date: 24 October 2001
UK Transmission Date: 29 August 2002 (E4)

Teleplay: Aaron Sorkin
Story: Eli Attie, Gene Sperling
Director: Alex Graves
Cast: Miguel Sandoval (Victor Campos)
Nicholas Pryor (Clement Rollins) Edmund L Shaff (Bill Horton)
Max Chalawsky (Kinnis) Félix Solis (Hammaker)
Andrea C Robinson (Barbara) Tom McCarthy (Thomas)
Stephanie Cantu (Reporter) Nadia Akakowsky (Reporter)

Special Prosecutor Rollins isn't nasty enough. 'We need a different enemy,' CJ tells Babish. Sam is concerned about the loyalty of a noted Californian Democrat. The governor of Wyoming is upset that the president won't put out a forest fire. Ainsley fixes up Donna with a Republican.

A View from the Hill: There's some concern on the Hill about how soft the press has been with Rollins, particularly regarding his relationship to the White House. Democrats are worried that Republicans will use this as an excuse to start their own hearings earlier than expected.

American History X: Article 1 section 7 of the Constitution states: 'Every Bill which shall have passed the House of Representatives and the Senate shall, before it becomes a law, be presented to the President: If he approves he shall sign it, but if not he shall return it, with his Objections to that House.'

Politics of Revelation: The first round of subpoenas reveals a lot of middle names: Abigail Ann Bartlet, Elizabeth Bartlet Weston, Eleanor Emily Bartlet, Zoey Patricia Bartlet, Leo Thomas McGarry and Toby Zachary Ziegler.

Politics of Expediency: Victor Campos wants the president's support on a complete amnesty for all undocumented immigrants from the Americas. Sam says they can't back a bill that treats Hispanic immigrants differently; Connie persuades him otherwise.

A Little Learning is a Dangerous Thing: Donna stayed up all night before her nineteenth-century English literature midterm. And passed.

Office Gossip: CJ runs a whispering campaign to get the press on Rollins' back about being too friendly with the White House.

Denial, Thy Name is Josh: When Sam was four he wanted to be a fireman. At the same age, Josh wanted to be a ballerina. He doesn't like to talk about it.

The Conspiracy Starts at Closing Time: Babish says the president is thinking of waiving executive privilege. Rollins wonders whether he's also waiving attorney–client privilege, spousal privilege and doctor–patient privilege.

References: The *Wall Street Journal*, FedEx, Yellowstone National Park (see **8**, 'Enemies'), Adolphe Adam's 1841 ballet *Giselle*, the Indiana Pacers and the Cleveland Cavaliers, LexisNexis research systems and Robin Hood. CJ alludes to Johnny Cash's 'Folsom Prison Blues' ('we need to be investigated by someone who wants to kill us just to watch us *die*'). The scene of Bruno and Leo discussing Sam while Sam's still in the room is very similar to a famous sequence in *Friends* involving Chandler.

'You May Remember Me From Such Films and TV Series As . . .': Mark Feuerstein played Morgan Farwell in *What*

Women Want and was in *Caroline in the City* and *Once and Again*. Miguel Sandoval appeared in *Blow*, *Get Shorty*, *Jurassic Park*, *Sid and Nancy* and *Do the Right Thing*. Nicholas Pryor was in *Carriers*, *Less than Zero*, *Airplane!* and played Chancellor Arnold in *Beverly Hills 90210*. Edmund Shaff was in *Ed Wood*, *That's My Bush* and *Passions*. Max Chalawsky appeared in *Friends and Family*. Félix Solis was in *Empire*. Andrea Robinson appeared in *Nutty Professor II*.

Behind the Camera: Gene Sperling is a former head of the National Economic Council under President Clinton. Eli Attie was a speech writer for Al Gore.

Oh, Donna!: Given the job of boxing all subpoenaed documents, Donna is at her wits' end. 'I grew up on a farm,' she tells Josh, who replies: 'You grew up in a condo.' She insists it was *near* a farm: 'I was cute, I was peppy and I always did well on my nineteenth-century English literature midterm till you came along and *sucked* me into your life of white-collar crime . . . You know what they do to a girl like me on that cell block? I've seen those movies.' Josh says he has too. Later, Josh tells Sam that Donna is about three days away from unspooling; could he borrow some senior assistants from Communications to help her?

Sex and Drugs and Rock'n'Roll: Ainsley sets Donna up on a date with 'hot guy' Cliff Calley whom Ainsley went to law school with. He's just broken up with his girlfriend and is a Republican working for the Majority Counsel's office at the Ways and Means committee, though he's about to be transferred to House Government Oversight. He was educated at Choate, Brown and Harvard.

'Man, you've got a killer body, you know that?' Bruno asks CJ. She replies that she does, in fact, know this.

Cigarettes and Alcohol: CJ has a beer bottle at the climax, but nothing with which to open it.

Logic, Let Me Introduce You to This Window: Connie has a PhD in political economy from Oxford. However Oxford doctorates are called a DPhil. CJ notes Rollins was editor of *Yale Law Review*. The name of this publication is the *Yale Law Journal* (ironically, Gene Sperling is a former editor). There's talk of Bartlet's first veto (CJ confirms in **49**, 'On the Day Before' that the president has not vetoed a bill since taking office), but in **26**, 'In This White House', Sam was asked by Mark Gottfried why the president vetoed the bill. It doesn't sound like Bartlet followed Babish's advice in **41**, 'Bad Moon Rising' to select the most blood-spitting, Bartlet-hating, Republican in the bar. How does CJ know about Josh's ballerina dreams before Sam's had a chance to tell her? Bartlet has suddenly acquired more photos on his desk.

Quote/Unquote: Leo, on Josh and Toby: 'The two of you, when you don't like something, have a tendency to . . .' Josh: 'Show our displeasure?' Leo: 'Piss people off!'

CJ: 'We need someone perceived by the American people to be irresponsible, untrustworthy, partisan, ambitious, and thirsty for the limelight. Am I crazy, or is this not a job for the House of Representatives?'

Leo, on why the Congressional Black Caucus would oppose the estate tax: 'The first generation of black millionaires is about to die.'

Notes: 'The Governor of Wyoming was an inch and a half from calling me a pyromaniac tonight.' A well-structured episode, focusing on how devious CJ can be when she's cornered.

Ainsley says that Rollins is well respected and takes his duties seriously. Rollins was a University of Chicago Law School professor. Bill Horton is Secretary of the Interior. Jack Buckland (see **49**, 'On the Day Before') is mentioned. Bruno, who called her 'red-headed girl' last episode, still doesn't know Margaret's name (he thinks it's Gertrude).

Critique: 'The characters themselves are highly produced,' noted the *New York Times*. 'From the pot-smoking hooker who graduates law school to President Bartlet with his Nobel in economics, everyone is brilliant – and they're even better people. In fact, the only time they go slightly astray is when their Talmudic sense of right-and-wrong is blinded by that awful failing: loyalty. When that happens, they burn with shame, then march right back and apologise.'

Cast and Crew Comments: For this episode, Rob Lowe had to learn a little Spanish. 'As you might guess, Sam doesn't just speak regular Spanish,' Lowe says. 'I tend to torture Rob a little,' Sorkin told *Entertainment Weekly*.

49
On the Day Before

US Transmission Date: 31 October 2001
UK Transmission Date: 29 August 2002 (E4)

Teleplay: Aaron Sorkin
Story: Paul Redford, Nanda Chitre
Director: Christopher Misiano
Cast: Kevin Tighe (Jack Buckland) H Richard Greene (Robert Royce)
Cliff De Young (Kimball) Scott Michael Campbell (Donald Dolan)
John F O'Donohue (Koveleski) Mary Mara (Sherri Wexler)
Steven J Levy (Jonathan) Ana Mercedes (Sally) Elizabeth Taheri (Pam)

The President vetoes the estate-tax repeal. The staff attempt to counter the Republicans' override threats. Josh faces a governor threatening to challenge Bartlet. Charlie is offered legal immunity in the MS investigations. CJ has difficulties with an aggressive TV reporter.

A View from the Hill: There's a rule against exhibitions on the House floor. To buy some time before the crucial vote, a Democrat displays a poster. Another objects and the Chair has to rule, followed by a vote – this buys twenty minutes. When, later, more time is needed Josh suggests having a Democrat call for a journal vote which will require the House to approve the previous day's activity. If that doesn't work, a member can attach an amendment to the override vote. Donna asks, 'What kind of amendment?' Josh says it doesn't matter, 'To qualify for the estate-tax repeal, estates have to have Astroturf.' 'It's hard to figure why Congress can't get anything done,' Donna notes sarcastically.

American History X: 'Walk softly and carry a big stick' is a quote from Theodore Roosevelt.

Politics of Compromise: For his support in the vote, the White House is willing to offer Tennessee Democrat Kimball a one-year moratorium on an increase in grazing fees, support for an increase in production flexibility contracts, a promise not to lower agricultural export subsidies and to discuss a tougher FDA crackdown on the illegal use of antibiotics in milk. Sam suggests they offer the same deal to Pennsylvania Republican Royce. He, it turns out, is a moderate who is embarrassed by the estate-tax anyway but gives Toby and Sam some sage advice about people in their own party. He eventually agrees to vote with them in exchange for a promise to put up a weak Democrat against him in the next election.

The Conspiracy Starts at Closing Time: After the suicide bombings, the Israelis attack the Abu Sneni Bab and Al-Sheik neighbourhoods in Hebron, a police station in Ramallah and *Al-Watan*, the Hamas newspaper.

References: Tony Bennett and Tom Jones (neither of whom Josh resembles), biochemist and Nobel prize winner Dr Kary B Mullis, ricotta-based pasta dish Cheese Gnocchi and chévre brioche, the Periodic Table, PLO leader Yasser Arafat, the Heisman Trophy (annually awarded to the most outstanding college footballer in the US) and the New York Marathon. Boston Celtic's legend Bill Russell and coach Red Auerbach, statesman Oliver Wendell Holmes (1841–1935) and the Jewish day of atonement, Yom Kippur.

'You May Remember Me From Such Films and TV Series As . . .': Kevin Tighe was Dave Blalock in *Murder One* and Sport Sullivan in *Eight Men Out*. H Richard Greene played

Mr Cooper in *The Wonder Years*. Cliff DeYoung was Marty Lawrence in *Suicide King* and appeared in *The Craft*, *Nails* and *F/X*. Scott Campbell appeared in *Flubber* and *Fair Game*. John O'Donohue was in *NYPD Blue* and *As Good as it Gets*. Mary Mara can be seen in *ER*, *Law & Order*, *Blue Steel* and *K-PAX*. Thomas Kopache was in *Stigmata* and *Leaving Las Vegas*. Jeff Mooring was David in *Sports Night*. Rick Cramer appeared in *Spy Hard*. Richard Saxton was in *Bounce*.

Logic, Let Me Introduce You to This Window: Would the Privacy Act really prevent CJ telling a reporter the names of the American victims of the terrorist attack? The *Indianapolis Post-Dispatch* is not a real newspaper.

Quote/Unquote: CJ, on chemists: 'You gotta be a cryptographer to talk to these guys. They speak in combinations of letters that don't spell anything but end up meaning table salt.'

CJ, to the annoying Sherri: 'I changed my clothes because I didn't think it was appropriate to talk about the death of two teenagers while wearing a ball gown. And you knew that. Because you're stupid, but you're not *stupid*.'

Notes: 'You can't ask forgiveness of God until you've asked forgiveness of people on the day before.' Some delicious moments in this, but a sluggish middle section sees the third season continuing to run on the spot somewhat.

Bill Hutchinson (see **1**, 'The West Wing') is mentioned. Jack Buckland, Governor of Indiana (see **48**, 'Ways and Means'), has a meeting with Josh where Josh suggests he may be an interesting nominee for Labor Secretary when the current incumbent, Carl Reed, retires in three months. Donna tells Josh that she got together with Mark again after their initial date (see **48**, 'Ways and Means' and **50**, 'War Crimes').

Cast and Crew Comments: The cast emerged from a reading of the script in early August to be told of a real suicide bombing in Jerusalem in which an American had

been killed. 'It was mind-blowing,' Richard Schiff told
Daily Variety. 'Hopefully this is the last time nonfiction
reflects our fiction.' Sadly it was not. Leo wondering if
there could be an 'Afghan connection' would have horrible
resonance by the time the episode was finally broadcast.

50
War Crimes

US Transmission Date: 7 November 2001
UK Transmission Date: 5 September 2002 (E4)

Teleplay: Aaron Sorkin
Story: Allison Abner
Director: Alex Graves
Cast: Michael O'Keefe (Will Sawyer) Gerald McRaney (Alan Adamley)
Bob Glouberman (Terry Beckwith) Chris Ufland (Benton)
Mary Ostrow (Sharon) Keith Pillow (Klesko) Marcy Goldman (Reporter)

Donna gives a deposition to the House committee. The
president and Hoynes clash over gun control. Leo and an
Air Force general argue about an international war-crimes
court. Sam hears proposals to abolish the penny.

American History X: Operation Rolling Thunder (1965–68)
was the sustained bombing campaign of North Vietnam.
In September 1966 Leo was flying F-105s for the 355th
Tactical Fighter Wing. Alan Adamley was his Forward Air
Commander. During one raid, unbeknown to Leo, a
civilian target (a dam) was bombed and there were eleven
casualties.

Politics of Expediency: After a shooting in a church in
Texas, Leo advises Bartlet to send Hoynes to his home
state. Hoynes, who is more pro-guns than his president, is
reluctant. Hoynes is a hero in Texas, notes Bartlet, though
Hoynes disagrees, suggesting that his associations with the
more liberal president have weakened him. 'It's not easy
being my vice president' Bartlet says. It is, however, the
only way Hoynes will get the Democratic nomination in

four years. Hoynes realises this, but adds that the only way Bartlet can win this time around, is if Hoynes is on the ticket with him. The president acknowledges that this is true and Hoynes agrees to represent him in Texas. Like it or not, they're stuck together in an uneasy alliance.

A Little Learning is a Dangerous Thing: Sam becomes embroiled in discussions on the abolition of the cent. Two thirds of cents produced in the last thirty years have dropped out of circulation. The Mint gets letters containing cents from citizens who found them on the street and mailed them back to help with the national debt. Sam notes that cents can't even be put in tollbooths, except in Illinois (Toby suggests that's because it's Abraham Lincoln's home state).

Real War Crimes: The infamous Operation Paperclip saw the US repatriate numerous Nazi scientists at the end of World War Two. The most noteable of Paperclip's luminaries was Wernher von Braun, inventor of the V-2 rockets and wanted by the British for war crimes, but spirited to America to aid in the development of guided missiles and, ultimately, the space programme.

The Gospel According to the Bartlets: He feels the homily in a church service 'lacked panache'. Abbey says it concerned Ephesians 5:21. 'Husbands, *love* your wives, as Christ *loved* the church and gave himself up for her.' She skips over the part that says, 'Wives, be subject to your husbands as to the Lord,' because 'it's *stupid*'. Bartlet notes St Paul writes 'be subject unto one another'. In this age of 24-hour cable crap devoted to feeding the voyeuristic gluttony of the American public hooked on a bad soap opera that's passing itself off as important, Bartlet notes, people should be able to find some relevance in this.

Oh, Donna!: She tells Sam that Josh is still pissed with her (see **49**, 'On the Day Before'). At her deposition, Cliff tells the rest of the committee that he's met Donna 'socially on several occasions'. She is asked whether she keeps a photo album. She doesn't, but clarifies that she *does* keep photos.

She doesn't have a scrapbook either but keeps cards and letters from her father. The next question is 'do you keep a diary?' She says she doesn't. Later, Cliff tells her that when he stayed the night (she implies that they slept together) he saw what looked like a diary. Donna angrily brushes him off but later tells Josh that she *does* have one – it contains little concerning her work at the White House but lots of personal stuff. She is upset that her lie might have endangered the president. Josh arranges for Cliff to read the diary to confirm that it contains nothing incriminating. 'If I read any of this in the newspaper,' Josh notes, 'I've got the entries for October 4th and 5th,' which, presumably, are the dates Donna was with Cliff.

The Conspiracy Starts at Closing Time: Cliff tells Donna about several laws she's violating: Lying to Congress, Obstruction of Proceedings before Departments, Agencies and Committees and Contempt of Congress. All carry heavy jail sentences.

References: The *San Francisco Chronicle*, Oakland Raiders, Detroit Lions, Green Bay Packers and Indianapolis Colts, Pizzahouse classic 'Volare' by Modugno and Migliaci. Martin Sheen does his impression of Frank Sinatra and misquotes 'You Make Me Feel So Young'. Also Larry King, the NRA, the Convention Center in San Antonio, Prince Sultan Bin-Abd-al-Aziz Al Sa'ud of Saudi Arabia and *Rambo*.

'You May Remember Me From Such Films and TV Series As . . .': Michael O'Keefe was Fred in *Roseanne* and appeared in *Caddyshack* and *Finders Keepers*. Gerald McRaney was in *Night of Bloody Horror* and *Touched By An Angel*. Bob Glouberman was in *Spin City*. Chris Ufland appeared in *Rules of Engagement*. Mary Ostrow was in *The X-Files*. Marcy Goldman's movies include *Airplane!*

Sex and Drugs and Rock'n'Roll: Bartlet offers Hoynes a beer. He seemingly doesn't know that his vice president is a former alcoholic (see **2**, '"Post Hoc, Ergo Propter Hoc"'). On Sunday after church Bartlet and his brother always share a beer.

Logic, Let Me Introduce You to This Window: Leo flew an F-105 Fighterchief in Vietnam. There's no such plane; the F-105 was known as the Thunderchief.

Quote/Unquote: Abbey: '*You're* an oratorical snob.' Bartlet: 'Yes I am. And God loves me for it.' Abbey: 'You said He was sending you to hell.' Bartlet: 'For other stuff.'

Hoynes: 'We're not going to get anywhere by treating gun owners like psychopaths. Particularly in the South where guns are a tradition.' Bartlet: 'That's not good enough ... We tamed the frontier, John. We did that already.'

Leo: 'We set up Nuremberg ... And that was fine until we realised the Cold War threat was going to take precedence. So when the German rocket scientists came here to help us get into space we looked the other way while SS officers followed behind, protected by American intelligence services.'

Adamley: 'All wars are crimes.'

Notes: 'Last month in Idaho, a man killed six members of his family, including his pregnant wife. You know why the liberal intelligentsia didn't go crazy? Cos he did it with an axe. You think we need axe control?' At last, after a few episodes that have failed to fully satisfy, a *real* touch of class. Best episode of the season thus far, by a distance. Best bits: Jed and Abbey's amusing deconstruction of Ephesians. Toby's loyalty speech. Adamley telling Leo he once committed a war crime. Josh brilliantly keeping Donna out of jail.

CJ's laptop quacks when she has email. Will Sawyer has recently been kicked out of Myanmar after the local military put a bounty on his head while he was investigating narcotics trafficking. He claims to have been made a God by the Bau tribe of Fiji (he's the only white man ever to witness their sacrificial rites). Fitzwallace is mentioned. Hoynes alludes to Millie Griffiths and the marijuana controversy (see **37**, 'Ellie').

Critique: Foreign correspondent Sawyer, temporarily assigned to the White House 'goes off with typical bombast about "the Larry King-ization of everything from Monica to Gary Condit," [and concludes that] TV has abandoned the notion of reporting altogether,' Sorkin told Peter de Jonge. 'The implication is that real news is something that happens somewhere else, not here. But, [after 11 September] Bosnia has come to our front-yard.'

Cast and Crew Comments: 'I'm only working on my second episode now, but you can sense the integrity on this show,' Mark Feuerstein told the *New York Times*. 'We're actors who believe in what we're doing, rather than politicians who only wind-up being performers.'

Did You Know?: When told of a rumour that Abbey will become hooked on prescription drugs later this season, Stockard Channing told *Toronto Star*: 'I've got Episode 5 here. Nobody knows what's in 6. If those Internet people know something else, then they know more than Aaron Sorkin!'

51
Gone Quiet

US Transmission Date: 14 November 2001
UK Transmission Date: 5 September 2002 (E4)

Teleplay: Aaron Sorkin
Story: Julia Dahl and Laura Glasser
Director: Jon Hutman
Cast: Valerie Mahaffey (Tawny Cryer)

A navy submarine has 'gone quiet' off North Korea. Sam and Bruno argue over advertising money. Babish quizzes Abbey about malpractice suits. Toby trades art critique with a Congresswoman.

American History X: Bartlet asks why America is still fighting North Korea when no one else is interested. 'Sixteen countries were involved in that police action,' Albie replies. 'Colombia's fighting a drug war, Ethiopia's trying to feed itself, Belgium and the Netherlands [have] got cheese and chocolate to make.' Also, the USS *Pueblo* incident in 1968 (Albie says 'I was there', referring to Hal Holbrook's Emmy-winning role in the TV movie *Pueblo*), the *Glomar* and Project Jennifer (a disastrous covert CIA operation tto raise a sunken Soviet nuclear submarine in the Pacific), USS *Gudgeon* (which, in 1957, was involved in a skirmish with Soviet destroyers) and an incident concerning the USS *Wasp* in the Solomon Islands.

A Little Learning is a Dangerous Thing: The Majority Leader (see **33**, 'The Leadership Breakfast') in Cleveland, when asked why he wants to be president, makes a hash of his reply.

The Encyclopedic Mind of Josiah Bartlet PhD: When Romans ran for Consul, he tells a less-than-interested Charlie, they wore white togas to show intent.

Art for Art's Sake: The forthcoming budget is set to include an additional $105 million for National Parks security, the same amount as the previous budget for National Endowment for the Arts (see **12**, 'He Shall, from Time to Time . . .') Toby meets sour-faced-but-cute Tawny, who describes various works funded by current NEA chair, Oakenwood. These include *Throne* by Rayne Billings (Polaroids of his dysfunctional family on the lavatory), *One Horse, Two Horse* by Mark Moloney (two TVs, one with footage of stallions, the other showing *The God-father*), *Slut* a one-word poem by Jules Waltz, a female performance artist who sings naked and covered in chocolate, *Hold the Lettuce* by Lydia Benedict (two bacon cheeseburgers constructed from Rottweiler dung), the work of Lisa Mulberry (who specialises in placing genitalia in anatomically incorrect positions) and a piece by Andrew Hawkins which involves him destroying all his belongings outside a Starbucks in Haight Ashbury (Sam: 'I've done that a couple of times. I didn't know there was funding available'). Toby likens Tawny's attitude to Germany in 1937 when the Nazis banned 'degenerate art' (victims of

this included Edvard Munch, Frank Marc and Paul Klee).
He eventually agrees to get rid of Oakenwood in return for
the NEA budget.

Denial, Thy Name is Abbey: Babish asks Abbey about
Jonathan Hawkings, Nina Alva, Maurice Blustein and
Jessica Nording. These were all patients involved in
malpractice suits against her. There have been seven
altogether: four were dismissed as nuisance suits, two went
to court, one was settled. Another witness is Arlene
Neiderlander, the wife of a patient on whom Abbey
performed a coronary artery bypass graft and who subsequently died of liver infection. A New York judge dismissed the case. Abbey asks how any of this falls under the
purview of the Investigating Committee. Then she realises:
'They don't have a criminal case against the president . . .
But they can develop one against me.' In focusing on her,
they can distract the president from governing.

Carol's Record Collection: She and CJ have a discussion
about the lyrics of Right Said Fred's 'I'm Too Sexy'.

References: Basketball superstar Dikembe Mutombo, *Le
Monde*, the America's Cup yacht race, 'Zip-a-dee-doo-dah'
from *Song of the South*, Schweppes Bitter Lemon, Bud-
weiser Clydesdales horses, cubist master Pablo Picasso
(1881–1973), French Impressionist Claude Monet (1840–
1926), Buckley v. Valeo (1976) which ruled that campaign-
finance laws only apply to communications that advocate
the election or defeat of a clearly identified candidate,
Pericles (see **3**, 'A Proportional Response'), Greek sculptor
Phidias, Florentine ruler Lorenzo Medici (1449–92), Leonardo da Vinci (1452–1519), Elizabeth I (1533–1603) and
William Shakespeare (1564–1616).

'You May Remember Me From Such Films As . . .': Hal
Holbrook's movies include *The Firm*, *Wall Street*, *The Fog*
and *Capricorn One*. Valerie Mahaffey was in *Senior Trip*
and *After Amy*.

Oh, Donna!: Josh dictates a letter concerning a transgression of Donna's involving some elderly White House visitors. In it, Josh regrets that matters escalated to a point where she felt it necessary to call the Park Police. 'Type that,' he says tersely. Donna asks if she can use his computer since hers is damaged: 'One of them poured Wheatena on the keyboard.'

Logic, Let Me Introduce You to This Window: There's no Seawolf class submarine named the *Portland* (only three such subs exist: the *Seawolf*, the *Connecticut* and the *Jimmy Carter*). Albie refers to 'the USS *Glomar*', however the *Hughes Glomar Explorer* (see **American History X**) was publicly listed as a research vessel owned by Summa Corporation and never had a USS designation.

Quote/Unquote: Oliver: 'Nature, like a woman, will seduce you with its sights, its scents and its touch. And then it breaks your ankle. Also like a woman.' Abbey: 'What the hell kind of dates are you going on?'

Bartlet on Albie Duncan: 'He'll be good to have around for morale, cos he's Mr Happy-Fun-Guy!'

Toby, to Tawny: 'I don't know where you get the idea that taxpayers shouldn't have to pay for anything of which they disapprove. Lots of them don't like tanks.'

Sam: 'Why are you so bent on countering these *idiot* leaflets?' Bruno: 'Because I'm *tired* of working for candidates who make me think I should be embarrassed to believe what I believe. I'm tired of getting them elected. Because somebody came along and said "liberal" means 'soft-on-crime, soft-on-drugs, soft-on-Communism, soft-on-defence, and we're gonna tax you back to the Stone Age . . .' And instead of saying, "Well, excuse me, you right-wing, reactionary, xenophobic, homophobic, *anti*-education, *anti*-choice, *pro*-gun, *Leave it to Beaver* trip-back-to-the-50s," we cowered in the corner and said, "Please don't hurt me." *No more.*'

Notes: 'This is one of those things we've talked about that sounds worse than it is because of your inexperience with

the military.' Another funny, inventive episode. Best bits:
CJ joyfully reworking 'I'm Too Sexy' for Toby's benefit.
Albie's vicious sarcasm. Toby's hilarious battle with
Tawny.

Sam refers to the president's opinion of soft money (see
21, 'Lies, Damn Lies and Statistics'). State Department
liaison Peter (presumably, Henry – see **46**, 'Manchester
Part 1') is recovering from heart surgery. His deputy,
Albie, has been at State since Truman and has an uneasy
relationship with Bartlet. Connie describes herself a 'sa-
vant-like'.

Did You Know?: Stockard Channing told *ET Online* that
she injured her foot while hiking. She became wheelchair
bound, with four pins and a metal plate in her ankle.
Sorkin managed to work her injury into the story. 'The
first lady fell and broke her ankle, it's really quite simple!'

52
The Indians in the Lobby

US Transmission Date: 21 November 2001
UK Transmission Date: 12 September 2002 (E4)

Teleplay: Allison Abner, Kevin Falls, Aaron Sorkin
Story: Allison Abner
Director: Paris Barclay
Cast: Gary Farmer (Jack Lone Feather)
Georgina Lightning (Maggie Morningstar-Charles)
Armando Pucci (Alberto Fedrigotti) Jenny Gago (Bernice Collette)
Shashawnee Hall (Russell Angler) Dave Hager (Mark Faragut)
Patrick O'Connell (Officer)

Thanksgiving. Bartlet is talking about turkeys to whoever
will listen (and everyone has to, including the Butterball
Hotline). Two Stockbridge-Munsee Indians arrive for a
cancelled meeting and refuse to leave.

American History X: Bartlet doesn't like Camp David, the
president's mountain retreat. He says Bess Truman (1885–
1982) thought it was 'dull'.

Politics of Dishonour: Maggie Morningstar-Charles and Jack Lone Feather had a meeting arranged with Jacob Cutler of Intergovernmental Affairs. But he had to cancel. CJ apologises and offers to reschedule. They say they'll wait, Jack adding 'you can forcibly remove us. I've noticed correspondents from the *Times*, Reuters, CNN and the *Miami Herald* are here.' CJ asks, 'This has something to do with us screwing you out of all your land, doesn't it?' The Treaty of Washington (1856) moved their tribe from New York to Wisconsin. The government agreed to protect the reservation, provide education and health care and recognise them as a sovereign nation. But the Dawes Act (1887) forced them to sell the land. Proposed by Congressman Henry Dawes, this noted: 'To be civilized, you must cultivate the land, wear civilized clothes, drive Studebaker wagons and drink whiskey.' The 1934 Indian Reorganization Act allowed the tribes to buy back this land and, if they put it in a trust like a national park, it would never be taken away. They have been waiting for an answer on their application for this from the Department of the Interior for fifteen years. CJ manages to persuade them to rearrange the meeting.

A Little Learning is a Dangerous Thing: The method of calculating the poverty level in the US was devised in 1963 by an Eastern European immigrant named Molly Orshansky who worked for the Department of Social Security.

The Encyclopedic Mind of Josiah Bartlet PhD: CJ tells him that, somewhere during the discussion of anise, coriander and the other fifteen spices he uses to baste a turkey, she lost consciousness. Bartlet is *not* amused: 'You know that line you're not supposed to cross with the president . . .?'

Talking Turkey: Seeking advice about how to cook his turkey, Bartlet calls the Butterball Hotline. He identifies himself as Joe Bethersonton of 11454 Prudre Street, Fargo, 50504. The operator says Jed's voice sounds familiar. He explains: 'I do radio commercials for . . . products.' He asks if stuffing should be cooked *inside* a turkey. It can be, he is told, or baked in a casserole dish. 'If I cook it inside the turkey, is there a chance I could kill my guests?' *Salmonella* and *Campylobacter jejuna* are discussed ('I think you made the second bacteria up,' notes Bartlet). To avoid this he should cook all the ingredients first: sauté vegetables, fry sausage or oysters, etc. The president assures the operator that he has an accurate thermometer: 'It was presented to me as a gift from the sous chef to the King of . . . auto-sales. In Fargo.' When he gets off the phone, Jed tells Toby and Charlie: 'That was excellent. We should do that once a week.'

The Conspiracy Starts at Closing Time: A thirteen-year-old boy in Georgia shot his teacher in the head. His parents immediately got the boy out of the country and Interpol arrested him in Rome. The state Governor wants the boy back, but Italy won't extradite to a country with the death penalty. 'You stand hand-in-hand with . . . Somalia,' notes Alberto, the Italian *Chargé d'Affaires*. Josh flies to Atlanta to meet De Kalb county DA Mark Faragut, a prospective Democrat candidate for Senator. 'Italy can't tell me how to prosecute my case,' he says. Josh replies: 'The Georgia Fourth is tough enough for a Democrat without appearing as if he's against the death penalty . . . The only way to combat that is with TV time.' Guarantee he won't seek the death penalty and Mark will have his campaign bankrolled.

References: FedEx, Italian fascist dictator Benito Mussolini (1883–1945), YMCA and *The Little Red Lighthouse and the Great Grey Bridge* by Hildergarde H Swift. Wolverine is the nickname of Michigan University students. Bruno's hero is showman PT Barnum (1810–91).

'You May Remember Me From Such Films and TV Series As . . .': Gary Farmer was in *Route 666* and *Sioux City*. Georgina Lightning appeared in *Backroads*. Armando Pucci was in *Dream Lover*. Jenny Gago appeared in *The Cross*, *Innerspace* and *Alien Nation*. Shashawnee Hall's movies include *Point of Origin* and *Nightmare on Elm Street*. Dave Hager appeared in *Double Jeopardy*.

Oh, Donna!: She's booked Josh on a flight that gets him to his mother's for Thanksgiving. Josh says he thought he was going to Connecticut because that's where the house is. Donna points out his mother moved to Palm Beach ten months ago: 'You forgot where your mother lives?' Josh insists: 'I'm from Connecticut. Like a swallow to Capistrano . . .' Donna says she will tell his mother he forgot. Josh replies: 'You're the girl I made fun of in elementary school, you know that?' Donna does.

Logic, Let Me Introduce You to This Window: The zip codes for Fargo are 58102 and 58103. Josh *must* know that the Bishop of Rome is the Pope? Atlanta airport looks uncannily like LAX. Josh correctly names five US/Canadian border states. This could be an attempt to rectify the impression of **45**, 'Isaac and Ishmael' that Sorkin doesn't know his geography. De Kalb County is mispronounced throughout the episode. It should, apparently, be 'Da-Kab.' The US Supreme Court has held that if a defendant is under sixteen when an offence is committed, the death penalty isn't applicable. The president is, as he often tells people, an educated man – surely he's heard of the dangers of undercooked meat before now?

Quote/Unquote: Sam: 'Turns out we've got four million new poor people.' Josh: 'Since when?' Sam: 'Yesterday.' Josh: 'I'm not an expert, but wouldn't we have a better chance of getting re-elected if we could say there are four million *fewer* poor people? Hang on. I *am* an expert.'

Toby says the Office of Management Budgets are preparing a new formula to calculate the poverty level. Bruno: 'Show of hands?'

CJ: 'How do you keep fighting these smaller injustices when they're all from the mother of injustices?' Maggie: 'What's the alternative?'

Notes: 'It's a lawyer and a Michigan Wolverine. I think we can take 'em. We always do.' A fine attempt at a comedy-centric episode. Bartlet's call to the Butterball Hotline is a series highlight, as is Josh's meeting with Alberto and full marks for the courage of *not* taking easy options over the Indian storyline (not using right-on soundbites concerning native Americans for a start).

Bartlet speaks four languages though his French is seemingly limited (he calls Abbey 'my little cheese'). Toby has nieces and nephews (see **22**, 'What Kind of Day Has it Been' and **38**, 'Somebody's Going to Emergency, Somebody's Going to Jail'). CJ says she has pardoned the turkey (see **30**, 'Shibboleth') and been to her dentist (see **15**, 'Celestial Navigation'). René, the White House head chef, is mentioned (Mario's replacement, presumably. See **2**, ' "Post Hoc, Ergo Propter Hoc" '). Reporter Mark is Canadian (there's reference to Canadian Thanksgiving: second Monday in October). Bruno, as a teenager, raced sailboats (he crewed Larchmont to Nassau on a 58-foot sloop called *Candice*).

Did You Know?: The episode's original title was 'The Butterball Hotline'.

53
The Women of Qumar

US Transmission Date: 28 November 2001
UK Transmission Date: 19 September 2002 (E4)

Teleplay: Aaron Sorkin
Story: Felicia Wilson, Laura Glasser, Julia Dahl
Director: Alex Graves
Cast: Christian Clemenson (Evan Woodkirk) Dinah Lenney (Mary Klein)
Ty Burrell (Tom Starks) Bradley White (Man)
Bruce Kirby (Barney Lang) Sid Conrad (Ed Ramsey)
Bill Erwin (Ronald Kruickshank) Fort Atkinson (Grant)
Michael Canavan (Flynn) James Hornbeck (Bedrosian)
Stan Sellers (Califf) Larry Cox (Aide) Dean White (Aide)
Kim Sykes (Secretary)

CJ argues with the president on whether to make public a possible outbreak of mad cow disease. She is outraged about US arms sales to a Gulf state that oppresses its women. Josh meets a women's group lobbyist over the wording of a treaty concerning prostitution.

A View from the Hill: A politician named Segal is upset about the time and money spent by a town in Virginia complying with the Americans with Disabilities Act. The president asks if employees in wheelchairs are supposed to work in the parking lot.

American History X: The president is to speak at a Smithsonian exhibition commemorating the sixtieth anniversary of Pearl Harbor, but a veterans' group objects to the exhibition. They are troubled by a commentary about racist propaganda posters (one poster called 'The Sowers', for instance, portrays the Japanese as hulking barbarians). The representatives of the group, Barney, Ed and Ronald, are concerned the overreaching message is of a vengeful America and a victimised Japan. Ed says the museum claims 63,000 American lives would have been lost if they'd invaded the Japanese mainland in 1945. Over objections that such a scenario could never have happened, CJ asks the veterans to imagine that Germany, despite being defeated in the war had, nevertheless, been able to hang on to France and possibly Italy, thus continuing to exist as a recognised government. Ed says the Americans would never have allowed it. CJ replies: 'We did it in Cambodia. You're protesting because you think the Smithsonian isn't paying proper respect to what you and the soldiers of the Tenth Armoured Third Army risked and lost your lives for. How would you feel in the hypothetical I just described, if we were selling tanks, missiles and fighter jets to the Nazis?'

Politics of Worst Case Scenario: A herd of cattle in Ogallala, Nebraska was accidentally given banned feed eighteen months ago. One of the cows is now showing neurological damage. Tissue is sent to the UK for testing. The first round of tests in Iowa showed a presumptive positive for mad cow disease. Leo asks for the worst-case scenario. 'We declare a national state of emergency and a Class One recall on all consumer beef.' The second they announce a positive case, Bartlet notes, 'we lose $3.6 billion in beef exports, fast food is deserted, supermarkets pull beef'.

A Little Learning is a Dangerous Thing: After the Civil War, veterans had to visit Washington personally to get their pensions. They waited for a clerk to look through records until their papers were found. They were bound with red tape, hence the term 'red tape'.

The Encyclopedic Mind of Josiah Bartlet PhD: Charlie is taking an exam in modern American history. Bartlet thinks he should study the Crusades, the fall of the Roman Empire from Theodosius to Justinian and the Visigoths – 'Modern history is another word for television.' He will, he says, get Charlie a copy of a speech George Perkins Marsh used in 1845 to rouse the agricultural community of Rutland, Vermont. And then a study on the word 'ecology' as coined by German biologist, Ernst Haeckel.

The Nuisance Suit Starts at Closing Time: Some months previously the president was asked whether the dangers of airbags outweighed the benefits. His reply was: 'Everything has risks. Your car could drive into a lake and your seatbelt jams, but no one's saying don't wear your seatbelt.' A couple attending the fundraiser were in an accident. The man was not wearing his seatbelt and was killed and his partner is now suing the president for contributory negligence. 'Aren't lawsuits against the president the equivalent of *insane*?' Toby asks, citing a guy who's suing Bartlet because of the CIA-sponsored radio transmissions in his bridgework. Another litigant wants an alien from the planet Xanadu removed from his front yard and a couple are suing for all back taxes because taxes are unconstitutional.

References: The *Rocky Mountain News*, the Central Veterinary Laboratory in Addlestone Surrey, *Weekly Standard*, Dodger Stadium, the Boston Celtics, the *Clean*

Water Act (1972), *Nintendo*, Coke and Pepsi, explorer
Amerigo Vespucci (1451–1512), Easy-Bake Ovens, the
Washington Times, the Women's Suffrage movement, the
Child Support Enforcement Act, the Rotary Club, Popeye,
the Doctrine of Sovereign Immunity, first lady Eleanor
Roosevelt (1884–1962) and apartheid.

**'You May Remember Me From Such Films and TV Series
As . . .':** Mary-Louise Parker's movies include *Five Senses*,
Fried Green Tomatoes and *Red Dragon*. Christian Clemen-
son appeared in *Armageddon*, *Apollo 13*, *The Big Lebowski*,
The Fisher King, *Broadcast News* and *Buffy*. Dinah Lenney
was in *ER*. Ty Burrell appeared in *Evolution*. Bradley
White was in *Pay It Forward*. Bruce Kirby played Sgt
Kramer in *Columbo* and Sgt Vine in *Kojak*. Sid Conrad
was in *Wisdom*. Bill Erwin's CV includes *Dennis the
Menace*, *Growing Pains*, *The Twilight Zone*, *The Waltons*
and *Gunsmoke*. Fort Atkinson appeared in *Striking Distance*. James Hornbeck was in *Seduced*. Stan Sellers'
movies include *Doctor Dolittle*. Larry Cox appeared in
Heathers. Kim Sykes was in *The Crow*.

Oh, Donna!: 'You've worked as a prostitute,' Josh suggests
to Donna. 'Wouldn't legalising prostitution allow women
to unionise and access to social services and health care
benefits?' Donna replies: 'You think if you make prostitution legal, then prostitutes are going to suddenly want
everyone to *know* they're prostitutes? I'll be back on my
street corner.'

Sex and Drugs and Rock'n'Roll: Amy asks if Josh is dating
his assistant. Josh denies this. Amy continues: 'I heard you
might be. She's cute.'

Logic, Let Me Introduce You to This Window: Mad cow
disease is never once referred to by its proper name: bovine
spongiform encephalopathy (BSE). Qumar, of course,
doesn't exist. Are there such things as pig-pickin' festivals?
Josh says prostitution is legal in Germany, Turkey and the
Netherlands. It's also legal in various forms in Italy,
Norway, Canada and Singapore. The George Perkins

Marsh speech Bartlet mentions was from 1847 not 1845. Amy says she knows of no little girl who says 'I want to be a prostitute when I grow up.' It was, in fact, alleged that when the movie *Pretty Woman* was popular in the early 1990s that's exactly what many teenage girls *were* saying.

Quote/Unquote: Toby wonders if murder is going to overtake health care and education on the campaign trail. Sam: 'No, you're right, cos health care and education are much sexier.'

Josh, after his meeting with Amy: 'The appointments aren't going to be held up. At least not by Lady *Godiva*.' Donna: 'Tell me she wasn't bare breasted, at least outside your imagination.'

CJ asks how Josh's meeting with Amy went. Josh: 'I showed her who's boss.' CJ: 'Who'd it turn out to be?' Josh: 'It's still unclear.'

Notes: 'Every time we make one of these deals with a place like Qumar I feel the women around here look at me funny.' Worst episode in some time, spending a lot of energy saying not much. Turning CJ into a shrill champion of the rights of Islamic women in the face of some of the views expressed in **45**, 'Isaac and Ishmael' is particularly unfortunate.

Sam's father (see **38**, 'Somebody's Going to Emergency, Somebody's Going to Jail') is a member of the Elks.

Cast and Crew Comments: The BSE storyline unintentionally paralleled the autumn 2001 US anthrax scares. Despite, according to Thomas Schlamme in *TV Guide Online*, pressure to remove it from the networks, the plot stayed.

Did You Know?: Although it's filmed in Hollywood, according to *US Today*, the *West Wing* cast are doing their best to help Washington's economy by making thirty second public service announcements encouraging tourism in the capital.

54
Bartlet For America

US Transmission Date: 12 December 2001
UK Transmission Date: 26 September 2002 (E4)

Writer: Aaron Sorkin
Director: Thomas Schlamme
Cast: Steven Gilborn (Paul Dearborn)
Doug Ballard (Governor of Tennessee) Todd Waring (Rathburn)
Mark Hutter (Congressman) Ashley L Clark (Alan) Carlos Jacott (Allen)
Randy Thompson (CEO Donor) Dennis Haskins (CEO Donor)
Ellis E Williams (Reverend Al Skyler)
David St James (Congressman Gibson) Greta Sesheta (Congresswoman)
Joe O'Connor (Calhoun)[108] Judy Kain (Event Planner)
Thomas Carrington (Congressional Staffer)

It's two days before Christmas, but no one at the White House feels much festive spirit following a racist threat to firebomb black churches in Tennessee. Leo and his new $650-an-hour lawyer are on Capitol Hill, to testify before the House committee.

Backstory: Leo has known Bartlet for 32 years, clarifying the approximation given in **1**, 'The West Wing'. He notes that they became close friends eleven years ago (circa 1990). Leo first approached Bartlet about running for president 'four years ago last month' (roughly November 1997), which *just* fits in with the timescale established in **23**, 'In The Shadow of Two Gunmen'. Their first meeting concerning this took place at the New Hampshire Statehouse in Concord. A second meeting occurred later at the Marriott Hotel. At neither of these did Bartlet mention his MS.

Upon winning the Democratic nomination, Bartlet (with advice from others, notably Leo), decided to make John Hoynes his running mate. At this meeting, Bartlet told Hoynes that he had MS. As a consequence, Hoynes didn't accept the job offer immediately.

---

[108] Joe O'Connor previously appeared in **17**, 'The White House Pro-Am' playing a (nameless) Congressman.

On 30 October 1998, in St Louis, just prior to the third and final televised election debate, Bartlet had a mild attack during which he collapsed. The doctor's said it was an inner-ear infection. At this time, Leo was meeting with two potential donors to the campaign, one of whom was future Congressman Gibson. After their meeting, Leo got drunk and Gibson, returning to the room to retrieve his briefcase, saw this. The only other people who know about the incident are Bartlet and Josh.

American History X: Bartlet mentions that Thomas Hilton started a fishing village at the mouth of the Piscataqua River in 1623, making a nonsense of the slogan, 'New Hampshire: It's What's New!'

During the hearing there's a reference to Edith Galt Wilson (1872–1961), the second wife of Woodrow Wilson (1856–1924), the 28th president. Aided by her doctors, Mrs Wilson effectively ran the US for several months while her husband recovered from a stroke.

Politics of Deviancy: As one member of the committee prepares to metaphorically, as Bartlet notes, 'spank Abbey', the president delivers a sad little homily on what men do to women.

The Conspiracy Starts at Closing Time: The FBI apprehend a suspect in the church arsons, one Gilbert Murdoch, who was stopped outside Chattanooga for a failing brake light. Murdoch panicked, believing he was being pulled over for planning to make a Molotov cocktail. Mike Casper notes that it took agents almost twenty minutes to establish a conspiracy to firebomb churches.

References: Jordan is wearing an Armani suit, and not spandex, as Leo tells the president. There's an allusion to Sly Stone's 'It's a Family Affair', while Bartlet misquotes Simon and Garfunkel's 'The 59th Street Bridge Song (Feelin' Groovy)'. Bartlet refers to occasions when previous presidents – Eisenhower in 1957 and Kennedy in 1961 – overruled governors concerning law-enforcement issues. Also, the Grammy awards, the AFT, Article 2, Section 1,

Clause 6, of the US Constitution and the 25th Amendment, both concerning the fitness of a president to lead and the Civil Rights Act of 1964.

'You May Remember Me From Such Films and TV Series As . . .': Joanna Gleason played Morgan Winslow in *Diff'rent Strokes*, appeared in *The Wedding Planner*, *Hannah and Her Sisters* and *F/X2* and provides voice work on *King of the Hill*. Steven Gilborn was Harold Morgan in *Ellen* and Mr Collins in *The Wonder Years*. Doug Ballard's CV includes *Oh Baby*, *Sunset Grill* and *Northern Exposure*. Todd Waring was in *Splash Too*. Mark Hutter appeared in *Hotel* and *Exposed*. Ashley L Clark was in *Friends*. Carlos Jacott played the agent in *Being John Malkovich* and also appeared in *She's All That*, *It's a Shame About Ray*, *Angel*, *The Last Days of Disco*, *She Spies* and *Grosse Pointe Blank*. He was also Ramon the Pool Guy in *Seinfeld*. Randy Thompson played Dr Kriegal in *Buffy*, and appeared in *Singles*, *Charmed*, *Roswell* and *The Montana Run* (which he also wrote and directed). Dennis Haskins played Richard Balding in *Saved By The Bell*. Ellis E Williams's movies include *Jackie Brown*. David St James was in *My Sister's Keeper*. Greta Sesheta's CV includes *Alias*. Judy Kain was in *Trevor* and *Grosse Pointe*.

Oh, Donna!: Mike Casper tells Donna that he would be hitting on her if he weren't at the White House on FBI business.

Cigarettes and Alcohol: Leo extols the virtues of the sound that an ice cube makes when dropped into a whisky glass. And, also, of Johnnie Walker Blue Label, sixty-year-old Scotch that costs $30 a glass. Leo and Joanna arrange a dinner date for Christmas Eve.

Logic, Let Me Introduce You to This Window: Leo notes that 30 October, the day of the last debate, was 'eight days before the election', which would place it on 6 November. However, if Bartlet was elected in 1998 (see **24**, 'In The Shadow of Two Gunmen' Part 2) and the election was carried out as per the US Constitution (on the Tuesday after the first Monday in November), then the election should have been in 4 November. Gibson calls Congressman Bruno Phil, yet on the television coverage of the hearings his first name is given as Joseph. Screwball comedies were more of a 1930s Hollywood phenomenon. The 23rd December 2001 is a Sunday, so it's unlikely that a house committee would be meeting on such a day. Leo, seemingly, lied to Karen Larson in **13**, 'Take Out The Trash Day' when he said he hadn't had a drink in six years.

Quote/Unquote: Bartlet, on Leo and Jordan: 'I like you and her. It's like a fifties screwball comedy.'

Leo: 'Do you have any idea how many alcoholics are in Mensa? You think it's a lack of willpower? That's like thinking somebody with anorexia nervosa has an over-developed sense of vanity.'

Cliff, to Gibson: 'This is why good people hate us . . . If you proceed with this line of questioning, I will resign this committee and wait in the tall grass for you, Congressman.'

Notes: 'If Jed Bartlet had told you about his health . . . would you have still thought it was a good idea for him to run?' An outstanding example of *The West Wing*'s ability to create big drama from a minimalist setting. A piece of *bijoux* courtroom theatre that could have drowned in a *faux-naïf* avalanche of cheap slogans in lesser hands. Instead, thanks to John Spencer's brilliant performance, 'Bartlet For America' works on every level.

Bartlet's Christmas present to Leo is a frame holding the crumpled cocktail napkin upon which Leo wrote *Bartlet for America* four years ago. Josh reminds Leo of the story of the man who fell into a hole (see **32**, 'Noël'). Leo still drinks tomato juice (see **20**, 'Mandatory Minimums'). His previous job title was 'General Chairman *Bartlet For America*'. Leo's grandfather was an alcoholic, like his father (see **13**, 'Take Out The Trash Day'). Gibson mentions the president's collapsing in the Oval Office (see **12**, 'He Shall, from Time to Time . . .') There's a brief shot of Sam's well-thumbed Filoxfax.

Critique: 'On domestic policy, it is impossible for lefties like me not to be stirred to tears by the show, as Bartlett [sic] and the crew stand up to Christian fundamentalists, protect social security, fight child poverty and fend off the incursions of the US's especially rabid right-wing,' noted Johann Hari. 'Yet look at what has happened to *The West Wing*'s depiction of US foreign policy. Even a fictional character who is seen as so left-wing that he is unelectable spouts a chilling, implicitly racist foreign policy.'

Awards: In this showpiece episode of the third season, John Spencer's performance in 'Bartlet For America' won him an Emmy award for Outstanding Supporting Actor in a Drama Series. Lauren Schaffer's editing and Thomas Del Ruth's cinematography were also nominated. The latter also won an American Society of Cinematographers Award for his work on this episode.

Did You Know?: Leo McGarry is, like John Spencer himself, a recovering alcoholic. 'But I hardly want to be the poster boy for sobriety,' the actor told *New York Newsday*. 'It's my personal journey, and I have a hard time with the responsibility that putting the truth out there gives you.'

55
H.Con – 172

US Transmission Date: 9 January 2002
UK Transmission Date: 3 October 2002 (E4)

Teleplay: Aaron Sorkin
Story: Eli Attie
Director: Vincent Misiano
Cast: Kinga Philipps (Waitress)

Cliff makes Leo an offer regarding the MS affair, which Leo wants to refuse, no matter what its personal implications may be. Josh is looking for *any* excuse to see Amy; a photographer has written a tell-all book and Sam wants to refute its allegations; and Charlie gives the president a present that touches him, and troubles everyone else.

A View From the Hill: Leo is offered a deal – an end to the hearings, in exchange for the president's accepting a joint resolution of censure from the House and the Senate.

American History X: Jordan gives Leo some examples of nonbinding joint resolutions from the 106th Congress. These include one in support of Ohio's state motto, one fostering friendship with the people of Mongolia, one recognising the contributions of Bristol, Tennessee, to country music and one in support of Little League baseball.

Leo mentions that when the British ambassador told the German foreign minister that they intended declaring hostilities over violation of Belgium's neutrality, in September 1914, the minister said, 'You're going to war over a piece of paper.' There's also a discussion on the joint resolution to censure Andrew Jackson in 1834 over his withholding documents relating to his removing funds from the Bank of the US. Jackson subsequently had the censure expunged in January 1837.

Politics of Compromise: Toby has liaised with various women's groups in preparation for the State of the Union address. Josh notes that America is one of only six countries that have no national policy regarding paid maternal leave. Amy replies that she's fine with this, since Papua New Guinea also doesn't have such a law.

A Little Learning is a Dangerous Thing: The forthcoming publication of a salacious book, *The Camera Doesn't Lie: What I Saw in the Bartlet White House* by Ron Berkhalt, has Sam working around the clock to find errors in it. Sam hired Berkhalt and subsequently fired him. Josh notes that Berkhalt was a buffoon and Toby vaguely remembers the author as a not very talented, unpleasant malcontent. Extracts from the book are discussed on several occasions. It describes Toby as 'the prickly, mumbling Communications Director, whose inner, bitter darkness spelled the break-up of the one marriage we know about'. It alleges that, on Carol's birthday, Charlie (and, presumably, other staffers) attended a séance at which those present tried to contact Margaret's dead grandmother. And the book alleges that, after the birth of his first two daughters, Bartlet wanted a son and consulted a book on how to choose the sex of your baby, which advised that the prospective father should avoid wearing jockstraps and other tight-fitting clothes, leading to several amusing conversations about the contents of the president's pants.

The Encyclopedic Mind of Josiah Bartlet PhD: Charlie buys Bartlet a copy of Herman Moll's 1709 map 'Canaan, Palestine or The Holy Land. Divided into the Twelve Tribes of Israel' at a flea market. Toby, CJ and Leo all advise the president not to hang it in the Oval Office, since it could be seen as insulting, given that it doesn't recognise the existence of Israel. Bartlet, in vain, appeals that it wouldn't, since Israel wouldn't be created for another 250 years.

References: The opening scene takes place in the Rayburn House Office Building. Also, the Head Start programme, the Teacher of the Year award, *Peter Pan* ('Never Land'), *Bewitched*, the Ritz-Carlton hotel chain, the character of Deep Throat from *All The President's Men*, and *How To Choose the Sex of Your Baby* by Dr Landrum B Shettles. There are references to the Russian ballet dancer Nijinsky (1890–1950), the American Medical Association, the *New York Post* and the *Washington Times* and Jay Leno. CJ sarcastically sings 'Cool' from *West Side Story* to an enraged Sam. The president's favourite movie is Anthony Harvey's 1968 epic *The Lion in Winter*, which Toby also greatly admires.

'You May Remember Me From Such Films as . . .': Kinga Philipps played Austin's mum in *Austin Powers in Goldmember* and appeared in *Tomcats*.

Oh, Donna!: She indulges in some playful teasing with Josh when he's waiting for a phone call from Amy.

Cigarettes and Alcohol: When meeting Amy, Josh orders an Absolut Martini, on the rocks, with two olives. Subsequently, Toby, CJ and Sam share bottles of Sam Adams beer in CJ's office.

Sex and Drugs and Rock'n'Roll: Josh has known Amy since they were at Harvard together. She dated Josh's roommate, Chris, and, according to Josh, the couple had lots of sex. Josh notes that he studied hard in high school, at Harvard and in law school. His IQ, he suggests, doesn't break the bank and he wanted to get into politics. He therefore feels that he missed out on stuff such as how to handle relationships. At the end of the episode, Amy kisses him, suggesting he might be about to get a crash course.

Logic, Let Me Introduce You to This Window: Jordan gets the position of the Washington Memorial wrong. It's in the middle of the Mall, not at the end. The episode title is not a form of terminology used in the House. In reality, a concurrent resolution would be called 'H.Con. Res. 172'. CJ's admission that she doesn't know which is Ed and which is Larry, if it isn't a joke, is an unbelievable statement for somebody who's worked with both for at least three years. Why is the federal section of the Georgetown Law Library open to the public at eleven o'clock on a Monday evening? Josh says that he knows *The Nutcracker*, but that he's never seen a ballet. Didn't he have a childhood ambition to *be* a ballerina (see **48**, 'Ways and Means')? When Toby is in CJ's office, reading about a basketball game, through the office window it's clearly daytime outside. It should be dark.

Quote/Unquote: Bartlet: 'How was your weekend?' Charlie: 'It was good, sir.' Bartlet: 'What did you do?' Charlie: 'I was here most of the time with you.'

Toby, to Sam on what's true in Berkhalt's book: 'My name *is* Toby Ziegler, and I *am* the communications director, though there's a typo in "communications" at one point.'

Bartlet, on the book: 'Fiction or nonfiction?' Toby: '*Science* fiction.'

Notes: 'I take a bullet for the president; he doesn't take one for me.' Another superb episode, balancing a very serious plot (the machinations surrounding getting the president to agree to the censure), with more frivolous ones (Sam and the tell-all book) and one that's downright *lightweight* (Josh and Amy's flirting). Good performance, and cracking dialogue, all round.

Toby and the president once played miniature golf. Toby's mother has been dead for twelve years (see **4**, 'Five Votes Down'). Josh has never been to Bosnia. He remembers when Amy threw a water balloon on his head (see **53**, 'The Women of Qumar'). Oliver Babish is mentioned.

Cast and Crew Comments: 'I wanted to wrap up [the MS storyline] now and explore new elements inside the Bartlet administration,' Aaron Sorkin told the *St Louis Post-Dispatch*. 'I don't think you'll find that the rest of the season will be lacking in idealism.'

Did You Know?: The events of 11 September 2001 cast some long shadows across the world. One, inevitably given its subject matter, touched *The West Wing*. At the time of the terrorist attacks, Aaron Sorkin was writing what was scheduled to be the sixth episode of the season, a Hallowe'en special. He immediately abandoned the script. He said it didn't feel right, that all of a sudden what artists and writers did seemed 'despicably silly'.

56
100,000 Airplanes

US Transmission Date: 16 January 2002
UK Transmission Date: 10 October 2002 (E4)

Writer: Aaron Sorkin
Director: David Nutter
Cast: Traylor Howard (Lisa) Nancy Linehan Charles (Oncologist)
Howard S Miller (Oncologist) Nicholas Hormann (Bobby)
Brian Baker (John Tandy) Charles Walker (Oncologist)
Marcus Eley (Bartender)

On State of the Union night, Sam is trailed by a *Vanity Fair* reporter, his ex-fiancée Lisa. The speech is to be delivered just two weeks after the president was forced to accept a Congressional censure and Bartlet demanded that a passage promising a cure for cancer within a decade be included.

Backstory: Lisa Sherbourne is Sam's ex-fiancée (see **23**, 'In the Shadow of Two Gunmen' Part 1). CJ asks if the reason that they *didn't* get married was that her name would have been Lisa Sherbourne-Seaborn. Sam tells Toby the reason was that Lisa didn't like him very much. He later tells Lisa, in response to the same question, that it was because he never felt that he was cool enough for her. Lisa replies that Sam thinks too little of her. She didn't leave him: *he* left her to work for Bartlet. Where, she believes, he's doing a great job.

A View From the Hill: Toby says the president, if he wished, could fulfil his constitutional obligation to keep Congress informed by buying that branch of the legislature a subscription to the *Wall Street Journal*.

American History X: Sam says that on 16 May 1940 Franklin Roosevelt ordered that 50,000 aeroplanes be built if the US was to be a force in any forthcoming war. The fact that this wildly ambitious target was not only reached but *doubled* during the next four years gives this episode its title. There are several references to John Kennedy's famous speech to a joint session of Congress on 25 May 1961, in which he promised to land a man on the moon before the end of the present decade.

A Little Learning is a Dangerous Thing: The president and Abbey entertain a group of oncologists for dinner. Bartlet is bored with the conversation until one of the doctors mentions that medical science is ten years, $25 billion and some luck away from curing cancer. This gives Bartlet an idea for his upcoming State of the Union speech. He's ultimately talked out of it for various nonmedical reasons: it's suggested that the idea would be considered too political, as though he were trying to gain sympathy after the censure.

In-Jokes: Following CJ's confession that she didn't know Ed from Larry in the previous episode, Lisa, introduced to the pair, asks which is which and they simultaneously reply that it doesn't matter. Another regular debate topic on several *West Wing* message boards is covered. Why is it that Ed and Larry are never seen separately? 'It's weird, isn't it?' notes Larry.

References: Allusions to *This Is Spinal Tap*, the Charlatans' 'How High?', HaHa's comedy club in Cleveland and Emily's List (see **24**, 'In The Shadow of Two Gunmen' Part 2). Also, *Vanity Fair*, Henry Kissinger (US secretary of state 1973–77), Microsoft's Bill Gates, the Reverend Jesse Jackson, Mr Rogers from the children's TV show *Mr Rogers' Neighborhood* and Mahatma Gandhi (1869–1948). Joey quotes Samuel Broder, a former director of the National Cancer Institute. Medical facilities referenced include Sloan-Kettering and Dana-Farber. Sam mentions *USA Today*, the fashion designer Tommy Hilfiger and Apollo 11's Tranquillity Base.

'You May Remember Me From Such Films and TV Series As . . .': Traylor Howard appeared in *Me, Myself & Irene* and *Dirty Work*. Nancy Linehan Charles's movies include *Minority Report* and *Dead Man on Campus*. Howard Miller was in *The Thirteenth Floor*, *CSI* and *Liar Liar*. Nicholas Hormann's CV includes *Kramer vs. Kramer* and *Seinfeld*. Charles Walker was in *Almost Famous*, *Charmed* and *Moonlighting*.

Oh, Donna!: Donna notes that second dates are when the wheels traditionally come off for Josh. When Josh stares wistfully at Joey at the party, Donna appears behind him and says, brutally, 'So many women, so little charm.'

Cigarettes and Alcohol: At the party, Amy drinks a glass of Chardonnay (as CJ also appears to later). A jilted Josh asks the barman for an ice and vodka. Sam orders a Jack Daniel's.

Sex and Drugs and Rock'n'Roll: Amy's new boyfriend, mentioned in the previous episode, is the Florida Democratic Congressman John Tandy. Toby suggests to Josh that they started dating shortly after Nan Lieberman announced that she was going to make a primary challenge to Tandy. Josh speculates that Tandy is using Amy to gain the female vote, a suggestion that Amy finds offensive. However there's a clear suggestion that she may suspect some truth in this.

Toby asks CJ to dance with him after Joey announces the impressive approval ratings for the president's speech. Following this, a happy CJ returns to her office and is in conversation with Carol when Sam walks in. 'Get on the couch. I'm going to do you, right now,' she says, merrily. Sam looks happy about this until CJ notes that she was still talking to Carol. Later, Sam says that if she was serious about what she was suggesting with Carol, he could just sit in the corner and watch.

Logic, Let Me Introduce You to This Window: Donna was apparently working from an outdated manual when she declared that regulations governing federal travel take six thousand words. Travel regulations had, as a correspondent to the *Government Executive Magazine*'s 'West Wing Watch' gleefully noted, 'been rewritten in plain English to deal with exactly the problem that Donna raised'. Sam asks when Congress last rebuked a sitting president? Toby replies during the Civil War. Although the Senate *did* pass a resolution condemning President Lincoln in 1864, it was not a joint resolution. Nor, for that matter, was an 1848 house resolution on James Polk. Donna asks Toby if he knows how many words are in the Gettysburg Address and the Ten Commandments. He replies 266 and 173, respectively. He's wrong, it should be 286 and 179. Once again, there are early-evening skies visible through a White House office window during a scene that's supposed to be taking place late in the evening (see **55**, 'H.Con – 172').

Quote/Unquote: Josh: 'Still trying to get waived into Generation X?' Lisa: 'Still a pompous jackass?' Josh: 'You betcha.'

CJ: 'You don't ask the school bully out to lunch the day after he stole your lunch money.'

Joey: 'The federal government shouldn't be directing scientific research.' Sam: 'Why?' Joey: 'Because you stink at it!'

Notes: 'I think ambition is good. I think overreaching is good. I think giving people a vision of government that's more than Social Security cheques and debt reduction is good.' The juxtaposition of the train-wrecked relationships of both Sam and Josh are central to this episode. Neither Amy nor Lisa is a particularly sympathetic character, and, if the intention was for the audience to empathise with the boys, then it works. But that's actually quite a dramatic cheat, and '100,000 Airplanes', despite some strong *realpolitik* ideas, is a rather shallow and narcissistic piece, with only some good acting to hold it together.

These events take place two weeks after the president accepted the house censure and, therefore, two weeks and a few days after the events of the previous episode. Sam knows enough sign language to thank Joey for her contribution to a conversation.

Cast and Crew Comments: 'Sometimes Aaron will give you a heads-up, but in this case it was just, "You've got a lot to do in the next show," ' Rob Lowe told Pat O'Brien. 'We had talked about Sam's fiancée [previously] and I always wondered why Sam didn't get married and what drove him to want to work for Bartlet. To have those questions [being] answered three years into the show was a surprise for me. I think the audience will like seeing that glimmer into his past.'

Did You Know?: Watch out in this episode for Ray Dewey, a Grammy-nominated composer and pianist who was also West Coast director of NBC's broadcast standards. He's the man playing 'The Surrey with the Fringe on Top' on the piano in Wilson's Grill. Dewey himself hadn't previously watched *The West Wing*, 'although, I understand it's a quality product,' he told Sarah Crump.

57
The Two Bartlets

US Transmission Date: 30 January 2002
UK Transmission Date: 17 October 2002 (E4)

Teleplay: Kevin Falls, Aaron Spelling
Story: Gene Sperling
Director: Alex Graves
Cast: Tom Knickerbocker (Civilian) Tom Porter (Officer)

The presidential race begins with the Iowa caucuses. Toby and CJ disagree about affirmative action, Donna tries to get out of jury duty and Sam meets a ufologist who tells him that most of the gold at Fort Knox has been replaced.

Backstory: This episode sees the first implications that CJ's father may be suffering from the initial stages of senility (finally dealt with a year later in 'The Long Goodbye'). After he fought in Korea, CJ's father became a teacher. Yet, according to a bitter CJ, each time there was an opportunity for career advancement, it took him an extra five years because invariably there was a less-qualified black woman around. Thus, instead of retiring as superintendent of the Ohio Valley Union Free School District, he retired as head of the Math Department at William Henry Harrison Junior High.

Florida's Governor Robert Ritchie (see **66**, 'Posse Comitatus', **72**, 'Game On') is mentioned for the first time. CJ hopes that he will be the Republican nominee in the forthcoming election, though Sam (and, seemingly, everyone else except Bartlet and Toby) believe it will be someone named Simon, rather than Ritchie.

A View From the Hill: A cloture motion (the process of closing a debate in the Senate by calling for a vote) is the only procedure by which the Senate can vote to end a debate after a specific amount of time, thus ending the threat of a filibuster.

Politics of Protest: Approximately forty protesters are in a live-target area close to a US warship off Puerto Rico. Their leader is Billy Molina, a young Hispanic actor who is a friend of Josh. Leo wants Josh to speak to Molina even after Josh tells him that if he didn't work at the White House he'd probably be with the protesters. In one of the highlights of the episode Josh tells a military officer that in five hundred years Puerto Rico has never determined its own destiny. He continues that the US military are using depleted-uranium shells, napalm and cluster bombs in the area and that Vieques has a cancer rate 25 per cent higher than the rest of Puerto Rico. Josh is ultimately able to make a deal with Billy.

A Little Learning is a Dangerous Thing: Toby once had a short-term job as a telemarketer.

The Encyclopedic Mind of Josiah Bartlet PhD: Toby suggests that Bartlet's reluctance to engage Ritchie is due to Bartlet's deep-seated nervousness about upsetting people with his intellect. Bartlet's father never liked him because he was *too smart*, Toby guesses, and suggests that Mr Bartlet (see **44**, 'Two Cathedrals') used to beat his son. Bartlet, reluctantly, confirms this is true and says it was a complicated relationship. Toby replies that this treatment was because Bartlet was smarter than his father. 'He didn't like you. *That's* why people hit each other.' Toby suggests that Bartlet believes, if he wins one more election, he'll finally erase these dreadful memories.

The Conspiracy Starts at Closing Time: Bob Engler (see **5**, 'The Crackpots and These Women') has another meeting with Sam at the behest of two Congressmen. He alleges that much of the gold inside Fort Knox has been removed and replaced by aliens from a crashed spacecraft, previously held at Papoose Lake, Nevada. The nearby Groom Lake facility is a slightly-less-secret-than-it-used-to-be USAF base, built in the 1950s to house America's U-2 spy planes. Also known as Area 51 (or 'Dreamland'), it is home for numerous 'black-ops' experimental aircraft programmes (including the F-117 stealth fighter). The site and its surrounding area are also associated – to varying levels of credibility – with numerous UFO sightings and conspiracy theories, including the infamous 1947 'Roswell incident' which Bob and Sam discuss at some length. (Sam repeats the 'official' explanation that the crashed aircraft was actually a weather balloon – something that even the US military aren't sticking to any more.) Engler's father, who recently died, was a multiple PhD who spent his life researching this alleged conspiracy. The town and its associated mythology are a key element in the backstory of TV series such as *The X-Files*, *Dark Skies*, *Stargate SG-1* and *Roswell*.

References: 'Safe Haven' laws, which exist in Texas, Louisiana and Minnesota, allow mothers to leave their newborn children at a hospital with no questions asked, avoiding charges of child abandonment. The episode includes references to Hamlet and Ophelia, the Freedom to Farm Act, various butter sculptures at the Iowa State Fair, including the butter cow, butter Elvis and butter Last Supper. Also, Marcel Duchamp (1887–1968), whom CJ calls the father of Dadaism, Obi-Wan Kenobi from *Star Wars*, William Henry Harrison (1773–1841), the ninth president of the US, the verdict in the OJ Simpson trial and Dungeons & Dragons. Toby alludes to *The Strange Case of Dr Jekyll and Mr Hyde* and mentions the Spanish maxim '*Quando dio vuole castigarci ci manda quello che desideriamo*' ('When the gods wish to punish us, they answer our prayers').

'You May Remember Me From Such Films and TV Series As . . .': Tom Knickerbocker was in *Rules of Engagement* and *Murder One*.

Oh, Donna!: Donna's ability to embarrass Josh is again demonstrated as they have a public discussion about how powerful a man he is and Donna wonders whether he's been zapped by all the 'lovemaking' he's been doing with Amy.

Cigarettes and Alcohol: Bartlet and Toby share some bourbon.

Sex and Drugs and Rock'n'Roll: Josh has a visit from Amy in the early hours. She's still keen to defend Tandy from Josh's insinuations, but reveals that, after Tandy proposed to her, she declined and the couple have stopped seeing each other. When Josh looks nervous at this news, Amy notes that she and Josh have spent four nights together and that she isn't a pathetic stalker. Josh says they've spent *six* nights together and then, for some reason, asks her to leave and call him in thirty seconds because, 'That's where the *real* conversation always takes place.' As soon as she leaves, the phone rings. Josh answers and begins listing their nights together: on the steps of his apartment when Amy kissed him (see **55**, 'H.Con – 172'), when she came over after the State of the Union; at Amy's house when she played a bootleg tape of the Rolling Stones at Wembley Stadium, put on a feather boa and sang 'Honky Tonk Woman'; and another occasion involving 'a variety of hosiery'. Sadly, he doesn't get any further with the description, because Leo stops him.

Disillusioned after his brush with the military, Josh asks Amy if she'd like to go on vacation to Tahiti, where they can dance to UB40. Amy points out that reggae is Caribbean music, but agrees. Ultimately, Josh has to cancel, but he makes it up to Amy by turning his apartment into a Tahitian-style club, with 'Red Red Wine' playing on the stereo. He offers her a Samoan Fog Cutter (which includes three kinds of rum and Bacardi 451) or a Navy grog. Afterwards, presumably, they have some noisy sex. But we don't get to see that.

Logic, Let Me Introduce You to This Window: CJ suggests that Toby's father was in the army, something that the subsequent episode 'Holy Night' would seem to contradict. Josh throws one switch in his apartment and not only do all the lights come on, but the stereo kicks into life. Quite a wiring job.

Quote/Unquote: Toby, on Bartlet's proposed comments: 'I've read it twice and I don't even know where you stand on affirmative action.' Bartlet: 'I was trying to avoid a quote.' Toby: 'As well as nouns and pronouns?'

  Toby: 'It's one thing that Ritchie came out for the Pennsylvania referendum today. But the manner in which he articulated it . . . His staff was cringing, I promise you. And *we* let it go.'

Notes: 'There's always been a concern about the two Bartlets: the absent-minded professor . . . Disarming, unthreatening, good for all time zones. And the Nobel Laureate, still searching for salvation: Lonely, frustrated, lethal.' Up to the final few moments, this is mainly a Josh episode (love his disgusting coffee-making performance) with some nice bits and pieces (particularly Sam's meeting with the UFO-obsessed Bob), but nothing *too* dramatic. Then the heavyweights enter and Toby's psychoanalysis of an apoplectic Bartlet is *a sight to see*.

  Josh still wears the oversized pyjamas CJ bought him in **25**, 'The Midterms'. Leo is still living at a hotel (see **8**, 'Enemies'). Amy has a basset hound called Henry, whom she leaves with her sister whenever she's out of town.

Cast and Crew Comments: 'It's a very difficult confrontation that doesn't go very well because I get personal,' Richard Schiff noted, regarding Toby's criticising the president for the way he is running his campaign.

Did You Know?: When Aaron Sorkin wrote a sequence that allowed Dulé Hill to display his tap-dancing prowess, he expected the actor to be delighted. 'I told him I'd rather not,' Hill told *TV Guide*. 'I understood completely,' added Sorkin. 'Dulé really wants to make his mark as an actor.'

58
Night Five

US Transmission Date: 6 February 2002
UK Transmission Date: 24 October 2002 (E4)

Writer: Aaron Sorkin
Director: Christopher Misiano

Cast: Alanna Ubach (Celia) Carmen Argenziano (Leonard Wallace)
Nancy Cassaro (Janet Price) Basil Wallace (McKonnen Loboko)
Paul Fitzgerald (Casey Reed)

In five nights since his argument with Toby, the president hasn't slept. Stanley Keyworth's advice is sought. Toby clashes with his ex-wife over an upcoming foreign-policy statement, a reporter is missing in the Congo and a mouthy temp accuses Sam of sexism.

A View From the Hill: Sam asks Ainsley to look at a consolidated appropriations act that the White House wants to drop into the president's UN speech. It authorises the payment of $926 million in UN dues in exchange for a reduction in peacekeeping assessments.

American History X: Josh notes that the White House was designed by the Irish architect James Hoban and was built largely by slaves. He mentions the *Resolute* desk, made from timbers of the HMS *Resolute* and presented to Rutherford Hayes by Queen Victoria. When James Buchanan (1791–1868) was visited by the future Edward VII (1841–1910), then Prince of Wales, it was decided there wasn't enough room for guests, but it took another forty years to move all the offices out of the Residence. Leo asks whether Josh showed Stanley the soot stains on the North Portico from when the British torched the place. He adds that, when Dolly Madison heard cannon fire, she evacuated the building, but she'd already set the table for dinner. The British soldiers arrived, ate, then set the building ablaze.

Politics of Rad-Fem: Celia Walton, a sassy intern, suggests that Sam talked to Ainsley in a demeaning way. Sam is troubled and asks Ainsley if she felt insulted by his comments. Ainsley says she understood the metaphor. A lengthy discussion follows among the trio, with contributions from Ginger and Bonnie, and a few pithy asides from Charlie. Ainsley declares that Sam isn't a sexist. Celia's surprised that Ainsley is willing to let her sexuality diminish her power. Ainsley says that all women don't think alike. She likes it when guys tease her – it's an inadvertent show of respect. She also says that she *likes* sex. Thus, her sexuality doesn't diminish her power: it enhances it. Celia asks what kind of feminism that represents. Ginger notes it's often called 'lipstick' or 'stiletto' feminism. Sexual revolution, Ainsley continues, gets in the way of *actual* revolution. Nonsense issues distract attention from real ones: pay equity, childcare, genuine sexual harassment. She then tells a thoroughly chastened Celia to stop taking the fun out of her day.

A Little Learning is a Dangerous Thing: The president's UN speech includes the phrase 'the crushing yoke of Islamic fanaticism'. Andi, as a member of the House International Relations Committee, is outraged. She notes that America doesn't have a monopoly on what's right. The US Constitution defends religious pluralism, she continues, it doesn't reduce all of Islam to fanaticism. Neither does the speech, Toby replies. But grotesque oppression isn't acceptable just because it's been institutionalised. Andi has drafted an insert, which she'd like included in the speech, that states that the US's goal isn't to preach American values. She suggests that America has no staunch allies in the Arab world, just reluctant ones – a coalition held together with duct tape. Toby suggests that the US has bent over backwards not to offend the Arab world. Instead of blowing Iraq back to the Dark Ages for harbouring terrorists and trying to develop nuclear weapons, it imposed economic sanctions and was reviled by Arabs. When the US sent American soldiers to protect Saudi Arabia, it was suggested that it was *desecrating* holy land. When the president recently praised the Islamic people as faithful and hardworking, he was denounced in the Arab press as knowing nothing about Islam. Ultimately, however, Toby agrees to look at the softer wording.

The Troubled Mind of Josiah Bartlet PhD: Bartlet admits his insomnia to Stanley (see **32**, 'Noël'), who points out he's a trauma specialist, not an expert in sleep disorders. Stanley asks if Bartlet has tried taking a sleeping pill. He did, on the third night; it didn't work until the middle of a security briefing the following morning. Stanley asks how many cigarettes Bartlet smokes a day, since nicotine can interfere with sleep patterns, and queries how much sleep Bartlet normally gets. Jed replies four or five hours on a good night. Stanley notes that, having covered physical, lifestyle and environmental factors, they are now left with psychological. Is the president depressed? Bartlet says he isn't. Stanley wonders if there's any stress in Bartlet's job and then realises how silly that question is.

Bartlet doesn't like the concept of stress, feeling it's a Madison Avenue word. He has a job he likes and his family's healthy: 'Stress is for *other people*.' Stanley then wonders what happened four nights ago. Bartlet eventually admits that Toby suggested that Bartlet's father never liked him. After a discussion about how it mustn't be easy being Jed Bartlet, the president asks if it isn't good for a person to keep setting goals. Stanley says it is, but it's tricky for someone who's still trying to get his father to stop hitting him. He compares Bartlet with President Lincoln who, Stanley suggests, did what he thought was right, even though it meant losing *half the country*. He thinks that Bartlet sometimes doesn't do what he believes in if it means losing Michigan. Stanley agrees to see the president again.

The Conspiracy Starts at Closing Time: Bill Price, a journalist who often criticised the administration, has gone missing in the Congo. The US embassy in Kinshasa confirms that a Belgian TV crew, filming outside Goma, saw an American captured by MaiMai rebels. A deal is brokered to stop the Congolese exporting columbite-tantalite to Rwanda. Unfortunately, Price has already been killed by his captors.

References: Nellie Furtado's *Woah Nellie*, the Austin Powers movies ('you bet, baby'), the Federalist Society, the comedian duo Bud Abbott (1897–1974) and Lou Costello (1906–59), the *International Herald-Tribune*, Arthur Miller and his play *Death of a Salesman* and the Girl Scouts.

'You May Remember Me From Such Films and TV Series As . . .': Alanna Ubach's movies include *Legally Blonde*, *Clockwatchers* and *Freeway*. One of this author's favourite actors, Carmen Argenziano, boasts a CV that includes *Swordfish*, *Gone in Sixty Seconds*, *A Murder of Crows*, *The Godfather Part II*, *Melrose Place*, *24*, *Caged Heat*, *The Jesus Trip*, *Kojak* and *The Rockford Files*. He is best known as Jacob Carter in *Stargate SG-1*. Nancy Cassaro was in *Goodfellas*. She also wrote the screenplay for *The Devil and Daniel Webster*. Basil Wallace appeared in *Time of Fear*. Paul Fitzgerald was in *Roswell*.

Oh, Donna!: Donna is offered a job with an Internet start-up, CapitolScoop.com by a college friend, Casey Reid. Casey says that Donna has been Josh Lyman's traffic cop, which is like having an MA in power brokering. He scribbles something on the back of the business card and hands it to Donna. She asks if this is their operating budget? He replies, 'It's your starting salary.' Donna ultimately decides not to take the job.

Sexism and Drugs and Rock'n'Roll: Charlie has a basket-ball injury sustained while playing Deanna. Your *little* sister, Sam gleefully notes. Charlie points out that she plays varsity. Sam agrees. *Girls'* varsity.

Logic, Let Me Introduce You to This Window: For Stanley's supposedly secret meeting with the president, a lot of people seem to be 'in the know' (including Sam and, more worryingly, a driver). 'They' hate America, according to Andi and Toby's conversation. It's never made . clear exactly whom this sweeping generalisation encompasses. It's an established fact that people all over the world hate or, at least, resent (to varying degrees) the US for a number of reasons, most of which are not the illogical, selfish ones that many American commentators suggest. Are all Ameri-can and Muslim values mutually exclusive, as Toby suggests? Why is Charlie in the White House after mid-night when the president is in the Residence? Charlie suggests that his sister is in high school (or possibly college). Although never specifically stated, both **3**, 'A Proportional Response', and **7**, 'The State Dinner', implied that Deanna was much younger than this.

Quote/Unquote: Sam: 'I was having a good night until, like, three minutes ago.'

Bartlet on his week: 'Things are blowing up everywhere and I've chosen the General Assembly of the UN to define a tougher foreign policy. Not *unusually* stressful, no.'

Andi: 'What's Egypt going to think? Or Pakistan?' Toby: 'That freedom and democracy are coming soon to a theatre near them.'

Toby: 'I don't remember having to explain to Italians that our problem wasn't with them, but with Mussolini. Why does the US have to take every Arab country out for an ice-cream cone? They'll like us when we win.'

Notes: 'I've been having trouble sleeping.' Listening to Toby and Andi's furious argument about US policy in the Middle East, it's difficult not to regard Toby's hawkish (and out-of-character) language as having been influenced by media attacks on Aaron Sorkin's script for **45**, 'Isaac and Ishmael'. That is, of course, if one accepts that Sorkin's views are the same as those expressed by Toby, which is always a dangerous assumption when dealing with dramatic fiction. Some of the points Toby makes *are* valid, and many of those that Andi makes in response are wishy-washy nonsense (something missed by the more outspoken reviews of this episode, particularly one very harsh one on *Television Without Pity*). However, once again *The West Wing* displays a frighteningly right-wing US foreign policy and, in light of the subsequent real-life war in Iraq, a shockingly poor grasp of just *why* America is so disliked by so many.

Toby and Bartlet haven't spoken since the events of **57**, 'The Two Bartlets'. Stanley Keyworth charges $375 an hour for his services.

Cast and Crew Comments: 'That idea – exploring the demons in all of us, using the president of the United

States – is something that will not be left aside,' Thomas Schlamme told the *Houston Chronicle*. 'Whether it's a shrink or a relationship with his wife or someone on the staff, some deeper exploration of the president's psyche is something we don't stop doing.' However, Schlamme added, 'It's not going to be *The Sopranos*, where every episode the president goes upstairs and has a session.'

Did You Know?: An NBC trailer for this episode was pulled after one initial screening when some viewers complained about the disturbing resemblance of the plot to the real-life plight of Daniel Pearl, the *Wall Street Journal* reporter who was taken hostage on 23 January in Pakistan. His captors threatened to kill Pearl unless Pakistani prisoners at Guantanamo Bay were set free (a threat they subsequently carried out). 'It could seem distasteful,' said NBC representative John Miller. 'We hadn't made the connection to Pearl until [the trailer] aired last Wednesday and people called in.'

59
Hartsfield's Landing

US Transmission Date: 27 February 2002
UK Transmission Date: 31 October 2002 (E4)

Writer: Aaron Sorkin
Director: Vincent Misiano
Cast: James Keane (Registrar) Lionel D Carson (Security Guard)
Matthew Yang King (Staffer) Dan Sachoff (Reporter)
Teddy Lane Jr (Agent) JP Hubbell (Agent) Jack Choy (Civilian)

On the day before the New Hampshire primary the president plays a game of diplomatic and military chess with the Chinese government over Taiwan while playing *actual* chess with Toby and Sam. In New Hampshire, the town of Hartsfield's Landing will vote at midnight and Josh is determined that Bartlet will not lose.

American History X: Hartsfield's Landing is a town in New Hampshire, population 63. While the rest of the state goes to the polls at 8 a.m., all of the 42 registered voters of Hartsfield vote at one minute past midnight. Hartsfield has, according to CJ, accurately predicted the winner of every presidential election since William Taft. In reality, two New Hampshire hamlets, Hart's Location and Dixville North, vote this way.

A Little Learning is a Dangerous Thing: Charlie notes that, for the third time in two months, a copy of the president's private schedule was found in the press room. He is therefore making anyone obtaining a copy sign for it. From this, he and CJ indulge in a (frankly ludicrous) episode-long game of one-upmanship, which reaches epic proportions by the climax.

The Encyclopedic Mind of Josiah Bartlet PhD: The president was given a number of chess sets by the Indian prime minister and gives them out as gifts – specifically to Sam and Toby for their work on the State of the Union speech. The set given to Sam is hand-carved camel bone and once belonged to Tansen, a musician who was a favourite at the sixteenth-century Mogul court of Emperor Akbar. Inviting Sam to a game, the president notes that he is using the Fibonacci opening while they have a fascinating discussion concerning the differences between India and China. The set given to Toby once belonged to Jawaharial Nehru (1889–1964), who played chess with Lord Louie Montbatton (1900–79) while discussing India's independence.

Bartlet attempts to distract Sam by giving an example of free association, mentioning the Charles River in Boston and stating that the Hudson is not a river but a tidal estuary. While shuttling between various high-level meetings, Bartlet plays both Sam and Toby (*almost* settling his differences with the latter – see **57**, 'The Two Bartlets' – though they have another pointed discussion about intelligence and Bartlet's father).

The Conspiracy Starts at Closing Time: Taiwan is getting ready to test-fire three Patriot missiles. China's reaction is to accelerate its military exercises in the area. The Taiwan

Relations Act (1979) may oblige the US to become involved if the situation escalates. Sam eventually realises the deal the president has brokered with the Chinese is an agreement not to sell Taiwan Aegis destroyers for a period of ten years. But Sam notes that Aegis technology isn't an item the US wants Taiwan to have and, furthermore, Taiwan can't afford them. Thus, everyone's face has been saved by Bartlet's agreeing not to sell something he wasn't going to sell anyway.

References: Allusions to Ching Chuang Kang Air Base, the *Xinhua* agency, the seventh-inning stretch in baseball, the Export–Import Bank and the February 1972 Shanghai Communiqué between Richard Nixon and Mao Tse Tung, which states that America acknowledges, but doesn't necessarily endorse, the One China. Also, Sigmund Freud (1856–1939), Krazy Glue, Charles Dickens (1812–70), 'Marion the Librarian' from *The Music Man* and Quemoy and Matsu in the Formosa Strait. The chess imagery probably derives from *The Thomas Crown Affair*.

'You May Remember Me From Such Films and TV Series As . . .': James Keane's movies include *Apocalypse Now*, *Close Encounters of the Third Kind*, *Pleasantville* and *Bulworth*. Matthew Yang King was in *Friends*. Dan Sachoff's CV includes *Sibling Rivalry*. Teddy Lane appeared in *CSI*, *Buffy* and *Gang Related*. JP Hubbell was in *ER*.

Oh, Donna!: Josh receives an email from the daughter of a couple of Hartsfield's Landing residents – the Flenderses – which suggests that her parents are going to vote Republican. Josh, therefore, sends Donna to Lafayette Park with a mobile phone to call the defecting family and persuade them to support Bartlet. Donna spends most of the episode getting to the root cause of the Flenderses' dissatisfaction (Bartlet being economic with the truth over his MS). Finally, Josh calls her back inside, noting that the Flenderses have a right, in a democracy, to vote for whomever they chose.

Logic, Let Me Introduce You to This Window: CJ notes that Bartlet is giving the press an essay on the history of chess. Unfortunately, he gets most of it wrong – most sources suggest that chess was actually invented in China rather than India. Charlemagne didn't become king of the Franks until 768, and not 760 as Bartlet claims. After Toby's first move, Bartlet notes it's 'the Evans gambit' (a variant on the Giuoco Piano opening). However this chess opening cannot be identified until seven moves have been made (four by white and three by black). There are several references to Taiwan's first ever free elections. Until the mid-nineties Taiwan *was* a highly repressive, albeit pro-America, one-party state. However, democracy has existed in the country since then. CJ notes that Jack Norworth and Albert von Tilzer wrote 'Take Me Out to the Ballgame' and 'Shine On, Harvest Moon'. However, though Norworth *did* provide the lyric for the latter, his wife, Nora Bayer-Norworth, and not Tilzer, wrote the music.

Quote/Unquote: CJ, to Charlie: 'The anal-retentive side of you isn't going to help you get girls.'

Bartlet: 'I don't want to be killed.' Toby: 'Then make this election about smart. And not. Make it about engaged. And not. Qualified and not. Make it about heavyweight. You're a heavyweight.'

Bartlet: 'Sam, you're going to run for president one day. Don't be scared. I believe in you. That's checkmate.'

Notes: 'See the whole board . . .' A beautifully structured play about *games*, which is, in many ways, a conceptual sequel to **21**, 'Lies, Damn Lies, and Statistics'. Several online fans objected to the obvious symbolism of the episode's chess metaphor. But, just because something is obvious, it doesn't mean it's unworthy and, in Bartlet's scenes with Sam (as much *his* protégé as Josh is to Leo), we have some of the finest *West Wing* moments. Only the embarrassing Charlie–CJ subplot reduces the episode's impact.

Bartlet was taught chess by a school friend, David Wheaton. Bartlet had a crush on his sister. Wheaton was stabbed to death on a trip to San Francisco attempting to stop a man from beating up a woman. Toby remembers a story that Abbey once told him about Bartlet's receiving his Nobel Prize from King Gustav in Stockholm and then spending the rest of the evening proudly telling the king about how well Ellie was doing in maths and about her having scored two goals for her soccer team. Candidates for the Republican nomination, besides Ritchie, include Daniel, Weston and Kalmbach.

Did You Know?: When Martin Sheen first met his wife, Janet Templeton, she was still an art student. 'We didn't hit it off,' Sheen told Jacqueline Cutler. 'She didn't care for me. I pursued her and I knew if I could get her to see me in a play she would be chasing me. That's exactly what happened.' The couple married in December 1961.

60
Dead Irish Writers

US Transmission Date: 6 March 2002
UK Transmission Date: 7 November 2002 (E4)

Teleplay: Aaron Sorkin
Story: Paul Redford
Director: Alex Graves
Cast: Hector Elizondo (Dalton Millgate) Robin Thomas (Jack Enlow)
Jerry Lambert (Chuck Kane)

The first lady is having a birthday party as she contemplates the probable loss of her medical licence the next day. The president is visited by Lord Marbury, who argues against a meeting with a former Irish terrorist. Donna discovers that she's really Canadian and Sam meets a senator who is blocking the funding of a controversial scientific project.

A View From the Hill: Particle physicist Dalton Millgate was Sam's teacher for a semester. Now he's having trouble securing funding for a superconducting supercollider. Sam plans to put him in touch with Senator Jack Enlow, who's on the authorising subcommittee. Enlow wishes to know what the benefits of the project are. Millgate notes that great achievement has no road map, citing the pioneering discoveries of X-ray and penicillin. Neither was discovered with a practical objective in mind. When the electron was discovered in 1897, it was useless, yet now we have a world *run* by electronics. Enlow agrees to withdraw his objections but still doesn't think that the project will ever see the light of day.

Politics of the Irish Question: Marbury arrives with instructions that Sinn Féin politician Brendan McGann cannot visit the White House during their St Patrick's Day dinner. Bartlet dumps the problem on to Leo and Leo on to Toby. Toby notes that Sinn Féin is a recognised political party. It's the political wing of the IRA, Marbury replies. The US are honouring a man allied with car bombers and murderers. The IRA recently backed out of its promise to destroy its weapons, as agreed in the Good Friday Accord. Marbury suggests that, in world terms, America is a child involving itself in a centuries-old conflict without sufficient regard for history. He quotes Kipling (who warned to expect the blame 'of those ye better, and the hate of those ye guard'). Toby responds with James Joyce ('History is a nightmare from which I'm trying to awake') and Marbury counters with a quotation from Eugene O'Neill's *A Moon for the Misbegotten*: 'There is no present or future, only the past happening over and over again.'

The Encyclopedic Mind of Josiah Bartlet PhD: He's not very good at crosswords, judging by the opening scene.

Original Sin: Marbury notes that, for Americans, the worst blot on their collective psyche is slavery and their unfortunate history with their aborigines. For Britain, it's Ireland. Toby notes that Ireland has given America several presidents (those of Irish heritage include Andrew Jackson, James Polk, James Buchanan, Ulysses S Grant, William McKinley, Woodrow Wilson, John Kennedy, Richard Nixon, Ronald Reagan and Bill Clinton), a lot of Boston Democrats and half the New York police force.

References: Charlie refers to Booker T's 'Time is Tight'. The doctrines of social Darwinism and libertarianism, Mardi Gras, Lent, Lenox china, *The Great Gatsby*, the *Manchester Union Leader*, Amtrak, CNN's *Crossfire*, 'Danny Boy', the etymology of the word 'toast' via the House of Stuarts, the 1643 toasts by members of the Middle Temple to Princess Elizabeth pledging to die in her service. Also, Fruit Loops, non-Hodgkins lymphoma, Yasir Arafat, King Baudouin of Belgium, Betaseron, 'Yankee Doodle Dandy' by George M Cohan, Winston Churchill, Franz Joseph Haydn (1732–1809) and Wolfgang Amadeus Mozart (1756–91). There's a misquotation of the biblical text concerning 'sins of the father' (alluded to in Exodus 20, Leviticus 26, Psalm 79, Isaiah 65 and Daniel 9, among others).

'You May Remember Me From Such Films and TV Series As . . .': Hector Elizondo's CV includes *Chicago Hope*, *Samantha* and *Runaway Bride*. Robin Thomas was in *The Banger Sisters*, *Jade* and *Midnight Caller*. Jerry Lambert played Fred in *The Geena Davis Show*.

Oh, Donna!: The Secret Service, via a routine background check on the party guests, discover that Donna is actually Canadian (and is developing a massive inferiority complex). Donna notes that she was born in Warroad, Minnesota, but the border has recently been redrawn and *now* that's part of Manitoba. Josh ultimately discovers the INS has a grandfather clause and that, if Donna passes a three-part literacy test and an American-history exam, and fills out a one-page form, she can be an American again.

Cigarettes and Alcohol: Lord Marbury and Toby share a bottle of Lagavulin, a sixteen-year-old single-malt whisky. Bartlet mentions two fine wines to be served at the party, the '97 Willamette Valley Pinot Noir and the '94 Hogue Cellars Zinfandel. Abbey decides to get drunk and takes CJ, Amy and Donna with her.

Logic, Let Me Introduce You to This Window: The president's rather loud talking during the Canadian national anthem (and the fact that various people in the room are *not* standing) seems rather disrespectful. Marbury calls himself *England*'s ambassador. He should be *Britain*'s. And would the British ambassador to the US really say to the first lady *in public* that her breasts are magnificent, even if he *is* a close personal friend? The pancreas doesn't produce hydrochloric acid: it's the parietal cells in the stomach lining that do (you really worry that Abbey, a *doctor*, doesn't know that). Toby makes the ignorant assumption that over four hundred years of Irish civil war has *anything* to do with religion when noting that recognising McGann will make 'the Protestants' accept they have to negotiate with someone. The Irish question is one of politics (Republican versus Loyalist), *not* religion (Catholic versus Protestant), and part of the reason that it's been going on for so long is the inability of many people to grasp that basic fact. Interesting to note that, in *The West Wing* universe, the 1998 Good Friday Accord still happened with, presumably, Bartlet instead of Bill Clinton as a major player in its drafting. The Donna-as-Canadian plot is completely illogical. Citizenship depends on many factors, such as the citizenship of Donna's parents and the fact she has an American birth certificate, not where the border is *now*.

Quote/Unquote: Josh: 'You went over my head and you did it behind my back.' Amy: 'Quite the contortionist am I.'

Bartlet: 'In my house, anyone who uses one word when they could have used ten just isn't trying hard.'

Bartlet, with the Canadian national anthem playing: 'I was gone forty-five minutes. They were all Americans when I left.' Donna: 'I know exactly how you feel, Mr President.'

Notes: 'Sometimes you like to talk, and I think that's great. But sometimes you're Abbey and sometimes you're my boss.' A quite entertaining mess, frankly. The Toby/ Marbury subplot is a highlight for the acting, but is historically inaccurate and very hypocritical in light of some of Toby's attitudes expressed in **58**, 'Night Five' (and further exposing the ludicrousness of some of the things

Sam said concerning the claim that terrorism never achieved anything in **45**, 'Isaac and Ishmael'). Abbey and the girls' little get-together is fun but rather inconsequential.

CJ doesn't have a cat. She *could* get one, but she's not wild about them. Sam was bad at physics (and still is). Marbury's full title is John, Lord Marbury, Earl of Croy, Marquess of Needham and Dolby, Baronet of Brycey. Chuck Kane head of Intergovernmental Affairs at the Treasury, Mark Rothman and Robbie Gill are on the short list for the post of deputy political director on the forthcoming election campaign. Amy lists some of Abbey's many achievements as first lady: expanding Medicare to cover mammograms, cancer clinical trials (money that, Amy suggests, could have gone into Viagra), stopping the cutting of infant nutrition programmes, childhood immunisations and work on juvenile diabetes. Donna and CJ inadvertently help Abbey to decide to voluntarily forfeit her medical licence for the duration of her stay in the White House.

Critique: 'Toby's agenda is Ireland, and we're in luck because he's conducting it with Britain's irrepressible ambassador, Lord John Marbury, who's always a welcome sight,' wrote *TV Guide*. 'Rees makes Marbury both outrageous and instantly likeable (to everyone but Leo), and his appearances always provide both substance and comic relief.'

Awards: For her performance in this episode, Stockard Channing won an Emmy for Outstanding Supporting Actress in a Drama Series.

Did You Know?: Brad Whitford is a cousin of Michigan Republican Congressman Nick Smith.

61
The U.S. Poet Laureate

US Transmission Date: 27 March 2002
UK Transmission Date: 14 November 2002 (E4)

Teleplay: Aaron Sorkin
Story: Laura Glasser
Director: Christopher Misiano
Cast: Laura Dern (Tabatha Fortis) Yolanda Lloyd Delgado (Terri)
Beth Littleford (Leslie) James Eckhouse (Bud Wachtell)
David Gautreaux (Reporter #3) Christopher Michael (Floor Manager)
Tim Haldeman (Barnett) Jennifer Marley (Student)

On an open mike, the president makes a disparaging
remark about his potential Republican opponent. Toby
tries to prevent the newly appointed poet laureate from
making a speech against America's lack of support for a
landmines treaty. Josh is delighted by the fact that he has
his own unofficial website, then gets trapped in the murky
world of fandom.

A View From the Hill: The president is due to make a
speech concerning using cleaner-burning fuels, America
becoming less dependent on oil and other pro-
environmental issues.

Poet's Corner: Toby, who has a noticeable crush on the
new poet laureate, Tabatha Forits, attempts to smooth
difficulties with her on the thorny issue of landmines.
Having described her own, horrific, experiences (seeing a
boy blown to pieces in Banja Luka), Tabatha agrees to
attend a dinner in her honour at the White House and
produce some uncontroversial stanzas on the American
Experience. In return, Toby will ensure she gets time to
speak to the president and express her concerns.

A Little Learning is a Dangerous Thing: Aaron Sorkin had
already sparred with posters on the website *Television
Without Pity* (previously mightybigtv.com) on several
occasions. Here, he strikes back with a vengeance. When
Josh discovers a fan-based, but actually hypercritical,
website devoted to him – LemonLyman.com – he becomes
tangled in its Byzantine politics, despite Donna's warnings.
Then (like Sorkin before him) he sees one of his posts end
up in the press. Josh's tormentor, the site moderator, is
portrayed as a chain-smoking dictator – a vicious slap at

Sorkin's own nemeses on *Television Without Pity*. Josh notes that she seems to pride herself in organisational skills and discipline, is very big on scolding, telling posters when they've posted in the wrong threads, or to stop using capital letters and that she doesn't have time to repeat herself, when *clearly* she does. That's called being a control freak, notes Donna. Josh posts a sarcastic reply and is drowned in hostile messages, some even suggesting that an offhand comment about using Sanskrit was a racist dig at Egyptians.

The majority of the real-world site's posters were actually quite amused and some even *flattered* by all this. But a few – mainly those in positions of power – took distinct umbrage. 'Glark' (probably not his/her real name), the technical director of *TWP*, responded, 'If we at *TWP* are the TV critic terrorists and we've gotten under his skin enough that he's changing the way he writes and shoehorning these plots into the show then the terrorists have already won.'

The Encyclopedic Mind of Josiah Bartlet PhD: Bartlet wrote a book entitled *Theory and Design of Macroeconomics in Developing Nations*. CJ notes that the president graduated *summa cum laude* from Notre Dame with a major in American studies and a minor in theology. He received a master's degree and a doctorate at the London School of Economics and an honorary doctorate in humane letters at Dartmouth University, where he was a tenured professor.

The Conspiracy Starts at Closing Time: Bartlet tells CJ that he admired the way she handled his public gaffe. CJ points out that at least it got the press talking about whether Ritchie actually *is* smart enough to be president and didn't seem to have hurt the president's reputation. She did, however, think Bartlet's use of a gun metaphor was unusual. She asks if it's possible that Bartlet *saw* that the green light was still on when he made his comments. Bartlet says nothing.

References: Name-checks for Edmond Rostand's *Cyrano de Bergerac*, explorers Ferdinand Magellan (1480–1521, the first man to lead an expedition to circumnavigate the globe), Vasco Nuñez de Balboa (1475–1519, the discoverer of the Pacific Ocean) and Jacques Cousteau (1910–97). Also, *Close Encounters of the Third Kind*, Clark Clifford (the special counsel to President Truman), TV shows *Meet the Press*, *Nightline*, *Capital Gang* and *Inside Politics*, the federal page of the *Washington Post*, Bob Dylan (and his use of blank verse), the Harvard Alumni Association, the Big Eat Conference, the Miranda Warning which advises those arrested of their rights, the Folger Library, John Quincy Adams and Woodrow Wilson. Bartlet sings Hoagy Carmichael's 'Makin' Whoopee' and gets the words wrong. Josh mentions William Golding's *Lord of the Flies*. CJ compares the LemonLyman.com website to the asylum in *One Flew Over the Cuckoo's Nest* and mentions the characters of Nurse Ratched, McMurphy and Chief Bromden. Tabatha's lecture was on various poets considered too rebellious to have been laureate, including Adrienne Rich, Anne Sexton and Allen Ginsberg (whose *Howl* (1956) is quoted). A poster for a production of *As You Like It* can be briefly glimpsed.

'You May Remember Me From Such Films and TV Series As . . .': One of the finest actresses of her generation, Laura Dern played Lulu in *Wild At Heart* and Sandy in *Blue Velvet*, and appeared in *Fat Man and Little Boy*, *Jurassic Park* and *I Am Sam*. Yolanda Lloyd Delgado's CV includes *Roswell* and *The Young and the Restless*. Beth Littleford played Deirdre in *Spin City*. James Eckhouse's movies include *Cathedral* and *84 Charing Cross Road*. David Gautreaux was in *Melrose Place* and *L.A. Law*. Tim Haldeman appeared in *Dante's Peak*, *Kung Fu* and *Happy Days*.

Satire: Happiness is Toby's default position. Allegedly.

Sex and Drugs and Rock'n'Roll: Donna notes that on LemonLymon.com there is a 'Josh Fantasy Date' section, where women (and several men) describe what they'd do with Josh if they got the chance. Josh looks appalled. Welcome to the world of fan fiction, pal.

Logic, Let Me Introduce You to This Window: How can Josh immediately post on to a moderated Internet forum? One usually has to register for these things – get a username and a password etc. Dartmouth isn't a university: it's a college. Toby suggests that the US created the international landmines treaty in the first place. In reality, it originated in Canada. Carol, seemingly, doesn't have anything better to do than spend time pulling together a one-page memo for CJ, the sole purpose of which is to educate Charlie on a minor matter. The timescale of the Congress debate on Bartlet's comments is confused, with Bartlet telling Leo that the Democrats should yield all their floor time and leave the Republicans whingeing to themselves happening two days after Leo first said the debate was going to take place.

Quote/Unquote: CJ: 'It's the classic Washington scandal. We screwed up by telling the truth.'

Donna, on the contributors to Josh's website: 'You don't know these people.' Josh: 'What's wrong with them?' Donna: '*Nobody knows*.'

CJ, on Josh's posting online again: 'If you do, I'll shove a motherboard so far up your ass . . .' Josh: 'Technically speaking, I outrank you.' CJ: '*So far up your ass . . .*'

Tabatha: 'An artist's job is to captivate you for however long we ask for your attention. If we stumble into truth, we got lucky.'

Notes: 'We may be talking about a .22-calibre mind in a .357 Magnum world.' A very frustrating episode, which contains quality ideas and gorgeous acting but keeps getting itself drawn into rhetoric and shallow posturing. As someone who has suffered from ignorant online attacks, this author fully appreciates how tempting it must've been for Sorkin to use the canvas at his disposal to attempt to rubbish picky, overly critical fandoms. To be fair, on occasions *Television Without Pity* do rather deserve to be taken down a peg or two for their self-righteousness. In fan-community terms, however, they're hardly the annoying overgrown school bullies that some series manage to acquire. Nevertheless, as a general rule, you piss off your fans *at your peril*. Sorkin sometimes seems like a dog with a bone when it comes to making enemies – a year later, in 'Arctic Radar', he'd *still* be making sarcastic comments about TV fans.

Bartlet claims not to know Governor Ritchie well. The news programmes he appears on are *Sunrise Cincinnati* and *Good Morning Philadelphia*. CJ reminds reporters that she went to Berkeley (see **3**, 'A Proportional Response'). Sam suggests that Ainsley is slightly to the right of the Kaiser. Ainsley has a new office, not in the basement and with *actual* windows. She got her law degree at Harvard. Ritchie has authored a book, *A Promise to Lead*, in which he advocates drilling the Arctic National Wildlife Reserve in Alaska as a possible source for oil.

Trivia: The scene of Richard Schiff and Laura Dern in front of a Georgetown auditorium, was actually filmed at Occidental College's Thorne Hall in Los Angeles.

Did You Know?: Asked to gauge the value of having the issue of landmines turn up in a *West Wing* episode, the Vietnam Veterans of America Foundation president, Bobby Muller, said, 'It's of extraordinary importance. The cultural mechanisms are critical to any campaign.'

62
Stirred

US Transmission Date: 3 April 2002
UK Transmission Date: 21 November 2002 (E4)

Teleplay: Aaron Sorkin & Eli Attie
Story: Dee Dee Myers
Director: Jeremy Kagan
Cast: David Dunard (AA member) Randy Oglesby (AA member)
Felton Perry (AA member) Jim Jansen (Bill Fisher)

A truck bearing uranium crashes in Idaho. Meanwhile there are discussions on whether Bartlet should keep Hoynes as his running mate. Donna asks Josh for a presidential proclamation honouring the retirement of her favourite teacher.

A View From the Hill: The Internet Education Act is due before the Health, Education and Welfare Committee tomorrow. The committee intends to eliminate the Technology Challenge Fund, aimed at the rural poor and the vice president's pet project for the last decade. Sam is asked to meet Hoynes and help save the bill. Sam notes that the problem is the committee's chairman, who bears a grudge because Hoynes attacked him. Hoynes points out that the administration *asked* him to attack the chairman. Sam tells Hoynes that what the committee really want is Hoynes's name removed from the bill. In the interests of passing a piece of legislation that he believes in, Hoynes agrees.

American History X: Donna refers to Lincoln's Emancipation Proclamation made on 1 January 1863. There are also references to Paul Revere (see **30**, 'Shibboleth'), the revolutionary hero General Casimir Pulaski (1747–79), Daniel Webster (see **42**, 'The Fall's Gonna Kill You') and former Vice President Aaron Burr (1756–1836) and his deadly duel with Treasury Secretary Alexander Hamilton (1755–1804). Larry suggests that nobody knew Eisenhower's political leanings until he ran for president as a Republican. CJ adds that Ulysses Grant voted only once in his life and that was for someone from the other party.

Politics of Expediency: Josh organises a meeting at which alternatives to Hoynes are discussed. With Ritchie as Bartlet's presidential opponent, Bruno doesn't think that Hoynes can win Texas for the Democrats as he did four years ago. If Bartlet loses both Texas and Florida, that's a third of the entire electoral vote. If they've lost the South anyway, it's argued, then why not have someone who will win Bartlet more votes in the North and West. The main suggestions for a replacement are Fitzwallace and Leo. Hoynes himself is practical about these ideas but Bartlet notes that he has always liked Hoynes far more than Hoynes believed (see **50**, 'War Crimes'). Ultimately, he decides to keep Hoynes for one overwhelming reason – because Bartlet could die.

A Little Learning is a Dangerous Thing: Donna's twelfth-grade English teacher was Molly Marillo, who is retiring. Josh fondly remembers *his* American-history teacher, Mr Feig, who died four years ago.

The Encyclopedic Mind of Josiah Bartlet PhD: The president fills in Charlie's tax self-assessment form for him. Charlie earns $35,000 a year, receives $4,000 in benefits related to his mother and donates $1,400 to charitable causes including the First Baptist Church, the Salvation Army, the Police Benevolent Fund and the Big Brothers and Sisters of Washington. Charlie believes he should be due a rebate of $700 and intends to buy a DVD/MP3 player and *On Her Majesty's Secret Service*. However, due to some labyrinthine loophole, instead of being refunded, Charlie actually *owes* $400. In a thoughtful gesture, Bartlet tells Charlie that, when he gets home, he'll find the DVD, along with the Bond movie and a copy of Gilbert and Sullivan's *Yeoman of the Guard* on CD (see **27**, 'And it's Surely to Their Credit') waiting for him.

The Conspiracy Starts at Closing Time: A heavy-haul vehicle carrying depleted-uranium fuel rods crashes in Idaho. It was hit, head-on, by another truck in a tunnel. The town of Elk Horn is nearby, with a population of 20,000.

References: Allusions to the Washington Capitals ice hockey team, the drug czar from the Office of National Drug Control Policy, the Mr Moto novels of John P Marquand (1893–1960), National Digestive Diseases Awareness Week, National Sewing Month, the Internet search engine Google, Labatts lager, Tostitos snack food, VISA, the Willard Hotel, the Lone Ranger's pal Tonto, Etch-a-Sketch, the clothes store Banana Republic, John

Fowles's *The Collector*, *Bring It On*, *The Bicycle Thief*, the Aberdeen Proving Ground in Maryland and the song 'Let's Call the Whole Thing Off'.

'You May Remember Me From Such Films and TV Series As . . .': David Dunard appeared in *Militia* and *Auggie Rose*. Randy Oglesby was in *Pearl Harbor*, *Independence Day* and *Enterprise*. Jim Jansen's CV includes *That's My Bush!*, *Parker Lewis Can't Lose*, *The X-Files* and *Artificial Intelligence: AI*. Tim Van Pelt was in *Contagion*.

Oh, Donna!: Donna never has a bad hair day. One of her hometown friends, with whom she's still in contact, is Sally Seidelman.

Cigarettes and Alcohol: Leo attends AA meetings organised by Hoynes every Thursday (see **4**, 'Five Votes Down'). Hoynes never told the president that he, himself, is a recovering alcoholic, assuming that Bartlet knew via Leo. Hoynes tells Bartlet that he had his last drink when he was 22. His family, like Leo's, had a history of alcoholism.

Logic, Let Me Introduce You to This Window: The deputy chief of the White House Staff doesn't know how a presidential proclamation works? Not likely, is it? Why is Charlie buying *On Her Majesty's Secret Service* specifically on eBay rather than through any outlet? It's not a particularly rare, obscure or expensive DVD. Bartlet discusses the effect of shaking a traditional martini made with gin, with sarcastic reference to James Bond. The reason a martini is stirred, rather than shaken, is to avoid chipping the ice. However, Bond's drinks are made with vodka and gin and, therefore, this doesn't apply. Ian Fleming even gave a lengthy rationale for Bond's preferred preparation in *Casino Royale*. Fuel rods are never made from depleted uranium.

Bartlet refers to *Beowulf* as a classic of Middle English. It was actually written in Old English. Martin Sheen mispronounces the word 'cavalry'. Regarding the banning of Shakespeare's *Twelfth Night*, Associated Press reported, in March 1996, that schools in Merrimack,

New Hampshire, had removed the play from their curriculum after the school board passed a 'prohibition of alternative lifestyle instruction' act. (*Twelfth Night* includes a romantic subplot involving a young woman disguised as a boy.) In 1999 the board members who had passed this ridiculous law were voted out and the play is back on the syllabus. Hoynes says that now he's removed his name from the Internet bill, the Democrats can't campaign on it as one of their achievements. Why not? The original drafts would still be associated with Hoynes.

Quote/Unquote: Sam: 'My idea's totally inviable?' Josh: 'You're a Democrat, it's a pretty big club.'

Josh, on Hoynes running as an independent: 'To do that, he'd be the craziest vice president since Aaron Burr. And Burr *shot* a guy!'

Charlie: 'Economists just make it up as they go along, don't they?' Bartlet: 'Yeh.'

Notes: 'I'm in the Oval Office with the President of the United States. And it's because of you.' Best episode of the third season, 'Stirred' is a dramatically satisfying collection of impressions on the idealism and the skulduggery that go hand in hand for those in power. The juxtaposition of Donna's selfishly naïve obsession with rewarding someone special to her and the sinister machinations surrounding Hoynes's position is a true masterstroke. A brilliantly claustrophobic and minimalist atmosphere is created and the dialogue *glows*. This is *The West Wing* at its finest.

Bruno and Doug are mentioned (the latter for the first time in almost a season). The housing and urban development secretary is Bill Fisher. Presumably, he replaced the sacked Debbie O'Leary (see **15**, 'Celestial Navigation'). He has ambitions to be the next governor of New Jersey.

Critique: Christopher Klose, a Washington political consultant whose firm produces television and radio ads, told the *Las Vegas Review-Journal* that viewers realise *The West Wing* is entertainment. But he added that it could add to a general concern about nuclear waste. 'It's not quite on the par of Homer Simpson working at a nuclear power plant,' noted Klose. 'But it's somewhere between that and being treated like a statement of fact.'

Did You Know?: The obvious inspiration for this episode's nuclear-accident subplot was the state of Nevada's campaign to stop federal government plans to entomb the nation's spent nuclear fuel at Yucca Mountain, ninety miles northwest of Las Vegas. 'I think somebody will probably monitor [the episode]. If it comes out with something totally misleading, we probably would have something to say,' noted Mitch Singer, a spokesman for the Nuclear Energy Institute. 'It's a safe bet that with Martin Sheen as president, it's not going to come out singing the praises of the nuclear industry,' Singer added. Sheen, of course, is no stranger to nuclear issues. He has been arrested at least seventy times for involvement in protests on issues such as nuclear disarmament and homelessness and has participated in protests at the gates of the Nevada Test Site.

'This film might as well have been produced in Las Vegas. It is part of a calculated campaign being waged by opponents of Yucca Mountain,' said David Blee, a representative of Atlanta-based NAC International.

63
Enemies, Foreign and Domestic

US Transmission Date: 1 May 2002
UK Transmission Date: 28 November 2002 (E4)

Writers: Paul Redford, Aaron Sorkin
Director: Alex Graves
Cast: Ian McShane (Nickolai) Peter Scolari (Jake Kimball)
Gregory Itzin (State Department Officer) Bill Cobbs (Alan Tatum)
Svetlana Efremova (Ludmilla) George Tasudis (George)
Valarie Pettiford (Janice) Damien Leake (Dr Tatum) Lee Faranda (Aide)

After criticising the Saudis, CJ receives a death threat. Bartlet is to meet the Russian president. However,

Fitzwallace has intelligence that the Russians are building a nuclear facility in Iran.

American History X: Franklin Roosevelt, while running for president, gave a budget speech on 19 October 1932 in Pittsburgh. Attending was a young boy, Alan Tatum, who wrote to Roosevelt's aide, Tom Farley. By a series of circumstances so unlikely as to be wildly improbable, the letter arrives, 69 years late, on Charlie's desk.

Politics of Outrage: CJ notes that in Saudi Arabia women aren't allowed to drive or be in the company of any man other than a close relative, and have to adhere to a dress code that would make a Maryknoll nun look like Malibu Barbie. They beheaded 121 people last year for robbery, rape and trafficking, she continues. They have no free press, elected government or political parties, and the royal family allows the religious police to beat women publicly.

Politics of Freedom: Asked to provide press credentials to a Russian journalist, Ludmilla Koss, critical of the Chagorin government, Toby discovers the woman's reputation for writing salacious articles. We have people like you on cable and the Internet, Toby tells her. Everyone on the ideological spectrum rolls their eyes when such so-called journalists are mentioned. He notes that Americans take the concept of a free press for granted but, angrily, asks how Ludmilla can treat it with such contempt.

A Little Learning is a Dangerous Thing: As a prelim to the forthcoming summit with Chagorin, Sam meets two Russian officials, Nikolai Ivanovich and George Kowzlowski. Once minor matters (such as the president's wearing a coat) are dealt with, the officials present Sam with a suggested wording of a joint statement. This, they claim, they wrote themselves. The statement is actually a coded message from Chagorin to Bartlet making the president aware that the Russian administration are building Iran a nuclear reactor and that Chagorin does not support this.

Sam got a letter asking whether he'd like to donate his

brain to a medical school in Grenada. There are days when he seriously considers accepting.

The Conspiracy Starts at Closing Time: One of the president's biggest campaign contributors is Jake Kimball, the CEO of Antares, a computer chip manufacturer. The company have recently discovered a potential fault in 80 million of their chips and are about to recall them. This will effectively bankrupt Antares and leave 98,000 workers (75,000 in the US) jobless. Leo wants Bartlet to help, which he is reluctant to do because it may be seen as a favour for a friend. He cannot agree to guarantee a loan to the company, but does say that the government will remain Antares's biggest customer. In return, Kimball is asked not to make further contributions to Bartlet or any other Democrat.

References: Freedonia and Lydia the Tattooed Lady from the Marx Brothers' *Duck Soup* and 'Hooray for Captain Spalding' from *Animal Crackers*. Also Tammany Hall (the popular name for the Democratic political machine in Manhattan), the League of Women Voters, Mantyniemi (the residence of Finland's president), the *Novaya Gazetta*, the composer Peter Tchaikovsky, the 1986 nuclear disaster at Chernobyl, Jean Valjean from *Les Misérables* and the *National Enquirer*. CJ quotes from *Julius Caesar* ('Brutus is an honourable man'). There are allusions to *Alice in Wonderland*, Stolichnaya vodka, the Russian Duma, the computer game Pong, *Candid Camera* and the train *The Spirit of St Louis*.

'You May Remember Me From Such Films and TV Series As . . .': Mark Harmon played Sam Crawford in *Moonlighting*. He also appeared in *Centennial*, *The Presidio*, *St Elsewhere* and *Local Boys*. Ian McShane is known to British readers from *Lovejoy* and to Americans from *Dallas*. His CV also includes *Space: 1999*, *Funeral Games*, *Villain*, *The Last of Sheila*, *Roots*, *Jesus of Nazareth* (as Judas) and *Yesterday's Hero*. Peter Scolari was in *Good Time Girls*, *Newhart* and *From the Earth To the Moon*.

Gregory Itzin appeared in *Murder One* and *Airplane!*. Bill Cobbs was in *Fluke*, *Bird*, *Trading Places* and *The People Under The Stairs*. Svetlana Efremova's movies include *Prince of Central Park*. George Tasudis appeared in *Fugly*. Valerie Pettiford was in *Glitter* and *The District*. Damien Leake's CV includes *Mighty Joe Young*, *Ask Harriet*, *Highlander* and *Looking For Richard*.

CJ's Email Headers: These include 'Message from a friend', 'Can I get a plug somewhere?', 'Die CJ, Die – from all Saudi Arabia', 'I hate you!!!' and 'American lies, lies, lies.'

Logic, Let Me Introduce You to This Window: Couldn't the casting department find any Russian actors and, thus, spare us Ian McShane providing the cheesiest Russian accent since Sean Connery in *Hunt for the Red October*? CJ, seemingly, only had four emails on the day she made her anti-Saudi comments. The photos that Ron shows CJ to prove that she's being stalked were, he says, sent in an email. But they appear to be glossy photographs as opposed to prints from a computer. The subplot concerning the boy who wrote a letter to Roosevelt is quite touching and beautifully played, but it's logically flawed.

Quote/Unquote: Toby: 'You don't ban those who supported your opponent: you make them wallow in their loserdom by covering your victory. You sit them in the front row [and] give them a *hat*!'

Ron, on CJ's death-threat: 'Muslim extremists don't get personal. They don't know your name; they don't care . . . He wants *you*. Why doesn't he want me?'

Nikolai: 'I don't know what "frumpy" is, but onomatopoeically, it sounds right.' Sam: 'It's hard not to like a guy who doesn't know "frumpy", but knows "onomatopoeia".'

Bartlet: 'Last time a member of my staff got a death threat, they missed him and hit *me*!'

Notes: 'You don't get to put a bomb in Iran. There are no other issues.' An interesting episode, with an oddly watchable collection of subplots. It's noticeable that, whenever Charlie is given something to do, one of the other regulars usually loses out in terms of screen time (in this case, it's Josh). Best bits: Sam with the Russians and Toby and Ludmilla's confrontation.

This episode begins on 29 April 2002. During his election campaign Bartlet made a budget speech in San Diego. He suffers badly from the effects of jet lag. The president gets a couple of thousand weird letters each day. Josh has had experience with death threats. CJ tells Ron Butterfield that she gets a lot of hate mail: after the president, she's the most visible person in the administration. She's assigned a four-person Secret Service detail led by Simon Donovan. CJ's niece is mentioned (see **64**, 'The Black Vera Wang'). Toby's never been scuba diving, but he's seen pictures and it looks fun. He tells Ludmilla that he's 44 (this is contradicted in 'Holy Night', which states that Toby was born in 1954). Abbey is said to like shrimp. Carol reads the AP/Reuters section of the *White House International Information* website.

Cast and Crew Comments: It didn't take Mark Harmon long to accept the guest role of Simon. 'I got a scene faxed to me by my agent late on a Wednesday afternoon, and Thursday morning I was working,' Harmon told Rick Porter. 'I appreciate that I'm in very rare air here,' he added. 'So often the formula [of a series] gets changed by outside pressures, but they've been able [to create an atmosphere] where it's all about the work. This train is moving fast, and you're expected to keep up.'

Did You Know?: CJ's comments were based on a genuine incident in Makkah, Saudi Arabia, on 11 March 2002. Islamic Mutawwa'in religious enforcers reportedly interfered with firefighters and refused to let approximately fifteen girls leave a burning building because they weren't wearing the required *hijab* (head coverings) and *abayas* (robes).

64
The Black Vera Wang

US Transmission Date: 8 May 2002
UK Transmission Date: 5 December 2002 (E4)

Teleplay: Aaron Sorkin
Director: Christopher Misiano
Cast: Patrick Breen (Kevin Kahn) Evan Rachel Wood (Hogan Cregg)
Gerry Becker (Network News Director)
Leon Russom (Network News Director)
Michael Holden (Network News Director) Ned Schmidtke (Admiral)
Kate Palmer (Assistant) Maggie Baird (Carney) Steve Tom (General)
Ivy Jones (Martha) David Katz (Assistant)
William J Jones (Secret Service Agent) David Burtka (Bruce)

Bartlet's security advisers try to pinpoint the location of a predicted terrorist attack. CJ tries to get used to her bodyguard, Simon. Toby meets with TV network executives over future political convention coverage. Sam is used by an old friend for political gain.

American History X: There are allusions to Andrew Jackson, to the 1896 election campaign between William McKinlay (1843–1901) and William Jennings Bryan (1860–1925) and to the latter's famous 'Cross of Gold' speech.

Politics of Conspiracy: Fitzwallace tells Bartlet that a credible threat suggests an attack on a US military installation in the next 48 hours. The NSA has been monitoring a terrorist cell in Syria and confirming that intelligence has been received from sources in Kazakhstan. Leo asks which targets are most vulnerable and Fitzwallace lists a navy fleet in Bahrain and Al Jaber, Incirlik and Seeb North Air Bases. A subsequent update of the potential targets adds several homeland sites, including the White House itself. Mohammed Sabeh, a leader of a Bahji cell, is believed to be in the US. The actual target is subsequently revealed to be Fort Point and the Golden Gate Bridge in San Francisco, but disaster is averted when a terrorist is arrested in Oakland. Fitzwallace tells Bartlet that, following the Helsinki meeting, the Russians have interrogated a Chechnyan prisoner. He worked with an operative who claimed to report directly to Abdul Shareef, the Qumari defence minister (see **53**, 'The Women of Qumar', **65**, 'We Killed Yamamoto', **66**, 'Posse Comitatus').

The Intrigue Starts at Closing Time: Ginger gives Sam a videotape that arrived anonymously. Sam and Ginger speculate on whether it contains porn. It turns out to be a TV ad attacking the president as dishonest and secretive. Bruno suggests that the Ritchie camp sent them the video to warn about what would happen in the event of an attack on Ritchie. He says that every campaign has an advert like this in reserve. CJ believes that they didn't when Bartlet ran for president, but Sam and Toby note that, actually, they *did*. Sam offers to meet Kevin Kahn, one of Ritchie's aides who's an old friend, privately. Bruno dismisses the idea but Sam meets Kahn anyway and, in doing so, has the contents of their discussion leaked to the press, to Bruno's fury.

References: These include Madison Square Garden, the Harlem Boys Choir, Dean Martin, the Royal National company, 'Secret Agent Man', Barneys store, Clyde's Old Ebbitt restaurant, designer Vera Wang, the Kennedy School of Government, Nabisco, Tiny Tim and Miss Vicki, the National Archives and the Supreme Court. Sam alludes to *The Adventures of Rocky and Bullwinkle*.

'You May Remember Me From Such Films and TV Series As . . .': Evan Rachel Wood played Emily in *Little Secrets*, Chloe in *Profiler* and Kylie in *Practical Magic*. She also appeared in *American Gothic*. Patrick Breen's CV includes *Oz*, *Men in Black* and *Galaxy Quest*. Gerry Becker was Stanley in *Man on the Moon*, Nathan Reed in *Angel* and Nixon in *Ally McBeal*. He also appeared in *Stonewall*, *Mystery Men*, *Hoffa*, *Mickey Blue Eyes*, *When Billie Beat Bobby* and *Donnie Brasco*. Leon Russom was in *Behind Enemy Lines* and *He Said, She Said*. Kate Palmer was in

Family Law. Maggie Baird appeared in *Manic*, *Charmed* and *Picket Fences*. Steve Tom's CV includes *The Kid*, *Scrubs* and *Gilmore Girls*. Ivy Jones appeared in *Scissors* and *The Waltons*. David Katz was in *Die Hard*. William Jones appeared in *USA High*. David Burtka's movies include *24 Nights*.

Oh, Donna!: Josh's present for Donna is some moose meat, which he got from the Finnish Office of Protocol. Donna subsequently gives this to an intern named Bruce (why she does so is never revealed). Bruce puts the item up for sale on eBay. Josh tells Donna to sack the intern, but she won't, even buying the meat back from Bruce for $210.

Sex and Drugs and Rock'n'Roll: CJ tells Carol that she's acting strangely around Simon, clarifying that her niece is going to a junior prom. Carol guesses that CJ doesn't want to be known as somebody with a niece old enough to be attending a senior prom.

Logic, Let Me Introduce You to This Window: Fort Myer is in Virginia, not Maryland. Bartlet mentions which Shakespeare plays make up the *War of the Roses*. He misses out *Richard III*, but includes *Henry VIII* in error. There aren't any Barneys stores in Washington. Toby's suggestion that the administration will use antitrust laws to force the networks into covering the Democrat and Republican conventions would probably be a nonstarter. During his confrontation with Kevin, Sam pushes him in the chest. That's, technically, assault – so why doesn't Kevin report this? One can hardly think of a more humiliating story for the White House than that one of its senior staff has been arrested for brawling in the street.

Quote/Unquote: Sam: 'I don't like eating things where the cartoon character can talk. And, you know, hatch a plan.'

News Director: 'We'll show the acceptance speeches. And the balloons. The balloons aren't news, but they're nice television.'

Bruno: 'You forgot that all warfare is based on deception. One of these days, you guys are going to listen to me, or you're going to find out what the crappy end of an Inauguration Day feels like.'

Notes: 'I want you to start getting into a mental place where you can order an unidentified plane shot down.' An oddly structured episode, with two major storylines (CJ's stalker and Bartlet's terrorism problems) drowned in really inconsequential stuff (the Donna plot, especially). Best bit: Toby and Bruno growling at each other about TV coverage.

This episode takes place nine days after the previous one, the staff having spent the last six days in Helsinki. CJ's car is a blue 1965 Mustang. The Secret Service are still using the codename Flamingo for her (see **10**, 'In Excelsis Deo') and she *still* hates it. Her niece is called Hogan and is approximately sixteen. CJ explains Hogan's name, noting that her older brothers are golf crazy (she's named after Ben Hogan). Her stalker uses the email address bill182@aol.com. Sam's father is mentioned. Simon went to college on a military scholarship. He was a Chicago police officer and joined the Secret Service nine years ago. He was on Bartlet's protection detail at Rosslyn (see **22**, 'What Kind of Day Has it Been'). Bruno still has problems remembering Margaret's name so he buys her a name necklace. Ritchie's running mate is Jeff Heston.

Did You Know?: 'We have pages coming down daily,' Mark Harmon noted concerning the hectic shooting schedule for *The West Wing*. 'We just started the finale, yet there are still scenes from [previous episodes] that I have to shoot.'

65
We Killed Yamamoto

US Transmission Date: 15 May 2002
UK Transmission Date: 12 December 2002 (E4)

Writer: Aaron Sorkin
Director: Thomas Schlamme
Cast: Juan Garcia (Rick Pintero) Christopher Curry (Colonel Lee)
Annika Peterson (Jane) Nicki Micheaux (Muriel)

Bob Morrisey (Harry Conroy) Harry S Murphy (Witness)
Kevin Brief (Democrat) Roz Witt (Democrat)
Howard Lockie (Democrat) Kim Brockington (Agent Thayer)

While Bartlet, Leo and Fitzwallace grapple with the moral absolutes of a planned assassination, Josh and Amy argue over a welfare-reform bill. Donna represents the White House in North Dakota, Charlie's asked to find a replacement for Mrs Landingham and CJ and Simon's relationship develops.

A View From the Hill: The Working Toward Independence Act is ready to leave committee. Josh is told that an additional billion dollars for childcare has been found. However, this is dependent upon $300 million more for marriage incentives and a rise in the weekly working requirements to 38 hours. When Josh tells Amy about this, she promises to wreck the bill, while simultaneously dumping Josh's phone in a pot of stew. Josh tells her that for every vote on the left she obtains to defeat the bill, he has to negotiate a vote on the right. Amy responds that she's been phoning the Bible belt to tell conservatives how weak the abstinence provisions are. Josh points out that there's an election coming in November and that Amy is part of the Democratic Party. Amy replies that it doesn't matter who wins if Bartlet gets there by selling out.

American History X: Fitzwallace tells Leo about the Battle of Agincourt (1415) and, for anyone who didn't know, observes it was between the French and the British.

A Little Learning is a Dangerous Thing: Simon notes that CJ's stalker sent her a Trojan horse virus in an email. This allowed the stalker to read all CJ's computer files.

The Encyclopedic Mind of Josiah Bartlet PhD: Leo suggests that Bartlet's belief in moral absolutes is his biggest flaw as a liberal.

The Conspiracy Starts at Closing Time: A money trail has been established to the man captured trying to bomb San Francisco. The payment leads to a bank owned by Abdul

Shareef. Similar money transfers took place around the time of other terrorist attacks. Shareef's diplomatic immunity can be set aside, but the US would be obligated to inform the sultan of Qumar about their intentions to arrest Shareef, and the sultan is Shareef's brother. Treaties signed with Britain when Qumar was a crown protectorate are also discussed. Bartlet concludes that he wants Shareef to stand trial in a US court, and, if they have to stick heroin on his plane to get him there, that's an option. However, it's subsequently discovered that the evidence of the Chechnyan prisoner was extracted under torture. His testimony would, therefore, be inadmissible in any court. So, Fitzwallace and Leo come up with another plan. Kill Shareef.

References: The title refers to the downing by American forces of a plane carrying Japanese Admiral Isorku Yamamoto (1884–1943). Also, Al Capone, *Flashdance*, the NSA Echelon surveillance network, the director Werner Fassbinder (1945–82), Agent 99 Maxwell's female partner in *Get Smart*, Dulles Airport, Mount Rushmore, the New York Mets and the Yankees, *Bride & Groom* magazine, *Leave It To Beaver*, William Pitt (1759–1806), the attack on Pearl Harbor, the German theologian Dietrich Bonhoeffer (1906–45) and the film producer Sherry Lansing. Simon wears a West Point sweatshirt. Bartlet notes that Machiavelli's *Il Principe* justifies every act of oppression.

'You May Remember Me From Such Films and TV Series As . . .': Kurt Fuller appeared in *That's My Bush!*, *Wayne's World*, *Scary Movie* and *The Fan*. Juan Garcia was in *The Net* and *The Shield*. Christopher Curry's movies include *Red Dragon*, *Home Alone 3* and *Last Exit To Brooklyn*. William Thomas was in *The Cosby Show* and *Bruce Almighty*. Annika Peterson's CV includes *Sam the Man* and *Boomtown*. Nicki Micheaux appeared in *Six Feet Under*, *Sweet Jane* and *Soul Food*. Bob Morrisey was in *The Book of Stars* and *Buffy*. SE Perry was in *Dreaming In Black & White*. Harry Murphy's movies include *Calendar Girl*. Kevin Brief was in *Shteps* and *Grounded for Life*. Roz

Witt appeared in *The Hollywood Sign* and *Gilmore Girls*.
Howard Lockie was in *Purgatory House*. Kim Brockington
played Felicia in *The Guiding Light*.

Oh, Donna!: Josh lies in bed on a Sunday morning, wearing
a T-shirt and boxers, talking to Donna on the phone.
Meanwhile, Amy dances provocatively around the apartment and Josh describes this. Strange behaviour. Josh has
a mission for Donna: to attend a public meeting in North
Dakota to discuss changing the state's name.

Cigarettes and Alcohol: Amy drinks red wine as she
prepares a stew. Josh gets a bottle of beer from the fridge.

Logic, Let Me Introduce You to This Window: Fitzwallace
says that he's been a soldier for 38 years. A *sailor*, surely,
if he's an admiral? Donna complains how cold and isolated
Bismarck is. She was born in Minnesota and lived in
Wisconsin; both are *much* colder. One can understand why
Mrs Landingham is buried in Arlington National Cemetery, but there's no explanation as to why her husband,
Henry, is also. Why doesn't Charlie ride in the same car as
the president? Why do the Secret Service allow Bartlet's
limousine to have its window rolled down, thus providing
a target for snipers? Who's responsible for a virus ending
up on CJ's hard drive? The White House IT people for not
making certain that all staff have up-to-date antivirus
protection, or CJ herself, for opening a file attachments?
Bartlet asks why Ritchie's commitments aren't known
before his staff get to the president's own schedule.
However, Bartlet also notes that *he* was the one responsible
for the charity event in the first place, so the date was,
presumably, of his own choosing.

Quote/Unquote: Amy: 'All women count on you, Josh. We
find you godlike.'

CJ, on the Secret Service gym: 'Is it a good gym?' Simon:
'We run alongside moving cars.'

Bartlet: 'True or false, Josh, my life would be better right
now if you and your girlfriend switched places.'

Notes: 'Can you tell when it's peacetime and wartime anymore?' Again, this is a case of simply too much going on. Some of the subplots seem important but, actually, go nowhere (Sam's state of mind, chiefly). Others seem inconsequential but are actually setting up major developments to come. The Amy–Josh stuff is annoying because, the politics aside, the switch from twee domestic scenes to childish bickering is too obvious. The good stuff (Leo and Fitzwallace on a changing world order), however, is *very* good.

Bartlet mentions Josh's mistake over tobacco (see **46**, 'Manchester' Part 1). During Toby's first campaign, questions were aimed at his candidate – running for Bronx Borough president – about tax returns. A press conference was called. Toby didn't want this to last long, so he turned off the air conditioning to keep reporters from becoming comfortable. Unfortunately, this strategy backfired when the candidate fainted. At Rosslyn, Simon shot and killed one of the shooters, Ray Beckwith (see **23**, 'In The Shadow of Two Gunmen' Part 1). The White House gym closes at 7 p.m. America has no extradition treaty with Qumar.

Soundtrack: Two classic Van Morrison songs are heard in Amy's apartment (both seemingly on the radio – must be an oldies station): 'Caravan' and 'Moondance'.

Cast and Crew Comments: 'The dreary lecture show that followed Sep 11 was an intellectual's attempt to evade the truth by avoiding the emotions Sep 11 elicited,' wrote Peggy Noonan in a *Wall Street Journal* exposé concerning her time on the show. 'It yielded lifeless drama ... Bad men did bad things, leaving us wounded and furious. A prim little history of terrorism that was wholly sombre and yet lacked seriousness was what no one needed.'

Trivia: The final sequence to be shot was the scene of CJ being escorted home by Simon. It was filmed on a block in Greenwich Village, New York, three days prior to transmission.

Did You Know?: When Martin Sheen first arrived in New York as an aspiring actor, in February 1959, he had just a couple of hundred dollars to sustain him. Sheen notes that, during those early days, he slept in subway stations and took odd jobs as a soda jerk in the Bronx and as a stock boy at American Express.

66
Posse Comitatus

US Transmission Date: 22 May 2002
UK Transmission Date: 19 December 2002 (E4)

Writers: Aaron Sorkin
Director: Alex Graves
Cast: Armin Shimerman (Richard III) Fred Sanders (Ted)
Wren T Brown (Man in Josh's meeting)
Ken Thorley (Man in Josh's meeting) Basil Hoffman (Congressman)
Al No'mani (Abdul Shareef) Al Faris (Translator)
John David Conti (Howell) Nate Reese (Cantwell)
Paul Norwood (Bristola) Heidi Anderson (Waitress)
William Dennis Hunt (Duke of York) Jeanie Hackett (Queen Margaret)
Orlando Seale (Young Clifford) Douglas Weston (Bedford)
Adrian Diamond (Young Boy) Glenn Kubota (Grocer)
Karen Tsen Lee (Reporter) Ted Koch (Reporter)
Mark Gerald Douglas (Agent) Lisa Datz (Agent) James Villani (Thug).
Chorus: Joshua Wolf Coleman, Charles Currier, Russell Edge, Joshua
Fardon, Richard Gould, Rob Nagle, Kevin Owers, Graham Shiels,
Richard Soto

Bartlet makes his decision regarding Shareef. At the *War of the Roses* performance, Bartlet encounters Governor Ritchie, his Republican rival in the upcoming election. When Josh supports a key welfare reform bill that Amy opposes, their relationship is threatened.

A View From the Hill: *Griswold/Buxton v. Connecticut* (1965) was a landmark case in which the director of the Planned Parenthood League of Connecticut, and its medical director, a licensed physician, were convicted as accessories for giving married persons advice on how to prevent conception. The Supreme Court overturned the decision.

Having been on the brink of losing the welfare bill vote, Josh plays his trump card and gives Brenda (Amy's boss) a position as chair of the platform committee. The bill is passed by eight votes. Outmanoeuvred, Amy intends to resign her job on Monday.

Politics of Assassination: In 1976, President Ford issued Executive Order 11905, which, effectively, outlawed political assassination. The president is the only person who can order a covert action. Leo notes that an executive order comes from the president, and he can ignore it if he chooses. Also, because of the *Posse Comitatus* Act (1878), an assassination cannot be carried out either by the military, or on American soil. A so-called 'Gang of Eight' – majority and minority leaders in both houses and the chair and ranking member on each body's intelligence committee – are informed of the plan.

Politics of Tragedy: Having caught CJ's stalker (off screen, annoyingly), Simon wanders into a Broadway deli to buy a Milky Way chocolate bar, and, tragically, finds himself in the middle of a bungled armed robbery. He's shot and killed.

A Little Learning is a Dangerous Thing: Kevin Kahn informs the press that the president is meeting with Ritchie in New York. Sam suggests telling the press that Bartlet can't meet with Ritchie as he has to work on the welfare bill, which the Florida delegation is holding up.

The Encyclopedic Mind of Josiah Bartlet PhD: At the theatre, when Bartlet and Ritchie meet, Bartlet hopes they will have a great debate. How many different ways will you find to call me stupid? asks Ritchie. Bartlet insists that he wasn't, though he adds that Ritchie has turned being unengaged into a Zenlike artform. If it seems, at times, that Bartlet doesn't like Ritchie, he continues, that's the only reason. Ritchie responds, sarcastically, that Bartlet is 'a superior sonovabitch'. He's an academic elitist snob, Hollywood, weak, liberal and can't be trusted. And, if it appears that Ritchie doesn't like Bartlet, these are just some of the many reasons why.

The Conspiracy Starts at Closing Time: At the episode's climax, three men shoot and kill Abdul Shareef on a landing strip in Bermuda.

References: Allusions to New York City Hall, the National Security Act, the RAF, *Gannett News*, Jack Kent Cooke (1912–97), the owner of the Washington Redskins, Christ's College at Cambridge, Bally's hotel in Las Vegas, the Swingle Singers and the Major Deegan Expressway. The centrefielder for the New York Yankees, Bernie Williams, is indeed an accomplished classic guitarist. Scenes from *Henry VI, Part 1* and *Part 3* are enacted. Posters outside the theatre include *Les Misérables*, *Mamma Mia*, *The Full Monty* and *Rent*.

'You May Remember Me From Such Films and TV Series As . . .': James Brolin's movies include *Von Ryan's Express*, *A Guy Thing*, *The Boston Strangler* and *Capricorn One*. Armin Shimerman played Pascal on *Beauty and the Beast*, Quark in *Star Trek: Deep Space 9* and Principal Snyder in *Buffy the Vampire Slayer*. He also appeared in *Stargate SG-1*, *Ally McBeal*, *Blind Date*, *The Hitcher* and *Stardust Memories*. Lily Tomlin's CV includes *Rowan and Martin's Laugh-In*, *Nashville*, *Nine To Five* and *All of Me*. Andrew McFarlane was Joseph in *Hot Boyz*. Fred Sanders appeared in *Godzilla*, *Sea of Love* and *Felicity*. Wren Brown was in *Flipper*, *Chameleon* and *I'm Gonna Git You Sucka*. Ken Thorley played Mr Mott in *Star Trek: The Next Generation* and appeared in *Buffy* and *Grace Under Fire*. Basil Hoffman's CV includes *Switch*, *My Favorite Year*, *The Electric Horseman* and *Hill Street Blues*. Al No'mani was in *Three Kings*. Al Faris appeared in *Alias* and *The Interrogation*. John David Conti's movies include *The Runner*. Nate Reese appeared in *The Shield* and *Son of the Beach*. Paul Norwood was in *Judging Amy*. Heidi Anderson's movies include *Children of a Laughing God*. William Hunt played the Emperor Wang in *Flesh Gordon* and appeared in *Chaplin*. Jeanie Hackett was in *Shopping*. Orlando Seale's movies include *Sleepy Hollow*. Douglas Weston was in *Guardian*. Ted Koch appeared in *Hannibal*.

Glenn Kubota was in *North*. James Villani's CV includes *Hang Time*. Mark Gerald Douglas was in *Hitting the Ground*. Kevin Owers was in *Titanic*. Russell Edge appeared in *Boomtown*.

Oh, Amy!: For breakfast, she orders an egg-white omelette and burned toast. Strange girl.

Sex and Drugs and Rock'n'Roll: Asked to find a replacement for Mrs Landingham, Charlie contacts Debbie Fiderer (formerly DeLaGuardia, mentioned in **3**, 'A Proportional Response') who first hired Charlie. Having held a number of executive secretary roles, she was fired from the White House (Charlie suggests this was directly related to his employment) and has spent the last year as an alpaca farmer. She turns up for her first interview with Bartlet stoned, but Charlie assures her that she'll have a second chance (see **68**, '20 Hours in America' Part 2).

Logic, Let Me Introduce You to This Window: The song that the company are singing is 'Patriotic Chorus' written by Stephen Oliver in 1983 for an RSC production of *The Life and Adventures of Nicholas Nickelby*. Bartlet couldn't, therefore, have remembered it from his own college days as he suggests to Stanley. It's odd that CJ cracks jokes to the press about Josh's problems in getting the welfare bill passed. Because the murder of Shareef takes place in Bermuda, three people in Britain were aware of it in advance. Presumably the prime minister, the defence secretary and . . . the Queen? As head of state in Bermuda she *should* be told. Is someone (even someone important, like Shareef) allowed to bring two bodyguards with him into the Oval Office? Simon – a highly-trained Secret Service agent – doesn't secure the location of the robbery that he stumbles into. Criminally, he doesn't look around the store just in case there's a second gunman hiding in one of the aisles. CJ leaves the theatre on Broadway and, the next time we see her, she's sitting in Times Square (over a mile away), crying. That's quite a walk in high-heeled shoes. While Amy and Josh are bickering, the phone rings.

Amy picks it up, doesn't say anything, then tells Josh that Simon is dead. Presumably it's Donna calling and she's *very lucky* that it wasn't a wrong number.

Quote/Unquote: Sam, to the press, on Ritchie's late appearance: 'If ninety per cent of success is showing up, we're just happy there's somebody standing up for the other ten.'

Bartlet, to Ritchie: 'In the future, if you're wondering, "Crime, boy, I don't know," is when I decided to kick your ass.'

Notes: 'You're killing Shareef?' A fantastic end to the season, with a clever juxtaposition of the play-within-a-play idea that Shakespeare used so often. The final ten minutes are quite brilliant TV (albeit, once you start to pick at the loose threads of the episode, it threatens to come to pieces in your hands). Best Bit: Bartlet's confrontation with Ritchie.

Bartlet signed an executive order prohibiting political assassinations. He tells Stanley that he's been sleeping much better since the events of **58**, 'Night Five'. Leo says that, whenever he's with Mallory in a seafood restaurant, she names the lobsters to keep Leo from eating them. Sam notes that Ritchie argues baseball is what ordinary Americans watch. Toby replies that there's nothing ordinary about the people at Yankee Stadium. Simon has spent three years working as a Big Brother.

Critique: 'There may have been something a little off, a little dated, about Bartlet's political enemies trying to exploit his health problems,' noted the *Ain't It Cool* website. 'The storyline, which took up most of the season's first half, was plotted before Sept 11, and manifested one of those very rare occasions when the series fell out of synch with the national *zeitgeist*. But those who abandoned *West Wing* before midseason missed a fantastic rebound.'

Soundtrack: The late Jeff Buckley's heartbreaking version of Leonard Cohen's 'Hallelujah' accompanies the aftermath to Simon's murder.

Cast and Crew Comments: Aaron Sorkin subsequently commented that Simon's death was much protested by all the female staffers working on the show. Mark Harmon himself recalled that Aaron Sorkin said during a read-through prior to the final episode, 'We're going to have Michael O'Neill back, which generally means someone is going to die!' 'Mike's a friend of mine,' Harmon said. 'It was fun to work with him as a Secret Service guy on this. We had a good time when we were shooting [the death scene].'

Trivia: Much of the season finale was filmed in New York. Locations include the presidential motorcade roaring through Times Square, and numerous sequences around Schubert Alley and the Booth Theater on 45th Street. Most of the cast stayed at an East Side hotel – except for John Spencer, who remained at his midtown apartment and spent time with his partner, the Broadway actress Patti Mariano. With the season wrapped, Spencer participated in the AIDS Walk New York in Central Park.

Did You Know?: John Spencer is a bit of a workaholic in real life. In fact, the actor hasn't taken a holiday in two years. However, all that changed in 2002, when Spencer instructed his agent not to send him any scripts. 'An actor can get seduced by good material,' he told *TV Guide*. So, how does Spencer relax? Apparently, by representing *The West Wing* at the Monte Carlo Television Festival and shooting promos for Channel 4 in the UK, while attending Wimbledon. This may sound like work, but Spencer doesn't consider it as such. 'It's a great way to fly first class for free,' he notes.

The West Wing – Season Four (2002–2003)

John Wells Television/Warner Bros. Television
(A Time/Warner Entertainment Company)
Created by Aaron Sorkin
Producers: Neal Ahern Jr, Paul Redford, Kristin Harms, Llewelyn Wells
Co-Executive Producers: Alex Graves, Christopher Misiano, Kevin Falls
Associated Producers: Patrick Ward, Mindy Kanaskie
Executive Producers: Aaron Sorkin, Thomas Schlamme, John Wells
Advisers: Dee Dee Myers, Gene Sperling
Executive Story Editor: Eli Attie
Theme and Music: WG Snuffy Walden

Regular Cast:
Martin Sheen (President Josiah Bartlet) John Spencer (Leo McGarry)
Bradley Whitford (Josh Lyman) Richard Schiff (Toby Ziegler)
Rob Lowe (Sam Seaborn) Allison Janney (CJ Cregg)
Janel Moloney (Donna Moss) Kathryn Joosten (Delores Landingham 71)
NiCole Robinson (Margaret[109] 67–72) Allison Smith (Mallory O'Brien 68)
Devika Parikh (Bonnie 73–74)
Melissa Fitzgerald (Carol 67–69, 71, 73–74)
Peter James Smith (Ed 68–69, 71, 73–74)
William Duffy (Larry 67–69, 71, 73–74) Reneé Estevez (Nancy 67–68)
Dulé Hill (Charlie Young)
John Amos (Admiral Percy Fitzwallace 67–69, 71)
Kim Webster (Ginger 67–68, 70–74) Ivan Allen (Roger Salier[110] 73)
Penny Griego (DC Anchor[111] 73)
Stockard Channing (Abigail Bartlet 68, 72–74)
Charles Noland (Steve 69, 73) Kris Narmont (Katie Witt 67–70, 72–73)
Marlee Matlin (Joey Lucas 71) Bill O'Brien (Kenny Thurman 71)
Ralph Meyering Jr (Tom 70) Kathleen York (Andi Wyatt 71, 73)
Anna Deavere Smith (Nancy McNally 67–68)
Randolph Brooks (Arthur Leeds 68)
Timothy Davis-Reed (Mark 67–69, 72–73)
George Coe (Howard Stackhouse 70)
Glenn Morshower (Mike Chysler 69, 71)
Ron Silver (Bruno Gianelli 67–69, 74) Victor McCay (Henry 67–68)
Rick Cramer (Aide 71)
Thomas Kopache (National Security Adviser 69, 71, 74)

---

[109] Uncredited in **69**, 'College Kids'.
[110] Credited as Anchor in **73**, 'Election Night'.
[111] Credited as Anchor in **73**, 'Election Night'.

Mary-Louise Parker (Amy Gardner 69–71, 74)
Joanna Gleason (Jordan Kendall 69, 72, 74)
Clark Gregg (Mike Casper 69–70) Tim Van Pelt (Harry[112] 72)
SE Perry (Marine Officer 67, 69) Lily Tomlin (Debbie Fiderer 68–69, 73)
James Brolin (Robert Ritchie 72)
Andrew McFarlane (Anthony Marcus 68, 70, 73)
John Gallagher Jr (Tyler 67–68) Larry Cox (Staffer 67, 69)
John P Connolly (Matt Kelley 68–69) Hal Holbrook (Albie Duncan 72)
Joshua Malina (Will Bailey 72–74) Danica McKellar (Elsie Snuffin 72–74)
Ashleigh Olden (Sharon 72–73) Christian Slater (Jack Reese 73–74)

67
20 Hours in America
Part 1

US Transmission Date: 25 September 2002
UK Transmission Date: 22 July 2003 (E4)

Writer: Aaron Sorkin
Director: Christopher Misiano
Cast: Amy Adams (Cathy) Joan MacIntosh (Meredith Walker)
Valorie Armstrong (Mrs Harrison) Art Chudabala (Peter Lien)
Alan Dale (Mitch Bryce) Danielle Harris (Kiki)
Ernestine Jackson (Fiona) Joel Marsh Garland (Cap)
Marina Gonzalez Palmier (Civilian) Dan Gerrity (Civilian)
Jack Tate (Civilian) Tori Reid (Aide)
Constance Pfeiffer (Elderly Woman) Ron Newell (Store Manager)
Rohn Thomas (Sy) Tommy Lafitte (Earl) Danielle Jones (Friend)
Jennifer Armour (Friend #2) Amy Harmon (Volunteer)
Harry O'Toole (Man at Counter)

Toby, Josh and Donna have a lousy day when the motorcade leaves them stranded in Indiana.

A View From the Hill: Fitz suggests that, following the events of **66**, 'Posse Comitatus', now might be a good time for the administration to reconsider its position on the international war crimes tribunal (see **50**, 'War Crimes').

Bartlet meets Peter Lien, a 34-year-old from Texas, who is the first Vietnam refugee to reach Congress. He's replacing Congressman Jim Corr.

---

[112] Credited as Congressman in **72**, 'Game On'.

Politics of Stupidity: At an event attended by Abbey in Madison, twenty women dressed in aprons and carrying rolling pins were also there. This was in protest over a statement made by the first lady on LA TV that with the suspension of her medical licence, she is now just a wife and mother. Bruno and CJ have a lengthy discussion on the ridiculousness of the issue.

A Little Learning is a Dangerous Thing: Josh and Toby throw stones into a steel can and have a bet: the first to miss, each time he says his name for the rest of the day, has to follow it with 'I work at the White House.' Amusingly, Toby loses.

Having had to do Josh's job for the day, Sam asks Ginger if there is a condensed index of all knowledge available. Ginger notes that they usually just ask Margaret.

The Encyclopedic Mind of Josiah Bartlet PhD: The president's forthcoming speeches will tackle sustainable growth in Michigan, new economy in Ohio and information technology in Pennsylvania. Josh objects to Toby's strategy (seemingly agreed with Bruno) to make the election about intellect. No matter how subliminal, Josh notes, the election cannot be a national therapy session.

The Conspiracy Starts at Closing Time: A month ago, a Qumari investigation into Shareef's missing plane was reopened. Fitwallace tells Leo that the plane was left in 27 pieces, scattered among other wrecks, buried in underwater landslides and limestone cliffs within the Bermuda Triangle. If anyone ever did find the plane, there's no evidence left of anything untoward. SEALS and Special Ops carried out the job.

References: After addressing Air Wing One at Reynolds Air Base, a military choir sings 'The Battle Hymn of the Republic'. Bartlet recently described Ritchie as a 'Potemkin-President' meaning something that appears elaborate and impressive but in actual fact lacks substance. The term comes from Grigori Aleksandrovich Potemkin (1739–91), who had elaborate fake villages constructed for Catherine the Great's tours of the Ukraine and the Crimea. Also, CNN, CBS, ABC, NBC, Texaco and Shell, the men's health guru Jack La Lanne, the conductor Arturo Toscanini, *Lost in Space* ('Danger, Will Robinson'), *Reader's Digest*, the right-wing commentators Phyllis Schlafly and Ann Coulter (author of *Treason: Liberal Treachery from the Cold War to the War on Terror*), the economist Milton Friedman and Herbert Hoover. Allusions to *Reach for the Stars* and Emerson, Lake and Palmer's *Brain Salad Surgery*. Donna discusses the song 'I Don't Like Mondays' with Josh. Originally a hit for the Boomtown Rats in 1978, it was inspired by a real-life murder committed by schoolgirl Brenda Spencer in Cleveland. Tori Amos's rather hysterical version of the song is played during the next episode.[113] Sam wears a Princeton T-shirt.

'You May Remember Me From Such Films and TV Series As . . .': Amy Adams played Beth in *Buffy* and appeared in *Drop Dead Gorgeous* and *Catch Me If You Can*. Joan MacIntosh was in *Fresh Horses*. Valorie Armstrong was the eponymous *Naughty Nurse* and appeared in *Pretty Woman* and *Santa Barbara*. Art Chudabala's CV includes *Strange Days* and *The Stöned Age*. The Australian actor Alan Dale is best known as Jim Robinson in *Neighbours*. He also played the villainous Vice President Prescott in *24* and appeared in *The X-Files*. Danielle Harris was Molly in *Roseanne* and Suzi in *Poor White Trash*. Her movies include *City Slickers*, *Halloween 4* and *Don't Tell Mom the Babysitter's Dead*. John Gallagher was in *Pieces of April*. Ernestine Jackson appeared in *Girls Town*. Joel Garland's CV includes *Snipes* and *Witchblade*. Marina Palmier was in *Highway to Hell*. Dan Gerrity's movies include *See Jane Run* and *Jawbreaker*. Jack Tate appeared in *Martians Go Home*. Tori Reid was in *For Real* and *Passions*. Constance Pfeifer appeared in *The American Scream*. Rohn Thomas's movies include *The Shawshank Redemption*. Tommy

---

[113] This was much to the delight of the song's author, Bob Geldof, who watched the episode while waiting to go on stage in Boston.

Lafitte was in *Out of the Black*. Danielle Jones's CV includes *Ozone*.

Oh, Donna!: Josh tells Cathy that Donna's nervous. When they were in Tennessee recently two staffers were left behind when the motorcade left. Donna suggests that they were never heard from again.

Sex and Drugs and Rock'n'Roll: Toby and Josh have a borderline-lewd conversation about the lovely Cathy, little realising that her boyfriend, Cap, is sitting next to them.

Time As An Abstract: Currently, 77 of 92 Indiana counties do not recognise daylight-saving time, as the rest of the Eastern time zone does each spring. These are on New York time from late October until April and on Chicago time the rest of the year. 'There's always some quirky story about Indiana's time zones,' noted Indiana Commerce Department's spokesman Jeff Harris after this episode broadcast. 'It's usually played in a humorous light, which isn't always the best thing for Indiana, but that's the reality we deal with.'

Logic, Let Me Introduce You to This Window: Isn't Ginger rather casually dressed for work? The pilot of *Air Force One* is always a colonel and not a general. Is Bartlet's mobile phone a secure line considering the nature of his conversation with Leo? Josh tells Cathy that Bartlet has his blood pressure taken each morning and, if it's high, Toby isn't allowed to be in the president's sight. He's probably joking but, if he isn't, is that the kind of information he would casually disclose? The *Milwaukee Sentinel* is actually called the *Milwaukee Journal Sentinel*. Ed and Larry's bet on how long it would take the president to lose his temper in a meeting is, surely, a sacking offence.

Quote/Unquote: Cathy: 'These guys work for Bartlet.' Sy: 'Didn't vote for him the first time. Don't plan to the second time.'

Sam's voicemail message: 'I'm sleeping for a few hours right now so you can leave a message or, if you really need me, you can shout into the machine and I'll wake up.'

Bruno: ' "Elitist feminist"? You can't do that to the English language.'

Josh: 'That's Ritchie's way of saying, ". . . it's great Bartlet's a Nobel Prize winner. When I'm elected, I'm gonna hire me some of those." ' Toby: 'What he's saying is, "Eastern education isn't for real men, but . . . I'll have *Jews* for the money stuff." '

Notes: 'We were waylaid by some mean schoolgirls.' Lots of nice ideas, and some terrific comedy (Josh and Toby's insane overreaction to getting stuck in Indiana, Josh waking Sam up) but the entire episode feels a bit empty. A disappointing start to the season.

Bartlet is soon to visit Seoul. He has seen the great Wall of China. CJ tells Charlie that Simon was a Big Brother to a teenager named Anthony Marcus. She has been trying to spend some time with Anthony, but he's rather hostile towards her, associating CJ with Simon's death. Charlie notes that he did that for a while with some of the cops his mother worked with. CJ loves dry rub, an Indiana meat speciality. Mitch Bryce is the energy secretary. Two of the potential replacements for Mrs Landingham are Meredith Walker and Mrs Harrison. But neither seems to impress the president. Donald McKittridge is director of the Office of White House Personnel. Sarah Wissinger (see **4**, 'Five Votes Down') has a meeting with Bartlet. Steak sandwiches are being served on *Air Force One*. Ritchie's wife is called Janet. CJ has a running joke with the press corps concerning all of the things that Ritchie has said in speeches that he is not. These include a scientist, a doctor and, bizarrely, Chinese.

Cast and Crew Comments: 'We're going to be moving buses and a lot of stuff around,' noted Christopher Misiano as he prepared for the shoot. 'It's really ambitious.'

Aaron Sorkin told Rob Owen that the *Planes, Trains and Automobiles*-style story was inspired by an assistant to President Clinton, Kris Engskov, who had the same job as Charlie. 'A couple years ago, he told Dulé that the motorcade leaves when the president gets in the car. It doesn't wait for anybody. The Secret Service can't have the president sitting there, so it's not uncommon to have people left behind. He talked about running in to buy a postcard and coming out and there was nothing there. That was too good to be true, so I wrote an episode about it.'

Did You Know?: The Indiana location for this episode was actually filmed in Pennsylvania, much of it on Jeff and Roberta McConnell's 400-acre dairy farm in Washington Township, Lawrence County. The shoot was the first extensive Hollywood production in Pennsylvania since *The Mothman Prophecies* in 2001. Neal Ahern said that he and his crew scouted locations in Indiana, Texas, North Carolina and Maryland, but the work of Dawn Keezer at the Pittsburgh Film Office sold the producers on the area. Keezer drove producers on their scouting trip of over 400 miles in a single day. 'I scouted with Tommy Schlamme on July 19,' noted Ahern. 'He said, "Neal, we're staying here." '

A day of shooting was planned for 24 August but torrential rain caused a postponement. The Bridgeville Public Library, a former Penn Central Railroad station, was used for the exteriors shot on 26 August. 'We picked this spot because Bridgeville has a very unused railroad track. It was easy to buy the track and the six-car train for a day,' noted assistant location manager Steve Hough. The local press was full of articles over the following weeks with dozens of stories of people who had brief appearances in this episode. Rudy Vrbanic of Creekside, the only licensed crop-dusting pilot in western Pennsylvania, was one such, appearing along with his single-engine Piper plane. Vrbanic's wife, Bonnie, also appeared as an extra. 'The people couldn't have been nicer, and the location couldn't have been more beautiful,' noted Aaron Sorkin. 'The footage looks terrific. It was a very, very successful trip.' Between takes on the location shoot, Martin Sheen entertained extras with his rendition of Elvis's 'Love Me Tender'. 'Don't give up the day job,' noted one, dryly.

68
20 Hours in America
Part 2

US Transmission Date: 25 September 2002
UK Transmission Date: 29 July 2003 (E4)

Writer: Aaron Sorkin
Director: Christopher Misiano
Cast: Don Perry (Muriel Keith) Allan Wasserman (Donald McKittridge)
David Early (Bartender) Aaron Marcus (Deskman)
Jeff Gage (Train Conductor) Susan Allenbach (Driver)
Robert Noble (Butler) John Fletcher (Photographer)
Thomas Crawford (Bill Lacey) Albert Owens (Senator)
Mary-Pat Green (Senator)

The president interviews Debbie Fiderer again. Fitzwallace and Nancy McNally worry about what the Qumaris know about Shareef's death. Toby meets a man in a bar who could change the administration's tax policy.

A View From the Hill: The president is due to attend a DNC fundraiser at the Capital Hilton.

Two Guys Walk Into a Bar: Toby meets Matt Kelley. He's been taking his daughter to view colleges and tells Toby his life story and about how he's struggling to make ends meet. Matt spends much time thinking about what would happen if he injured himself and was unable to work. It should be hard, he notes, putting one's daughter through college – that's a man's accomplishment. But it should be a little easier.

A Little Learning is a Dangerous Thing: Concerning the attacks on Abbey over her TV statement, CJ says that she wanted her office to issue a statement to those complaining, saying, You're annoying, shut up; but Bruno told her to think of something else.

According to Toby, who is seemingly keeping a list of Ritchie's most embarrassing gaffs, the governor thinks that Sarajevo and Bosnia are two different countries and that Mexico is part of NATO.

Sam compares working in the Oval Office to chaos theory with patterns and great beauty emerging from randomness. He tells Mallory that he loves Josh like a brother and knows that he's a world-class political mind, but, until today, he didn't know that Josh was *smarter* than Sam.

The Encyclopedic Mind of Josiah Bartlet PhD: Sam notes that the president is asking his secretarial candidates about their memories and speculates it may be because short-term memory loss is a symptom of MS.

The Conspiracy Starts at Closing Time: When Debbie alerted Josh to Charlie's potential (see **3**, 'A Proportional Response'), the other person in with a chance of getting the job was David Dweck. He is the son of Brian Dweck, CFO of Colfax and contributor to Representative Mark McKittridge, whose brother is Donald, the director of the White House Office of Presidential Personnel. McKittridge promptly fired Debbie.

CJ reports that two pipe bombs were set off inside the Geiger Indoor Arena, the swimming team's facility at Kennison State University. The women's team was hosting a meet with Illinois, Michigan and Minnesota. Forty-four people are dead, and a hundred injured.

Bartlet is told that in the next 48 hours the Qumari rescue team will announce that they've recovered a military-issue Israeli-made parachute from close to the Shareef crash site.

References: The name of the French premier with whom Bartlet dined at the Élysée Palace was D'Atier, a reference to *The American President*. He refers to Abbey as Medea, the mythical devotee of Hecate from *Jason and the Argonauts*. Also, Alfred Nobel, the Nikkei index, James Bond, *The Bad Seed*, *Dr. Strangelove*, *Camelot*, Kikkoman Chinese food, the *New Yorker*, Benjamin Disraeli (1804–81) and an allusion to *A Streetcar Named Desire*. 'The streets of heaven are too crowded with angels' is a quote from Tom Hanks's 1994 Oscar acceptance speech. There's an allusion to TS Eliot, via Oscar Wilde ('Good writers borrow, great writers steal'). Leo and Margaret have a discussion about a cooking show that appears to be one hosted by Nigella Lawson. The background music heard in the bar is Dion's 'The Wanderer', where an Indianapolis Colts banner can be seen.

'You May Remember Me From Such Films and TV Series As . . .': John Connolly appeared in *Sessions* and *Any Day Now*. Don Perry was in *Bank Robber*, *Ricochet*, *Doppelgänger* and *Cheers*. Allan Wasserman's movies include *Shooting LA* and *Big*. David Early was in *The Dark Half* and *The Silence of the Lambs*. Aaron Marcus appeared in *Stage Fright*. Jeff Gage's movies include *Bullethead*. Susan Allenbach was in *Random Hearts*. Thomas Crawford's CV includes *Apollo 13*, *Outbreak*, *CSI* and *Angel*. Albert Owens appeared in *Air Force One*. Mary-Pat Green was in *XXX* and *Married . . . With Children*.

Oh, Donna!: Arriving at an airport hotel soaking wet, Donna innocently asks at the desk if she can hire a room for herself and the two men with her for half an hour. Josh interjects that their plane has been delayed before the man can call the police.

Cigarettes and Alcohol: Toby drinks a Jack Daniel's on the rocks and Josh a beer in the bar.

Sex and Drugs and Rock'n'Roll: Charlie tells Debbie that, in the event that the president and the first lady need some private time, the staff have euphemisms. They list such occasions as 'barbecuing'.

Mallory isn't living in New York any more. Richard (her ice-hockey-playing boyfriend) was traded to Chicago Blackhawks, but she and Richard have, in any case, split up.

Logic, Let Me Introduce You to This Window: *Technically*, the Great Depression didn't start on 24 October 1929, as Bartlet states, but five days later ('Black Tuesday') when the stock market collapsed completely. Toby is angry that

Ritchie seemingly believed that Neville Chamberlain led England in World War Two. Actually, he *did* – at least, a small portion of it, until his resignation in May 1940. Charlie tells Debbie that the president has five secretaries, four of whom funnel their work through the executive secretary. She seems surprised by this. She was in Personnel at the White House, so surely she'd know. CJ says Central Savings Time instead of Central Daylight Time. Swimming meetings are seldom held in September – it's a winter sport. Also, it doesn't seem likely that CJ would be the first source for the news of the pipe bomb (or a source of nongovernment news at all, for that matter). That's not her job. That's what TV companies pay anchors a lot of money for. Terrible crime though it is, it hasn't anything directly to do with Washington or the Bartlet administration.

Quote/Unquote: Charlie: 'We're going to have to reschedule the photo op for tomorrow.' Mr Keith: 'Oh. Why?' Charlie: 'You're spooking-the-hell out of the president.'

Fitzwallace: 'There was no call.' Leo: 'Why are they saying there is? It's to provoke a response, right? And they're using the Act Five scene from *Hamlet*? Are these *Batman* villains?'

Bartlet: 'What I lack in memory, I more than make up for with exceptional powers of deductive reasoning.' Debbie: 'That come with tights and a cape?'

Notes: 'Three hundred IQ points between them, they can't find their way home. I swear to God, if Donna wasn't there, they'd have to buy a house.' A more satisfying collection of plots than the first part. There are several fine moments: Bartlet's conversation with Charlie about superstition, Donna knocking some sense into Toby and Josh. Only the Qumar subplot weights the episode with somewhat unnecessary baggage.

Having asked Charlie if he would consider being a Big Brother to Anthony last episode, CJ now asks Sam. Sam's workload will make this impossible. After Anthony verbally abuses CJ, Charlie decides that the kid needs some discipline and tells Anthony that, at nine o'clock on Saturday mornings, Charlie eats breakfast at Cosmo's on Delaware, comes to the White House for an hour and does office work, and then goes to St Jude's for an hour to play basketball. He expects Anthony to be there on the Saturday coming.

Cast and Crew Comments: 'When I came back to begin writing the show, I suddenly felt comfortable in my chair again,' noted Aaron Sorkin. 'The show felt right. I think that the cast and crew felt that way, too.'

Did You Know?: The final scene for the episode was filmed at sunrise on the Virginia side of the Memorial Bridge as Brad Whitford, Richard Schiff and Janel Maloney exit an airport van and start walking towards the bridge. The production utilised a thirty-foot Technocrane and an insert car and process trailer to film the interior scenes in the airport van.

69
College Kids

US Transmission Date: 2 October 2002
UK Transmission Date: 5 August 2003 (E4)

Teleplay: Aaron Sorkin
Story: Debora Cahn, Mark Goffman
Director: Alex Graves
Cast: Alex Paez (David) Pam Shaddock (Jan)
Mary Kathleen Gordon (Woman)
Special Musical Appearances: Barenaked Ladies, Aimee Mann

Bartlet reacts to the Qumari situation by having Leo hire a lawyer. Josh is upset that Amy has accepted a job with a rival to the president. The approval process for Debbie hits a snag.

A View From the Hill: In the DC district court the case *Sullivan v. Commission on Presidential Debates, ABC, CBS, NBC News* is heard. This involves the 'Third-party 15%

rule', which excludes minority parties from televised debates and is in support of Independent nominee Howard Stackhouse (see **39**, 'The Stackhouse Filibuster'). Against all expectations, the judge upholds the case, leaving the White House seeking cause for appeal.

Politics of Legality: Jordan Elaine Kendall was born in Lincoln, Nebraska, attended the Maxwell School of Diplomacy and International Relations, was counsel in delegations to the UN and to the UN itself and is currently a partner in Whitcombe, Whylie, Hawking, Harrison and Kendall. She's a specialist in international law and has handled several high-profile cases (including the citizenship case of a Cuban baseball player, Orlando Ruiz, the defence of a chemical company in a wrongful-death suit and Leo in **54**, 'Bartlet for America'). Jordan is told of the circumstances behind Shareef's assassination and debates the likely implications with Leo and Bartlet. She has trouble foreseeing the exact consequences on the international stage, largely because most of international law doesn't exist yet.

Politics of Taxation: Following their discussions with Matt Kelley in the last episode, Josh and Toby simultaneously hit on a bright idea after reading a newspaper story about a company called Redstar and a $35 million retention bonus they gave to an executive called Wadkins. Josh notes that Congress has ended the deductibility of salaries over a million dollars but that this excluded items deemed by the IRS to be incentive-based. In other words, *bonuses* are tax-deductible. College costs are a much better use of capital, they agree.

Politics of Recreation: The episode recreates Rock The Vote's annual Patrick Lippert Awards, dedicated to entertainers and activists who work to inspire and educate youth.

A Little Learning is a Dangerous Thing: Qumar (capital, Jabal Nafusah), geographically, is roughly where southern Iran is in reality.

In school, Ellie had a teacher named Mr Pordie who had no interest in nuance, according to Bartlet. When he asked why there's conflict in the Middle East, Ellie stated it was a centuries-old religious conflict involving land and culture. Mr Pordie, alternatively, believed it was because the region is incredibly hot.

Donna gives Josh a precise little essay on why there are too many football players on university scholarships.

The Conspiracy Starts at Closing Time: Mike Casper (see **54**, 'Bartlet For America') is still the White House liaison with the FBI. He shows the president a letter written by the group claiming responsibility for the pipe bomb mentioned in the previous episode and promising further atrocities in the next 48 hours. The letter bears the hallmarks of a group of right-wing separatists called the Liberationist Cause, a splinter group of the Patriot Brotherhood, who have their own website. Bartlet notes that the Internet has been a phenomenal tool for hate groups. Law-enforcement people in Johnson County, Iowa, surrounded a house when they had been tipped off that several men had been buying pseudoephedrine. This, when mixed with tractor starter fluid, produces methamphetamine. The deputies were shot at when they approached the house, the occupants of which are linked to the Patriot Brotherhood.

Fitzwallace tells the president that, in response to Qumari attempts to blame Israel for Shareef's death, they will leak a story that Shareef is alive and living in Libya while planning to overthrow the Sultan. The CIA will manufacture documents, photographs, audio messages and even a body double if necessary.

References: Bartlet alludes to the street gangs in *West Side Story*. Also, the Arab TV service Al-Jazeera, Hizbollah, the Battle Creek Air National Guard Base, Title IX of the Educational Amendments of 1972, which bans sexual discrimination in schools, SF-86 the questionnaire covering national security, the philosopher Thomas Paine (1737–1809), author of *The Rights of Man*, a quotation from Psalms 30 ('Joy cometh in the morning'), the Arctic explorer Robert Scott (1868–1912), *Don Quixote de la Mancha*, Barnum and Bailey, the Libertarian and Natural Law Parties, Chernobyl and Dr Martin Luther King (1929–68). Bartlet and Fitzwallace both allude to a maxim first used by Desiderius Erasmus (1466–1536) and later popularised by HG Wells (1866–1946): among the blind, the one-eyed man is king.

'You May Remember Me From Such Films and TV Series As …': Alex Paez's CV includes *CSI: Miami* and *Charmed*. Pam Shaddock was in *Emma's Wish*.

Sex and Drugs and Rock'n'Roll: At the rally, Barenaked Ladies perform 'One Week' and Aimee Mann sings James Taylor's 'Shed a Little Light'. Also on the bill are Chrissie Hynde (seemingly without the Pretenders), Sixpence None the Richer, Aaron Neville, Diamondback Whale, Daisy Chain, Next Big Thing, the Cruel Shoes and Single-Cell Paramecium. Except the last, whom Donna made up.

Logic, Let Me Introduce You to This Window: The president enters the Lansing auditorium, in which he will make his speech at the back, and walks through the audience to the stage. Surely the Secret Service wouldn't allow such an unsecured entrance. Josh refers to soccer (that's football for everyone else on Planet Earth) as a woman's sport. That's how the game is seen in America, thanks to the women's World Cup success of the US team in 1999. Several billion Brazilians, Argentineans, Africans, Italians, Spaniards, Germans, French, British etc. might *just* disagree with that assessment. Shouldn't Debbie's written threat to poison the president, even if it *was* in jest, *automatically* exclude her from being considered for the job? Would a White House press secretary really appear at a public event in jeans and a T-shirt with an exposed midriff? CJ describes Barenaked Ladies as helping American democracy, which is considerate of them, as the band is Canadian.

Quote/Unquote: Bruno: 'I'm not comfortable with a federal judge being even a little bit crazy.'

CJ: 'Democracy by favouristic fiat, a bureaucratic junta that is clearly prohibited under federal law.' Toby: 'There's no way "favouristic" is a word.' Sam: 'We agree with you, Toby, we just don't think it's grounds for an appeal!'

Josh: 'Why isn't college tuition tax-deductible?' Sam: 'I don't know. Why do "flammable" and "inflammable" mean the same thing?'

Notes: 'There's evil in the world, there'll always be, we can't do anything about that. But there's violence in our schools, too much mayhem in our culture. We *can* do something about that.' After an ordinary couple of episodes, at last the *real West Wing* shows itself. Cleverly allowing the bombastic *major* issues, like Qumar and the pipe bombing, to carry the bulk of the episode, it's the pithy little diversions (like the TV debate court case) that are the winners here.

Leo orders an egg salad sandwich on a Kaiser roll, unless it's Milos making the potato salad. He tells Jordan about the secret ingredient Milos puts in the salad that makes Leo crave it beyond indulgence. Bartlet notes that Article 51 of the UN Charter gives every nation the right to wage war to defend itself. Amy has a new job, running Stackhouse's debate preparation team. CJ repeats what Bartlet said in **22**, 'What Kind of Day Has it Been': 'decisions are made by those who show up'.

Cast and Crew Comments: 'I would do anything for *West Wing* and Aaron,' noted Aimee Mann. 'I got the call at the last minute. They wanted Joan Armatrading, but she couldn't make it because of a visa problem. They said, "We want you to do this James Taylor song." We did it as fast as we could and tried to replicate the original version.'

Did You Know?: The Hollywood producer Lawrence Bender, active in Rock The Vote, held a fundraiser and viewing party on the night this episode was broadcast. Bender invited guests to pay a minimum $250 to watch it at his home. The party, in Bel-Air, raised an estimated $100,000 for the organisation. For Aaron Sorkin, watching

150 people react to his show was torture. 'It's like that dream you have when you find yourself in front of a bunch of people, totally naked.'

70
The Red Mass

US Transmission Date: 9 October 2002
UK Transmission Date: 12 August 2003 (E4)

Teleplay: Aaron Sorkin
Story: Eli Attie
Director: Vincent Misiano
Cast: Malachi Throne (Ben Yosef) Deborah May (Janet)
Robin Bartlett (Susan Thomas) John Cothran Jr (Civilian Advisor)
Larry Brandenburg (Jackson) Hilary Salvatore (Emily)
Becky Meister (Sally) Richard Green (Jerry) Lynn Tufeld (Grace)
Joe Marinelli (Morris) Brandon Noll (Staffer) Joe Cosgrove (Cardinal)
Noel Conlon (Weaver) Helen Duffy (White)

Bartlet ponders the consequences of the FBI's storming the siege in Idaho. The staff try to negotiate with the Ritchie camp for more televised debates.

A View From the Hill: Horton Wilde, the Democrat running in the California 47th district (Orange County), has suffered his fourth heart attack (see **71**, 'Debate Camp', **72**, 'Game On').

Amy asks Josh for his opinion on Stackhouse. Josh replies that he's always liked the senator and would vote for him, but he's not on the ballot in Connecticut. Or 22 other states. Amy subsequently tells Stackhouse that she believes he remains an extraordinary, energetic, compassionate and courageous public servant, but that she'll be voting for Bartlet.

Politics of Murder: The Israeli foreign minister, Ben Yosef, is a friend of Leo's and presents him with a yarmulke and the Medal of David. Yosef's plane is subsequently shot down over the Lebanon, seemingly by the Qumaris.

Politics of Debate: The White House want five televised debates covering the economy, foreign policy, global threats and national security, the environment and strengthening family life, which would include healthcare and education. The Ritchie camp want just two and, by dragging their feet, seem to have achieved their aim, the format being, in the president's opinion, nothing more than a joint press conference. However, CJ and Sam suggest a different offer: a single *proper* debate at which *they* can set the rules, giving Bartlet the chance to cross-examine Ritchie (see **72**, 'Game On') and the moderator the right to demand an answer in the case of procrastination. Toby is concerned that the president may have a bad night, but determines to make sure that won't happen.

A Little Learning is a Dangerous Thing: The Supreme Court convenes on the first Monday in October, the day before the Red Mass is held for the members of the court, which the Cabinet, Congress and the president attend. Anthony asks Charlie about the law covering separation of church and state. Charlie gives Anthony a copy of the Constitution and suggests he find out himself. Later, Charlie asks the president the same question. It *is* a Constitutional issue, Bartlet notes, but it was the intention of the founders not to have a national religion and not to have the government encourage a national display of piety as a substitute for real action.

The Conspiracy Starts at Closing Time: The house in Iowa containing the armed separatists has been surrounded for eleven days. The plan was to wait for them to surrender, but one of the children in the house is sick, so Bartlet orders the FBI to storm the building. Mike Casper confirms that the raid was successful: high explosives, steel pipes, fuses and blueprints for the KSU swimming pool were seized, one terrorist was killed and the sick boy rushed to hospital.

References: The music played during the Mass is Vivaldi's 'Gloria'. Also, Matthew 6 ('a servant of two masters'), the

New York Mets, the Shrine of the Immaculate Conception, Thornton Wilder's *The Skin of Our Teeth*, Immanuel Kant's *A Critique of Practical Reason*, *The Republic* by Plato, Robert Frost's 'Mending Wall' ('Good fences make good neighbors'), *Agence France*, Ben Gurion Airport and the Roman orators and statesmen Cicero, Lentulus, Caesar and Cato. Bartlet refers to the Italian economist Vilfredo Pareto's observations that 80 per cent of the land is owned by 20 per cent of the people.

'You May Remember Me From Such Films and TV Series As …': Malachi Throne was in *Star Trek*, *The High Chaparral*, *The Bionic Woman* and *Catch Me If You Can*. Deborah May appeared in *Nurse Betty* and *ER*. Robin Bartlett's CV includes *Mad About You*, *Sophie's Choice* and *Heaven's Gate*. John Cothran was in *Sin's Kitchen*, *Spawn*, *Charmed* and *24*. Larry Brandenburg appeared in *Fargo* and *Field of Dreams*. Hilary Salvatore's movies include *Bring It On* and *American Pie*. Becky Meister appeared in *Magicians*. Richard Green was in *Mulholland Drive*. Noel Conlon's CV includes *Courage* and *Knight Rider*. Helen Duffy was in *Hijacking Hollywood*.

Oh, Donna!: Josh asks Donna what she's doing tomorrow, Saturday. Donna plans to go bike riding, meet friends for lunch, then get a manicure. Josh wants her to attend a seminar given by a self-help guru, Teddy Tomba, author of *Owning Yourself*, *Leasing Yourself* and *Connecting With Yourself*, who's been advising Ritchie. After attending, Donna kids Josh that it was a singular experience but then admits that it was, actually, idiotic. However, she considers Tomba may be a buffoon, but he's harmless, unlike a guy called Fern, who sat next to her. She refers to the seminar as a 'there, but for the grace of God society' (see **9**, 'The Short List').

Sex and Drugs and Rock'n'Roll: Ritchie makes a speech at the AMA, during which he calls for abstinence and proposes amending the law to stop inner-city needle-exchange programmes. This is designed purely to get

Stackhouse to comment, which will in turn force the president on to the subject. Won't Josh figure this out in five minutes? Amy is asked. Amy says *Donna* will figure it out in five minutes. Toby would like someone to ask Ritchie whether he's aware that needle exchange costs $9,000 for each infection stopped, while treating someone with HIV costs $200,000. Bruno believes if Bartlet comes out in favour of needle exchange that will put three states back into play: Ohio, Michigan and Maine. After Bartlet's speech at the Mass, Stackhouse graciously praises Bartlet and tells him that he has decided not to run and will endorse the president. Bartlet uses the opportunity to speak to the press about needle exchange.

Quote/Unquote: Josh: 'There comes a day when every man realises he's never gonna become a major-league ball player.' Donna: 'And you're just having that day *today*?'

Josh: 'You got a mouthful of wise ass today, doncha?' Donna: 'I located the light switch.' Josh: 'Could you locate it *again*?'

Josh: '[With] the fifty life-and-death matters that walk across [the president's] desk every day, I don't know if he's thinking about Immanuel Kant ... if he does, I am [certain] he's doing his best to reach for all of it, not just the McNuggets.'

Bartlet: 'A coach once told me the hardest thing to do in sports is to walk into your Super Bowl locker room at half-time and change the strategy that got you there 'cos it's no longer working.'

Notes: 'I know how Ritchie's going to win this election.' Another episode touched with *magnificence*. The juxtaposition between Stackhouse – a man who will never be president but, one feels, would have made a great one – and Bartlet is cleverly played. Donna and Josh's debate on literature, with the subtext of Ritchie's (and, by logical extension, George Bush's) reduction of intellect to soundbite-sized chunks of inanity, is inspired. The scene in which Leo wonders what winning is caught much flak for its seemingly racist assumption that everything in the world would be all right with an American flag flying over Mecca. Nevertheless, it does accurately portray the confusion at the heart of post-9/11 US attitudes to foreign policy: if you want to defeat your enemy, first, you've got to sing his song.

Bartlet feels he's never been liked in Maine. Leo has some Scottish ancestry. He describes Sam as one of the big minds of his generation. Josh has been advised to take flying lessons because it will relax him. Donna studied modern poetry.

Cast and Crew Comments: Concerning the drop in *The West Wing*'s ratings during the early part of Season Four, Thomas Schlamme told the *Chicago Sun-Times*, 'Some of that was the election [storyline], these were not our best episodes [and] some of it was that we got hit with *The Bachelor* and people started to leave, given an excuse.'

Did You Know?: When Bartlet is talking about the upcoming campaign, a football game can be seen on TV in the background. It's actually a Canadian CFL match featuring the Calgary Stampeders.

71
Debate Camp

US Transmission Date: 16 October 2002
UK Transmission Date: 19 August 2003 (E4)

Teleplay: Aaron Sorkin
Story: William Sind, Michael Oates Palmer
Director: Paris Barclay
Cast: Jeffrey Pierce (Jeff Johnson) Bruce French (Bill Stark)
Eyal Podell (Gordon) Bill Ferrell (Guard) Nicole Lyn (Intern)
Lance Baldwin (Date)

As the staff prepare Bartlet for the presidential debate, a question about a failed attorney-general nomination leads to memories of the administration's first weeks in office. As Toby seeks advice on how to revive his marriage to Andi,

Joey Lucas reports that the president is likely to lose New Hampshire.

A View From the Hill: The administration's first choice for attorney-general, Cornell Rooker, was a conservative African-American from Miami. Bartlet withdrew the nomination just days after taking office, when Rooker's support of racial profiling became public (after Danny Concannon broke the story) and it was clear that Congress would block the appointment.

Politics of Prayer: CJ held her first press briefing two days after Bartlet's inauguration. She used mnemonic skills to remember all the reporters' names. She also met Bill Stark of *Kingspeak*, a magazine with a circulation of 600,000 Christian evangelicals. She was told that on 10 December the readers would be praying for her.

A Little Learning is a Dangerous Thing: Josh refers to the fact that Scandinavia has a very high rate of suicides per head of population.

The Encyclopedic Mind of Josiah Bartlet PhD: During the flashback to Bartlet's first days in office, we observe a conversation with Mrs Landingham concerning items from the National Gallery or the Smithsonian that the White House could borrow. Leonardo da Vinci's *Madonna and Child with Pomegranate* and Botticelli's *Adoration of the Magi* are discussed, though the president's first choice, *Apollo 11*, seemingly wasn't on offer.

The Conspiracy Starts at Closing Time: Eight Israeli thunderfighters (Boeing F-15E Strike Eagles) attacked two terrorist bases in Qumar in retaliation for the murder of Ben Yosef. While no Qumari institutions were destroyed, Qumar considers this attack to be an act of war. Thirty thousand troops are said to be massing on the Syrian border. Meanwhile, the *Mastico*, a Qumari cargo ship, is in the Mediterranean, heading for Lebanon, carrying weapons and explosives, clearly intended to arm the Bahji. Bartlet orders Fitzwallace to stop the ship.

References: The song that Sam and company sing after dinner is 'Gaudeamus Igitur'. Also mentioned, the Marx Brothers, Hizbollah, the Urban League, La Raza, the Kremlin, the fashion designer Celia Yang, *Bambi*, the Clampetts from *The Beverly Hillbillies*, Abraham Lincoln, Cher and Sonny, the Phillips Andover Academy, the *Playboy* owner Hugh Hefner, Don Imus, Howard Stern and the *New York Times*. There's a possible allusion to *Buffy the Vampire Slayer* ('Bite me!'). Amy mentions the white cliffs of Dover and alludes to the Tour de France.

'You May Remember Me From Such Films and TV Series As . . .': Jeffrey Pierce was in *Big Apple* and *Astronauts*. Bruce French's CV includes *Mr Deeds*, *Passions*, *Jagged Edge* and *Helter Skelter*. Eyal Podell played Roland in *Charmed* and appeared in *The Chaos Factor* and *Deep Blue Sea*. Bill Ferrell's movies include *Blue Streak*. Nicole Lyn was in *Bless the Child* and *Relic Hunter*. Lance Baldwin appeared in *All My Children*.

Oh, Donna!: Shortly before Bartlet's inauguration, Donna was invited to the White House for lunch by her Republican predecessor, Jeff Johnson. He mentioned to Donna that there's an XW-9 warhead in a silo below the Eisenhower putting green. Johnson then arranged for Donna to be interviewed by his girlfriend, a writer with the teen magazine *21*, where Donna mentioned this fact. After publication, an amused Josh convinces Donna that she's been set up, but subsequently someone claiming to be from the NSA arrives and notes that Donna has hit a little close to home with her revelations. It then transpires that the officer is Michael – a friend of Donna's who works in the staff secretary's office (and has his own band).

Sex and Drugs and Rock'n'Roll: Toby and Andi were still married when the administration took office in January 1999. They must, therefore, have divorced sometime during the summer, prior to **1**, 'Pilot'. The couple wanted children but Andi's immune system made a pregnancy improbable and Toby suggested adoption or surrogacy.

However, after some years of fertilisation treatment, seemingly with Toby's sperm, Andi is now pregnant with twins. Toby is overjoyed (well, as close as Toby can get to joy) and wishes to kick-start the marriage, something that Andi rejects out of hand.

Logic, Let Me Introduce You to This Window: Joey Lucas believes that Bartlet cannot win New Hampshire. It would have to be an extraordinary election in which a president lost his home state but won elsewhere. It would also be fairly unusual for a Democrat not to take all of New England and *still* win. Would the Donna of 1999 (a few months after being the meek girl seen in **23**, 'In The Shadow of Two Gunmen' Part 1, and, indeed, some time prior to being the relatively meek girl seen in **1**, 'Pilot') be confident enough to pull the stunt that she did on Josh? The debate camp is said to be taking place over 48 hours. Seemingly, therefore, the 24 hours that Toby asked CJ to clear from the president's schedule in the previous episode wasn't enough. Ohio no longer has 21 electoral votes: as of 2000 it has only 20.

Quote/Unquote: Bartlet: 'We are, as always, one bad bottle of tequila away from all-out war in West Asia.'

Josh: 'If you asked the president which he'd rather win, New Hampshire or the election, he'd have to think before he answered.' And: 'So a radical feminist is saying women should stay home with the kids?'

Andi, to Toby: 'They draw blood from you – like a rabid dog – clean it, thank goodness, and give me injections of your blood cells to build up tolerance. You know how you're always saying you wish people were more like you?'

Leo: ' "We'll worry about tomorrow, tomorrow"? We said that *yesterday*.'

Notes: 'It's our second day. How do you think it's going so far?' Maybe I'm a sucker for flashback episodes, but this, like several previous examples, works surprisingly well in giving the audience a taste of life before the series began. The revelation that *West Wing*'s major contribution to

Western civilisation, *pedconferencing*, began simply because most of the staff kept getting lost in the White House's many corridors is cleverly played, while most of the other subplots work to one degree or another.

The debate camp takes place at the Saybrook Institute for Public Policy in Faith, North Carolina. Bartlet's inauguration was on 20 January 1999. Josh played the lead in *Li'l Abner* in the eighth grade. He was good but, he alleges, everyone else wasn't. He would vouch for Donna with his life. Sam does a reasonable Bartlet impression. Amy is a keen cyclist. The previous president's deputy chief of staff was called McConnell. Horton Wilde (see **70**, 'The Red Mass') has died.

Cast and Crew Comments: 'I won't pretend that I don't know who Bush is,' says Aaron Sorkin, 'but I was interested in writing about a demonisation of intellect. Which didn't start with Bush–Gore – it didn't even start with Eisenhower–Stevenson. It's peculiarly American: being tagged as the smartest kid in your class turns into both a sense of arrogance and a sense of weakness.'

Did You Know?: ThinkFilm producers Stephanie Antosca and Jonathan Zurer managed all aspects of this episode's location filming in Washington, including casting extras and renting equipment. The September trip included scenes with Mary-Louise Parker riding a bike (attached to a golf-cart rig designed by the key grips Tom Nichols and Brian Leach) near the Jefferson Memorial, having dinner with a local actor, Lance Baldwin, at Signatures Restaurant in Market Square, and entering her apartment located in Dupont Circle.

72
Game On

US Transmission Date: 30 October 2002
UK Transmission Date: 26 August 2003 (E4)

Writer: Aaron Sorkin, Paul Redford
Director: Alex Graves

Cast: Tony Amendola (Ali Nissir) John Aniston (Alexander Thompson)
Paige Orr (Karen) Trent Trail (Lawrence) Tomiko Martinez (Staffer)
Amy Bruckner (Sally) Gia Cross (Girl) Ashley Benson (Girl)
Alison Robertson (Carrie) Jason McCune (Jonathan) Ted Davis (Bobby)
Michael Raysses (Ted) Stephanie Venditto (June) Anita Dashiell (Joe)
Ross Shimabuku (Derek) Mary McDonough (Beth) Nick Jameson (Chet)
Scott Facher (Stage Manager) Amy Parks (Tammy)
Stacy Reed (Girl in Bar) Steve Stapenhorst (Martin)

In San Diego, Bartlet faces Ritchie in a live TV debate. Leo
and Jordan meet a Qumari politician to avert the escalating crisis. Sam tries to persuade Horton Wilde's team to
end their campaign.

A View From the Hill: Sam is sent to give the president's
condolences to Wilde's widow, Kay, and to close down his
campaign. Unfortunately, due to California law, a dead
candidate must remain on the ballot. The campaign
director, Will Bailey, sees an opportunity to discuss
important ideas. The candidate may be dead, but what he
believed in isn't, Bailey notes. That metaphor alone is
reason to carry on. A reporter asks what happens if, by
some miracle, Wilde wins. He's told that a special election
would be held within ninety days. The Republican opponent, Chuck Webb, is a seven-term Congressman who,
according to Will, is on the board of the NRA and once
challenged another Congressman to a fistfight over an
amendment to make stalkers submit to background checks
before buying guns. He's joined protests designed to
frighten pregnant women. The point of this, Will concludes, is that there are worse things in the world than no
longer being alive.

Politics of Complexity: After a North Carolina Democrat
declares his support for Ritchie on defence, CJ asks
cantankerous State Department veteran Albie Duncan (see
51, 'Gone Quiet') to speak on the president's behalf.
Bartlet will be attacked on China and must defend trade
goals versus human-rights violations. Duncan notes that
trade's essential for human rights. Instead of isolating
China, the US makes them live by the same global trading

rules as everyone else and, as a bonus, gains 1.2 billion consumers for American products. CJ is delighted with his reply but Duncan says the situation is complicated. The president, he continues, knows that political prisoners will be sewing soccer balls whether the US sells China cheeseburgers or not, so why not sell them cheeseburgers anyway? He notes that 3,700 years ago, in the Chang dynasty, when a king died, his luckier slaves were beheaded. The unlucky ones were buried alive. As far as political repression goes, *this* is progress. After the debate, CJ encourages Duncan to give a much fuller answer than mere soundbites because, as she says, the president just reminded everyone that complexity isn't a vice.

A Little Learning is a Dangerous Thing: Several references are made to an impressive speech given by the governor of California, Gabe Tillman, at the Stanford Club. It was written by Will Bailey, with jokes supplied by Elsie Snuffin.

The Encyclopedic Mind of Josiah Bartlet PhD: The opening sequence features Toby being convinced by Leo that the president is suffering a confidence crisis. Leo suggests that, in a forthcoming two-minute-drill, Toby be supportive of whatever Bartlet says. Toby tells the rest of the staff to do so but, when Bartlet gives a stumbling answer relating to capital punishment, he's unable to contain himself any longer, thus winning a smirking Bartlet several $10 bets with the rest of the staff.

The Conspiracy Starts at Closing Time: Leo tells Jordan that the navy have stopped the *Mastico* with warning shots. He notes that Qumar's price for backing down changes daily. Yesterday, they wanted THAAD missile technology; today it's the release from US jails of convicted Bahji operatives. Jordan suggests they quietly get Ali Nissir, from the General Assembly, to come to Washington. After sparring around Ben Yosef's assassination, Nissir suggests to Leo that a charade is taking place. Leo laughs and asks if Nissir believes that the president would *lose* votes if he admitted complicity in Shareef's death. To sweep all fifty states, Leo suggests, Bartlet would need to do only two things: blow the Sultan's brains out in Times Square, then walk across the street to Nathan's for a hot dog. He tells Nissir that the *Mastico will* return to port, that Qumar will cease and desist *any* disinformation campaign concerning Israel. And, sometime next year, the Sultan will propose a peace plan and win the Nobel Prize.

References: Sam impersonates George Bailey, as played by Jimmy Stewart in *It's a Wonderful Life*, and alludes to Hughie Cannon's 'Bill Bailey'. Donna misquotes a famous line from *Twelve Angry Men*. Also, the Suffragettes, CNN's *Inside Politics*, Republican presidential candidate Wendell Wilkie (1892–1944), the *San Jose Mercury News*, the *Orange County Post-Gazette*, Winston Churchill, the Visigoths, the Boland Amendment, the Geneva Convention, the Spanish conquistador Francisco Pizarro (1478–1541), the Moscow Circus, one of *the* great boxing matches – Muhammad Ali versus George Foreman in Zaïre (now the Democratic Republic of the Congo) in 1975, the Grand Canyon and Las Vegas's Tropicana Casino. The song playing in the Laguna Beach bar is 'Midnight Confession' by Grass Roots. The sequence supposedly at Newport Beach was actually filmed on LA's Venice Beach. Sam has trouble folding an AAA California state map. Anaheim's 405 Freeway is mentioned.

'You May Remember Me From Such Films and TV Series As . . .': Josh Malina played Jeremy Goodwin in *Sports Night*. He also appeared in *Sliders*, *A Few Good Men* and *It's a Shame About Ray*. Danica McKeller was Winnie Cooper in *The Wonder Years*. Her movies include *Sex and the Teenage Mind*, *Reality School* and *Speechless* (which she also wrote and directed). Tony Amendola played Bra'tac in *Stargate SG-1*, Sorrel in *Kindred: The Embraced*, Carl Jasper in *Cradle Will Rock* and Sanchez in *Blow*. He also appeared in *Seinfeld*, *Angel*, *24* and *She-Wolf of London*. John Aniston was in *Kojak* and *Days of Our Lives*. His daughter is the *Friends* star Jennifer. Ashleigh Olden appeared in *Undressed*. Paige Orr's movies include *The Good Things*. Tomiko Martinez was in *Faux Pas*. Alison Robertson played Elsa in *Definite Maybe*. Stephanie Venditto appeared in *After Sex*. Mary Beth McDonough was Erin in *The Waltons*. Amy Parks appeared as Maureen in *Rats*. Steve Stapenhorst's movies include *Malcolm X* and *Space Cowboys*. Ross Shimabuku is a sports anchor with KTBK in Phoenix.

It's a Tie!: Bartlet decides to wear his lucky tie for the debate. In the previous campaign, Bartlet set his own tie on fire while having a cigarette moments before going on TV. Josh gave Bartlet his and this tie is, now, considered lucky. Unfortunately, it got damaged at the cleaners'. Charlie spends the episode attempting to procure a duplicate. Ultimately, Bartlet says he isn't worried – but confides to Abbey that his sudden need for a new tie was the spark that helped him win the debate last time. Abbey, who feels that she hasn't done enough to help Jed in this election, cuts his tie with scissors, forcing him to borrow Josh's yet again.

Sex and Drugs and Rock'n'Roll: Before going on stage, Bartlet slaps Abbey, hard, on the arse.

Logic, Let Me Introduce You to This Window: If, as subsequently revealed, Elsie is Will's sister, then why has she a different surname? Given her apparent age, and Will's protective attitude towards her, she seems unlikely to be married. Additionally, Will tells Sam he's the youngest in his family, but Elsie is *clearly* younger than Will. How long has Albie Duncan been at the State Department? He says thirty years, but Toby notes he's been there since Eisenhower's administration, which is over *forty* years. In **51**, 'Gone Quiet', Bartlet said he'd been at State even longer, since Truman's era (which ended in 1952). Both the ten-word answers that Josh gives Leo on defence and crime are more than ten words, *considerably* so in the case of the second one. It was the Shang dynasty, not the Chang, as Duncan says.

That Debate, in Full: The biggest philosophical difference between Ritchie and Bartlet concerns the role of the federal government, it's suggested. Ritchie responds that the Department of Education isn't needed, before making racist comments about Eskimo poetry. He suggests that the president will now use a big word: 'unfunded mandate'. Bartlet replies that is actually *two* words, not one. He continues that there *are* times when America is fifty states and other occasions when it's one country. Florida, for example, didn't fight Germany in World War Two or establish civil rights. The state, Bartlet notes, received $12.6 billion in federal money last year from New Yorkers, Nebraskans and Alaskans (with their Eskimo poetry), from a total budget of $50 billion. He therefore asks one simple question: can they have it back?

Later, the moderator suggests many economists believe tax cuts, which are central to Ritchie's economic agenda, could harm the economy. Is now the time to cut taxes? 'You bet it is,' Ritchie replies, glibly, stating that the Americans know how to spend their money better than the government. That's the ten-word answer that Josh has been searching for, Bartlet replies. Such soundbites can win political campaigns, he continues. So, what are the next ten words of Ritchie's answer? the president asks. His taxes are too high, so are Bartlet's. *How*, exactly, are these cuts to be paid for? Ritchie doesn't reply.

Quote/Unquote: CJ: 'He's not a little bit crazy?' Toby: 'Duncan? No. No. No . . . A little bit.'

Bartlet: 'I don't think Americans are tired of partisan politics, I think they're tired of hearing career politicians *diss* partisan politics . . . Partisan politics . . . *guarantees* that the minority opinion is heard. As a lifelong possessor of minority opinions, I appreciate it.'

Bartlet: '[Sometimes] there's a day with an *absolute* right and an *absolute* wrong, but those days almost always include body counts. Other than that, there aren't . . . many *un-nuanced* moments in leading a country that's way too big for ten words.'

Notes: 'It depends who shows up. If it's Uncle Fluffy, we've got problems. If it's the president . . . It could be a sight to see.' What a *glorious* piece of dramatic writing. From the hilarious opening scenes, 'Game On' is Aaron Sorkin's mission statement in one 45-minute burst of energy. A story about pride (Leo's scenes with Bartlet), agenda and duty (Sam's debates with Will) and the complexities of politics (CJ's conversation with Albie). The camerawork is brilliant, particularly when the staff enjoy their moment of triumph after the debate, but the highlight of the episode is their joyous reaction to Bartlet's first, diamond-sharp comment to Ritchie ('It's not gonna be Uncle Fluffy,' notes a delighted CJ). In some ways, sadly, 'Game On' defines the ultimate liberal fantasy of *The West Wing*, particularly as Bartlet *wipes the floor* with Sorkin's Bush clone, Ritchie. A decent, intelligent president who has a vision greater than the plastic, one-dimensional, 'ten-words-or-fewer'-dominated political world that we *actually* live in. The real fantasy, of course, is that Bartlet *gets elected*. Some fans bitterly complained that Ritchie was little more than a straw man, there only to remind us that intelligence should be our first weapon. But there are, as Will notes, many worse things to be.

Bartlet's daughter, Ellie, is 27 (see **37**, 'Ellie'). Leo reminds Jordan that he flew fighters over the demilitarised zone in Korea. Sam has written speeches for senators, movie stars and the king of Belgium. Sam tells Will that, should the Wilde campaign succeed, he will run in the re-election. He notes that he was *magna cum laude* graduate of Princeton and editor of the *Duke Law Review*. He's worked the DCCC, had seven years at Gage Whitney, and for the last four served as deputy communications director and senior counsel. He grew up two streets from the bar in which they're talking. Debbie is currently on a three-day crash course in 'everything' at the Maxwell School. Jordan is said to be special counsel to the Office of the Chief-of-Staff. Will grew up in Brussels, where his father, Thomas Bailey, was the supreme commander of NATO. Elsie previously worked as a TV sitcom writer.

Cast and Crew Comments: 'That episode was patterned after actual presidential debates. We had access to thousands of feet of documentary and newsreel footage,' noted the cinematographer Thomas Del Ruth. 'Before we shot the debate scenes, I saw an amalgam clip that the editors put together of the debates between Kennedy and Nixon, Johnson and Goldwater and Carter and Reagan. We studied details, including their mannerisms and other subtext that audiences might interpret.'

Did You Know?: 'When it was really looking like Rob would be leaving, which got us all very sad, we had a meeting,' Aaron Sorkin told Rob Kushman. 'In the two minutes it took me to get back to my office, I called Tommy [Schlamme], and said I'm absolutely convinced we have to get Josh Malina. Amazingly, after that phone call, I opened my email, and there was an email from Josh.'

'Just that day,' Malina added, 'I read in *Variety* that Rob was planning to leave. I thought I'd do a little fishing expedition. I think I said, "What about using someone who's less attractive and would work for less money?"' 'I emailed him back,' Sorkin continued. 'I said, "OK. I'll have you on the show."'

73
Election Night

US Transmission Date: 6 November 2002
UK Transmission Date: 2 September 2003 (E4)

Teleplay: Aaron Sorkin
Story: David Gerken, David Handelman
Director: Lisa Linka Glatter
Cast: Omar Benson Miller (Orlando Kettles)
Megan Cavanagh (Alleged Voter) Kaarina Aufranc (Alleged Voter)
Kris Iyer (Doctor) Richard Saxton (Anahiem Anchor)[114]
Lynette Romero (Anahiem Anchor) Christopher Schauble (Anchor)
Mindy Thomas (Anchor) Howard Mann (Senior Citizen)

---

[114] Richard Saxton played 'Boston Anchor' in three previous episodes.

Don Dowe (Technician) Ron Ostrow (John)
MariaLazam Hanson (Passer-by) Derek Thompson (Man)
Leesa Severun (Michelle) Ron Morehouse (Bow Tie)
Michael Mulheren (Alleged Voter)[115]

The election arrives as Bartlet's staff begin counting exit-poll votes across the country. Especially in Orange County, where the Congressional result has important implications for both Sam and Will Bailey.

A View From the Hill: Josh tells Sam that, in California, the late Horton Wilde is losing by just 88 votes with three hours' voting remaining. There was a low Republican turnout because Bartlet won in the Midwest, low supporter turnout because Webb didn't have an opponent, the DNC stopped campaigning a week ago, so the Republicans left town. They never saw the exit polls that Will Bailey was seeing. Also, there was an actual El Niño storm (which Will seems to believe he caused himself by, in the episode's best scene, shouting at the sky).

Politics of Humour: In revenge for the stunt that Josh was part of in **72**, 'Game On', Toby arranges an election day practical joke. An acting troupe play confused voters who convince Josh they all intended to vote for Bartlet but have, mistakenly, voted for someone else, or spoiled their ballots. This is almost certainly a sarcastic comment on the farcical climax to the real 2000 election in Florida.

A Little Learning is a Dangerous Thing: Debbie has instituted several new rules and conveyed them to the staff via email. One is that senior staff may not attend meetings without their briefing memos. Another is that they must attend meetings on time, or they won't be allowed in, something that Josh falls foul of. She notes that, during the past three hundred working days, the president has finished work at an average of 10.20 p.m. As a consequence, he hasn't had a decent night's sleep in four years. She also intends to be responsible for placing all the president's calls.

---

[115] Uncredited.

The Conspiracy Starts at Closing Time: Bartlet suffers from severe shaking in his car and, later, briefly loses his sight while completing his re-election speech, something that only Abbey notices. It seems that his MS is becoming progressively worse. There are going to be more days like this, Abbey notes, but lots of smart people are going to help him.

References: *Dragnet* ('just the facts, ma'am'), *Roll Call*, Don Quixote's follower Sancho Panza, Joe McCarthy (see **5**, 'The Crackpots and These Women'), *Angel* ('yet, somehow, I don't care'), Officer Krupke from *West Side Story*, the crime novelist Mickey Spillane, the black visionary Frederick Douglass (1818–95), the Friars Club, *Cinderella*, Honoré de Balzac (1799–1850) and *Meet the Press* and its host Tim Russert. Richie Havens's version of Bob Dylan's 'The Times They Are A-Changin'' is heard. There's a possible oblique allusion to the close-run 1960 Kennedy–Nixon election and the controversial Chicago ballot therein. One of the actors drinks a Starbuck's coffee. Bartlet refers to Chapter 659, Section 43, of the New Hampshire election code dealing with the distribution of campaign materials.

'You May Remember Me From Such Films and TV Series As . . .': Christian Slater played Daniel Malloy in *Interview with the Vampire*, Clarence in *True Romance*, George in *Kuffs*, Lucky Luciano in *Mobsters*, Will Scarlett in *Robin Hood: Prince of Thieves*, Mark in *Pump Up the Volume* and Jason in *Heathers*. His CV also includes *Who Is Cletis Tout?*, *3000 Miles To Graceland*, *Very Bad Things* (which he also produced), *Star Trek VI: The Undiscovered Country*, *Young Guns II*, *The Name of the Rose* and *Alias*. He directed *Museum of Love*.

Omar Benson Miller appeared in *8 Mile*. Megan Cavanagh was in *Three Shots*, *That Darn Cat* and *Home Improvements*. Kaarina Aufranc's CV includes *Deadly Swarm* and *CSI*. Kris Iyer was in *Some Girl* and *Buffy*. Lynette Romero is a newscaster on KTLA. Similarly, Christopher Schauble is a KNBC anchor on *Today in LA*.

Howard Mann appeared in *Space*, *Wholly Moses* and *Laverne and Shirley*. Don Dowe's movies include *Carnival of Wolves* and *Bad Girls From Mars*. Ron Ostrow was in *Sports Night*, *The Rat Pack* and *Firefly*. Ron Morehouse appeared in *Boston Public*. Michael Mulheren's CV includes *Bringing Out the Dead* and *Law & Order*.

Oh, Donna!: She calls Josh Pumpkin Patch. Donna wants to get the president to sign her absentee ballot, as he'll be the first winner she's ever voted for. Josh notes that she actually voted for Ritchie. And every other Republican in Wisconsin. Donna tries to rectify this by finding a Ritchie voter to swap votes. After some hours, and much hilarity, she finally meets Lieutenant Commander Jack Reese, a navy officer, who's just been transferred to Nancy McNally's office. He agrees to vote for the president instead of Ritchie.

Cigarettes and Alcohol: There's a lengthy (and rather pointless) subplot about Charlie and a football-playing friend of Anthony's who got stopped with a can of Pabst beer in his car. Bartlet has a whisky to celebrate winning in New Hampshire.

Logic, Let Me Introduce You to This Window: A woman going down on the escalator tells Josh, who's going up, that she voted for Bartlet. How, mere seconds later, can she be at the *top* of the escalator with the rest of the acting troupe when they reveal to Josh that he's been set up? Why is Josh worried about rain in Oregon, the state with the biggest postal vote in the entire US?

Quote/Unquote: Toby, on foregone conclusions: 'D'you wanna tempt the wrath of the *whatever*, from high atop *the thing*?'

CJ, to Toby: 'I know better than to stick my face in your personal life, except, you know, for sport . . .'

Donna, to a Ritchie supporter: 'Maybe it says that, even with the president's supporters accidentally voting for the wrong candidate, you're still gonna get creamed, you little fascist! *This is an honour thing!*'

Notes: 'You're going to win New Hampshire.' Something of an anticlimax, really, as the result of the election is, dramatically, never in question. There are several fine scenes (Donna's subplot, especially), but, after a run of great episodes, 'Election Night' sees the series, somewhat, treading water.

Sam and Donna share coffee and a banana muffin in the street outside the polling station.

Critique: 'Much fun, particularly at Josh and Donna's expense, is had with America's insanely muddled electoral system,' noted Quentin Cooper. 'As the votes are counted there's time for a little rain-making and some goat-theft, as well as a cameo from Christian Slater. *The West Wing* at its magnificent best.'

Cast and Crew Comments: 'Aaron called and offered me the role,' noted Christian Slater. 'It was something I could not say no to. I just *love* that show.'

Did You Know?: As an aspiring young actress in Florida, Kris Murphy used her real name, Kristy Zlock, before heading for LA with a name-change.

74
Process Stories

US Transmission Date: 13 November 2002
UK Transmission Date: 9 September 2003 (E4)

Teleplay: Aaron Sorkin
Story: Paula Yoo, Lauren Schmidt
Director: Christopher Misiano
Cast: Tobin Bell (Colonel Whitcomb) Gina Hecht (Julie)
Victor Raider-Wexler (Bernie) Wendy Braun (Gail)
Nick Jameson (Martin) Tim Silva (George) Marc Lynn (Whitaker)
Christopher May (TomWyatt) Diane Hsu (Campaign Aide)
Rae Ritke (Ashley) Symba Smith (Annette)

The president wasn't the only election winner: the late Horton Wilde also won, which puts Sam in a delicate position. Andi was a winner, too, but Toby remains worried about how her pregnancy will play, politically. A coup is developing in Venezuela, and it's the first night in the White House for Donna's new friend, Jack Reese.

A View From the Hill: Andi won her Congressional race in Maryland with a whopping 85 per cent of the vote. She and Toby discuss the Fourteenth Amendment.

American History X: There are references to Louisiana's being the only state that still operates under the Napoleonic legal code and the Independence War battles of Lexington and Concord.

Politics of Credit: Chris Whitaker, an Illinois pollster whom Bruno contracted, appears on several TV programmes taking credit for the energy strategy that helped to win the election. CJ is keen that the credit be given where it's deserved, to Bruno. But Bruno himself doesn't care. He was hired to win the election, he's done that and now all he wants is to get drunk and dance with the pretty ladies at the victory party. However, Whitaker makes the mistake of attending the party where CJ collars him and notes, sarcastically, that she's grateful for the process story that he has created, which will take the media's attention away from important stuff. To show her gratitude, she adds, she will call the major news outlets and forward all of Whitaker's confidential memos to the president. Of which, of course, there are none.

A Little Learning is a Dangerous Thing: Donna and Jack have a lengthy discussion about the president's attempts to cut Pentagon procurement, much of which involves why ashtrays on submarines are specifically designed to break, not shatter.

The Encyclopedic Mind of Josiah Bartlet PhD: He spends the episode showing off his knowledge of sturgeon, caviar and voting histories to his wife.

The Conspiracy Starts at Closing Time: Amy tells Josh that Sam should run in the California 47th. She adds that, once the euphoria of victory has died down, the White House is going to be dealing with an angry minority of House Democrats who feel that the president didn't do enough for them in the election. Those complaining would be silenced if the president were to send a top lieutenant, still flush with victory, on a suicide mission to Orange County. Having called Will Bailey for some polling information, Josh agrees. Amy tells Sam that she'll help him raise money and that he'll be the best-funded Democrat ever to run in the district.

References: Bartlet plays Dean Martin's 'Love Me, My Love' as he and Abbey attempt to get passionate while being constantly interrupted. Leo and Jordan dance to Julia Fordham's cover of the standard 'Someone to Watch Over Me' and later listen to WNKW radio's *The Music of Your Life* and an instrumental version of 'There, I Said It Again'. There's a mass chorus in CJ's office of the traditional New Orleans bordello ballad 'The House of the Rising Sun' (best known from the Animals' 1964 hit version). Anouk's 'It's a Shame' is playing at Andi's victory party. Also, Lazarus, whom, in John 11, Jesus raised from the dead, ABC news anchor Sam Donaldson, Manolos footwear, Disney's *California Adventure*, the author Mark Twain (1835–1910) and the Convention on the International Trade on Endangered Species. When Toby tells Jed and Abbey about Andi's pregnancy, Bartlet misquotes *Fiddler on the Roof*, while Leo alludes to *The Untouchables*. There are numerous references to the Greek mathematician Aristotle (384–322 BCE). Abbey does a cunning Marilyn Monroe impression. CJ has a lava lamp in her office.

'You May Remember Me From Such Films and TV Series As . . .': Tobin Bell played David Ferrie in *Ruby* and appeared in *Goodfellas*, *Serial Killer*, *Stargate SG-1* and *Malice*.

Oh, Donna!: As Sam bemoans the 'probable improbability' of Wilde's victory, Donna is stumped for an answer and simply asks if he wants some cake.

Cigarettes and Alcohol: Jed and Abbey prepare to have Stoli Cristal – a most elegant vodka – with their supper.

Sex and Drugs and Rock'n'Roll: Bruno tells CJ that carloads of women from the WLC and the Women's Action Network have come to the party and are unloading at the Northwest Executive Entrance. CJ sees Donna, and suggests that she may wish to tell Josh. At this point Josh comes shooting through the doors and races towards the Executive Entrance. 'He knows,' notes Donna.

Logic, Let Me Introduce You to This Window: The Badlands (another name for the Dakotas) is referenced along with the fact that Sitting Bull (1831–90) is buried there. Actually two different towns on either side of the North–South Dakota border both claim to have the remains of the Sioux chief. How does Jack Reese know where the Situation Room is when he's been in the White House for only five minutes and couldn't even find his own office when he arrived? Also, shouldn't he salute his superior officers when he enters the meeting? Are submariners really allowed to smoke on nuclear attack submarines? One of the Venezuelan generals is referred to first as Rojas and later as Reyes.

Quote/Unquote: Andi: 'I'm going to get sued. The Citizens' League for a Rooty-Tooty Freedom Liberty. They'll work out of a strip mall in Sarasota but they'll be curiously well funded.'

Bruno: 'That's the brunette named Annette.' CJ: 'Wouldn't you just give anything if she was from Tibet?'

Bartlet: 'You're young, Charlie. Don't you want to be having fun right now?' Charlie: 'Yes, sir. But I work for you.'

Notes: 'The process matters more than the outcome. *That's* what we wanted. Therein endeth the lesson.' A fabulous episode about how, in getting what you want, the way in which you achieve this is often far more important than what you end up with. The Leo/Jordan sequences are some of the finest ever moments of *The West Wing* – touching, poetic, mature, dripping with sexual tension. And that's just one subplot in an episode full of such elegant themes. The uncharismatic Donna/Jack Reese sections aren't as well crafted but, even here, there's dialogue to admire, while each of the regulars gets a little moment to shine in the spotlight. Best bit: Sam, discovering the delicious ironies of life, watching himself being announced as the potential candidate in the California 47th in front of a group of, suddenly speechless, colleagues.

It's been a glorious but strange and, at times, frustrating four years in the company of these characters. The future lies, seemingly, in a different direction altogether. And that's why this book ends here, with victory achieved against overwhelming odds.

Sam once worked on a State Assembly election in Manhattan. Amy likes shrimp. The president of Venezuela is called Ignacio. The two generals leading the coup d'état are Martinez and Rojas, backing a rival politician named Luna. The president's forces still hold the PDVSA refinery at Punto Fijo.

Critique: 'Jeers to fading from office,' noted *TV Guide* in early 2003. 'World events have left NBC's *West Wing* looking irrelevant, never more so than when the political drama goes into high dudgeon over events in fictional Qumar. We haven't cared less about a nation since *Dynasty* discovered Moldavia.'

Cast and Crew Comments: 'At this point in my life, if anyone had told me that I'd be doing this show, I wouldn't have believed it,' Martin Sheen told *St Paul Pioneer Press*. 'I have never been happier in my life or more satisfied with my career and the people I work with.'

Did You Know?: Why is Rob Lowe really leaving? 'It's entirely a money situation,' Aaron Sorkin told *TV Guide*. 'It has nothing to do with anything else. Nobody's the villain. It's a business situation.' Sorkin continues to praise Lowe's performances: 'I just want to be clear. There's nobody at NBC, nobody at Warner Bros and nobody on the show that wants Rob to leave. Sam Seaborn isn't going to die, so the door is always gonna be open. The chances of Rob staying? I talk to Rob every day and everybody wants him to keep doing the show.'

The West Wing and the Internet

Like most TV series, *The West Wing* has a flourishing fan community on the Internet, with many websites devoted to it. These are some of the most interesting. Disclaimer: Websites are transitory things and this information, though accurate when written, may be woefully out of date by publication.

The West Wing Continuity Guide (http://westwing. bewarne.com/) is a gorgeous collection of character profiles, background details, quotes, discontinuities and links, with lots of contributions from readers. A visual and conceptual treat.

The West Wing Episode Guide (http://www. westwingepguide.com/) This fantastic resource, with episode descriptions, full acting credits, information links and a plethora of press quotes, is an absolute gem.

Television Without Pity (www.televisionwithoutpity. com/) features loads of *West Wing* information, including detailed (and very opinionated) episode synopses, transcripts of interviews and a stimulating forum on which Aaron Sorkin has occasionally answered questions from fans.

The world of fan fiction requires a book of its own, and *The West Wing* is no different from many other series in featuring *tons* of it. Lots of this is 'shipper-fic, relationship-based erotica, about the characters – most of which proves that everyone seems to want Josh and Donna coupled up! *The West Wing FanFic Archives* (http:// westwingstories.com/) is, as the name suggests, packed with lots of Josh–Donna and CJ–Toby romance. As with all fanfic, lots of these tales are terrifically well written. And some are appalling. The similarly named *Wing Wing Fan-Fiction Archive* (http://blake.prohosting.com/wwffa/) covers much the same ground with categories such as

'Romance', 'Angst', 'Missing Scenes', 'Humor' and 'Future Events'. *The Josh Lyman Fiction Archive* (www. angelfire.com/il/Cindyshomepage/Josh.html) is self-explanatory. Broad-minded adult readers may be interested in *The Left Wing* (www.ma-at.net/LeftWing/) a tasteful 'Slash' site (homoerotica – much of it written by women, a high percentage of which is *excellent*). This features the expected quota of Josh–Sam stories, but far more featuring Sam and Toby than this author ever wants to contemplate.

The West Wing Episode Resource (http://www. angelfire.com/ky3/westwingresource) is another fine site featuring episode reviews, news and comments.

Lastly, for UK readers, http://web.ukonline.co.uk/ fringedwellers/westwing.htm features amusing and often perceptive episode commentaries by a group of UK-based fans.

Select Bibliography

Abejo, Jerry, ' "Accurate" map of the world gets boost from *West Wing*', *Knight Ridder Newspapers*, 6 March 2001.

Adalian, Josef, and Schneider, Michael, 'Plots are hot-spots for Net', *Daily Variety*, 23 September 2001.

Allemang, John, 'The money is the message', *Globe and Mail*, 2 March 2000.

Allemang, John, 'Who wants to be a *West Wing* survivor? Not Kelly', *Globe and Mail*, 17 July 2000.

Anderson, Roger, 'From the Clinton White House to NBC's *West Wing*', *Scripps Howard News Service*, 22 February 2000.

Anderson, Roger, 'Presidential Seal', *Fresno Bee*, 27 February 2000.

Archerd, Army, '*West Wing* snafu part for Hillary', *Daily Variety*, 25 August 2000.

Archerd, Army, '*West Wing* takes Middle-East angle', *Daily Variety*, 17 August 2001.

Atherton, Tony, 'Fantasy TV: The New Reality', *Ottawa Citizen*, 27 January 2000.

Atherton, Tony, 'Who got shot in *West Wing*?', *Ottawa Citizen*, 4 October 2000.

Aucoin, Don, '*West Wing* on alert', *Boston Globe*, 3 October 2001.

Ausiello, Michael, 'Backstage Scoop at the Emmys', *TV Guide*, 5 November 2001.

Ausiello, Michael, '*West Wing* rocked by Chandlergate!', *TV Guide*, 12 April 2003.

Ausiello, Michael, '*Friends* in high places', *TV Guide*, 19 April 2003.

Ausiello, Michael, '*West Wing* creator quits! What now?', *TV Guide*, 2 May 2003.

Baer, John, 'A prime-time success story', *Philadelphia Daily News*, 14 March 2001.

Ballerstero, Dana, 'Best Part: The Sheen Shine', *Hispanic*, July–August 2000.

Balz, Dan, 'Study Finds Disparity in Vote Counting', *International Herald Tribune*, 10 July 2001.

Barcley, Paris, 'A Woman of Influence', *Advocate*, 13 February 2001.

Barcley, Paris, 'A Few Good Stories', *Advocate*, 13 February 2001.

Bark, Ed, 'Sorkin's drug-subplot ending', *Dallas Morning News*, 22 July 2001.

Bark, Ed, 'Lowe's moving beyond politics, with no regrets', *Dallas Morning News*, 14 March 2003.

Barney, Chuck, '*West Wing* creator looks past finale to next season', *Contra Costa Times*, 17 July 2000.

Barton, David, 'Timothy Busfield will make a "Watergatey" return to *The West Wing*', *Sacramento Bee*, 3 December 2002.

Battaglio, Steven, 'Say it ain't so, Lowe', *New York Daily*, 6 September 2002.

Batz, Bob, '*West Wing* episode to feature Dayton', *Dayton Daily News*, 13 November 2002.

Bauder, David, 'A Death Riles *West Wing* Family', *Associated Press*, 13 June 2001.

Beck, Marilyn, Smith, Stacy Jenel, and DuBois, Stephanie, 'Political Maneuvering', *San Jose Mercury News*, 29 December 1999.

Belcher, Walt, 'Sorkin hears an earful from Mrs. Landingham fans', *Tampa Tribune*, 24 July 2001.

Belcher, Walt, '*West Wing, 7th Heaven*, bring news headlines', *Tampa Tribune*, 6 May 2002.

Bendavid, Naftali, 'NBC's White House drama *The West Wing* is generating buzz in Washington', *Chicago Tribune*, 28 September 1999.

Beschloss, Michael, 'Facing the Nation', *TV Guide*, 20 October 2001.

Betts, Hannah, 'And now, ladies, just for yourselves . . . When Harry met Garry', *The Times*, 7 July 2001.

Bianco, Robert, 'Isaac and Ishmael Review' *USA Today*, 4 October 2001.

Billin, Andrew, 'Perpetual Spin', *New Statesman*, 14 February 2000.

Binaculli, David, 'A program we can support', *New York Daily News*, 6 November 2000.

Blakey, Bob, '*West Wing* drama battles real scandal', *Calgary Herald*, 21 September 1999.

Bobbin, Jay, 'Beating around the Bush: Life goes on for Bradley Whitford and the cast of *The West Wing*', *TV Times*, 12 January 2000.

Boedeker, Hal, 'Viewer choice: thoughtful or thoughtless', *Orlando Sentinel*, 3 October 2001.

Bone, James, 'Declaration of Ignorance as American teenagers flunk July 4 Quiz', *The Times*, 4 July 2001.

Bottomley, Suzette, 'Conspiracy Theory', *Herald and Post*, 26 October 2000.

Boyer, Jay, 'Allison Janney: The softer side of CJ Cregg', *Orlando Sentinel*, 29 July 2003.

Bradlee, Benjamin C, 'Deep Throat: Washington's Best-Kept Secret', in *A Good Life*, Simon & Schuster, 1995.

Branegan, Jay, 'They could call it Wonk Wing', *Time*, 15 May 2000.

Brioux, Bill, '*West Wing* Shocker', *Toronto Sun*, 4 October 2000.

Brioux, Bill, 'Lowe on a high', *Toronto Sun*, 25 July 2003.

Brown, Scott and Rice, Lynette, 'The Killing Season', *Entertainment Weekly*, 25 May 2001.

Buckman, Adam, '*West Wing* wimps out on terror', *New York Post*, 4 October 2001.

'California assembly mourns TV character', *Associated Press*, 10 May 2001.

Campagna, Suzanne, 'True Romance', *Intergalactic Enquirer*, February 2001.

Carrillo, Jenny Cooney, 'Who's Who on *The West Wing*', *Radio Times*, 13 January 2001.

Carter, Bill, '*West Wing* Rushes Script Keyed to Attacks', *New York Times*, 22 September 2001.

Cassidy, Mike, 'Chatting up cast of *West Wing*', *San Jose Mercury News*, 15 August 2000.

Catlin, Roger, 'This is Not The Real World', *Hartford Courant*, 7 September 2002.

Catlin, Roger, 'The focus was 9/11', *Hartford Courant*, 13 September 2002.

Cioffi, Laure, 'Season premiere of *West Wing* is coming to Lawrence County', *Vindicator*, 9 August 2002.

Clark, Heather, 'Remember, *West Wing* is Fictional New Mexico', Associated Press, 3 April 2002.

Cleveland, Rick, 'WW Veteran', *Written By*, November 2000.

Cole, Burton, 'Rainstorm delays *West Wing* shoot', *Tribune Chronicle*, 24 August 2002.

Coleridge, Daniel R, 'Mark Harmon's *West Wing* Love', *TV Guide*, 8 May 2002.

Coleridge, Daniel R, '*Sport Night* star replaces Rob Lowe', *TV Guide*, 5 February 2003.

Cornell, Paul, Day, Martin, and Topping, Keith, *X-Treme Possibilities: A Comprehensively Expanded Rummage Through the X-Files*, Virgin Publishing, 1998.

Crowell, Susan, 'Tinseltown comes to Tiny Town', *Salem Farm and Dairy*, 29 August 2002.

Crump, Sarah, 'Former Rocky River man has spot high in Per's Andes', *Cleveland Plain Dealer*, 10 January 2002.

Cutler, Jacqueline, 'Martin Sheen: acting president, tireless activist', *St Paul Pioneer Press*, 15 December 2002.

Daswani, Kavita, 'South Asian actors find little support, lots of stereotypes', *Los Angeles Times*, 27 July 2001.

Davis, John H, *The Kennedys – Dynasty and Disaster 1948–1984*, McGraw-Hill, 1984.

Dawidziak, Mark, '*Wing* sets high bar for second term', *Cleveland Plain Dealer*, 1 October 2000.

Deans, Bob, '*West Wing* not unlike real thing?', *Palm Beach Post*, 18 October 2000.

Deggans, Eric, 'The brains behind the show', *St Petersberg Times*, 17 August 1999.

Deggans, Eric, 'New opponents to besiege *West Wing*', *St Petersberg Times*, 6 February 2001.

Deggans, Eric, 'Too subtle for the small screen', *St Petersberg Times*, 26 February 2001.

De Jonge, Peter, 'Aaron Sorkin Works His Way Through Crisis', *New York Times*, 28 October 2001.

De La Garza, Paul and Blaz, John, '*West Wing* focuses on Columbia', *St Petersberg Times*, 11 February 2001.

Dickerson, Justin, '*West Wing* Graduates at Georgetown', *Hoya*, 29 April 2003.

Droesch, Paul, 'The Capitol Gang', *TV Guide*, 4 October 2000.

Droesch, Paul, 'It's My Party', *TV Guide*, 6 March 2002.

Droesch, Paul, 'Executive Decision', *TV Guide*, 30 October 2002.

Dube, Francine, 'Ottowa insiders see selves in TV's idealistic *West Wing*', *National Post*, 18 May 2000.

Duffy, Mike, '*West Wing* twists in plot done on the fly', *Detroit Free Press*, 26 January 2000.

Duffy, Mike, '*West Wing* takes on terrorism', *Detroit Free Press*, 3 October 2001.

Dunphy, Tom, 'The President Acting', *Irish American*, October/November 2000.

Elber, Lynn, 'The voices of television: how sweet they sound', *Associated Press*, 27 December 1999.

Elber, Lynn, 'TV Shows hum with Walden's tunes', *Entertainment Today*, 5 March 2001.

Elber, Lynn, 'Older women like Mrs Landingham in *The West Wing* called endangered species', *Associated Press*, 14 May 2001.

Elber, Lynn, '*West Wing* ends season powerfully', *Associated Press*, 17 May 2001.

Elber, Lynn, '*West Wing* director part of new wave of TV makers', *Associated Press*, 19 May 2001.

Endrst, James, 'Undebateable: *West Wing* in a world of its own', *Hartford Courant*, 4 October 2000.

Feran, Tom, 'Drama shows politics can succeed on TV', *Cleveland Plain Dealer*, 22 September 1999.

Feran, Tom, 'President's collapse surprised fans', *Cleveland Plain Dealer*, 19 January 2000.

Feran, Tom, '*West Wing* insight on terrorism falls flat', *The Columbus Dispatch*, 4 October 2001.

Feschuk, Scott, 'The *West Wing* of desire', *National Post*, 9 February 2001.

Fink, Mitchell, 'Expect a *West* fling for series' Janney', *New York Daily News*, 19 January 2001.

Fiore, Faye, 'Washington cast an eye on Hollywood', *Los Angeles Times*, 15 July 2001.

Fiore, Faye, 'Politicos scramble for piece of *West Wing* action', *St Paul Pioneer Press*, 22 July 2001.

Fitzwater, Marlin, 'The Right Wing joins *The West Wing*', *People*, 6 November 2000.

'Foxy Lady', Jorja Fox interview, *TV Guide*, 8 December 2000.

Frey, Jennifer, with Roxanne Roberts and Lloyd Grove, 'Will the real president please stand up?' *Washington Post*, 1 May 2000.

Friend, Tad, '*West Wing* Watch: Snookered By Bush', *New Yorker*, 4 March 2002.

Garchik, Leah, 'The Rocco effect on Florida Recount', *San Francisco Chronicle*, 13 December 2000.

Garchik, Leah, 'Beating Around the Bushes', *San Francisco Chronicle*, 30 May 2003.

Gillin, Beth, and Shister, Gail, 'Terror of *West Wing*', *Philadelphia Inquirer*, 3 October 2001.

Goldstein, Patrick, 'On a *Wing* and a Prayer', *Los Angeles Times*, 10 October 1999.

Goodale, Gloria, 'Acting President', *Christian Science Monitor*, 3 March 2000.

Graham, Alison, 'Today's Choice', *Radio Times*, 13 January 2001.

Graham, Alison, 'Today's Choice,' *Radio Times*, 9 June 2001.

Gray, Ellen, 'The gay joke is becoming a staple of network TV', *Philadelphia Daily News*, 1 September 1999.

Gray, Ellen, 'A doctored plot', *Philadelphia Daily News*, 19 January 2000.

Gray, Ellen, '*Wing*'ed Angel', *Philadelphia Daily News*, 15 March 2000.

Gray, Ellen, 'Whose *Wing* is it, anyway?' *Philadelphia Daily News*, 4 October 2000.

Gray, Ellen, 'Councilman's kid a co-star', *Philadelphia Daily News*, 12 January 2001.

Gray, Ellen, 'With "best friends" like these . . .', *Philadelphia Daily News*, 28 February 2001.

Griwkowsky, Fish, 'Still at war with the world', *Edmonton Sun*, 30 November 2002.

Groppe, Maureen, '"President" to tackle Indiana time zone issue', *Greater Lafayette Journal and Courier*, 15 September 2002.

Grossman, Cathy Lynn, 'Lessons in entertainment', *USA Today*, 14 December 1999.

Grove, Lloyd, with Beth Berselli, 'The Reliable Source', *Washington Post*, 5 May 2000.

Grzebieniak, Mary, 'A weary day on the set of *West Wing*', *Vindicator*, 26 August 2002.

Hamilton, Kendall, 'Coast to Coast', *Newsweek*, 6 September 1999.

Hammer, Michael, 'The Rob Report', *Smoke*, September 1999.

Harada, Wayne, 'Former island TV guy turns up on *West Wing*', *Honolulu Advertiser*, 26 September 2002.

Hari, Johann, 'A frightening picture of American superiority: Even a fictional character seen as so left-wing that he is unelectable spouts a chilling foreign policy', *Independent*, 5 February 2003.

Harris, Emmylou, 'Will this president ban land mines?', *Boston Globe*, 27 March 2002.

Haught, Nancy, 'A true believer in *The West Wing*', *Atlanta Journal-Constitution*, 31 March 2001.

Heffernan, Greg, 'Martin Sheen: Catholic President on Prime Time', *St Anthony Messenger*, May 2000.

Heldenfels, RD, 'Lily and me', *Akron Beacon Journal*, 12 July 2003.

Helderman, Rosalind S, 'Town ready for its close up on *West Wing*', *Washington Post*, 22 August 2001.

Helderman, Rosalind S, '*West Wing* dismays the North', *Washington Post*, 27 August 2001.

Hochman, Steve, 'A Taste of *West Wing*'s Nonpartisan Politics', *Los Angeles Times*, 11 September 2000.

Holland, Ty, 'Head of the class', *TV Guide*, 28 October 2001.

Huff, Richard, 'WB Net Returns to Gender-Build on Initial Appeal Among Young Women', *New York Daily News*, 14 September 1999.

Huff, Richard, '*West Wing* to Confront WTC Terror', *New York Daily News*, 22 September 2001.

Hughes, Mike, 'This fall, *West Wing* gears up for re-election TV', *Gannett News Service*, 23 July 2001.

Isenberg, Barbara, 'From Zoey to Franny', *Los Angeles Times*, 15 June 2003.

Jackson, Terry, '*West Wing* cliffhanger dogs creator', *Miami Herald*, 19 July 2000.

Janney, Allison, 'Janney stands tall in drama's talented cast', interview by Phil Kloer, *Atlanta Journal-Constitution*, 4 October 2000.

Jeckell, Barry A, 'Mann, Ladies, to rock *West Wing*', *Billboard*, 7 October 2002.

Jicha, Tom, 'Sheen at home in *West Wing*', *South Florida Sun-Sentinal*, 19 January 2000.

Jicha, Tom, '*Wing* Commander', *South Florida Sun-Sentinal*, 19 July 2000.

Jicha, Tom, 'Lauderdale alum flies on *West Wing*', *South Florida Sun-Sentinal*, 30 April 2003.

Johnson, Adrienne M, 'From Raleigh to *The West Wing*', *Raleigh News Observer*, 15 November 2000.

Johnson, Allan, '*West Wing*'s Sorkin gives state-of-detox address', *Chicago Tribune*, 23 July 2001.

Johnson, Peter, 'Something squirrelly in *The West Wing*', *USA Today*, 3 May 2000.

Johnson, Peter, '*West Wing* delves into Bartlet's disease', *USA Today*, 3 April 2001.

Johnson, Steve, 'Episode a landmark, but too preachy', *Chicago Tribune*, 4 October 2001.

Johnson, Tricia, and Limpert, Ann, 'Burning Questions', *Entertainment Weekly*, 3 November 2000.

Judge, Michael, 'High Court Points the Way on Immigration', *Wall Street Journal*, 10 July 2001.

Jurkowitz, Mark, 'Getting President Bartlet's Ear', *Boston Globe*, 27 March 2002.

Kahn, Robert, '*West Wing* takes season finale to Broadway', *New York Newsday*, 15 May 2002.

Kaplan, Don, '*Wing* and a Prayer', *New York Post*, 31 July 1999.

Kaplan, Jonathan, 'Television's newest star: the 25th Amendment', *The Hill*, 28 May 2003.

Keck, William, 'Office Politics', *Entertainment Weekly*, 12 October 2001.

Keck, William, and Rice, Lynette, 'On the Air', *Entertainment Weekly*, 16 May 2003.

Keveney, Bill, '*West Wing* talent garners 18 Emmys', *Charlotte Observer*, 3 September 2000.

Kiesewetter, John, 'For a pacifist, Martin Sheen plays a pretty good president', *Cincinnati Enquirer*, 17 October 1999.

Kiesewetter, John, 'She's past *Wonder Years*', *Cincinnati Enquirer*, 29 October 2002.

King, Joshua, 'Do you recognize the Clinton West Wing in *The West Wing*?', *Atlantic Monthly*, March 2001.

Kinnes, Sally, 'Is Bartlet the Best President We've Never Had? Now Even He Has a Worthy Rival', *Sunday Times Culture*, 16 February 2003.

Klein, Naomi, 'Prime Time's political sedatives', *The Globe and Mail*, 17 May 2000.

Kronke, David, 'Wing Commanders', *TV Guide* (Canadian Edition), 20 November 1999.

Kruger, Henrik, *The Great Heroin Coup: Drugs, Intelligence & International Fascism*, South End Press, 1980.

Kurtz, Howard, 'Leaving Wonkville, entering Punditopolis', *Washington Post*, 21 August 2000.

Kushman, Rick, 'Inside *The West Wing*: A visit to the set of TV's most creative prime-time drama', *Sacramento Bee*, 25 February 2001.

Kushman, Rick, 'White House rookie', *Sacramento Bee*, 2 March 2003.

Lambert, Brian, 'Taking *Wing*', *St Paul Pioneer Press*, 1 October 2000.

Lambo, Ann-Margaret, 'NBC drama begins filming at Volant farm', *New Castle News*, 26 August 2002.

Lang, Charley, '*The West Wing*'s Special Guest Star', *Planet Out*, 15 November 2000.

Larue, William, '*West Wing* finale planned as setup for new season', *San Jose Mercury News*, 3 October 2000.

Lass, Frances, 'Today's Choice', *Radio Times*, 31 March 2001.

Lee, Luaine, 'Channing's *West Wing* role suits her wanderlust', *Minneapolis Star Tribune*, 5 May 2000.

Lehman, Chris, 'The Feel-Good Presidency: The pseudo-politics of *The West Wing*', *Atlantic Monthly*, March 2000.

Leith, Scott, 'Coke leads push to place products in movies', *Atlanta Journal-Constitution*, 29 October 2000.

Levesque, John, 'Sorkin's treatment of women gets more annoying', *Seattle Post-Intelligencer*, 12 February 2001.

Levin, Gary, '*West Wing* mirrors attacks in new episode', *USA Today*, 24 September 2001.

Levine, Stuart, 'Political repercussions', *Variety*, 13 June 2003.

Lewis, Scott D, 'Aimee Mann's World', *Oregonian*, 15 November 2002.

Liebenluft, Jacob, 'Whiffenpoofs to sing for *West Wing* president', *Yale Daily News*, 22 November 2002.

Liner, Elaine, '*ER*, *West Wing* rush to replace departed cast', *Corpus Christi Caller Times*, 18 January 2000.

Lipman, Lisa, '*The West Wing* creator talks about MS storyline', *Post and Courier*, 30 January 2000.

Lippman, Laura, 'The Loveable Liberal Behind Bush's Victory', *New York Times*, 31 December 2000.

Lipson, Karin, and Lovece, Frank, 'High Stakes TV', *New York Newsday*, 27 February 2000.

Littleton, Cynthia, '*West Wing* premiere postponed to address attacks' *Hollywood Reporter*, 21 September 2001.

Littleton, Cynthia, 'Third-season premiere of *West Wing* draws big numbers', *Hollywood Reporter*, 4 October 2001.

Littleton, Cynthia, Andreeva, Nellie, and Wallenstein, Andrew, 'Emmys: Nominees react', *Hollywood Reporter*, 18 July 2003.

Logan, Michael, 'Death Takes a Holiday', *TV Guide*, 7 July 2001.

Long, Karen and Bentrup, Cheri, 'Show to feature local restaurant', *Chicago Pioneer Press*, 27 November 2002.

Lowe, Rob, 'Lowe Flying High', interview by Phil Rosenthal, *Chicago Sun-Times*, 27 February 2001.

Lowe, Rob, 'Rob Lowe in the limelight', interview by Daniel R Coleridge, *TV Guide*, 28 February 2001.

Lowe, Rob, 'Rob Lowe stands out in latest *West Wing*', interview by Scott Pierce, *Deseret Times*, 28 February 2001.

Lowry, Brian, '*The West Wing* to Address Recent News Events', *Los Angeles Times*, 22 September 2001.

Lowry, Brian, '*The West Wing* is in a rush to wrap', *Los Angeles Times*, 2 October 2001.

Lowry, Brian, '*West Wing* give lessons on the effects of terrorism', *Los Angeles Times*, 4 October 2001.

McAllister, Bill, '*West Wing* included subplot for citizen stamp committee', *Linn's Stamp News*, 25 December 2000.

McCollum, Charlie, '*West Wing* adds episode reflective of real-life events', *San Jose Mercury News*, 1 October 2001.

McDaniel, Mike, 'Chaos will enter *The West Wing*', *Houston Chronicle*, 3 April 2001.

McDaniel, Mike, 'Wing-ding puts Thomas Schlamme in the spotlight', *Houston Chronicle*, 12 February 2002.

MacDonald, Ian, *Revolution in the Head* (second edition), Fourth Estate Ltd, 1997.

McGrory, Mary, '*West Wing* View', *Washington Post*, 7 April 2002.

McKay, John, '*West Wing* stars say they're in the dark about series cliffhanger', *Canadian Press*, 8 June 2000.

McKay, John, 'Deceased *West Wing* presidential secretary may return but unsure how or when', *Canadian Press*, 14 June 2001.

McKissack, Fred, '*The West Wing* is not a wet dream', *Progressive*, May 2000.

McKitrick, Ross, 'Prime-time fiction', *National Post*, 16 April 2003.

Maclear, Michael, *The Ten Thousand Day War: Vietnam 1945–1975*, Avon Books, 1981.

McLeod, Tyler, '*West Wing* finale shot down', *Calgary Sun*, 15 July 2000.

McLeod, Tyler, '*West Wing* takes us back from the cliff', *Calgary Sun*, 1 October 2000.

McTavish, Brian, 'From Shawnee Mission East to *The West Wing*', *Kansas City Star*, 6 October 2000.

Marrs, Jim, *Crossfire*, Pocket Books, 1993.

Mason, Charlie, 'Death Becomes Mrs. Landingham', *TV Guide*, 8 August 2001.

Mason, Dave, 'Lowe leaves *West Wing* for whatever's next', *Ventura County Star*, 27 November 2002.

Mathews, Jay, 'How My Daughter Rejected Caltech', *Washington Post*, 13 August 2002.

'Media Talk: Television Meets Reality in a Drama on Pardons', *New York Times*, 26 February 2001.

Miller, Matthew, 'The Real White House', *Brill's Content*, March 2000.

Mink, Eric, '*West Wing* Boldly Confronts Disease', *New York Daily News*, 19 January 2000.

Mink, Eric, '*Wing* Uses Net Asset', *New York Daily News*, 25 October 2000.

Moore, Frazier, 'Hail to the chief of *The West Wing*', *Associated Press*, 8 May 2000.

Moore, Frazier, 'Cupid has *West Wing* pair in limbo', *Associated Press*, 12 February 2001.

Moore, Patrick, *New Guide to the Planets*, Sidgwick & Jackson, 1993.

Moreira-Byers, Sherries, '*West Wing* to film in Volant', *Sharon Herald*, 6 August 2002.

Morgan, John, 'TV meets Reality: Brad Whitford lobbies for autism', *USA Today*, 24 May 2001.

Morrison, Patt, 'Cake is High in Irony, but Davis isn't Biting', *Los Angeles Times*, 15 April 2002.

Murphy, Mary, 'House Call', *TV Guide*, 22 July 2000.

Murphy, Mary, 'State of Disunion', *TV Guide*, 11 August 2001.

Murphy, Mary and Schwed, Mark, 'Broken *Wing*', *TV Guide*, 31 May 2003.

Noonan, Peggy, 'Break Out the Bubbly', *Wall Street Journal*, 1 March 2002.

Nussbaum, Emily, 'Confessions of a Spoiler Whore', *Slate*, 4 April 2002.

Oseid, Tammy J, 'Bit part, big step', *St Paul's Pioneer Press*, 23 September 2002.

Ouzounian, Richard, 'Stockard Channing takes wing', *Toronto Star*, 23 September 2001.

Owen, Rob, 'Sheen for President', *Pittsburgh Post-Gazette*, 19 September 1999.

Owen, Rob, '*West Wing* wins votes with viewers', *Pittsburgh Post-Gazette*, 23 February 2000.

Owen, Rob, 'Giving her all', *Pittsburgh Post-Gazette*, 25 July 2000.

Owen, Rob, '*West Wing* creator vetoed a Bush cameo', *Pittsburgh Post-Gazette*, 13 January 2001.

Owen, Rob, 'Religion portrayed in prime time rarely reflects reality', *Pittsburgh Post-Gazette*, 15 July 2001.

Owen, Rob, '*West Wing* to film here', *Pittsburgh Post-Gazette*, 31 July 2002.

Owen, Rob, 'Aaron Sorkin wants to put the fun back into *West Wing*', *Pittsburgh Post-Gazette*, 25 September 2002.

Parker, Penny, 'On the town', *Rocky Mountain News*, 12 February 2003.

Patterson, Bradley H, *The White House Staff: Inside The West Wing and Beyond*, Brookings Institute, 2000.

Peale, Cliff, 'Bananas according to TV', *Cincinnati Enquirer*, 13 February 2000.

Pennington, Gail, 'Hail to *The West Wing*', *St Louis Post-Dispatch*, 4 October 2000.

Pennington, Gail, '*West Wing*'s Sorkin has a lot to answer for', *St Louis Post-Dispatch*, 26 July 2001.

Pennington, Gail, '*West Wing* returns to nothin' but blue skies', *St Louis Post-Dispatch*, 29 January 2002.

Pergament, Alan, 'Much ado about *Kingpin*', *Buffalo News*, 22 January 2003.

Petrozzello, Donna, '*West Wing* premiere is life-or-death', *New York Daily News*, 4 October 2000.

Piccalo, Gina and Roug, Louise, 'Fund-Raiser Takes Flight With *West Wing*'s Help', *Los Angeles Times*, 4 October 2002.

Pierce, Scott D, 'What would *West Wing* be without a chief executive?', *Deseret News*, 12 April 2000.

Pierce, Scott D, 'TV relationships takes *Wing*', *Deseret News*, 20 December 2000.

Portman, Jamie, 'Top Secret', *Calgary Herald*, 8 February 2000.

Poniewozik, James, '*West Wing*: Terrorism 101', *Time*, 4 October 2001.

Pompa, Frank, 'A Nation Ablaze with Change', *USA Today*, 3 July 2001.

Powell, Betsy, 'Aaron Sorkin defends cliffhanger ending his hit *West Wing*', *Toronto Star*, 4 October 2000.

Procter, Emily, '*West Wing* conservative branches out', interview by Victoria Rohan, *Bergen Record*, 18 May 2001.

Procter, Emily, 'Ainsley role puts actress in tough spot', interview by Rob Owen, *Pittsburgh Post-Gazette*, 16 May 2001.

Rackman, Jane, 'Today's Choice', *Radio Times*, 27 January 2001.

Renzhofer, Martin, 'Premiere of *West Wing* finally answers questions about assassination attempt', *Salt Lake Tribune*, 4 October 2000.

'Ressem jury told not to watch *West Wing* TV show', *Seattle Times*, 3 April 2001.

Reynolds-Hughes, Bridin, 'Rehoboth Beach to be in the spotlight on NBC's *The West Wing*', *Cape Gazette*, 9 April 2001.

Rice, Lynette, 'School Daze', *Entertainment Weekly*, 28 September 2001.

Rice, Lynette, 'On the Air', *Entertainment Weekly*, 2 August 2002.

Rich, Joshua, 'Gaffe Time', *Entertainment Weekly*, 18 October 2000.

Roach, Mary, 'From rough seas to smooth sailing', *USA Weekend*, 21 November 1999.

Robins, Max J, 'Dramatic Differences in Tragedy's Wake', *TV Guide*, 6 October 2001.

Robinson, Olivia, 'How The West Was Lost: How America Fell Out of Love With The President', *TV & Satellite Week*, 19 July 2003.

Rode, Jenny, 'From BC to *West Wing*', *Battle Creek Examiner*, 4 October 2002.

Rohan, Virginia, 'A Capitol Hill liaison', *Bergen Record*, 15 December 1999.

Rohan, Virginia, '*West Wing* player keeps a cool head', *Bergen Record*, 4 October 2000.

Rohan, Virginia, 'Viewers seem to be gravitating towards "comfort programs"', *St Paul Pioneer Press*, 28 October 2001.

Rosenthal, Phil, '*W. Wing* heals after gun attack', *Chicago Sun-Times*, 17 July 2000.

Rosenthal, Phil, 'Shedding light on murky look of *West Wing*', *Chicago Sun-Times*, 15 January 2003.

Ross, Chauncey, 'Taking to the air', *Indiana Gazette*, 15 September 2002.

Rothman, Robin A, '*West Wing, 24* provide civics lesson', *Knight Ridder*, 30 May 2003.

Roush, Matt, 'Cheers and Jeers', *TV Guide*, 11 December 1999.

Roush, Matt, 'Shows of the Year '99', *TV Guide*, 25 December 1999.

Roush, Matt, 'The Roush Review: End Games', *TV Guide*, 16 June 2001.

Roush, Matt, 'Reality Check', *TV Guide*, 20 October 2001.

Rubinstein, Julian, 'Politically Correct', *US Magazine*, October 1999.

Rutenberg, Jim, 'Expletives? More coming on fall TV', *New York Times*, 3 September 2001.

Ryan, Andrew, 'Corridors of power', *Globe and Mail*, 16 December 2000.

Sachs, Andrea, 'A Day in the life of a *West Wing* extra', *Washington Post*, 5 July 2001.

Sangster, Jim and Bailey, David, *Friends Like Us: The Unofficial Guide to* Friends (revised edition), Virgin Publishing, 2000.

Sauerwein, Kristina, 'Unscripted Angst at Writers Guild Forum', *Los Angeles Times*, 10 June 2002.

Saunders, Dusty, 'Channel 9 studies 10 p.m. audience loss', *Rocky Mountain News*, 15 May 2000.

Saunders, Dusty, '*Wing* cliffhanger a sellout? Hang in there', *Rocky Mountain News*, 18 July 2000.

Schlesinger, Arthur A, *A Thousand Days: John F Kennedy in the White House*, Houghton Mifflin Co., 1965.

Schork, Robert and Barnett, Deanna, 'How the *West* has won', *Soap Opera Weekly*, 3 April 2001.

Schuler, Corrina, 'Mbeki's stance on AIDS confounds critics', *National Post*, 2 November 2000.

Schwed, Mark, 'Hollywood Grapevine', *TV Guide*, 22 June 2002.

Segal, David, 'Hearsay: The Lawyer's Column', *Washington Post*, 17 January 2000.

Seibel, Deborah Starr, 'Dulé Noted', *TV Guide*, 6 October 2001.

Sepinwell, Alan, '*West Wing* won't bask in glory as season opens with two-parter', *Newhouse News Service*, 31 July 2000.

Shales, Tom, '*The West Wing* assumes the role of moral compass', *Washington Post*, 4 October 2001.

Sheen, Martin, 'The Left Wing', interview by Andrew Ryan, *Globe and Mail*, 15 November 2000.

Sheen, Martin, 'Alcoholics Anonymous and jazz are the only important things the USA has exported', interview by Andrew Duncan, *Radio Times*, 17 February 2001.

Sheen, Martin, 'I Discovered What Faith And Love Are All About', interview by Dotson Rader, *Parade*, 2 December 2001.

Shister, Gail, '*West Wing* runs political gamut, holds the scandal', *Philadelphia Inquirer*, 2 August 1999.

Shister, Gail, 'Bush in a cameo role? No thanks, *West Wing* producers say', *Philadelphia Inquirer*, 12 January 2001.

Shister, Gail, 'PBS pays up more readily than *West Wing* for Olmos', *Philadelphia Inquirer*, 19 June 2001.

Shister, Gail, 'Airing of a timely *West Wing* may depend on events', *Philadelphia Inquirer*, 5 February 2002.

'Shoeless, but Decorum Intact', *New York Times*, 7 September 2001.

Smith, Liz, '*Wing* and a prayer', *Newsday*, 14 May 2003.

Snierson, Dan, Jensen, Jeff, and Daly, Steve, 'In the Wings', *Entertainment Weekly*, 13 June 2001.

Sollinger, Shannon, 'Only in Hollywood', *Loudoun Times-Mirror*, 28 August 2001.

Sorkin, Aaron, 'State of Disunion', interview by Mary Murphy, *TV Guide*, 11 August 2001.

Sorkin, Aaron, 'Script Sensation', interview by Brad Herzog, *Syracuse University Magazine*, Summer 2001.

Sorkin, Aaron, interview, *New York Times*, 28 October 2001.

Sorkin, Aaron, 'Sorkin on 9/11', *Written By*, November 2001.

'Sources say: A look behind the scenes', *Capital*, 8 April 2003.

Spitz, Bob, 'Profile', *Sky*, February 2001.

Sponagle, Michael, 'The *West* point', *Globe and Mail*, 11 March 2000.

Stanley, Alessandra, '*West Wing* Withdraws Ad', *New York Times*, 2 February 2002.

Starr, Alexander, 'Shoptalk: To tell the truth', *New York Times Magazine*, 22 October 2000.

Starr, Michael, 'CCNY Schiffs into gear with *Wing* Star', *New York Post*, 13 September 2000.

Starr, Michael, 'Maloney "Wings" it on hopeful legislation', *New York Post*, 13 December 2000.

Starr, Michael, 'The Starr Report', *New York Post*, 15 January 2001.

Stephanopoulos, George, *All Too Human: A Political Education*, Back Bay Books, 2000.

Stone, Oliver, and Sklar, Zachary, *JFK – The Book of the Film, a documented screenplay*, Applause Books, 1992.

Storm, Jonathan, 'White House is setting for highly touted NBC drama', *Philadelphia Inquirer*, 22 September 1999.

Summers, Anthony, *Conspiracy*, McGraw-Hill, 1980.

Takahashi, Corey, 'Reality Check', *Entertainment Weekly*, 2 June 2000.

Tasker, Fred, 'Life looks to art: *West Wing* about MS bias in workplace', *Miami Herald*, 19 May 2001.

Tetreault, Steve, Kalil, JM, and Faulstick, Britt, 'Nevada nuclear dump foes welcome *West Wing* episode about waste mishap', *Las Vegas Review-Journal*, 29 March 2002.

Thompson, Kevin D, 'The 25th Amendment on television', *Palm Beach Post*, 20 May 2003.

Thompson, Kevin D, 'NBC banks of *Joey* spin-off', *Palm Beach Post*, 26 July 2003.

Topping, Keith, *High Times: An Unofficial and Unauthorised Guide to* Roswell High, Virgin Publishing, 2001.

Topping, Keith, *Hollywood Vampire: The Revised and Updated Unofficial and Unauthorised Guide to* Angel, Virgin Publishing, 2001.

Topping, Keith, *Slayer: An Expanded and Updated Unofficial and Unauthorised Guide to* Buffy the Vampire Slayer, Virgin Publishing, 2002.

Topping, Keith, *A Day in the Life: The Unofficial and Unauthorised Guide to* 24, Telos Publishing, 2003.

Trafford, Abigail, 'Prime Time's Cure For Cancer', *Washington Post*, 29 January 2002.

Tucker, Ken, 'Meet the Prez', *Entertainment Weekly*, 25 February 2000.

Tucker, Ken, 'How the "West" was undone', *Entertainment Weekly*, 8 November 2002.

Varadarajan, Tunka, 'U.S.–India Ties Could Herald a Strategic Shift', *Wall Street Journal*, 10 July 2001.

Vejnoska, Jill, '*West Wing* offers somber civics lesson', *Atlanta Journal*, 4 October 2001.

Vejnoska, Jill, 'Busy Matheson has to phone it in', *Atlanta Journal*, 7 January 2003.

Wade, Treshea, 'Library to serve as train station in *West Wing* episode', *Tribune-Review*, 14 August 2002.

Waxman, Sharon, 'Hollywood pleads its case', *Washington Post*, 7 May 2000.

Waxman, Sharon, 'Art meets politics', *Washington Post*, 8 May 2000.

Waxman, Sharon, 'Inside *The West Wing*'s New World', *George*, November 2000.

Waxman, Sharon, 'Will *West Wing* go up in smoke?' *Washington Post*, 20 July 2001.

Weinrub, Bernard, '*The West Wing*: Leader of the Free World (Free TV that is)', *New York Times*, 17 October 2000.

Weinrub, Bernard, '*West Wing* Producer, a Union Leader, Rules Out Writers' Raise', *New York Times*, 26 June 2001.

Weiss, Norman, '"President" Sheen says he is not ready for real *West Wing*', *Daily Californian*, 12 February 2001.

'*West Wing* Alert', *Sydney Morning Herald*, 24 September 2001.

'*West Wing* checks out real thing', *Boston Globe*, 6 May 2000.

'*West Wing* Flap Ends', *Minneapolis Star Tribune*, 29 July 2001.

'*West Wing* redraws Vt.–Canadian border', *Associated Press*, 7 October 2001.

'*West Wing* returns with new writing team', *Reuters*, 24 June 2003.

'*West Wing* stars offered pay rise', *Metro*, 17 July 2001.

'What Girls Learn', *Entertainment Tonight Online*, 11 October 2001.

Whedon, Joss, 'Blood Lust', interview by Rob Francis, *DreamWatch*, issues 71–2, August/September 2000.

Whitford, Bradley, 'He's in no position for Josh-ing on *Wing*', interview by Donna Petrozzello, *New York Daily News*, 13 December 2000.

Whitford, Bradley, 'Whitford loves just Joshin', interview by Frazier Moore, *Associated Press*, 20 December 2000.

Whitford, Bradley, 'Meg Ryan's Bossy Co-Star', interview by Daniel R Coleridge, *TV Guide*, 14 March 2001.

Whitford, David, 'The secret life of an actor', *Esquire*, May 2001.

'Winging It', *Modern Maturity*, May/June 2001.

Wolf, Jeanne, with Michael Ausiello, '*West Wing*'s Career Schiff', *TV Guide*, 30 January 2002.

Wolfe, Jennifer, 'Martin Sheen's change of heart', *TV Guide*, 3 May 2000.

Wolff, Michael, 'Our remote-control president', *New York Magazine*, 4 December 2000.

Woodward, Bob, and Berstein, Carl, *All The President's Men*, Bloomsbury, 1974.

Wyman, Mark, 'A Fable For The Internet Age', *Shivers*, issue 68, August 1999.

York, Tara, 'Yale's Whiffenpoofs to appear on *The West Wing*', *New Haven Register*, 22 November 2002.

Young, Susan, 'The lowdown on Rob Lowe leaving *West Wing*', *Oakland Tribune*, 26 July 2002.

Zerisias, Antonia, 'Isaac and Ishmael review', *Toronto Star*, 4 October 2001.

Zinn, Howard, *A People's History of the United States*, Harper & Row, 1980.

Zoller Seitz, Matt, 'Mr. Sheen Goes to Washington', *Newark Star-Ledger*, 14 May 2000.

Zurawick, David, 'Sorkin faces up to a sorry spring', *Baltimore Sun*, 23 July 2001.

Zurawick, David, '*West Wing* returns with risky move', *Baltimore Sun*, 3 October 2001.

Zwecker, Bill, 'Fonda to Enquirer: That wasn't me!', *Chicago Sun-Times*, 14 November 2002.

Four More Years . . .?

Departures are regular occurrences in most TV shows, but the announcement, in October 2002, that Rob Lowe would be leaving *The West Wing* in March 2003 came as an unexpected blow to the series' fans. Aaron Sorkin explained that the 1999 *West Wing* pilot had been expensive to make and the producers, at that stage, didn't know whether the series would be a hit. Lowe and co-stars Allison Janney, Richard Schiff, John Spencer and Bradley Whitford were all asked to reduce significantly their expected salaries to be in the series. '*They* did, Rob *didn't*,' Sorkin told *TV Guide*. During Season Three, the other cast members' pay was reportedly raised from $30,000 per episode to $70,000, while Lowe himself was refused a rise. 'While it's possible to say, "Everybody else on the show got a raise except for Rob" the fact is Rob had *his* raise two years [before] everybody else,' added Sorkin. 'There is a plan in place and I'm sticking to it,' Sorkin told the *New York Daily*. 'Sam Seaborn isn't going to die. The door is always open [for his return].'

Lowe subsequently noted that he had expected a bigger send-off than the one he received. 'I would've liked to see Sam leave with a flourish,' Lowe told Bill Brioux. Instead, the character all but vanished after Bartlet's election victory in November, before returning for two final episodes in late February. 'It was confusing when the producers decided not to use me . . . But it was one of the greatest paid vacations I've ever had. I travelled the world and had a great time.'

Meanwhile, media sources were reporting that NBC believed *The West Wing*'s characters were seen as too liberal by viewers in a country that had, seemingly, moved to the right. At a time when America was preparing for a real-life war, the sight of a fictional president, Martin Sheen, appearing in controversial antiwar commercials was too much for some of the less broad-minded of Americans, many of whom bombarded NBC with demands that this 'traitor' and his show be dropped from their schedules. 'In a world where we accept high-profile people being paid to tell us about sneakers, soft drinks and cosmetics, surely we shouldn't have a problem with them talking for free about their feelings on going to war, or not,' Sorkin told Olivia Robinson.

The war with Iraq, however, served to heighten America's rediscovered sense of patriotism. Not surprisingly, the liberal leanings of the Bartlet administration caused some viewers to vote with their remotes. Within weeks, *The West Wing* had lost around 3 million viewers. The network, reportedly, wanted juicier storylines to woo the viewers back. To add to the series' problems, it had a new, and dangerous, rival in its Wednesday night time-slot, ABC's popular reality show *The Bachelor*. Sorkin, seemingly, attempted to give the network what it wanted.

President Bartlet's second term began with 'Swiss Diplomacy'. John Hoynes is already manoeuvring for the next election. Meanwhile, the fifteen-year-old son of an Iranian leader needs a heart transplant and can get it only in America. In 'Arctic Radar', Sam heads to California to begin his Congressional campaign, leaving Toby needing speechwriting help. Sam's suggestion is Will Bailey. The 2002 Christmas episode, 'Holy Night', saw the return of Danny Concannon, on the trail of a story that could have apocalyptic repercussions on the White House. We meet Toby's father and discover that Mr Ziegler has a dark past. Also, Zoey returns, accompanied by a new French boyfriend, much to Charlie's distress.

On the administration's agenda in 'Guns Not Butter' is a foreign-aid bill and it's up to Josh to see it passed. 'The Long Goodbye' was written by playwright Jon Robin Baitz. CJ returns to Dayton, Ohio, to speak at a high school reunion. The visit includes the sobering reality of her father's escalating Alzheimer's disease. The two-part 'Inauguration' sees a genocide in a remote African country. The president's wish to intervene doesn't meet with universal approval, while Will Bailey's work on the inaugural address makes quite an impression. En route to California to campaign for Sam, Bartlet and staff debate whether to announce a controversial tax plan that may damage Sam's campaign in 'The California 47th'. The story concludes in 'Red Haven's on Fire', as a special-ops mission to rescue three captive American soldiers in Africa goes horribly wrong.

Meanwhile, the first lady gets a new chief of staff – Amy Gardner. Amy's first day sees her attempting to have the president veto his own foreign-aid bill, in 'Privateers'. 'Angel Maintenance' begins with *Air Force One* about to land in Washington when an indicator leads the crew to believe that the landing gears have not activated. *Friends'* Matthew Perry begins a two-episode stint as Joe Quincy, a lawyer who joins the staff in 'Evidence of Things Not Seen', when a shooting outside the White House leads to the building's being locked down.

'Life on Mars' details a complex series of events, which ultimately reveal a sex scandal that forces the resignation of Hoynes. In 'Commencement', terrorists kidnap Bartlet's daughter, Zoey. Andi refuses to remarry Toby, minutes before her waters break and she gives birth to twins. 'Twenty Five' sees Bartlet temporarily standing down from the presidency in favour of the Republican, speaker of the house, Glen Walken (John Goodman).

For Aaron Sorkin, the end of the season was fittingly presidential. His co-workers were gathered on the Oval Office set, preparing to shoot the swearing in of a new president, when word came to adjourn to the Roosevelt Room. Sorkin, the man who had written 86 of the show's 89 episodes, then delivered his bombshell: he was leaving the show. 'There was a stunned silence,' recalled Josh Malina. 'It was an emotional holocaust,' added Bradley Whitford. Asked what he would do next, Sorkin said, 'I honestly have no idea.' Thomas Schlamme was already scheduled to leave at the end of season four. 'We felt a bit like we'd been orphaned for a few days, but, after the initial shock, we determined to regroup and get behind our producer John Wells,' noted Martin Sheen. 'We have a solid staff. We still need a new head writer and there is *no* other Aaron Sorkin. But we'll find our way.'

'We've had ups and downs on the show,' John Wells told *TV Guide*, 'and we've always tried to encourage Aaron to stay. Because he writes so many of them, he's always expressed the sense that he was starting to run out of steam. I have some sympathy for him.' Wells, a regular writer on *ER*, will, reportedly, handle the early episodes of Season Five until a new writing staff is in place. Meanwhile, in terms of casting, *The X-Files*' Annabeth Gish will be introduced as the president's eldest daughter, Elizabeth, while the new vice president will be played by Gary Cole, previously best known for *Midnight Caller* and *American Gothic*. *Bring It On* star Jesse Bradford will also appear as an intern.

'I don't think there's a huge change in the show,' NBC executive Jeff Zucker told journalists at the annual Television Critics Association press tour. 'What John has brought to the first two scripts [of Season Five] is some incredible, emotional moments,' Zucker continued. 'You're going to be quite taken with how gut-wrenching and emotional it is.'

The early episodes of Season Five look likely to tie up the loose ends left at the previous year's dramatic climax. After that, *The West Wing* will find itself telling its stories in a much-changed world, in a hostile political climate and with its inspirational show-runner now gone. With any other series, one wouldn't put too much money on a fighting outcome, but with the extraordinary cast that *The West Wing* has, we all know that *anything* is possible.

HOLLYWOOD VAMPIRE
AN EXPANDED AND UPDATED UNOFFICIAL AND UNAUTHORISED GUIDE TO *ANGEL*

Keith Topping

Angel returned from Hell with his soul intact, but the price he paid was his relationship with Buffy Summers and his life in Sunnydale. In order to atone for his sins, he now fights for humanity in the dark, seedy underworld of the superficially glamorous city of LA.

In *Hollywood Vampire*, Keith Topping explores the world of Angel, Cordelia, Wesley, Gunn, Fred and Lorne as they fight their own personal demons and the loneliness of the Big City in their search for redemption. This essential unofficial fan bible covers the first four series of the show, episode by episode, encompassing the highlights, the shared history of *Buffy* and *Angel*, the novels and the websites. It also draws attention to logic flaws and points out pop-culture references.

ISBN 0 7535 0807 9

Other TV titles available from Virgin:

MANHATTAN DATING GAME
AN UNOFFICIAL AND UNAUTHORISED GUIDE TO EVERY EPISODE OF *SEX AND THE CITY*

Jim Smith

Manhattan – and four successful career women tiptoe round the dating minefield armed only with mascara, Manolos and some truly Machiavellian schemes.

Sex and the City is the award-winning hit comedy that candidly explores the social and sexual lives of four single New York City women. *Manhattan Dating Game* analyses their experiences as they seek fulfilment in the Big Apple. Episode by episode, covering every season and the highlights of each episode, this unofficial and intimate guide is your essential overview of the lives of Carrie, Charlotte, Miranda and Sam.

Coming Soon

ISBN 0 7535 0925 3

SLAYER
Keith Topping

With its literal representations of teenage horrors, *the Vampire Slayer* has touched on a universal truth. bestselling unofficial guides to the surreal world of nydale, Keith Topping analyses each episode, prese the highlights in categories such as: A Little Learnin Dangerous Thing, I Just *Love* Your Accent and D Thy Name is Joyce. He unearths pop culture refe and soundtrack information and draws attention t times logic flies out of the window, along with sectio the original feature film, the novels and websites.

'Topping's terrific tome adopts the perfect attitud this fizzing phenomenon . . . He rattles through each episode with focus on teen-angst metapho the brilliant feminist subtexts, and the dazzling u of "valley speak" . . . Colour me stunned.' *Uncu*

Seasons 1–5   ISBN 0 7535 0631 9
Season 6   ISBN 0 7535 0738 2

Coming Soon

Season 7   ISBN 0 7535 0844 3

SECRET IDENTITIES
AN UNOFFICIAL AND UNAUTHORISED
GUIDE TO *ALIAS*

Mark Clapham and Lance Parkin

Alias, the hit espionage TV series, mixes high-tech spy action, glamorous disguises, shocking plot twists and an ongoing family saga into one of the most clever and entertaining television shows in years.

Secret agent Sydney Bristow thinks that the agency she works for, SD-6, is a branch of the CIA and that their aim is the safety of the country. When Sydney discovers that SD-6 is really a criminal organisation she becomes a double agent for the real CIA. So begins a dangerous life of secrets and deceptions.

This essential unofficial guide to *Alias* covers each episode of the first two seasons, exploring and evaluating them, analysing and explaining each aspect of the complex plotlines and revealing the hidden clues in each episode.

ISBN 0 7535 0896 6